Exploring
Macroeconomics

Third Canadian Edition

Robert L. Sexton
Pepperdine University

Peter N. Fortura
Algonquin College

Colin C. Kovacs
Algonquin College

NELSON / EDUCATION

NELSON / EDUCATION

Exploring Macroeconomics, Third Canadian Edition

by Robert L. Sexton, Peter N. Fortura, and Colin C. Kovacs

Vice President, Editorial Higher Education:
Anne Williams

Executive Editor:
Amie Plourde

Editorial Consultant:
Rod Banister

Senior Developmental Editor:
Katherine Goodes, My Editor Inc.

Photo Researcher:
David Strand

Permissions Coordinator:
David Strand

Content Production Manager:
Lila Campbell

Production Service:
Integra Software Services Pvt. Ltd.

Copy Editor:
June Trusty

Proofreader:
Integra Software Services Pvt. Ltd.

Indexer:
Integra Software Services Pvt. Ltd.

Manufacturing Manager:
Joanne McNeil

Design Director:
Ken Phipps

Managing Designer:
Franca Amore

Interior Design Modifications:
Eugene Lo

Interior Design Image Credits:
Debate boxes: © David Marchal/iStockphoto; *Business Connection* boxes: © TommL/iStockphoto

Cover Design:
Sharon Lucas

Cover Image:
Denkou Images/Cultura/Getty Images

Compositor:
Integra Software Services Pvt. Ltd.

Printer:
RR Donnelley

Library and Archives Canada Cataloguing in Publication Data

Sexton, Robert L.
Exploring macroeconomics / Robert L. Sexton, Peter N. Fortura, Colin C. Kovacs. — 3rd Canadian ed.

Previously published as part of: Exploring Economics.
1st Canadian ed.
Includes bibliographical references and index.

ISBN 978-0-17-650976-7

1. Macroeconomics—Textbooks. I. Fortura, Peter II. Kovacs, Colin C. III. Sexton, Robert L. Exploring economics. IV. Title.

HB172.5.S49 2012
339   C2011-908696-4

ISBN 13: 978-0-17-650976-7
ISBN 10: 0-17-650976-3

To Cynthia, Laura, and Nicholas

P.N.F.

To Lindsay, Rowan, Seth, and Myles

C.C.K.

To Elizabeth, Katherine, and Tommy

R.L.S.

Brief Contents

Detailed Contents

About the Authors

Robert L. Sexton is Distinguished Professor of Economics at Pepperdine University. Professor Sexton has also been a Visiting Professor at the University of California at Los Angeles in the Anderson Graduate School of Management and the Department of Economics. He also played the role of an assistant coach in the movie *Benchwarmers* (2006).

Professor Sexton's research ranges across many fields of economics: economics education, labour economics, environmental economics, law and economics, and economic history. He has written several books and been published in many top economic journals such as the *American Economic Review, Southern Economic Journal, Economics Letters, Journal of Urban Economics,* and the *Journal of Economic Education.* Professor Sexton has also written more than 100 other articles that have appeared in books, magazines, and newspapers.

He received the Pepperdine Professor of the Year Award in 1991 and 1997, and the Howard A. White Memorial Teaching Award in 1994; he was named a Harriet and Charles Luckman Teaching Fellow in 1994.

Professor Sexton resides in Agoura Hills, California, with his wife, Julie, and their three children, Elizabeth, Katherine, and Tommy.

Peter N. Fortura earned his undergraduate degree from Brock University, where he was awarded the Vice-Chancellor's Medal for academic achievement, and his graduate degree (Master of Arts) from the University of Western Ontario. He has taught economics at Algonquin College in Ottawa for over 20 years. Prior to that, he was an economist in the International Department of the Bank of Canada in Ottawa.

He has published articles on Canadian housing prices, Canada's automotive industry, and Canada's international competitiveness. As well, he is the author of the *Study Guide to Accompany Principles of Macroeconomics,* by Mankiw, Kneebone, McKenzie, and Rowe (Nelson Education, 5th edition), and the co-author of the statistics textbook *Contemporary Business Statistics with Canadian Applications* (Pearson, 3rd edition).

He lives in Ottawa with his wife, Cynthia, and their children, Laura and Nicholas.

Colin C. Kovacs received his Master of Arts degree from Queen's University after completing his Bachelor of Arts at the University of Western Ontario. He has taught economics, statistics, and finance for nearly 20 years at both the DeVry College of Technology in Toronto and Algonquin College in Ottawa. His research papers have included *Determinants of Labour Force Participation Among Older Males in Canada,* and *Minimum Wage—The Past and Future for Ontario.*

He lives in Ottawa with his wife, Lindsay, and their children, Rowan, Seth, and Myles.

Preface

Exploring Macroeconomics, Third Canadian Edition, offers students a lively, back-to-the-basics approach designed to take the intimidation out of economics. With its short, self-contained active learning units and its carefully chosen pedagogy, graphs, and photos, this text helps students master and retain the principles of economics. In addition, the current-events focus and modular format of presenting information makes *Exploring Macroeconomics* a very student-accessible and user-friendly text. Driven by more than 60 years combined of experience teaching the economic principles course, Bob Sexton, Peter Fortura, and Colin Kovacs' dedication and enthusiasm shine through in *Exploring Macroeconomics.*

NEW TO THE THIRD CANADIAN EDITION
Overall Highlights

The third Canadian edition of *Exploring Macroeconomics* remains a separate split-edition with the third Canadian edition of *Exploring Microeconomics* that it is designed to accompany. With this edition, particular attention has been paid to the structure and lay-out of each chapter to ensure that the material is presented in as clear and consistent a manner as possible. The chapter section opening questions now align to headings in the section, to section check boxes, and to the Summary section in the Chapter In Review cards.

Also new to this edition are the Chapter In Review cards located at the back of the textbook. A quick study tool for students, these detachable review cards give students a summary overview of key chapter concepts at a glance and contain a chapter summary, key graphs, and key term/concept definitions.

End-of-chapter review questions have expanded to more than double the number of questions and problems. The Study Guide has been moved to become part of the Test Yourself quizzes in CourseMate.

Two new education features are being introduced in this edition—**Debate** and **Business Connection** boxes. Strategically placed in each chapter, the *Debate* features are designed to prompt in-class discussion and self-exploration. Students are presented with a defined topic with both "for" and "against" arguments intended to spark class-room interaction and analysis that is centred on key chapter topics. The *Business Connection* features, also located in every chapter, will be particularly appreciated by students enrolled in an introductory economics course as required by their business program. Specifically designed to highlight the link between economic theory and business principles, these boxes will not only strengthen a student's comprehension of key economic concepts, they will promote a deeper understanding of fundamental business ideas.

Finally, where relevant, additional Canadian content has been added and all statistical information has been updated. Most notably, chapter sections on economic fluctuations, fiscal policy, and monetary policy have been expanded to detail the impact of the global financial crisis on the Canadian economy in 2008–2009. This investigation extends to an examination of the unprecedented efforts of the Canadian government to mitigate the impact of the resulting recession in Canada.

CHAPTER HIGHLIGHTS

Chapter 1: The Role and Method of Economics

This chapter has undergone meaningful redesign to better attract the reader to the subject area. As well, additional illustrations of key introductory concepts have been added to help get the student off on the right foot.

Chapter 3: Supply and Demand

Greater detail has been added to the explanation and illustration of both demand shifters and supply shifters.

Chapter 5: Introduction to the Macroeconomy

The topic of price indexes—specifically the Consumer Price Index (CPI)—has been included in this chapter, providing a more comprehensive discussion of both real gross domestic product and inflation. Expanding the business cycle topic is a commentary about the 2008–2009 recession in Canada.

Chapter 10: Fiscal Policy

The Government of Canada's response to the 2008–2009 recession is evaluated.

Chapter 11: Money and the Banking System

T-accounts now accompany the topic of "How Banks Create Money."

Chapter 13: Monetary Policy

A clearer description of Bank of Canada policy options—specifically the targeting of the overnight interest rate—is now provided by this chapter. The Bank of Canada's response to the 2008–2009 recession is also discussed.

FEATURES OF THE BOOK

The Section-by-Section Approach

Exploring Macroeconomics uses a section-by-section approach in which economic ideas and concepts are presented in short, self-contained units rather than in large blocks of text. Each chapter is composed of approximately six to eight bite-sized sections, typically presented in two to eight pages that include all of the relevant graphs, tables, applications, features, photos, and definitions for the topic at hand. Our enthusiasm for and dedication to this approach stems from studying research on *learning theory*, which indicates that students retain information much better when it is broken down into short, intense, and exciting bursts of "digestible" information. Students prefer information divided into smaller, self-contained sections that are less overwhelming, more manageable, and easier to review before going on to new material. In short, students will be more successful in mastering and retaining economic principles using this approach, which is distinctly more compatible with modern communication styles.

But students aren't the only ones to benefit from this approach. The self-contained sections allow instructors greater flexibility in planning their courses. They can simply select or delete sections of the text as it fits their syllabus.

Learning Tools

Key Questions   Each section begins with key questions designed to preview ideas and to pique students' interest in the material to come. These questions are then used to structure the section material that follows, each question being prominently displayed as a section heading, with additional subheadings provided as needed. In addition to ensuring a clear instructional layout of each section and chapter, these key questions can also be used by students as a review resource. After reading the section material, if students are able to answer the key questions, they can go forward with confidence.

section 13.1

Money, Interest Rates, and Aggregate Demand

- What determines the money market?
- How does the Bank of Canada affect RGDP in the short run?
- Does the Bank of Canada target the money supply or the interest rate?
- Which interest rate does the Bank of Canada target?
- Does the Bank of Canada influence the real interest rate in the short run?

SECTION CHECK

- The money market is the market where money demand and money supply determine the equilibrium interest rate. Money demand has three possible motives: transaction purposes, precautionary reasons, and asset purposes. The quantity of money demanded varies inversely with interest rates and directly with income. The supply of money is effectively almost perfectly inelastic with respect to interest rates over their plausible range, as controlled by Bank of Canada policies.
- When the Bank of Canada sells bonds to the private sector or raises its target for the overnight interest rate, this leads to a reduction in the money supply, which in turn leads to a higher interest rate and a reduction in aggregate demand, at least in the short run. When the Bank of Canada buys bonds or lowers its target for the overnight interest rate, the money supply increases. The increase in the money supply will lead to lower interest rates and an increase in aggregate demand.

Section Checks   A *Section Check* appears at the end of each section and is designed to summarize the answers to the key questions posed at the beginning of the section. The summaries provided by the *Section Check* give students an opportunity to evaluate their understanding of major ideas before proceeding.

Exhibits   Graphs, tables, and charts are used throughout *Exploring Macroeconomics* to illustrate, clarify, and reinforce economic principles. Text exhibits are designed to be as clear and simple as possible and are carefully coordinated with the text material.

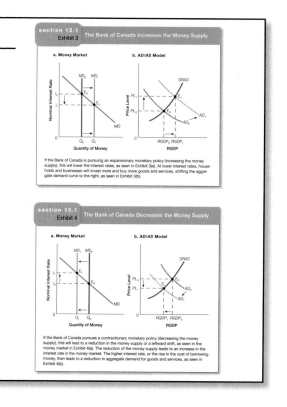

section 13.1
Exhibit 3   The Bank of Canada Increases the Money Supply

a. Money Market

b. AD/AS Model

If the Bank of Canada is pursuing an expansionary monetary policy (increasing the money supply), this will lower the interest rates, as seen in Exhibit 3(a). At lower interest rates, households and businesses will invest more and buy more goods and services, shifting the aggregate demand curve to the right, as seen in Exhibit 3(b).

section 13.1
Exhibit 4   The Bank of Canada Decreases the Money Supply

a. Money Market

b. AD/AS Model

If the Bank of Canada pursues a contractionary monetary policy (decreasing the money supply), this will lead to a reduction in the money supply or a leftward shift, as seen in the money market in Exhibit 4(a). The reduction of the money supply leads to an increase in the interest rate in the money market. The higher interest rate, or the rise in the cost of borrowing money, then leads to a reduction in aggregate demand for goods and services, as seen in Exhibit 4(b).

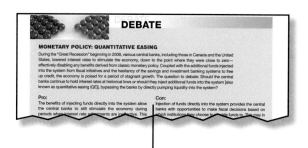

DEBATE

MONETARY POLICY: QUANTITATIVE EASING

During the "Great Recession" beginning in 2008, various central banks, including those in Canada and the United States, lowered interest rates to stimulate the economy, down to the point where they were close to zero—effectively disabling any benefits derived from classic monetary policy. Coupled with the additional funds injected into the system from fiscal initiatives and the hesitancy of the savings and investment banking systems to free up credit, the economy is poised for a period of stagnant growth. The question to debate: Should the central banks continue to hold interest rates at historical lows or should they inject additional funds into the system [also known as quantitative easing (QE)], bypassing the banks by directly pumping liquidity into the system?

Pro:
The benefits of injecting funds directly into the system allow the central banks to still stimulate the economy during periods when interest rate adjustments are ineffective. This

Con:
Injection of funds directly into the system provides the central banks with opportunities to make fiscal decisions based on which institutions they choose to provide funds to. This may in

Debate Features   *Debate* features, located in each chapter of the textbook, are designed to provide students with an opportunity to develop and express their opinions about a variety of economic issues. The "for" and "against" arguments that accompany each debate topic make it easy to use these features to initiate in-class discussions. By engaging in informal debate regarding current economic policy, students will be able to link course content to current events as well as to their own personal lives.

Business Connection Features *Business Connection* features are designed to help students see the link between economic theory and business fundamentals. Located in each chapter of the text, these features help students better understand the reasoning behind the empirical validity of economic theory, and they also aid in the grounding of abstract economic theory in more "modern" business principles.

Business CONNECTION

GETTING A JUMP ON INFLATION

Monetary policies are policies whereby the government controls the nation's money supply. In Canada this control is delegated to the Bank of Canada. The Bank of Canada's policies with respect to the money supply have a direct impact on short-run real interest rates, and accordingly on at least two of the components of aggregate demand—consumer expenditure and business investment. Business with an eye on revenues is always concerned about the demand for its goods or services. Many businesses selling big-ticket items such as cars and appliances find revenues extremely sensitive to interest rates, as purchasers often need to finance purchases with borrowed funds.

Sales are also very sensitive to overall demand resulting from the government's fiscal policies. How can business read the road ahead regarding fiscal and monetary policies? The fact is that this area of macroeconomics is fraught with complexity. Policymakers experience great difficulty predicting the impact that various policy initiatives will have on the economy and in forecasting when the expected outcomes will materialize. For businesses, it is almost impossible to gauge the collective impact that government and central bank policy decisions will have on costs of operations, revenue levels, and profitability. Nevertheless, there are some pockets of reliable theory in this area. The Phillips curve is one such theory. Let's examine this theory.

The work of economist A. H. Phillips suggests that there is a trade-off between inflation and unemployment in the

short term. Essentially, the cost of lower unemployment appears to be greater inflation, and the cost of greater price stability appears to be higher unemployment. How can firms use this theory to their advantage? Phillips theory maintains that when governments faced with a recessionary gap engage in expansionary monetary policy to reduce unemployment, the result in the near term will be a gradual increase in the rate of inflation. As attempts are made to further reduce unemployment, the rate of inflation is likely to increase more sharply.

Because of this trade-off relationship, where possible, those firms with an awareness of this relationship should seek to enter into long-term contracts for all significant factors of production, labour, land, equipment, and other resources as the economy signals improvement. Ideally, such contracts should be secured early in the business cycle, as the cost of the factors are likely to increase sharply as governments attempt to reduce unemployment at the expense of inflation. If the government is successful, the economy will move to a higher level of employment, eventually resulting in scarcity of many factors of production and increased costs for these factors.

Those firms that anticipate such a development will reap benefits on two fronts. First, their unit costs will increase at a rate lower than others in their respective industries. Second, they will have the capacity to enjoy increases in revenue due to increased demand resulting from lower unemployment. All of this should increase a firm's acceleration toward higher profit margins, at least in the short term.

In 1993, the North American Free Trade Agreement (NAFTA) was passed. This lowered the trade barriers between Mexico, Canada, and the United States. Proponents of freer trade, especially economists, viewed the agreement as a way to gain greater wealth through specialization and trade for all three countries. Opponents thought the agreement would take away Canadian and U.S. jobs and lower living standards.

WHO BENEFITS AND WHO LOSES WHEN A COUNTRY BECOMES AN IMPORTER?

Now suppose that our economy does not produce shirts as well as other countries of the world. In other words, other countries have a comparative advantage in producing shirts. This means that the domestic price for shirts is above the world price. This scenario is illustrated in Exhibit 3. At the new, lower world price, the domestic producer will supply quantity Q^S_{AT}. However, at the lower world price, the domestic producers will not produce

section 14.4
Exhibit 3 Free Trade and Imports

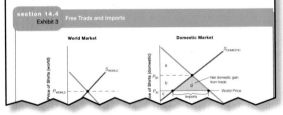

Photos *Exploring Macroeconomics* contains a large number of colourful pictures. They are not, however, mere decoration; rather, these photos are an integral part of the book, for both learning and motivational purposes. The photos are carefully placed where they reinforce important concepts, and they are accompanied by captions designed to encourage students to extend their understanding of particular ideas.

Scarcity and Resources

The scarce resources used in the production [...] four categories: labour, land, capital, and e[...]

Labour is the total of both physical a[...] tion of goods and services.

Land includes the "gifts of nature" [...] tion of goods and services. Trees, animal[...] ered to be "land" for our purposes, along [...] as land.

Capital is the equipment and struc[...] buildings, tools, machines, and factorie[...] invest in factories, machines, research an[...] potential to create more goods and servi[...] **capital,** the productive knowledge and [...] job training.

Entrepreneurship is the process of co[...] produce goods and services. Entreprene[...] what and how to produce goods and se[...] ways to improve production technique[...] chance to make a profit. It is this opportu[...] to take risks.

However, entrepreneurs are not nece[...] (cosmetics empire), or a Paul Desmarai[...] entrepreneurs when we try new products o[...] holds or our study time. Rather than money[...] enjoyment, additional time for recreation[...]

WHAT ARE GOODS AND SERV[...]

Goods are those items that we value or de[...] be seen, held, heard, tasted, or smelled. [...] willing to pay, such as legal services, medic[...] because they are less overtly visible, but the[...] goods and services, whether tangible or int[...] can be subjected to economic analysis. If [...] us, we will have to compete for those scarc[...] leads to competition for the available good[...]

labour
the physical and mental effort used by people in the production of goods and services

land
the natural resources used in the production of goods and services

capital
the equipment and structures used to produce goods and services

human capital
the productive knowledge and skill people receive from education and on-the-job training

entrepreneurship
the process of combining labour, land, and capital together to produce goods and services

goods
items we value or desire

service
an intangible act that people want

Marginal Key Terms When key terms and concepts are first introduced in the text, they are boldfaced and the definitions appear in the margin for ease of student learning.

For Your Review   Provided at the end of each chapter, these *For Your Review* problems allow students to test their understanding of chapter concepts. The *For Your Review* problems are organized into sections to match the corresponding sections in the text so that students and instructors can easily identify particular topics. To assist in the learning process, answers to all odd-numbered problems are provided at the back of the text. With a variety of both problems and application-style questions to choose from, *For Your Review* can also be used by instructors to assign homework directly from the text.

For Your Review

Section 1.1

1. Write your own definition of *economics*. What are the main elements of the definition?
2. Would the following topics be covered in microeconomics or macroeconomics?
   a. the effects of an increase in the supply of lumber on the home-building industry
   b. changes in the national unemployment rate
   c. the effect of interest rates on the machine-tool industry
   d. the effect of interest rates on the demand for investment goods
   e. the way a firm maximizes profits

Section 1.2

3. Are the following statements normative or positive, or do they contain both normative and positive statements?
   a. A higher income tax rate would generate increased tax revenues. Those extra revenues should be used to give more government aid to the poor.
   b. The study of physics is more valuable than the study of sociology, but both should be studied by all college students.
   c. An increase in the price of wheat will decrease the amount of wheat purchased. However, it will increase the amount of wheat supplied to the market.
   d. A decrease in the price of butter will increase the amount of butter purchased, but that would be bad because it would increase Canadians' cholesterol levels.
   e. The birth rate is reduced as economies urbanize, but that also leads to an increased average age of developing countries' populations.
4. Which of the following economic statements are positive and which are normative?
   a. A tax increase will increase unemployment.
   b. The government should reduce funding for social assistance programs.
   c. Tariffs on imported wine will lead to higher prices for domestic wine.
   d. A decrease in the capital gains tax rate will increase investment.
   e. Goods purchased on the Internet should be subject to provincial sales taxes.
   f. A reduction in interest rates will cause inflation.
5. The following statement represents which fallacy in thinking? Explain why. "I earn $12 per hour. If I am able to earn $12 per hour, everyone should be able to

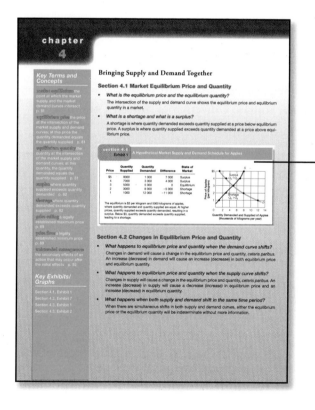

Chapter In Review Cards   Located at the back of the text, these detachable *Chapter In Review* cards are designed to give students a summary overview of key chapter concepts at a glance. Each *Chapter In Review* card will contain the following information:

- **Chapter Summary**   A point-form summary of each section's key questions, highlighting the most important concepts of each section, is provided.

- **Key Terms and Concepts**   A list of key terms and concepts is included that allows students to test their mastery of new concepts. Both the definition and page number are given for each term, so students can easily find the term in the chapter.

- **Key Graphs**   Given the importance and explanatory ability of graphical representations in economics, no review document would be complete without the inclusion of key graphs.

SUPPLEMENTARY MATERIALS
About NETA

⌐neta

The ***Nelson Education Teaching Advantage*** (**NETA**) program delivers research-based instructor resources that promote student engagement and higher-order thinking to enable the success of Canadian students and educators.

Instructors today face many challenges. Resources are limited, time is scarce, and a new kind of student has emerged: one who is juggling school with work, has gaps in his or her basic knowledge, and is immersed in technology in a way that has led to a completely new style of learning. In response, Nelson Education has gathered a group of dedicated instructors to advise us on the creation of richer and more flexible ancillaries that respond to the needs of today's teaching environments.

The members of our NETA editorial advisory board have experience across a variety of disciplines and are recognized for their commitment to teaching. They include

Norman Althouse, Haskayne School of Business, University of Calgary

Brenda Chant-Smith, Department of Psychology, Trent University

Scott Follows, F. C. Manning School of Business, Acadia University

Jon Houseman, Department of Biology, University of Ottawa

Glen Loppnow, Department of Chemistry, University of Alberta

Tanya Noel, Department of Biology, York University

Gary Poole, Senior Scholar, Centre for Health Education Scholarship, and Associate Director, School of Population and Public Health, University of British Columbia

Dan Pratt, Department of Educational Studies, University of British Columbia

Mercedes Rowinsky-Geurts, Department of Languages and Literatures, Wilfrid Laurier University

David DiBattista, Department of Psychology, Brock University

Roger Fisher, Ph.D.

In consultation with the NETA editorial advisory board, Nelson Education has completely rethought the structure, approaches, and formats of our key textbook ancillaries. We've also increased our investment in editorial support for our ancillary authors. The result is the *Nelson Education Teaching Advantage* and its key components: *NETA Engagement, NETA Assessment,* and *NETA Presentation.* Each component includes one or more ancillaries prepared according to our best practices and a document explaining the theory behind the practices.

NETA Engagement presents materials that help instructors deliver engaging content and activities to their classes. Instead of instructor's manuals that regurgitate chapter outlines and key terms from the text, *NETA Enriched Instructor's Manuals* (EIMs) provide genuine assistance to teachers. The EIMs answer questions like *What should students learn? Why should students care?* and *What are some common student misconceptions and stumbling blocks?* EIMs not only identify the topics that cause students the most difficulty, but also describe techniques and resources to help students master these concepts. Dr. Roger Fisher's *Instructor's Guide to Classroom Engagement* (IGCE) accompanies every *NETA Enriched Instructor's Manual.*

NETA Assessment relates to testing materials, not just Nelson's test banks and computerized test banks, but also in-text self-tests, study guides, Web quizzes, and homework programs like CourseMate. Under *NETA Assessment,* Nelson's authors create multiple-choice questions that reflect research-based best practices for constructing effective questions and testing, not just involving recall but engaging higher-order thinking. Our guidelines were developed by David DiBattista, a 3M National Teaching Fellow whose recent research as a professor of psychology at Brock University has focused on multiple-choice testing. All test bank authors receive training at workshops conducted by Professor DiBattista, as do the copy editors assigned to each test bank. A copy of *Multiple-Choice Tests: Getting Beyond Remembering*, Professor DiBattista's guide to writing effective tests, is included with every *Nelson Test Bank/Computerized Test Bank* package.

NETA Presentation has been developed to help instructors make the best use of PowerPoint® in their classrooms. With a clean and uncluttered design developed by Maureen Stone of StoneSoup Consulting, *NETA Presentation* features slides with improved readability, more multimedia and graphic materials, activities to use in class, and tips for instructors on the Notes page. A copy of *NETA Guidelines for Classroom Presentations* by Maureen Stone is included with each set of Microsoft PowerPoint® slides.

Instructor's Resource CD

Key instructor ancillaries are provided on the *Instructor's Resource CD* (ISBN-0176647724), giving instructors the ultimate tool for customizing lectures and presentations. The *Instructor's Resource CD* includes

- ***NETA Assessment***: The Test Bank was written by Russell Turner, Fleming College. It includes over 1300 multiple-choice questions written according to NETA guidelines for effective construction and development of higher-order questions. Also included are more than 260 true/false questions and over 100 essay-type questions. Test bank files are provided in Word format for easy editing and in PDF format for convenient printing, whatever your operating system.

    The *Computerized Test Bank* by ExamView® includes all of the questions from the *Test Bank*. The easy-to-use ExamView software is compatible with Microsoft Windows® and Apple Mac®. Create tests by selecting questions from the question bank, modifying these questions as desired, and adding new questions you write yourself. You can administer quizzes online and export tests to WebCT, Blackboard, and other formats.

- ***NETA Presentation***: Microsoft PowerPoint lecture slides average 40 slides per chapter. Authored by Sarah Arliss, Seneca College, many of the slides feature key figures, tables, and photographs from *Exploring Macroeconomics*, Third Canadian Edition. The NETA principles of clear design and engaging content have been incorporated throughout.

- ***Instructor's Manual***: The *Instructor's Manual* was written by Gary Tompkins, University of Regina. It is organized according to the textbook chapters and includes teaching tips, active learning exercises, and answers to all *For Your Review* exercises in the text.

- ***Image Bank***: This resource consists of digital copies of figures, short tables, and photographs used in the book. Instructors may use these images to create their own PowerPoint presentations.

Aplia™

aplia
Engage. Prepare. Educate.

Created by Paul Romer, a leading economist, Aplia enhances teaching and learning by providing online interactive tools and experiments that help economics students become "active learners." This application allows a tight content correlation between the third Canadian edition of *Exploring Macroeconomics* and Aplia's online tools.

Students Come to Class Prepared. It is proven that students do better in their course work if they come to class prepared. Aplia's activities are engaging and based on discovery learning, requiring students to take an active role in the learning process. When assigned online homework, students are more apt to read the text, come to class better prepared to participate in discussions, and be more able to relate to the economic concepts and theories presented. Learning by doing helps students feel involved, gain confidence in the materials, and see important concepts come to life.

Assign Homework in an Effective and Efficient Way. Now you can assign homework without increasing your workload! Together, the third Canadian edition of *Exploring Macroeconomics* and Aplia provide a superior combination of text and technology resources to give you multiple teaching and learning solutions. Through Aplia, you can assign problem sets and online activities that automatically give feedback and are tracked and graded, all without requiring additional effort. Since Aplia's assignments are closely integrated with the third Canadian edition of *Exploring Macroeconomics,* your students are applying to their homework what they have learned from the text.

More information can be found at www.aplia.com. Contact your local Nelson representative to package this exciting technology with your textbook.

CourseMate

CourseMate

Nelson Education's CourseMate brings course concepts to life with interactive learning and exam preparation tools that integrate with the printed textbook. CourseMate for *Exploring Macroeconomics,* Third Canadian Edition, provides an opportunity for students to activate their learning through a multitude of tools:

- Test Yourself quizzes
- Interactive quizzes
- Crossword puzzles
- Flashcards
- Student lecture note handouts
- Videos on economics
- Graphing tool
- Glossary
- and other general economics applications such as:
  - Careers in Economics
  - Education in Economics
  - Professional organizations in Economics
  - Economics news sources
  - Listing of general economics websites

CourseMate provides immediate feedback that enables students to connect results to the work they have just produced, decreasing their learning curve. It also encourages contact between students and faculty: You can monitor your students' level of engagement with CourseMate, correlating their efforts to their outcomes. You can even use CourseMate's quizzes to practise "just in time" teaching by tracking results in the Engagement Tracker and customizing your lesson plans to address student weaknesses.

Watch student comprehension and engagement soar as your class engages with CourseMate. Ask your Nelson representative for a demo today.

Acknowledgments

Producing the third Canadian edition of *Exploring Macroeconomics* has truly been a team effort. We would like to thank the editorial, production, and marketing teams at Nelson Education for their hard work and effort. First, our appreciation goes to Anne Williams, editorial director, who has provided the vision and leadership for the Canadian editions of the text.

We would like to extend special thanks to Rod Banister and Amie Plourde, acquisition editors at Nelson Education Limited, for their continuing support. We also thank Katherine Goodes, senior developmental editor at My Editor Inc., for her helpful advice and constant encouragement. This book reflects her hard work and effort. Thanks also to Susan Calvert, director of Content & Media Production; June Trusty, copy editor; and all the marketing and sales representatives at Nelson Education Ltd.

Finally, we would like to acknowledge the reviewers of the Canadian editions, past and present, for their comments and feedback:

Vick Barylak, *Sheridan College*
Aurelia Best, *Centennial College*
Jim Butko, *Niagara College*
Robert Dale, *Algonquin College*
Bruno Fullone, *George Brown College*
James Hnatchuk, *Champlain College Saint-Lambert*
Michael Leonard, *Kwantlen Polytechnic University*
Margaret Rose Olfert, *University of Saskatchewan*
Geoffrey Prince, *Centennial College*
Martha Spence, *Confederation College*
Carl Weston, *Mohawk College*

Their thoughtful suggestions were very important to us in providing input and useful examples for the third Canadian edition of this book.

P.N.F.
C.C.K.

chapter 1

The Role and Method of Economics

section 1.1

Economics: A Brief Introduction

- What is economics?
- Why study economics?
- What distinguishes macroeconomics from microeconomics?

WHAT IS ECONOMICS?

Some individuals think economics involves the study of the stock market and corporate finance, and it does—in part. Others think that economics is concerned with the wise use of money and other matters of personal finance, and it is—in part. Still others think that economics involves forecasting or predicting what business conditions will be like in the future, and again, it does—in part.

Growing Wants and Scarce Resources

Precisely defined, **economics** is the study of the allocation of our limited resources to satisfy our unlimited wants. **Resources** are inputs—such as land, human effort and skills, and machines and factories—used to produce goods and services. The problem is that our wants exceed our limited resources, a fact that we call *scarcity*. Scarcity forces us to make choices on how to best use our limited resources. This is **the economic problem:** Scarcity forces us to choose, and choices are costly because we must give up other opportunities that we value. This economizing problem is evident in every aspect of our lives. Choosing between a trip to the grocery store or the mall, or between finishing an assignment or going to a movie, can be understood more easily when one has a good handle on the "economic way of thinking."

Economics Is All Around Us

Although many things that we desire in life are considered to be "noneconomic," economics concerns anything that is considered worthwhile to some human being. For instance, love, sexual activity, and religion have value for most people. Even these have an

economics
the study of the allocation of our limited resources to satisfy our unlimited wants

resources
inputs used to produce goods and services

the economic problem
scarcity forces us to choose, and choices are costly because we must give up other opportunities that we value

The front pages of our daily newspapers are filled with articles related to economics—either directly or indirectly. News headlines might read: Gasoline Prices Soar; Stocks Rise; Stocks Fall; Prime Minister Vows to Increase National Defence Spending; Health-Care Costs Continue to Rise.

economic dimension. Consider religion, for example. Concern for spiritual matters has led to the development of institutions such as churches, mosques, and temples that provide religious and spiritual services. These services are goods that many people desire. Love and sex likewise have received economists' scrutiny. One product of love, the institution of the family, is an important economic decision-making unit. Also, sexual activity results in the birth of children, one of the most important "goods" that humans desire.

Even time has an economic dimension. In fact, perhaps the most precious single resource is time. We all have the same limited amount of time per day, and how we divide our time between work and leisure (including perhaps study, sleep, exercise, etc.) is a distinctly economic matter. If we choose more work, we must sacrifice leisure. If we choose to study, we must sacrifice time with friends, or time spent sleeping or watching TV. Virtually everything we decide to do, then, has an economic dimension.

Living in a world of scarcity means trade-offs. And it is important that we know what these trade-offs are so we can make better choices about the options available to us.

WHY STUDY ECONOMICS?

Among the many good reasons to study economics, perhaps the best reason is that so many of the things of concern in the world around us are at least partly economic in character. A quick look at newspaper headlines reveals the vast range of problems that are related to economics—global warming, health care, education, and social assistance. The study of economics improves your understanding of these concerns. A student of economics becomes aware that, at a basic level, much of economic life involves choosing among alternative possible courses of action—making choices between our conflicting wants and desires in a world of scarcity. Economics provides some clues as to how to intelligently evaluate these options and determine the most appropriate choices in given situations. But economists learn quickly that there are seldom easy, clear-cut solutions to the problems we face: The easy problems were solved long ago!

Many students take introductory college-level economics courses because these are part of the core curriculum requirements. But why do the committees that establish these requirements include economics? In part, economics helps develop a disciplined method of thinking about problems as opposed to simply memorizing solutions. The problem-solving tools you will develop by studying economics will prove valuable to you in both your personal and professional life, regardless of your career choice. In short, the study of economics provides a systematic, disciplined way of thinking.

Using This Stuff

The basic tools of economics are valuable to people in all walks of life and in all career paths. Newspaper reporters benefit from economics, because the problem-solving perspective it teaches trains them to ask intelligent questions whose answers will better inform their readers. Engineers, architects, and contractors usually have alternative ways to build. Architects learn to combine technical expertise and artistry with the limitations imposed by finite resources. That is, they learn how to evaluate their options from an economic perspective. Business owners face similar problems, because costs are a constraint in both creating and marketing a new product. Will the added cost of developing a new and improved product be outweighed by the added sales revenues that are expected to result? Economists can, however, pose these questions and provide criteria that business owners can use in evaluating the appropriateness of one design as compared to another. The point is that the economic way of thinking causes those in many types of fields to ask the right kind of questions.

WHAT DISTINGUISHES MACROECONOMICS FROM MICROECONOMICS?

Like psychology, sociology, anthropology, and political science, economics is considered a social science. Economics, like the other social sciences, is concerned with reaching generalizations about human behaviour. Economics is the study of people. It is the social science that studies the choices people make in a world of limited resources.

Economics and the other social sciences often complement one another. For example, a political scientist might examine the process that led to the adoption of a certain tax policy, whereas an economist might analyze the impact of that tax policy. Or, whereas a psychologist may try to figure out what makes the criminal mind work, an economist might study the factors causing a change in the crime rate. Social scientists, then, may be studying the same issue but from different perspectives.

Conventionally, we distinguish two main branches of economics: macroeconomics and microeconomics. **Macroeconomics** is the study of the **aggregate** or total economy; it looks at economic problems as they influence the whole of society. Topics covered in macroeconomics include discussions of inflation, unemployment, business cycles, and economic growth. **Microeconomics** is the study of the smaller units within the economy. Topics include the decision-making behaviour of firms and households and their interaction in markets for particular goods or services. Microeconomic topics also include discussions of health care, agricultural subsidies, the price of everyday items such as running shoes, the distribution of income, and the impact of labour unions on wages. To put it simply, microeconomics looks at the trees whereas macroeconomics looks at the forest.

macroeconomics
the study of the aggregate economy including the topics of inflation, unemployment, and economic growth

aggregate
the total amount—such as the aggregate level of output

microeconomics
the study of the smaller units within the economy including the topics of household and firm behaviour and how they interact in the marketplace

SECTION CHECK

- Economics is the study of the allocation of our limited resources to satisfy our unlimited wants.
- Economics is a problem-solving science that teaches you how to ask intelligent questions.
- Macroeconomics deals with the aggregate, or total, economy, while microeconomics focuses on smaller units within the economy.

Economic Theory

section

1.2

- What are economic theories?
- Why do we need to abstract?
- What is a hypothesis?
- What is the *ceteris paribus* assumption?
- Why are observations and predictions harder in the social sciences?
- What distinguishes between correlation and causation?
- What is the fallacy of composition?
- What are positive analysis and normative analysis?
- Why do economists disagree?

How is economic theory like a map? Because of the complexity of human behaviour, economists must abstract to focus on the most important components of a particular problem. This is similar to maps that highlight the important information (and assume away many minor details) to help people get from here to there.

stockex/GetStock.com

WHAT ARE ECONOMIC THEORIES?

A **theory** is an established explanation that accounts for known facts or phenomena. Specifically, economic theories are statements or propositions about patterns of human behaviour that are expected to take place under certain circumstances. These theories help us to sort out and understand the complexities of economic behaviour. We expect a good theory to explain and predict well. A good economic theory, then, should help us to better understand and, ideally, predict human economic behaviour.

WHY DO WE NEED TO ABSTRACT?

Economic theories cannot realistically include every event that has ever occurred. This is true for the same reason that a newspaper or history book does not include every world event that has ever happened. We must abstract. A road map of Canada may not include every creek, ridge, and valley between Calgary and Halifax—indeed, such an all-inclusive map would be too large to be of value. However, a small road map with major details will provide enough information to travel by car from Calgary to Halifax. Likewise, an economic theory provides a broad view, not a detailed examination, of human economic behaviour.

theory
an established explanation that accounts for known facts or phenomena

WHAT IS A HYPOTHESIS?

The beginning of any theory is a **hypothesis,** a testable proposition that makes some type of prediction about behaviour in response to certain changes in conditions. In economic theory, a hypothesis is a testable prediction about how people will behave or react to a change in economic circumstances. For example, if the price of compact discs (CDs) increased, we might hypothesize that fewer CDs would be sold, or if the price of CDs fell, we might hypothesize that more CDs would be sold. Once a hypothesis is stated, it is tested by comparing what it predicts will happen to what actually happens.

hypothesis
a testable proposition

Using Empirical Analysis

To see if a hypothesis is valid, we must engage in an **empirical analysis.** That is, we must examine the data to see if the hypothesis fits well with the facts. If the hypothesis is consistent with real-world observations, it is accepted; if it does not fit well with the facts, it is "back to the drawing board."

empirical analysis
the examination of data to see if the hypothesis fits well with the facts

Determining whether a hypothesis is acceptable is more difficult in economics than it is in the natural or physical sciences. Chemists, for example, can observe chemical reactions under laboratory conditions. They can alter the environment to meet the assumptions of the hypothesis and can readily manipulate the variables (chemicals, temperatures, and so on) crucial to the proposed relationship. Such controlled experimentation is seldom possible in economics. The laboratory of economists is usually the real world. Unlike a chemistry lab, economists cannot easily control all the other variables that might influence human behaviour.

From Hypothesis to Theory

After gathering their data, economic researchers must then evaluate the results to determine whether the hypothesis is supported or refuted. If supported, the hypothesis can then be tentatively accepted as an economic theory.

Economic theories are always on probation. A hypothesis is constantly being tested against empirical findings. Do the observed findings support the prediction? When a hypothesis survives a number of tests, it is accepted until it no longer predicts well.

WHAT IS THE *CETERIS PARIBUS* ASSUMPTION?

Virtually all economic theories share a condition usually expressed by use of the Latin expression ***ceteris paribus.*** This roughly means "let everything else be equal" or "holding everything else constant." In trying to assess the effect of one variable on another, we must isolate their relationship from other events that might also influence the situation that the theory tries to explain or predict. To make this clearer, we will illustrate this concept with a couple of examples.

ceteris paribus
holding everything else constant

Suppose you develop your own theory describing the relationship between studying and exam performance: If I study harder, I will perform better on the test. That sounds logical, right? Holding other things constant *(ceteris paribus),* this is likely to be true. However, what if you studied harder but inadvertently overslept the day of the exam? What if you were so sleepy during the test that you could not think clearly? Or what if you studied the wrong material? Although it may look as if additional studying did not improve your performance, the real problem may lie in the impact of other variables, such as sleep deficiency or how you studied.

WHY ARE OBSERVATIONS AND PREDICTIONS HARDER IN THE SOCIAL SCIENCES?

Working from observations, scientists try to make generalizations that will enable them to predict certain events. However, observation and prediction are more difficult in the social sciences than in physical sciences such as chemistry, physics, and astronomy. Why? The major reason for the difference in that the social scientists, including economists, are concerned with *human* behaviour. And human behaviour is more variable and often less readily predictable than the behaviour of experiments observed in a laboratory. However, by looking at the actions of a large group of people, economists can still make many reliable predictions about human behaviour.

Economists Predict on a Group Level

Economists' predictions usually refer to the collective behaviour of large groups rather than to that of specific individuals. Why is this? Looking at the behaviours of a large group allows economists to discern general patterns of actions. For example, consider what would happen if the price of air travel from Canada to Europe was drastically reduced, say from $1500 to $500, because of the invention of a more fuel-efficient jet. What type of predictions could we make about the effect of this price reduction on the buying habits of typical consumers?

Individual Behaviour

Let's look first at the responses of individuals. As a result of the price drop, some people will greatly increase their intercontinental travel, taking theatre weekends in London or week-log trips to France to indulge in French food. Some people, however, are terribly afraid to fly, and a price reduction will not influence their behaviour in the slightest. Others might detest Europe and, despite the lowered airfares, prefer to spend a few days in Vancouver, British Columbia, instead. A few people might respond to the airfare reduction in precisely the opposite way from ours: At the lower fare, they might make fewer trips to Europe, because they might believe (rightly or wrongly) that the price drop would be accompanied by a reduction in the quality of service, greater crowding, or reduced safety. In short, we cannot predict with any level of certainty how a given individual will respond to this airfare reduction.

Group Behaviour

Group behaviour is often more predictable than individual behaviour. When the weather gets colder, more firewood in sold. Some individuals may not buy firewood (e.g., if they don't have a fireplace in their home), but we can predict with great accuracy that a group of individuals will establish a pattern of buying more firewood. Similarly, while we cannot say what each individual will do, within a group of persons, we can predict with great accuracy that more flights to Europe from Toronto will be sold at lower prices, holding other things such as income and preferences constant. We cannot predict exactly how many more airline tickets will be sold at $500 than at $1500, but we can predict the direction of the impact and approximate the extent of the impact. By observing the relationship between the price of goods and services and the quantities people purchase in different places and during different time periods, it is possible to make some reliable generalizations about how much people will react to changes in the prices of goods and services. Economists use this larger picture of the group for most of their theoretical analysis.

WHAT DISTINGUISHES BETWEEN CORRELATION AND CAUSATION?

correlation
two events that usually occur together

causation
when one event causes another event to occur

Without a theory of causation, no scientist could sort out and understand the enormous complexity of the real world. But one must always be careful not to confuse correlation with causation. In other words, the fact that two events usually occur together (**correlation**) does not necessarily mean that one caused the other to occur (**causation**). For example, say a groundhog awakes after a long winter of hibernation, climbs out of his hole, sees his shadow, and then six weeks of bad weather ensue. Did the groundhog cause the bad weather? It is highly unlikely.

Perhaps the causality may run in the opposite direction. Although a rooster may always crow before the sun rises, it does not cause the sunrise; rather, the early light from the sunrise causes the rooster to crow.

The Positive Correlation between Ice Cream Sales and Crime

Did you know that when ice cream sales rise, so do crime rates? What do you think causes the two events to occur together? Some might think that the sugar "high" in the ice cream causes the higher crime rate. Excess sugar in a snack was actually used in court testimony in a murder case—the so-called "Twinkie defence." However, it is more likely that crime peaks in the summer because of weather, more people on vacation (leaving their homes vacant), teenagers out of school, and so on. It just happens that ice cream sales also peak in those months because of weather. The lesson: One must always be careful not to confuse correlation with causation and to be clear on the direction of the causation.

© Steve Estvanik/Shutterstock

People tend to drive slower when the roads are covered with ice. In addition, more traffic accidents occur when the roads are icy. So, does driving slower cause the number of accidents to rise? No, it is the icy roads that lead to both lower speeds and increased accidents.

WHAT IS THE FALLACY OF COMPOSITION?

One must also be careful with problems associated with aggregation (summing up all the parts), particularly the **fallacy of composition.** This fallacy states that even if something is true for an individual, it is not necessarily true for many individuals as a group. For example, say you are at a concert and you decide to stand up to get a better view of the stage. This works as long as no one else stands up. But what would happen if everyone stood up at the same time? Then, standing up would not let you see better. Hence, what may be true for an individual does not always hold true in the aggregate. The same can be said of arriving to class early to get a better parking place—what if everyone arrived early? Or studying harder to get a better grade in a class that is graded on a curve—what if everyone studied harder? All of these are examples of the fallacy of composition.

fallacy of composition
even if something is true for an individual, it is not necessarily true for a group

WHAT ARE POSITIVE ANALYSIS AND NORMATIVE ANALYSIS?

Positive Analysis

Most economists view themselves as scientists seeking the truth about the way people behave. They make speculations about economic behaviour, and then (ideally) they try to assess the validity of those predictions based on human experience. Their work emphasizes how people *do* behave, rather than how people *should* behave. In the role of scientist, an economist tries to observe, objectively, patterns of behaviour without reference to the appropriateness or inappropriateness of that behaviour. This objective, value-free approach, utilizing the scientific method, is called **positive analysis.** In positive analysis, we want to know the impact of variable A on variable B. We want to be able to test a hypothesis. For example, the following is a positive statement: If rent controls are imposed, vacancy rates will fall. This statement is testable. A positive statement does not have to be a true statement, but it does have to be a testable statement.

positive analysis
an objective, value-free approach, utilizing the scientific method

However, keep in mind that it is doubtful that even the most objective scientist can be totally value-free in his or her analysis. An economist may well emphasize data or evidence that supports his hypothesis, putting less weight on other evidence that might be contradictory. This, alas, is human nature. But a good economist/scientist strives to be as fair and objective as possible in evaluating evidence and in stating conclusions based on the evidence.

Normative Analysis

Like everyone, economists have opinions and make value judgments. When economists, or anyone else for that matter, express opinions about some economic policy or statement, they are indicating in part how they believe things should be, not just facts as to the way things are. **Normative analysis** is a subjective, biased approach, where one expresses opinions about the desirability of various actions. Normative statements involve judgments about what should be or what ought to happen. For example, one could judge that incomes

normative analysis
a subjective, biased approach

should be more equally distributed. If there is a change in tax policy that makes incomes more equal, there will be positive economic questions that can be investigated, such as how work behaviour will change. But we cannot say, as scientists, that such a policy is good or bad; rather, we can point to what will likely happen if the policy is adopted.

Positive versus Normative Statements

The distinction between positive and normative analysis is important. It is one thing to say that everyone should have universal health care, a normative statement, and quite another to say that universal health care would lead to greater worker productivity, a testable positive statement. It is important to distinguish between positive and normative analysis because many controversies in economics revolve around policy considerations that contain both. When economists start talking about how the economy should work rather than how it does work, they have entered the normative world of the policymaker.

WHY DO ECONOMISTS DISAGREE?

Although economists differ frequently on economic policy questions, there is probably less disagreement than the media would have you believe. Disagreement is common in most disciplines: Seismologists differ over predictions of earthquakes or volcanic eruption; historians can be at odds over the interpretation of historical events; psychologists disagree on proper ways to rear children; and nutritionists debate the merits of large doses of vitamin C.

The majority of disagreements in economics stem from normative issues, as differences in values or policy beliefs result in conflict. As we discussed earlier in this chapter, economists may emphasize specific facts over other facts when trying to develop support for their own hypothesis. As a result, disagreements can result when one economist gives weight to facts that have been minimized by another, and vice versa.

Freedom versus Fairness

Some economists are concerned about individual freedom and liberty, thinking that any encroachment on individual decision making is, other things equal, bad. People with this philosophic bent are inclined to be skeptical of any increased government involvement in the economy.

On the other hand, some economists are concerned with what they consider an unequal, "unfair," or unfortunate distribution of income, wealth, or power, and view governmental intervention as desirable in righting injustices that they believe exist in a market economy. To these persons, the threat to individual liberty alone is not sufficiently great to reject governmental intervention in the face of perceived economic injustice.

The Validity of an Economic Theory

Aside from philosophic differences, there is a second reason why economists may differ on any given policy question. Specifically, they may disagree as to the validity of a given economic theory for the policy in question. Suppose two economists have identical philosophical views that have led them to the same conclusion: To end injustice and hardship, unemployment should be reduced. To reach the objective, the first economist believes the government should lower taxes and increase spending, whereas the second economist believes increasing the amount of money in public hands by various banking policies will achieve the same results with fewer undesirable consequences. The two economists differ because the empirical evidence for economic theories about the cause of unemployment appears to conflict. Some evidence suggests government taxation and spending policies are effective in reducing unemployment, whereas other evidence suggests that the prime cause of unnecessary unemployment lies with faulty monetary policy. Still other evidence is consistent with the view that, over long periods, neither approach mentioned here is of much value in reducing unemployment, and that unemployment will be part of our existence no matter what macroeconomic policies we follow.

Economists Do Agree

Although you may not believe it after reading the previous discussion, economists don't always disagree. In fact, according to a survey among members of the American Economic Association, most economists agree on a wide range of issues, including rent control, import tariffs, export restrictions, the use of wage and price controls to curb inflation, and the minimum wage.

SECTION CHECK

- Economic theories are statements used to explain and predict patterns of human behaviour.
- Economic theories, through abstraction, provide a broad view of human economic behaviour.
- A hypothesis makes a prediction about human behaviour and is then tested.
- In order to isolate the effects of one variable on another, we use the *ceteris paribus* assumption.
- With its focus on human behaviour, which is more variable and less predictable, observation and prediction are more difficult in the social sciences.
- The fact that two events are related does not mean that one caused the other to occur.
- What is true for the individual is not necessarily true for the group.
- Positive analysis is objective and value-free, while normative analysis involves value judgements and opinions about the desirability of various actions.
- Most disagreement among economists stems from normative issues.

section
1.3

Scarcity

- What is scarcity?
- What are goods and services?

Most of economics is really knowing certain principles well and knowing when and how to apply them. In the following sections, some important tools are presented that will help you understand the economic way of thinking. These few basic ideas will repeatedly occur throughout the text. If you develop a good understanding of these principles and master the problem-solving skills inherent in them, they will serve you well for the rest of your life.

WHAT IS SCARCITY?

As we have already mentioned, economics is concerned primarily with **scarcity**—the situation that exists when human wants exceed available resources. We may want more "essential" items like food, clothing, schooling, and health care. We may want many other

scarcity
the situation exists when human wants exceed available resources

items, like vacations, cars, computers, and concert tickets. We may want more friendship, love, knowledge, and so on. We also may have many goals—perhaps an A in this class, a university education, and a great job. Unfortunately, people are not able to fulfill all of their wants—material desires and nonmaterial desires. And as long as human wants exceed available resources, scarcity will exist.

Scarcity and Resources

The scarce resources used in the production of goods and services can be grouped into four categories: labour, land, capital, and entrepreneurship.

Labour is the total of both physical and mental effort used by people in the production of goods and services.

Land includes the "gifts of nature" or the natural resources used in the production of goods and services. Trees, animals, water, minerals, and so on are all considered to be "land" for our purposes, along with the physical space normally thought of as land.

Capital is the equipment and structures used to produce goods and services. Office buildings, tools, machines, and factories are all considered capital goods. When we invest in factories, machines, research and development, or education, we increase the potential to create more goods and services in the future. Capital also includes **human capital,** the productive knowledge and skills people receive from education and on-the-job training.

Entrepreneurship is the process of combining labour, land, and capital together to produce goods and services. Entrepreneurs make the tough and risky decisions about what and how to produce goods and services. Entrepreneurs are always looking for new ways to improve production techniques or to create new products. They are lured by the chance to make a profit. It is this opportunity to make a profit that leads entrepreneurs to take risks.

However, entrepreneurs are not necessarily a Bill Gates (Microsoft), an Elizabeth Arden (cosmetics empire), or a Paul Desmarais (Power Corporation). In some sense, we are all entrepreneurs when we try new products or when we find better ways to manage our households or our study time. Rather than money, then, our profits might take the form of greater enjoyment, additional time for recreation, or better grades.

WHAT ARE GOODS AND SERVICES?

Goods are those items that we value or desire. Goods tend to be tangible—objects that can be seen, held, heard, tasted, or smelled. **Services** are intangible acts for which people are willing to pay, such as legal services, medical services, and dental care. Services are intangible because they are less overtly visible, but they are certainly no less valuable than goods. All goods and services, whether tangible or intangible, are produced from scarce resources and can be subjected to economic analysis. If there are not enough goods and services for all of us, we will have to compete for those scarce goods and services. That is, scarcity ultimately leads to competition for the available goods and services, a subject we will return to often in the text.

Bads

In contrast to goods, **bads** are those items that we do not desire or want. For most people, garbage, pollution, weeds, and crime are bads. People tend to eliminate or minimize bads, so they will often pay to have bads, like garbage, removed. The elimination of the bad—garbage removal, for example—is a good.

labour
the physical and mental effort used by people in the production of goods and services

land
the natural resources used in the production of goods and services

capital
the equipment and structures used to produce goods and services

human capital
the productive knowledge and skill people receive from education and on-the-job training

entrepreneurship
the process of combining labour, land, and capital together to produce goods and services

goods
items we value or desire

service
an intangible act that people want

bads
items that we do not desire or want

Business CONNECTION

ECONOMICS IN BUSINESS

Business students often wonder why they need to study economics. How will knowledge of economics help in making better business decisions? To appreciate the role of economics in business let's revisit the nature of business. A business is considered to be an organization that attempts to make a profit by providing goods or services. Fundamentally, there is agreement that the goal of a business is to earn a profit. OK, but what is profit? Generally, profit is what remains after an organization subtracts its business costs or expenses from its sales revenues. One may therefore conclude that a good business is a business that generates a reasonable profit after all its business costs or expenses are subtracted from its sales revenues.

We may also see business as an equation, $P = R - C$, where R is the revenue from sales, C represents the related costs and expenses incurred to provide the goods or services, and P is the residual profit. Clearly, for a business to generate a profit, the revenues—that is, the funds collected from the sales of goods or services—must be greater than the total costs incurred to provide these same goods or services. Running a successful business is similar to solving a problem.

First, a look at revenues: The amount of revenue collected by an organization depends on the quantity of goods or services sold and the price for each good or service. If this is the case, how do businesses know what prices to charge and how many units to sell? Will consumers buy at these prices? And if so, how many units will they buy?

These two essential questions must be addressed if the organization is to make a profit (a positive number for P) and avoid a loss (a negative number for P). Good news: The critical information on the right price and the right quantities to solve the problem of making a profit is buried in economic theories, principles, and laws—so stay tuned in to economics. As you study this social science, you will begin to uncover answers to the two vital questions: What price? What quantity?

Now, a look at costs: To earn profit a business needs to manage the costs associated with revenues. These costs include many factors, such as salaries and wages for labour, Internet charges, and rent for buildings. The costs for these inputs will depend on their scarcity, since scarce resources will be relatively more expensive than abundant resources. Since the goal of a business is usually to make a profit, success in business is achieved by ensuring that total costs are less than total revenues. This is where an understanding of the economic principle of marginal costs versus marginal benefits will be useful in making business decisions regarding costs and revenues. Some costs will vary with the quantity of goods or services produced and sold. Others, such as rent, may remain fixed regardless of the number of units sold. Once again, knowledge of economics will help you to answer those all-important questions about how many units to produce and at what cost in order to maximize profit, the primary goal of a business.

One final thought: The concept of opportunity costs will also apply, as entrepreneurs check to see if they are in the right business.

Everyone Faces Scarcity

We all face scarcity because we cannot have all of the goods and services that we desire. However, because we all have different wants and desires, scarcity affects everyone differently. For example, a child in a developing country may face a scarcity of food and clean drinking water, whereas a rich person may face a scarcity of garage space for his growing antique car collection. Likewise, a harried middle-class working mother may find time for exercise particularly scarce, whereas a pharmaceutical company may be concerned with the scarcity of the natural resources it uses in its production process. Although its effects vary, no one can escape scarcity.

SECTION CHECK

- Scarcity exists when our wants exceed the available resources of land, labour, capital, and entrepreneurship.
- Goods and services are things that we value.

Opportunity Cost

- Why do we have to make choices?
- What do we give up when we have to choose?
- Why are "free" lunches not free?

WHY DO WE HAVE TO MAKE CHOICES?

We may want nice homes, two luxury cars in every garage, wholesome and good-tasting food, a personal trainer, and a therapist, all enjoyed in a pristine environment with zero pollution. If we had unlimited resources, and thus an ability to produce all of the goods and services anyone wanted, we would not have to choose among those desires. If we did not have to make meaningful economic choices, the study of economics would not be necessary. The essence of economics is to understand fully the implications that scarcity has for wise decision making. This suggests another way to define economics: *Economics is the study of the choices we make among our many wants and desires.*

WHAT DO WE GIVE UP WHEN WE HAVE TO CHOOSE?

opportunity cost
the highest or best forgone opportunity resulting from a decision

We are all faced with scarcity and, as a consequence, we must make choices. Because none of us can "afford" to buy everything we want, each time we do decide to buy one good or service, we reduce our ability to buy other things we would also like to have. If you buy a new car this year, you may not be able to afford your next best choice—the vacation you've been planning. You must choose. The cost of the car to you is the value of the vacation that must be forgone. The highest or best forgone opportunity resulting from a decision is called the **opportunity cost.** For example, time spent running costs time that could have been spent doing something else that is valuable—perhaps spending time with friends or studying for an upcoming exam. Another way to put this is that "to choose is to lose" or "an opportunity cost is an opportunity lost." To get more of anything that is desirable, you must accept less of something else that you also value.

One of the reasons why vehicle drivers talk so much on their cellphones is that they have little else to do with their time while driving—a low opportunity cost. However, drivers should not use cellphones while driving because this is a distraction; by not giving full attention to their driving, they are giving up safety. Trade-offs are everywhere.

Bill Gates, Tiger Woods, and Mark Zuckerberg all quit university or college to pursue their dreams. Tiger Woods dropped out of Stanford to join the PGA golf tour. Bill Gates dropped out of Harvard to start a software company. Mark Zuckerberg also dropped out of Harvard to continue working on his social networking site Facebook. Staying in school would have cost each of them millions of dollars. We cannot say it would have been the wrong decision to stay in school, but it would have been costly. For each of them, the opportunity cost of staying in school was high.

Money Prices and Costs

If you go to the store to buy groceries, you have to pay for the items you buy. This amount is called the *money price*. It is an opportunity cost, because you could have used the money to purchase other goods and services. However, additional opportunity costs include the nonprice costs incurred to acquire the groceries—time spent getting to the grocery store, finding a parking space, actually shopping, and waiting in the checkout line. The nonprice costs are measured by assessing the sacrifice involved—the value you place on what you would have done with the time if you had not gone shopping. So the cost of grocery shopping is the price paid for the goods plus the nonprice costs incurred.

Remember that many costs do not involve money but are still costs. Do I major in accounting or human resources? Do I go to college or university? Should I get an M.B.A. now or work and wait a few years to go back to school?

Policymakers are unavoidably faced with opportunity costs too. Consider airline safety. Both money costs and time costs affect airline safety. New airline safety devices cost money (luggage inspection devices, fuel tank safeguards, new radar equipment, and so on), and time costs are quite relevant with the new safety checks. Time waiting in line costs time that could be spent doing something that is valuable. New airline safety requirements could also actually cost lives. If the new safety equipment costs are passed on in the form of higher airline ticket prices, people may choose to travel by car, which is far more dangerous per kilometre than air travel is. Opportunity costs are everywhere!

The Opportunity Cost of Going to College or Having a Child

The average person often does not correctly consider opportunity costs when thinking about costs. For example, the opportunity cost of going to college is not just the direct expense of tuition and books; of course, those expenses do involve an opportunity cost, because the money used for books and tuition could be used for other things that you value. But what about the nonmoney costs? That is, going to college also includes the opportunity cost of your time. Specifically, the time spent going to school is time that could have been spent on a job earning, say, $30 000 a year. And how often do people consider the opportunity cost of raising a child to the age of 18? There are the direct costs: food, visits to the dentist, clothes, piano lessons, and so on. But there are also additional costs incurred in rearing a child. Consider the cost if one parent chooses to give up his or her job to stay at home: Then, the time spent in child-rearing is time that could have been used making money and pursuing a career.

WHY ARE "FREE" LUNCHES NOT FREE?

The expression *there's no such thing as a free lunch* clarifies the relationship between scarcity and opportunity cost. Suppose the school cafeteria is offering "free" lunches today. Although the lunch is free to you, is it really free from society's perspective? The answer is no, because some of society's scarce resources will have been used in the preparation of the lunch. The issue is whether the resources that went into creating that lunch could have been used to produce something else of value. Clearly, the scarce resources that went into the production of the lunch like the labour and materials (food-service workers, lettuce, meat, plows, tractors, fertilizer, and so forth) could have been used in other ways. They had an opportunity cost, and thus were not free. Whenever you hear the word "free"—free libraries, free admission, and so on—an alarm should go off in your head. Very few things are free in the sense that they use none of society's scarce resources. So what does a free lunch really mean? It is, technically speaking, a "subsidized" lunch—a lunch using society's scarce resources, but one for which you personally do not have to pay.

SECTION CHECK

- ■ Scarcity means we all have to make choices.
- ■ When we are forced to choose, we give up the next highest-valued alternative.
- ■ Because the production of any good uses up some of society's resources, there is no such thing as a free lunch.

Marginal Thinking

- What do we mean by marginal thinking?
- What is the rule of rational choice?

WHAT DO WE MEAN BY MARGINAL THINKING?

Most choices involve how *much* of something to do, rather than whether or not to do something. It is not *whether* you eat, but *how much* you eat. Hopefully, the question is not *whether* to study this semester but instead *how much* to study this semester. For example, "If I studied a little more, I might be able to improve my grade," or "If I had a little better concentration when I was studying, I could improve my grade." This is what economists call **marginal thinking** because the focus is on the additional, or incremental, choices. Marginal choices involve the effects of adding to or subtracting from the current situation. In short, it is the small (or large) incremental changes to a plan of action.

marginal thinking
focusing on the additional, or incremental, choices

Always watch out for the difference between average and marginal costs. Suppose the cost to an airline of flying 250 passengers from Edmonton to Montreal was $100 000. The average cost per seat would be $400 (the total cost divided by the number of seats—$100 000/250). If ten people are on standby and willing to pay $300 for a seat on the flight, should the airline sell them a ticket? Yes! The unoccupied seats earn nothing for the airline. The airline pays the $400 average cost per seat regardless of whether or not someone is sitting in the seat. What the airline needs to focus on are the additional (marginal) costs of a few extra passengers. The marginal costs are minimal—slight wear and tear on the airplane, handling some extra baggage, and ten extra in-flight meals. In this case, thinking at the margin can increase total profits, even if it means selling at less than-average cost of production.

Another good example of marginal thinking is auctions. Prices are bid up marginally as the auctioneer calls out one price after another. When a bidder views the new price (the marginal cost) to be greater than the value she places on the good (the marginal benefit), she withdraws from further bidding.

WHAT IS THE RULE OF RATIONAL CHOICE?

In trying to make themselves better off, individuals will pursue an activity if the expected marginal benefits are greater than the expected marginal costs—this is the **rule of rational choice**. The term *expected* is used with marginal benefits and costs because the world is uncertain in many important respects, so the actual result of changing behaviour may not always make people better off—but on average it will. However, as a matter of rationality, people are assumed to engage only in behaviour that they think ahead of time will make them better off. That is, individuals will pursue an activity only if the expected marginal benefits are greater than the expected marginal costs, or $E(MB) > E(MC)$. This fairly unrestrictive and realistic view of individuals seeking self-betterment can be used to analyze a variety of social phenomena.

rule of rational choice
individuals will pursue an activity if the expected marginal benefits are greater than the expected marginal costs

Suppose that you have to get up for an 8 A.M. class but have been up very late. When the alarm goes off at 7 A.M., you are weighing the marginal benefits and marginal costs of an extra 15 minutes of sleep. If you perceive the marginal benefits of 15 minutes of sleep to be greater than the marginal costs of those extra minutes, you may choose to hit the snooze button. Or perhaps you may decide to blow off class completely. But it's unlikely you will choose that action if it is the day of the final exam, because it is now likely that the **net benefits**—the difference between the expected marginal benefits and expected marginal costs—of skipping class have changed. When people have opportunities to better themselves, they usually take them. And they will continue to seek those opportunities as long as they expect a net benefit from doing so.

net benefits
The difference between the expected marginal benefits and expected marginal costs

The rule of rational choice is simply the rule of being sensible, and most economists believe that individuals act *as if* they are sensible and apply the rule of rational choice to their daily lives. It is a rule that can help us understand our decision to study, walk, shop, exercise, clean house, cook, and perform just about every other action. It is also a rule that we will continue to use throughout the text because whether we are consumers, producers, or policymakers, we all must compare the expected marginal benefits and the expected marginal costs to determine the best level to consume, produce, or develop policies.

What would you be willing to give up to eliminate the rush-hour congestion you face? Think of the number of hours drivers waste each year sitting in traffic in Canada's largest cities. It costs the Canadian economy hundreds of millions of dollars a year in lost wages and wasted fuel.

Zero Pollution Would Be Too Costly

Let's use the concept of marginal thinking to evaluate pollution levels. We all know the benefits of a cleaner environment, but what would we have to give up—that is, what marginal costs would we have to incur—in order to achieve zero pollution? A lot! You could not drive a car, fly in a plane, or even ride a bike, especially if everybody else was riding bikes too (because congestion is a form of pollution). How would you get to school or work, or go to the movies or the grocery store? Everyone would

DEBATE

SHOULD WE VIEW ECONOMICS AS A RATIONAL SCIENCE?

Economics as a social science sometimes tries to explain economic principles and outcomes as predictable laws, and for the most part, it is successful. One of the keys to explaining economic principles is that people respond in predictable, rational, and self-interested ways. As this forms the foundation for many of our basic economic principles, we should be able to predict future outcomes based on past experiences—similar in nature to scientific methods and experimentation in the natural sciences. This leads us to our debate for this chapter: "Should we view economics as a rational science?"

Pro:
It is necessary to view economics as a rational science as this view forms the foundation for the basic principles of economic theory. Most economists believe that it is rational for people to anticipate the likely future consequences of their own behaviour; some would infer from this that a rational person would usually make decisions that are in their own self-interest. Such a theory provides a good base for the study of economics, and is useful when trying to forecast or explain future decisions.

Con:
While having a basic understanding of economics is useful, it becomes almost irrelevant because people don't always make rational decisions. For example, why would someone pay $10 for a "Pet Rock" when they can have their own pet rock simply by picking up a rock from the ground? Why do people buy company shares when the price is high? A rational person would not get caught up in hype. Because people make so many irrational decisions, isn't the foundation of economics unstable simply because of the irrational behaviour?

have to grow their own food because transporting, storing, and producing food uses machinery and equipment that pollutes. And even growing your own food would be a problem because many plants emit natural pollutants. We could go on and on. The point is *not* that we shouldn't be concerned about the environment; rather, we have to weigh the expected marginal benefits of a cleaner environment against the expected marginal costs of a cleaner environment. This is not to say the environment should not be cleaner, only that zero pollution levels would be far too costly in terms of what we would have to give up.

Optimal (Best) Levels of Safety

Just as we can have optimal (or best) levels of pollution that are greater than zero, it is also true for crime and safety. Take crime. What would it cost society to have zero crime? It would be prohibitively costly to divert a tremendous amount of our valuable resources toward the total elimination of crime. In fact, it would be impossible to eliminate crime totally. But it would also be costly to reduce crime significantly. Since lower crime rates are costly, society must decide how much it is willing to give up: The additional resources for crime prevention can come only from limited resources, which could be used to produce something else possibly valued even more.

The same is true for safer products. Nobody wants defective tires on their cars, or cars that are unsafe and roll over at low speeds. However, there are optimal amounts of safety that are greater than zero too. The issue is not safe versus unsafe products but rather *how much* safety consumers want. It is not risk versus no risk but rather *how much* risk are we willing to take? Additional safety can come only at higher costs. To make all products perfectly safe would be impossible, so we must weigh the benefits and costs of safer products. In fact, according to one U.S. study by Sam Peltzman, a University of Chicago economist, additional safety features in cars (mandatory safety belts, padded dashboards) in the late 1960s may have had little impact on highway fatalities. Peltzman found that making cars safer led to more reckless driving and more accidents. Although the safety regulations did result in fewer deaths per automobile accident, the total number of deaths remained unchanged because there were more accidents.

Reckless driving has benefits—getting somewhere more quickly—but it also has costs—possibly causing an accident or even a fatality. Rational people will compare the marginal benefits and marginal costs of safer driving and make the choices that they believe will get them to their destination safely. We would expect that even thrill-seekers would slow down if there were higher fines and/or increased law enforcement. It would change the benefit–cost equation for reckless driving (as would bad brakes, bald tires, and poor visibility). On the other hand, compulsory seat belts and air bags might cause motorists to drive more recklessly.

SECTION CHECK

- ■ Economists are usually interested in the effects of additional, or marginal, changes in a given situation.
- ■ The rule of rational choice states that individuals will pursue an activity if they expect the marginal benefits to be greater than the marginal costs, or $E(MB) > E(MC)$.
- ■ People make decisions based on what they expect to happen.
- ■ The optimal (best) levels of pollution, crime, and safety are greater than zero.

Incentives Matter

- Can we predict how people will respond to changes in incentives?
- What are positive and negative incentives?

CAN WE PREDICT HOW PEOPLE WILL RESPOND TO CHANGES IN INCENTIVES?

In acting rationally, people are responding to incentives. That is, they are reacting to the changes in expected marginal benefits and expected marginal costs. In fact, much of human behaviour can be explained and predicted as a response to incentives. Consider the economic view of crime. Why do criminals engage in their "occupation"? Presumably because the "job," even with its risks, is preferred to alternative forms of employment. For criminals, the benefits of their actions are higher and/or the opportunity costs of them are lower than is the case for noncriminals. In some cases, criminals cannot get a legitimate job at a wage they would find acceptable, so the cost of crime in terms of other income forgone may be quite low. At other times, the likelihood of being caught is small, so the expected cost is negligible. Also, for some, the moral cost of a crime is low, whereas for others it is high. The benefits, in terms of wealth gained, are clear. If the expected gains or benefits from committing a crime outweigh the expected costs, the activity is pursued. For most policy purposes, the primary concern is not what causes the level of crime to be what it is but, rather, what causes the level of crime to change. Changes in the crime rate can be largely explained in terms of such a benefit–cost framework. If the benefits of crime rise, say, in the form of larger real "hauls," and/or if the costs fall due to a reduced likelihood of being caught or of being imprisoned if caught, then economists would expect the amount of crime to rise. Likewise, economists would expect the crime rate to fall in response to increased police enforcement, stiffer punishments, or an increase in the employment rate. Whether this analysis tells the complete story is debatable, but the use of the economic framework in thinking about the problem provides valuable insight.

WHAT ARE POSITIVE AND NEGATIVE INCENTIVES?

Almost all of economics can be reduced to incentive [*E(MB)* versus *E(MC)*] stories, where consumers and producers are driven by incentives that affect expected costs or benefits. Prices, wages, profits, taxes, and subsidies are all examples of economic incentives. Incentives can be classified into two types: positive and negative. **Positive incentives** are those that either increase benefits or reduce costs and thus result in an increased level of the related activity or behaviour. **Negative incentives,** on the other hand, either reduce benefits or increase costs, resulting in a decreased level of the related activity or behaviour. For example, a tax on cars that emit lots of pollution (an increase in costs) would be a negative incentive that would lead to a reduction in emitted pollution. On the other hand, a subsidy (the opposite of a tax) for hybrid cars—part electric, part internal combustion—would be a positive incentive that would encourage greater production and consumption of hybrid cars. Human behaviour is influenced in predictable ways by such changes in economic incentives, and economists use this information to predict what will happen when the benefits and costs of any choice are changed. In short, economists study the incentives and consequences of particular actions.

positive incentives
incentives that either reduce costs or increase benefits resulting in an increase in the activity or behaviour

negative incentives
incentives that either increase costs or reduce benefits resulting in a decrease in the activity or behaviour

A subsidy for hybrid electric vehicles (HEVs) would be a positive incentive that would encourage greater production and consumption of these vehicles. Honda's Insight is expected to go 1100 kilometres on a single tank of gas; the Toyota Prius is expected to go about 700 kilometres.

© Jose Gil/Shutterstock

SECTION CHECK

■ People respond to incentives in predictable ways.
■ A positive incentive decreases costs or increases benefits, thus encouraging consumption or production, while a negative incentive increases costs or reduces benefits, thus discouraging consumption or production.

section

1.7

Specialization and Trade

■ Why do people specialize?
■ How do specialization and trade lead to greater wealth and prosperity?

WHY DO PEOPLE SPECIALIZE?

As you look around, you can see that people specialize in what they produce. They tend to dedicate their resources to one primary activity, whether it be child-rearing, driving a bus, or making bagels. Why is this? The answer, short and simple, is opportunity costs. By concentrating on the production of one, or a few, goods, individuals are **specializing.** This allows them to make the best use of (and thus gain the most benefit from) their limited resources. A person, a region, or a country can gain by specializing in the production of the good in which they have a comparative advantage. That is, if they can produce a good or service at a lower opportunity cost than others, we say that they have a **comparative advantage** in the production of that good or service.

For example, should a lawyer who types 100 words per minute hire an administrative assistant to type her legal documents if the assistant can type only 50 words per minute? The answer to this question depends on the particular comparative advantages of the lawyer and the administrative assistant. Consider a job that would take the lawyer five hours and the administrative assistant ten hours to complete. If the lawyer makes $100 an hour, and the administrative assistant earns $10 an hour, who has the comparative advantage?

specializing
concentrating on the production of one, or a few, goods

comparative advantage
occurs when a person or a country can produce a good or service at a lower opportunity cost than others can

If the lawyer types her own documents, it will cost $500 ($100 per hour × 5 hours). If she has the administrative assistant type her documents, it will cost $100 ($10 per hour × 10 hours). Clearly, then, the lawyer should hire the administrative assistant to type her documents because the administrative assistant has the comparative advantage (lower opportunity cost) in this case, despite being half as good in absolute terms.

We All Specialize

We all specialize to some extent and rely on others to produce most of the goods and services we want. The work that we choose to do reflects our specialization. For example, we may specialize in selling or fixing automobiles. The wages from that work can then be used to buy goods from a farmer who has chosen to specialize in the production of food. Likewise, the farmer can use the money earned from selling his produce to get his tractor fixed by someone who specializes in that activity.

Specialization is evident not only among individuals but among regions and countries as well. In fact, the story of the economic development of Canada involves specialization. Within Canada, the prairies with their wheat, the Maritime provinces of eastern Canada with their fishing fleets, and British Columbia with its lumber are all examples of regional specialization.

The Advantages of Specialization

In a small business, employees may perform a wide variety of tasks—from hiring to word processing to marketing. As the size of the company increases, each employee can perform a more specialized job, with a consequent increase in output per worker. The primary advantages of specialization are that employees acquire greater skill from repetition, they avoid wasted time in shifting from one task to another, and they do the types of work for which they are best suited. Specialization also promotes the use of specialized equipment for specialized tasks.

The advantages of specialization are seen throughout the workplace. For example, in larger firms, specialists conduct personnel relations and accounting is in the hands of full-time accountants; such jobs are too critical in large firms to be done by someone with half a dozen other tasks to perform. The owner of a small retail store selects the location for the store primarily through guesswork, placing it where she believes sales will be high or where an empty, low-rent building is available. In contrast, larger chains have store sites selected by experts who have experience in analyzing the factors that make different locations relatively more desirable, like traffic patterns, income levels, demographics, and so on.

HOW DO SPECIALIZATION AND TRADE LEAD TO GREATER WEALTH AND PROSPERITY?

Trade, or voluntary exchange, directly increases wealth by making both parties better off (or they wouldn't trade). It is the prospect of wealth-increasing exchange that leads to productive specialization. That is, trade increases wealth by allowing a person, a region, or a nation to specialize in those products that it produces at a lower opportunity cost and to trade for those products that others produce at a lower opportunity cost. That is, we trade with others because it frees up time and resources to do other things that we do better. For example, say Canada is better at producing wheat than Brazil, and Brazil is better at producing coffee than Canada. Canada and Brazil would each benefit if Canada produces wheat and trades some of it to Brazil for coffee. Coffee growers in Canada could grow coffee in expensive greenhouses, but it would result in higher coffee costs and prices, while leaving fewer resources available for employment in more productive jobs, such as wheat production. This is true for individuals, too.

Imagine Tom had 10 kilograms of tea and Katherine had 10 kilograms of coffee. However, Tom preferred coffee to tea and Katherine preferred tea to coffee. So if Tom traded his tea to Katherine for her coffee, both parties would be better off. Trade simply reallocates existing goods, and voluntary exchange increases wealth by making both parties better off, or they would not agree to trade.

In short, if we divide the tasks and produce what we do *relatively* best and trade for the rest, we will be better off than if we were self-sufficient—that is, without trade. Imagine life without trade, where you were completely self-sufficient—growing your own food, making your own clothes, working on your own car, building your own house. Do you think you would be better off?

SECTION CHECK

- Specialization is important for individuals, businesses, regions, and nations. It allows them to make the best use of their limited resources.
- Specialization and trade increase wealth by allowing a person, a region, or a nation to specialize in those products that it produces at a lower opportunity cost and to trade for those products that others produce at a lower opportunity cost.

section 1.8

Market Prices Coordinate Economic Activity

- How does a market system allocate scarce resources?
- What are the effects of price controls?
- What is a market failure?

HOW DOES A MARKET SYSTEM ALLOCATE SCARCE RESOURCES?

In a world of scarcity, competition is inescapable, and one method of allocating resources among competing uses is the market system. The market system provides a way for millions of producers and consumers to allocate scarce resources. For the most part, markets are efficient. To an economist, **efficiency** is achieved when the economy gets the most out of its scarce resources. In short, efficiency makes the economic pie as large as possible.

efficiency
getting the most from society's scarce resources

Buyers and sellers indicate their wants through their actions and inaction in the marketplace, and it is this collective "voice" that determines how resources are allocated. But how is this information communicated? Market prices serve as the language of the market system. By understanding what these market prices mean, you can get a better understanding of the vital function that the market system performs.

Markets may not always conform to your desired tastes and preferences. You may think that markets produce too many Chia Pets, fast foods, face-lifts, and Justin Bieber CDs. Some markets are illegal—the market for cocaine, the market for stolen body parts, and the market for child pornography. Markets do not come with a moral compass; they simply provide what buyers are willing and able to pay for and what sellers are willing and able to produce.

Market Prices Provide Important Information

Market prices communicate important information to both buyers and sellers. These prices communicate information about the relative availability of products to buyers, and they provide sellers with critical information about the relative value that consumers place on those products. In effect, market prices provide a way for both buyers and sellers to communicate about the relative value of resources. This communication results in a shifting of resources from those uses that are less valued to those that are more valued. We will see how this works beginning in Chapter 3.

The basis of a market economy is the voluntary exchange and the price system that guide people's choices and produce solutions to the questions of what goods to produce and how to produce and distribute them.

Take something as simple as the production of a pencil. Where did the wood come from? Perhaps British Columbia or Quebec. The graphite may have come from the mines in northern Ontario, and the rubber maybe from Malaysia. The paint, the glue, the metal piece that holds the eraser—who knows? The point is that market forces coordinated this activity among literally thousands of people, some of whom live in different countries and speak different languages. The market system brought these people together to make a pencil that sells for 25 cents at your bookstore. It all happened because the market system provided the incentive for people to pursue activities that benefit others. This same process produces millions of goods and services around the world from automobiles and computers to pencils and paper clips. The same is true of the iPod and iPhone. The entrepreneurs at Apple have learned how to combine almost 500 generic parts to make something of much greater value. The whole is greater than the sum of the parts.

In countries that do not rely on the market system, there is no clear communication between buyers and sellers. In the former Soviet Union, where quality was virtually nonexistent, there were shortages of quality goods and surpluses of low-quality goods. For example, there were thousands of tractors without spare parts and millions of pairs of shoes that were left on shelves because the sizes did not match those of the population.

WHAT ARE THE EFFECTS OF PRICE CONTROLS?

Government policies called **price controls** are government-mandated minimum or maximum prices that sometimes force prices above or below what they would be in a market economy. Unfortunately, these controls often harm the same people they are trying to help, in large part by short-circuiting the market's information transmission function. That is, price controls effectively strip the market price of its meaning for both buyers and sellers (which we will see in Chapters 3 and 4). A sales tax will also distort price signals, leading to a misallocation of resources (which we will see in Chapter 5).

price controls
government-mandated minimum or maximum prices

WHAT IS A MARKET FAILURE?

The market mechanism is a simple but effective and efficient general means of allocating resources among alternative uses. When the economy fails to allocate resources efficiently on its own, however, it is known as **market failure.** For example, a steel mill might put soot and other forms of "crud" into the air as a by-product of making steel. When it does this, it imposes costs on others not connected with using or producing steel from the steel mill. The soot may require homeowners to paint their homes more often, entailing a cost. And studies show that respiratory diseases are greater in areas with more severe air pollution, imposing costs and often shortening life itself. In addition, the steel mill might discharge chemicals into a stream, thus killing wildlife and spoiling

market failure
when the economy fails to allocate resources efficiently on its own

recreational activities for the local population. In this case, the steel factory emits too much pollution but does not bear the cost of its polluting actions. In other words, by transferring the pollution costs onto society, the firm has lowered its costs of production and is now producing more than the ideal output—this is inefficient because it is an overallocation of resources.

Markets can also produce too little of a good—research, for example. The government might decide to subsidize promising scientific research that may benefit many people—like cancer research.

Whether the market economy has produced too little (underallocation) or too much (overallocation), the government can improve society's well-being by intervening. The case of market failure will be taken up in more detail in Chapter 6.

In addition, we cannot depend on the market economy to always communicate accurately. Some firms may have market power to distort prices in their favour. For example, the only regional cement company in the area has the ability to charge a higher price and provide a lower-quality product than if the company was in a highly competitive market. In this case, the lack of competition can lead to higher prices and reduced product quality. And without adequate information, unscrupulous producers may be able to misrepresent their products to the disadvantage of unwary consumers.

The Market Distribution of Income

Sometimes a painful trade-off exists between how much an economy can produce efficiently and how that output is distributed—the degree of equality. There is no guarantee that the market economy will provide everyone with adequate amounts of food, shelter, and transportation. That is, not only does the market determine what goods are going to be produced, and in what quantities, but it also determines the distribution of output among members of society.

As with other aspects of government intervention, the degree-of-equity argument can generate some sharp disagreements. What is "fair" for one person may seem highly "unfair" to someone else. Although one person may find it terribly unfair for some individuals to earn many times the amount that other individuals who work equally hard earn, another person may find it highly unfair to ask one group, the relatively rich, to pay a much higher proportion of their income in taxes than another group.

SECTION CHECK

- Through voluntary exchange and the price system, the market system provides a way for producers and consumers to allocate scarce resources.
- Price controls sometimes force prices above or below what they would be in a market economy.
- A market failure occurs when an economy fails to allocate resources efficiently on its own.

A complete glossary of key terms and their definitions is available in CourseMate.

For Your Review

Section 1.1

1. Write your own definition of *economics.* What are the main elements of the definition?

2. Would the following topics be covered in microeconomics or macroeconomics?

   a. the effects of an increase in the supply of lumber on the home-building industry

   b. changes in the national unemployment rate

   c. the effect of interest rates on the machine-tool industry

   d. the effect of interest rates on the demand for investment goods

   e. the way a firm maximizes profits

Section 1.2

3. Are the following statements normative or positive, or do they contain both normative and positive statements?

   a. A higher income tax rate would generate increased tax revenues. Those extra revenues should be used to give more government aid to the poor.

   b. The study of physics is more valuable than the study of sociology, but both should be studied by all college students.

   c. An increase in the price of wheat will decrease the amount of wheat purchased. However, it will increase the amount of wheat supplied to the market.

   d. A decrease in the price of butter will increase the amount of butter purchased, but that would be bad because it would increase Canadians' cholesterol levels.

   e. The birth rate is reduced as economies urbanize, but that also leads to an increased average age of developing countries' populations.

4. Which of the following economic statements are positive and which are normative?

   a. A tax increase will increase unemployment.

   b. The government should reduce funding for social assistance programs.

   c. Tariffs on imported wine will lead to higher prices for domestic wine.

   d. A decrease in the capital gains tax rate will increase investment.

   e. Goods purchased on the Internet should be subject to provincial sales taxes.

   f. A reduction in interest rates will cause inflation.

5. The following statement represents which fallacy in thinking? Explain why.

   "I earn $12 per hour. If I am able to earn $12 per hour, everyone should be able to find work for at least that wage rate."

6. Do any of the following statements involve fallacies? If so, which ones do they involve?

   a. Because sitting in the back of classrooms is correlated with getting lower grades in the class, students should always sit closer to the front of the classroom.

   b. Historically, the stock market rises in years the NFC team wins the Super Bowl and falls when the AFC wins the Super Bowl. I am rooting for the NFC team to win for the sake of my investment portfolio.

   c. When a hockey team spends more to get better players, it is more successful, which proves that all the teams should spend more to get better players.

   d. Gasoline prices were higher last year than in 1970, yet people purchased more gas, which contradicts the law of demand.

   e. An increase in the amount of money I have will make me better off, but an increase in the supply of money in the economy will not make Canadians as a group better off.

Section 1.3

7. Explain the difference between poverty and scarcity.

8. The automotive revolution after World War II reduced the time involved for travel and shipping goods. This innovation allowed the Canadian economy to produce more goods and services since it freed resources involved in transportation for other uses. The transportation revolution also increased wants. Identify two ways in which vehicle manufacturers evoked new wants.

9. Which of the following goods are scarce?

   a. garbage

   b. salt water in the ocean

   c. clothes

   d. clean air in a big city

   e. dirty air in a big city

   f. public libraries

Section 1.4

10. The price of a one-way bus trip from Toronto to Ottawa is $150. Sarah, a school-teacher, pays the same price in February (during the school year) as in July (during her vacation), so the cost is the same in February as in July. Do you agree?

11. Pizza Pizza once ran a promotion that whenever the Ottawa Senators scored six goals or more, Pizza Pizza gave everyone with a ticket to that day's game a free slice of pizza. If holders of ticket stubs have to stand in line for ten minutes, is the slice of pizza really "free"?

12. List the opportunity costs of the following:

    a. going to college or university

    b. missing a lecture

    c. withdrawing and spending $100 from your savings account, which earns 5 percent interest annually

    d. going snowboarding on the weekend before final examinations

Section 1.5

13. Assume the total benefits to Mark from trips to a local amusement park during the year are given by the following schedule: 1 trip, $60; 2 trips, $115; 3 trips, $165; 4 trips, $200; 5 trips, $225; 6 or more trips, $240.

    a. What is Mark's marginal benefit of the third trip? The fifth trip?

    b. If the admission price to the amusement park was $45 per day, how many times would Mark be willing and able to go in a year? What if the price was $20 per day? Explain.

    c. If the amusement park offered a year-long pass for $200 rather than a per day admission price, would Mark be willing to buy one? If so, how many times would he go? Explain.

14. Assume the total cost of producing widgets was $4200 for 42 units; $4257 for 43 units; $4332 for 44 units; and $4420 for 45 units.

    a. What is the marginal cost of producing the 43rd unit? The 45th unit?

    b. If the widget producer could sell at $60 per unit however many he could produce, how many would he choose to produce? If he could sell at $80 per unit however many he could produce? Explain.

15. Imagine that you are trying to decide whether to cross a street without using the designated crosswalk at the traffic signal. What are the expected marginal benefits of crossing? What are the expected marginal costs? How would the following conditions change your benefit–cost equation?

    a. The street was busy.

    b. The street was empty and it was 3:00 A.M.

    c. You were in a huge hurry.

    d. There was a police officer 10 metres away.

    e. The closest crosswalk was 1 kilometre away.

    f. The closest crosswalk was 5 metres away.

Section 1.6

16. Which of the following are positive incentives? Negative incentives? Why?

    a. a fine for not cleaning up after your dog defecates in the park

    b. a trip to Hawaii paid for by your parents or significant other for earning an A in your economics course

    c. a higher tax on cigarettes and alcohol

    d. a subsidy for installing solar panels on your house

17. The penalty for drug trafficking in Singapore is death. Do you think there would be more drug traffickers in Singapore if the mandatory sentence was five years, with parole for good behaviour?

Section 1.7

18. Throughout history, many countries have chosen the path of autarky, choosing to not trade with other countries. Explain why this path would make a country poorer.

19. Farmer Fran can grow soybeans and corn. She can grow 1500 kilograms of soybeans or 3000 kilograms of corn on a hectare of her land for the same cost. The price of soybeans is $1.50 per kilogram and the price of corn is $0.60 per kilogram. Show the benefits to Fran of specialization. What should she specialize in?

20. Which region has a comparative advantage in the following goods?
    a. wheat: Colombia or Canada
    b. coffee: Colombia or Canada
    c. lumber: Alberta or British Columbia
    d. oil: Alberta or British Columbia

21. a. Why is it important that the country or region with the lower opportunity cost produce the good?
    b. How would you use the concept of comparative advantage to argue for reducing restrictions on trade between countries?

Section 1.8

22. Prices communicate information about the relative value of resources. Which of the following would cause the relative value and, hence, the price, of potatoes to rise?
    a. A fungus infestation wipes out half of the Prince Edward Island potato crop.
    b. The price of potato chips rises.
    c. Scientists find that eating potato chips makes you better-looking.
    d. The prices of wheat, rice, and other potato substitutes fall dramatically.

23. People communicate with each other in the market through the effect their decisions to buy or sell have on prices. Indicate how each of the following would affect prices by putting a check in the appropriate space.
    a. People who see an energetic and lovable Jack Russell terrier in a popular TV series want Jack Russell terriers as pets. The price of Jack Russell terriers ____Rises ____ Falls.
    b. Retirees flock to Tampa, Florida, to live. The price of housing in Tampa ____ Rises ____ Falls.
    c. Weather-related crop failures in Colombia and Costa Rica reduce coffee supplies. The price of coffee ____ Rises ____ Falls.
    d. Wheat fields in Alberta are replaced with oil rigs. The price of wheat ____ Rises ____ Falls.
    e. More and more students graduate from Canadian medical schools. The wages of Canadian doctors____ Rise ____ Fall.
    f. Canadians are driving more and they are driving bigger, gas-guzzling cars like sport utility vehicles. The price of gasoline _____ Rises _____ Falls.

Appendix

GRAPHS ARE AN IMPORTANT ECONOMIC TOOL

Sometimes the use of visual aids, such as graphs, greatly enhances our understanding of a theory. It is much the same as finding your way to a friend's house with the aid of a map rather than with detailed verbal or written instructions. Graphs are important tools for economists. They allow us to understand better the workings of the economy. To economists, a graph can be worth a thousand words. This text will use graphs throughout to enhance the understanding of important economic relationships. This appendix provides a guide on how to read and create your own graphs.

The most useful graph for our purposes is one that merely connects a vertical line (the **Y-axis**) with a horizontal line (the **X-axis**), as seen in Exhibit 1. The intersection of the two lines occurs at the origin, which is where the value of both variables is equal to zero. In Exhibit 1, the graph has four quadrants or "boxes." In this textbook we will be primarily concerned with the shaded box in the upper right-hand corner. This portion of the graph deals exclusively with positive numbers. Always keep in mind that moving to the right on the horizontal axis and up along the vertical axis each lead to higher values.

Y-axis
the vertical axis on a graph

X-axis
the horizontal axis on a graph

pie chart
a circle subdivided into proportionate slices that represent various quantities that add up to 100 percent

bar graph
represents data using vertical bars rising from the horizontal axis

time-series graph
shows changes in the value of a variable over time

USING GRAPHS AND CHARTS

Exhibit 2 presents three common types of graphs. A **pie chart** is a circle subdivided into proportionate slices that represent various quantities that add up to 100 percent. The pie chart in Exhibit 2(a) shows what college students earn. That is, each slice in the pie chart represents the percentage of college students in a particular earnings category.

A **bar graph** represents data using vertical bars rising from the horizontal axis. Exhibit 2(b) is a bar graph that shows the sales of wireless phone service by province for a new company that has just entered the Canadian market. The height of the line represents sales in millions of dollars. Bar graphs are used to show a comparison of the sizes of quantities of similar items.

Exhibit 2(c) is a **time-series graph.** This type of graph shows changes in the value of a variable over time. This is a visual tool that allows us to observe important trends over a certain time period. In Exhibit 2(c) we see a graph that shows trends in the stock price of Fly-by-Chance Airlines for the period January to December. The horizontal axis shows us the passage of time, and the vertical axis shows us the stock price in dollars per share.

appendix Exhibit 1 — **Plotting a Graph**

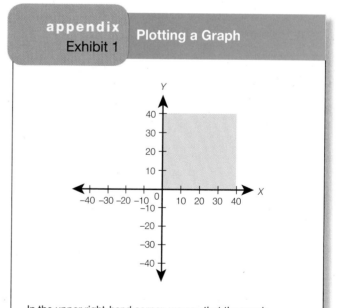

In the upper right-hand corner, we see that the graph includes a positive figure for the Y-axis and the X-axis. As we move to the right along the horizontal axis, the numerical values increase. As we move up along the vertical axis, the numerical values increase.

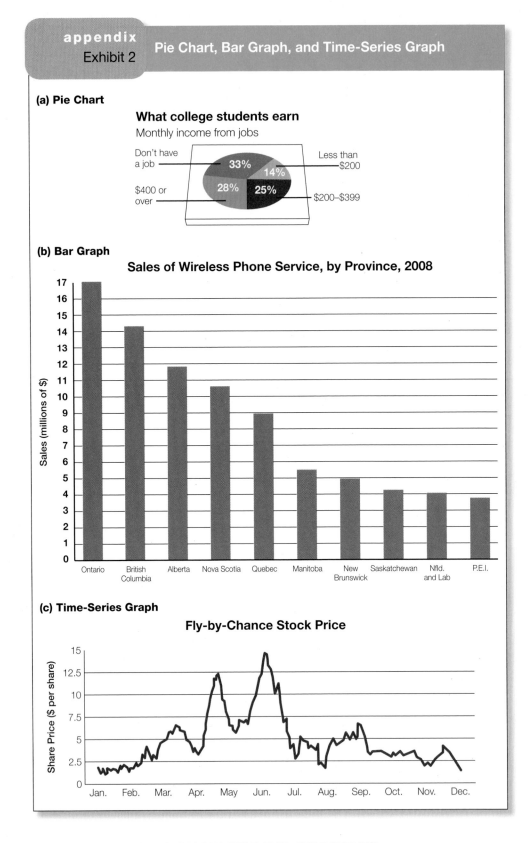

appendix
Exhibit 2   Pie Chart, Bar Graph, and Time-Series Graph

(a) Pie Chart

What college students earn
Monthly income from jobs

Don't have a job — 33%
Less than $200 — 14%
$400 or over — 28%
$200–$399 — 25%

(b) Bar Graph

Sales of Wireless Phone Service, by Province, 2008

Sales (millions of $) axis from 0 to 17

Ontario, British Columbia, Alberta, Nova Scotia, Quebec, Manitoba, New Brunswick, Saskatchewan, Nfld. and Lab, P.E.I.

(c) Time-Series Graph

Fly-by-Chance Stock Price

Share Price ($ per share) axis from 0 to 15

Jan. Feb. Mar. Apr. May Jun. Jul. Aug. Sep. Oct. Nov. Dec.

USING GRAPHS TO SHOW THE RELATIONSHIP BETWEEN TWO VARIABLES

variable
something that is measured by a number, such as your height

Although the graphs and chart in Exhibit 2 are important, they do not allow us to show the relationship between two variables (a **variable** is something that is measured by a number, such as your height). To more closely examine the structure and functions of graphs, let us consider the story of Katherine, an avid in-line skater who has aspirations of winning the Z Games next year. To get there, however, she will have to put in many hours of practice. But how many hours? In search of information about the practice habits of other skaters, she logged onto the Internet, where she pulled up the results of a study conducted by ESPM 3 that indicated the score of each Z Games competitor and the amount of practice time per week spent by each skater. The results of this study (see Exhibit 3) indicated that skaters had to practise 10 hours per week to receive a score of 4.0, 20 hours per week to receive a score of 6.0, 30 hours per week to get a score of 8.0, and 40 hours per week to get a perfect score of 10. What does this information tell Katherine? By using a graph, she can more clearly understand the relationship between practice time and overall score.

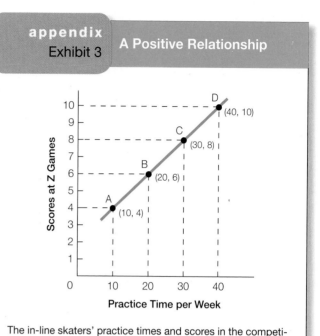

appendix Exhibit 3   A Positive Relationship

The in-line skaters' practice times and scores in the competition are plotted on the graph. Each participant is represented by a point. The graph shows that those skaters who practised the most scored the highest. This is called a *positive*, or *direct, relationship*.

A Positive Relationship

The study on scores and practice times revealed what is called a direct relationship, also called a positive relationship. A **positive relationship** means that the variables change in the same direction. That is, an increase in one variable (practice time) is accompanied by an increase in the other variable (overall score), or a decrease in one variable (practice time) is accompanied by a decrease in the other variable (overall score). In short, the variables change in the same direction.

positive relationship *when two variables change in the same direction*

A Negative Relationship

When two variables change in opposite directions, we say they are inversely related, or have a **negative relationship.** That is, when one variable rises, the other variable falls, or when one variable decreases, the other variable increases.

negative relationship *when two variables change in opposite directions*

Variables That Have a Maximum or a Minimum

Many relationships described in economic models have maximum or minimum values. For example, firms are always looking to make the maximum possible profits; one way they can achieve this is by minimizing their costs. Exhibits 4 and 5 show relationships that have maximum and minimum values.

Exhibit 4 shows the first case—a relationship that begins positive, reaches a maximum, and then ends with a negative relationship. This example of the relationship between tax rates and tax revenue shows what economists refer to as the *Laffer curve.* When the tax rate is zero, the government receives no tax revenue. As the tax rate rises, tax revenue increases because the government receives a larger percentage of people's incomes. In the exhibit, a tax rate of 50 percent generates the maximum tax revenue of $15 million. As the tax rate continues to rise, it may be the case that the incentive to earn more income begins to decline causing tax revenue to fall. If the tax rate was increased to 100 percent, there would be no incentive to earn income because it would all be taxed away; as a result, no tax revenue would be generated.

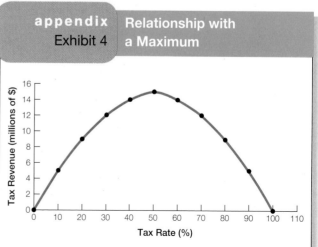

appendix Exhibit 4   Relationship with a Maximum

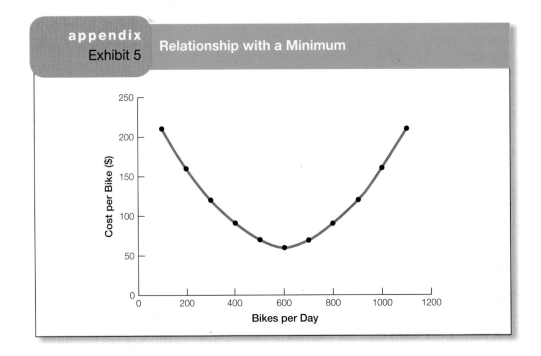

Exhibit 5 illustrates the opposite case—a relationship that begins negative, reaches a minimum, and then returns positive. Most economic costs are seen as following this relationship. As a bicycle manufacturer increases its output, per bike costs of production begin to fall, perhaps as workers develop special skills and the benefits of teamwork emerge. At a level of 600 bikes per day, the cost per bike is minimized at $60 per bike. However, as production is increased beyond 600 bikes per day, the cost per bike begins to rise, perhaps as the bike factory is forced to operate beyond its efficient capacity.

Variables That Are Not Related

There are still other situations in economics in which the change in one variable has no impact on the value of another variable. Exhibit 6 provides a graphical depiction of a curious relationship—a student's grade in economics and the lunar cycle. Since a

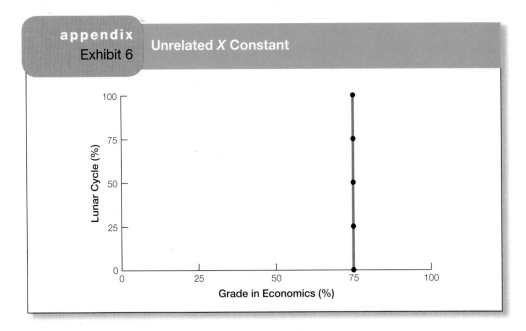

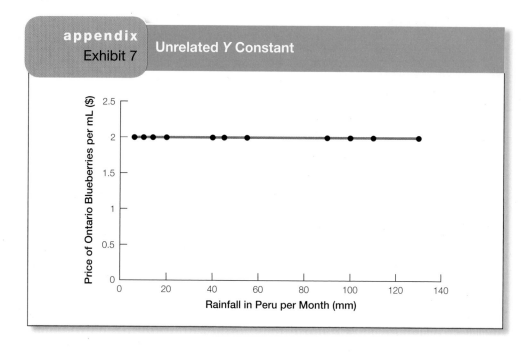

appendix
Exhibit 7 — Unrelated *Y* Constant

student's grade in economics is not affected by the lunar cycle, no relationship exists. If a student grade of 75 percent is plotted on the horizontal axis, with the lunar cycle plotted on the vertical axis, the curve is vertical.

Exhibit 7 illustrates another curious relationship—the price of blueberries grown in Ontario and the average rainfall in Peru. Since the price of blueberries grown in Ontario, plotted on the vertical axis, does not vary with the monthly rainfall in Peru, plotted on the horizontal axis, the curve is horizontal.

THE GRAPH OF A DEMAND CURVE

One of the most important graphs in all of economics is the demand curve. In Exhibit 8, we see Emily's individual demand curve for compact discs. It shows the price of CDs on the vertical axis and the quantity of CDs purchased per month on the horizontal axis. Every point in the space shown represents a price and quantity combination. The downward-sloping line, labelled *demand curve,* shows the different combinations of price and quantity purchased. Note that the higher you go up on the vertical (price) axis, the smaller the quantity purchased on the horizontal (quantity) axis, and the lower the price on the vertical axis, the greater the quantity purchased.

In Exhibit 8, we see that moving up the vertical price axis from the origin, the price of CDs increases from $5 to $25 in increments of $5. Moving out along the horizontal quantity axis, the quantity purchased increases from zero to five CDs per month. Point A represents a price of $25 and a quantity of one CD, point B represents a price of $20 and a quantity of two CDs, point C, $15 and a quantity of three CDs, and so on. When we connect all the points, we have what economists call a *curve*. As you can see, curves are sometimes drawn as straight lines for ease of illustration. Moving down along

appendix
Exhibit 8 — A Negative Relationship

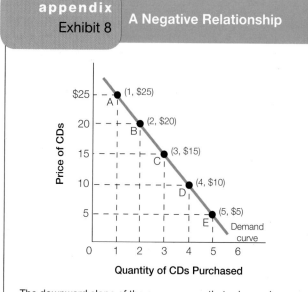

The downward slope of the curve means that price and quantity purchased are inversely, or negatively, related: when one increases, the other decreases. That is, moving down along the demand curve from point A to point E, we see that as price falls, the quantity purchased increases. Moving up along the demand curve from point E to point A, we see that as the price increases, the quantity purchased falls.

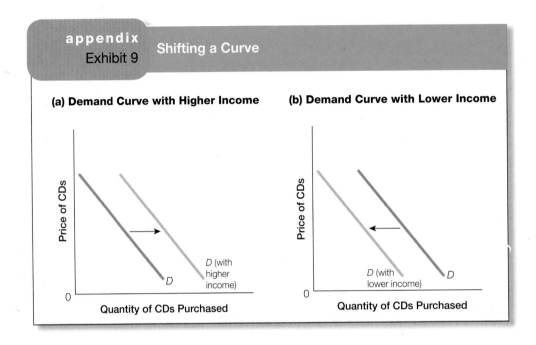

the curve, we see that as the price falls, a greater quantity is demanded; moving up the curve to higher prices, a smaller quantity is demanded. That is, when CDs become less expensive, Emily buys more CDs. When CDs become more expensive, Emily buys fewer CDs, perhaps choosing to go to the movies or buy a pizza instead.

USING GRAPHS TO SHOW THE RELATIONSHIP AMONG THREE VARIABLES

Although only two variables are shown on the axes, graphs can be used to show the relationship between three variables. For example, say we add a third variable—income—to our earlier example. Our three variables are now income, price, and quantity purchased. If Emily's income rises, say she gets a raise at work, she is now able and willing to buy more CDs than before at each possible price. As a result, the whole demand curve shifts outward (rightward) compared to the old curve. That is, she uses some of her additional income to buy more CDs. This is seen in the graph in Exhibit 9(a). On the other hand, if her income falls, say she quits her job to go back to school, she now has less income to buy CDs. This causes the whole demand curve to shift inward (leftward) compared to the old curve. This is seen in the graph in Exhibit 9(b).

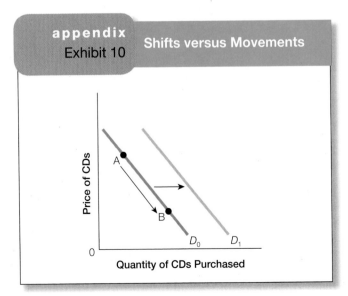

The Difference between a Movement along and a Shift in the Curve

It is important to remember the difference between a movement between one point and another along a curve and a shift in the whole curve. A change in one of the variables on the graph, like price or quantity purchased, will cause a movement along the curve, say from point A to point B, as shown in Exhibit 10. A change in one of the variables not shown (held constant in order to show only the relationship between price and quantity), like income in our example, will cause the whole curve to shift. The change from D_0 to D_1 in Exhibit 10 shows such a shift.

SLOPE

In economics, we sometimes refer to the steepness of the lines or curves on graphs as the **slope**—the ratio of the rise over the run. A slope can be either positive (upward sloping) or negative (downward sloping). A curve that is downward sloping represents an inverse, or negative, relationship between the two variables and slants downward from left to right, as seen in Exhibit 11(a). A curve that is upward sloping represents a direct, or positive, relationship between the two variables and slants upward from left to right, as seen in Exhibit 11(b). The numeric value of the slope shows the number of units of change of the Y-axis variable for each unit of change in the X-axis variable. Slope provides the direction (positive or negative) as well as the magnitude of the relationship between the two variables.

slope
the ratio of rise (change in the Y variable) over the run (change in the X variable)

Measuring the Slope of a Linear Curve

A straight-line curve is called a *linear curve*. The slope of a linear curve between two points measures the relative rates of change of two variables. Specifically, the slope of a linear curve can be defined as the ratio of the change in the Y value to the change in the X value. The slope can also be expressed as the ratio of the rise to the run, where the rise is the change in the Y variable (along the vertical axis) and the run is the change in the X variable (along the horizontal axis).

In Exhibit 12, we show two linear curves, one with a positive slope and one with a negative slope. In Exhibit 12(a), the slope of the positively sloped linear curve from point A to point B is 1/2, because the rise is 1 (from 2 to 3) and the run is 2 (from 1 to 3). In Exhibit 12(b), the negatively sloped linear curve has a slope of -4, a rise of -8 (a fall of 8 from 10 to 2) and a run of 2 (from 2 to 4), which gives us a slope of -4 ($-8/2$). Note the appropriate signs on the slopes: The negatively sloped line carries a minus sign and the positively sloped line, a plus sign.

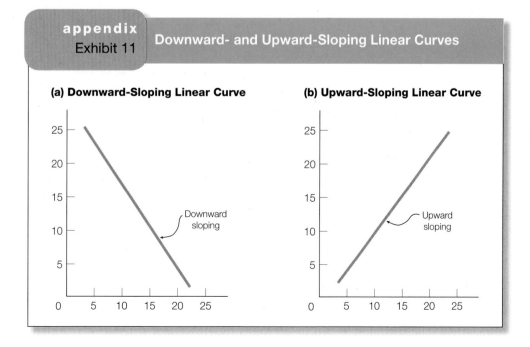

appendix Exhibit 11   **Downward- and Upward-Sloping Linear Curves**

(a) Downward-Sloping Linear Curve

Downward sloping

(b) Upward-Sloping Linear Curve

Upward sloping

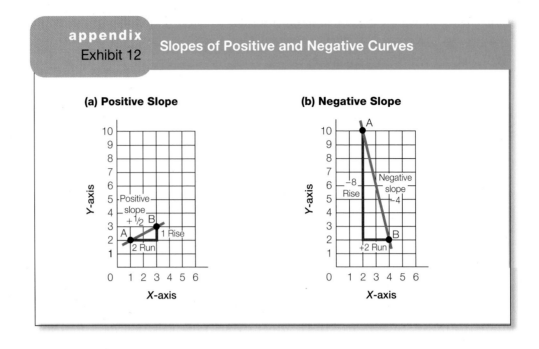

appendix Exhibit 12   Slopes of Positive and Negative Curves

(a) Positive Slope

(b) Negative Slope

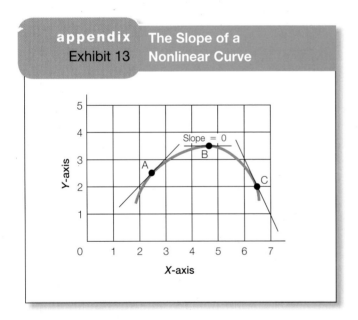

appendix Exhibit 13   The Slope of a Nonlinear Curve

Finding the Slope of a Nonlinear Curve

In Exhibit 13, we show the slope of a nonlinear curve. A nonlinear curve is a line that actually curves. Here the slope varies from point to point along the curve. However, we can find the slope of this curve at any given point by drawing a straight line tangent to that point on the curve. A tangency is when a straight line just touches the curve without actually crossing it. At point A, we see that the positively sloped line that is tangent to the curve has a slope of 1—the line rises one unit and runs one unit. At point B, the line is horizontal, so it has zero slope. At point C, we see a slope of −2 because the negatively sloped line has a rise of −2 units (a fall of two units) for every one unit run.

Remember, many students have problems with economics simply because they fail to understand graphs, so make sure that you understand this material before going on to Chapter 2.

Percentage Change

In economics, the determination of the percentage change in a quantity is a common calculation. The advantage of calculating percentage change (as opposed to simple absolute change) is that percentage change provides a more accurate measure of the magnitude of the change. For example, is an increase in price from $105 to $130 relatively larger or smaller than an increase in price from $50 to $75? In both cases, the difference (absolute increase) is the same at $25, but what about the relative (percentage) change?

The Formula for Percentage Change

The percentage change in a value that is originally x_0 and changes to x_1 can be expressed as follows:

$$\% \Delta = \left(\frac{X_1 - X_0}{X_0} \right) \times 100$$

So, is an increase in price from $105 to $130 relatively larger or smaller than an increase in price from $50 to $75?

The percentage increase in price from $105 to $130 is

$$\left(\frac{130 - 105}{105} \right) \times 100 = 23.81\%$$

The percentage increase in price from $50 to $75 is

$$\left(\frac{75 - 50}{50} \right) \times 100 = 50\%$$

Therefore, the increase in price from $50 to $75 is relatively larger than the increase in price from $105 to $130.

CourseMate

Access an interactive eBook and chapter-specific interactive learning tools, including flashcards, quizzes, a glossary, and more in CourseMate, accessed through **www.sextonmacro3ce.nelson.com**

chapter 2

Scarcity, Trade-Offs, and Production Possibilities

section 2.1

The Three Economic Questions Every Society Faces

- What is to be produced?
- How are the goods and services to be produced?
- Who will get the goods and services?

Collectively, our wants far outstrip what can be produced from nature's scarce resources. So how should we allocate those scarce resources? Some methods of resource allocation might seem bad and counterproductive, like the "survival of the fittest" competition that exists in the jungle. Physical violence has been used since the beginning of time, as people, regions, and countries attack one another to gain control over resources. One might argue that governments should allocate scarce resources on the basis of equal shares or according to need. However, this approach poses problems because of diverse individual preferences, the problem of ascertaining needs, and the negative work and investment incentives involved. In reality, society is made up of many approaches to resource allocation. For now, we will focus on one form of allocating goods and services found in most countries—the market system.

Because of scarcity, certain economic questions must be answered, regardless of the level of affluence of the society or its political structure. We will consider three fundamental questions that inevitably must be faced: (1) What is to be produced? (2) How are the goods and services to be produced? (3) Who will get the goods and services? These questions are unavoidable in a world of scarcity.

WHAT IS TO BE PRODUCED?

How do individuals control production decisions in market-oriented economies? Questions arise such as "Should we produce lots of cars and just a few school buildings, or relatively few cars and more school buildings?" The answer to this and other such questions is called **consumer sovereignty**—how consumers vote in economic affairs with their dollars (or pounds or yen) in a market economy. Consumer sovereignty explains how individual consumers in market economies determine what is to be produced.

Televisions, DVD players, cellphones, pagers, camcorders, and computers, for example, became part of our lives because consumers "voted" hundreds of dollars apiece on these goods. As they bought more colour TVs, consumers "voted" fewer dollars on black-and-white TVs. Similarly, vinyl record albums gave way to tapes and CDs to downloadable music as consumers voted for these items with their dollars. As consumers vote for more fuel-efficient cars and healthier foods, firms that want to remain profitable must listen and respond.

consumer sovereignty
consumers vote in economic affairs with their dollars in a market economy .

How Different Types of Economic Systems Answer the Question "What Is to Be Produced?"

Economies are organized in different ways to answer the question of what is to be produced. The dispute over the best way to answer this question has inflamed passions for centuries. Should central planning boards make the decisions, as in North Korea and Cuba? **Command economies** are economies where the government uses central planning to coordinate most economic activities. Under this type of regime, decisions about how many tractors or automobiles to produce are largely determined by a government official or committee associated with the central planning organization. That same group decides on the number and size of school buildings, refrigerators, shoes, and so on. Other countries—including Canada, the United States, much of Europe, and, increasingly, Asia and elsewhere—have largely adopted a decentralized decision-making process where literally millions of individual producers and consumers of goods and services determine what goods, and how many of them, will be produced. An economy that allocates goods and services through the private decisions of consumers, input suppliers, and firms is often referred to as a **market economy.** Actually, no nation has a pure market economy. Most countries, including Canada, are said to have a **mixed economy.** In such economies, the government and the private sector together determine the allocation of resources.

command economies
economies where the government uses central planning to coordinate most economic activities

market economy
an economy that allocates goods and services through the private decisions of consumers, input suppliers, and firms

mixed economy
an economy where government and the private sector together determine the allocation of resources

HOW ARE THE GOODS AND SERVICES TO BE PRODUCED?

All economies, regardless of their political structure, must decide how to produce the goods and services that they want—because of scarcity. Goods and services can generally be produced in several ways. For example, a ditch can be dug by many workers using their hands, by a few workers with shovels, or by one person with a backhoe. Someone must decide which method is most appropriate. The larger the quantity of the good and the more elaborate the form of capital, the more labour that is saved and is thus made available for other uses. (Remember, goods like shovels or large earthmoving machines used to produce goods and services are called *capital.*) From this example, you might be tempted to conclude that it is desirable to use the biggest, most elaborate form of capital. But would you really want to plant your spring flowers with huge earthmoving machinery? That is, the most capital-intensive method of production may not always be the best. The best method is the least-cost method.

The Best Form of Production

The best or "optimal" form of production will usually vary from one economy to the next. For example, earthmoving machinery is used in digging large ditches in Canada, the United States, and Europe, whereas in developing countries, such as India, China, or Pakistan, shovels are often used. Similarly, when a person in Canada cuts the grass, he or she may use a power lawn mower, whereas in a developing country, a hand mower might be used or grass might not be cut at all. Why do these "optimal" forms of production vary so drastically? Compared to capital, labour is relatively cheap and plentiful in developing countries but relatively scarce and expensive in Canada. In contrast, capital (machines and tools, mainly) is comparatively plentiful and cheap in Canada but scarcer and more costly in developing countries. That is, in developing countries, production would tend to be more **labour-intensive,** using a large amount of labour. In Canada, production would tend to be more **capital-intensive,** using a large amount of capital. Each nation tends to use the production processes that conserve its relatively scarce (and thus relatively more expensive) resources and use more of its relatively abundant resources.

labour-intensive
production that uses a large amount of labour

capital-intensive
production that uses a large amount of capital

WHO WILL GET THE GOODS AND SERVICES?

In every society, some mechanism must exist to determine how goods and services are to be distributed among the population. Who gets what? Why do some people get to consume or

Business CONNECTION

THE THREE ECONOMIC QUESTIONS EVERY ENTREPRENEUR FACES

Economics as a social science deals with how society allocates limited resources to satisfy unlimited wants. From a macroeconomic perspective, the Canadian government tries to increase economic growth by increasing Canada's gross domestic product, the GDP. It does so by supporting qualitative and quantitative improvements in the factors of production, land, labour, capital, and entrepreneurship. Of these factors, entrepreneurship is the most essential. At the microeconomic level, entrepreneurs attempt to earn a profit with the introduction of new goods or services. They face the same three key questions faced by all economies:

- What goods or service to produce?
- How should these goods or services be produced?
- Who are the potential buyers of these goods and services?

A business usually starts with the premise that consumers will want and will be able to buy the goods or services provided. Indeed, if the entrepreneurs are correct and consumers vote with dollars for the new products, there will be no difficulty generating sales revenue. Every year, an array of new products comes onto the market so entrepreneurs should be very much concerned with the first of the three economic questions.

The second question concerns how goods or services are produced. While you may not be concerned if robots are involved in assembling the parts in a smartphone, you might have some anxiety about robots providing your next haircut. The thoughtful entrepreneur with one eye on revenues and the other on costs must decide when to use labour, when to expend capital on machinery and equipment, or how to combine these resources. Faced with scarce resources, decisions regarding how much and what type of labour, equipment, and land or buildings to employ in operations must be addressed. How goods and services are produced will often determine their nature and quality, consumers' experience with the good or service, and the entrepreneur's cost of production. The successful entrepreneur is challenged to strike a delicate balance between the first two questions: What to produce and how.

While most of us can juggle two objects, what happens when we add a third, the question of for whom should the goods and services be produced? Here the entrepreneur needs insight regarding who might be willing and able to purchase the goods or services produced. For answers, entrepreneurs often conduct surveys. More broadly speaking, they will perform market research to gain the necessary insights to determine which consumers, which market segments, are likely to buy the new goods or services.

Successful entrepreneurs not motivated solely by profit usually build and operate profitable businesses. These resourceful, dedicated individuals bring enormous drive and creativity in building new enterprises. In the face of risks and uncertainties, they are constantly challenged to effectively and efficiently deal with the three economic questions of society.

use far more goods and services than others? This question of distribution is so important that wars and revolutions have been fought over it. Both the French and Russian Revolutions were concerned fundamentally with the distribution of goods and services. Even in societies where political questions are usually settled peacefully, the question of the distribution of income is an issue that always arouses strong emotional responses. As we will see, in a market economy with private ownership and control of the means of production, the amount of goods and services one is able to obtain depends on one's income, which depends on the quantity and quality of the scarce resources the individual controls. For example, Sidney Crosby makes a lot of money because he has unique and marketable skills as a hockey player.

To say that this may or may not be "fair" is an opinion at the centre of the *efficiency* versus *equity* dilemma in economics. As an economy, do you focus on getting the most you can from your scarce resources (efficiency), or should the emphasis be on equally distributing the benefits of those resources to all (equity)? Some economists believe that individual freedom and choice are central to economic well-being. When limitations are placed on these individual freedoms, these economists believe that economic efficiency will suffer.

On the other hand, some economists are concerned with the economic inequalities and unfairness created by production and distribution. For example, to these economists, government intervention is a valuable tool in making society more equitable.

Regardless of which side of the debate is chosen, one truth is certain: Decisions regarding the three economic questions raised in this section play a central role in shaping the efficiency and equity of an economy.

© Kojoku/Shutterstock

Avril Lavigne gets paid a lot of money because she controls a scarce resource: her talent and name recognition. As we will see in the next chapter, people's talents and other goods and services in limited supply relative to demand will command high prices.

SECTION CHECK

- Every economy has to decide what to produce. In a decentralized market economy, millions of buyers and sellers determine what and how much to produce. In a mixed economy, the government and the private sector determine the allocation of resources.
- The best form of production is the one that conserves the relatively scarce (more costly) resources and uses more of the abundant (less costly) resources. When capital is relatively scarce and labour is plentiful, production tends to be labour-intensive. When capital is relatively abundant and labour is relatively scarce, production tends to be capital-intensive.
- In a market economy, the amount of goods and services one is able to obtain depends on one's income. The amount of one's income depends on the quantity and the quality of the scarce resources that the individual controls.

The Circular Flow Model

- What are product markets?
- What are factor markets?
- What is the goods and services flow?
- What is the income flow?
- What is the circular flow model?

How do we explain how millions of people in an economy interact when it comes to buying, selling, producing, working, hiring, and so on? In a simple economy, there are two decision makers: the producers of goods and services, which we call *firms,* and households, the buyers of goods and services. Exchanges between these two decision makers take place in product markets and factor markets and involve flows of goods, services, and money.

WHAT ARE PRODUCT MARKETS?

product markets
the markets for consumer goods and services

Product markets are the markets for consumer goods and services. In the product market, households are buyers and firms are sellers. Households buy the goods and services that firms produce and sell.

WHAT ARE FACTOR MARKETS?

factor (input) markets
the market where households sell the use of their inputs (capital, land, labour, and entrepreneurship) to firms

Factor, or **input, markets** are the markets where households sell the use of their inputs (capital, land, labour, and entrepreneurship) to firms. In the factor markets, households are the sellers and the firms are the buyers.

WHAT IS THE GOODS AND SERVICES FLOW?

goods and services flow
the continuous flow of inputs and outputs in an economy

The **goods and services flow** represents the continuous flow of inputs and outputs in an economy. Households make inputs available to producers through the factor markets. These inputs are then turned into outputs which are then bought by households.

WHAT IS THE INCOME FLOW?

income flow
the continuous flow of income and expenditure in an economy

The **income flow** represents the continuous flow of income and expenditure in an economy. Households receive money payments from firms as compensation for the labour, land, capital, and entrepreneurship needed to produce goods and services. These payments take the form of wages (salaries), rent, interest payments, and profits, respectively. The payments from households to firms are for the purchase of goods and services.

WHAT IS THE CIRCULAR FLOW MODEL?

circular flow model of income and output
an illustration of the continuous flow of goods, services, inputs, and payments between firms and households

The simple **circular flow model of income and output** is an illustration of the continuous flow of goods, services, inputs, and payments between firms and households. A simple depiction of the model is presented in Exhibit 1. In the top half of the exhibit, the product market, households purchase goods and services that firms have produced. In the lower half of the exhibit, the factor (or input) market, households sell the inputs that firms use to produce goods and services. The income flow (going clockwise in Exhibit 1) describes how households receive income—money income—and use that income to buy goods and services—consumption spending. The goods and services flow (going counterclockwise in Exhibit 1) details how households supply inputs—capital, land, labour, and entrepreneurship—to firms that use them in the production of outputs—goods and services.

Let's take a simple example to see how the circular flow model works. Suppose a teacher's supply of labour generates personal income in the form of wages (the factor market), which she can use to buy automobiles, vacations, food, and other goods (the product market). Suppose she buys an automobile (product market); the automobile dealer now has revenue to pay for his inputs (factor market)—wages to workers, purchase of new cars to replenish his inventory, rent for his building, and so on. So we see that in the simple circular flow model, income flows from firms to households (factor markets) and spending flows from households to firms (product markets). The simple circular flow model shows how households and firms interact in product markets and in factor markets and how product markets and factor markets are interrelated.

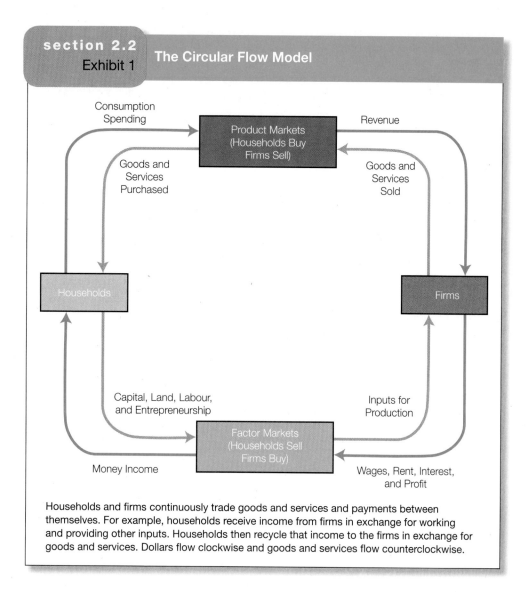

section 2.2

Exhibit 1   **The Circular Flow Model**

Households and firms continuously trade goods and services and payments between themselves. For example, households receive income from firms in exchange for working and providing other inputs. Households then recycle that income to the firms in exchange for goods and services. Dollars flow clockwise and goods and services flow counterclockwise.

The circular flow model can become much more complex but here it is presented merely to introduce the major markets and players in the economy. For example, the model can be extended to show the role of government, the financial sector, and foreign markets. Our simple model also does not show how firms and households send some of their income to the government for taxes or how households save some of their income for savings. Households are not the only buyers in the economy—firms, government, and foreigners buy some of the goods and services.

SECTION CHECK

- In the product market, households are buyers and firms are sellers.
- In the factor markets, households are the sellers and firms are the buyers.
- The goods and services flow represents the continuous flow of inputs and outputs in an economy.
- The income flow represents the continuous flow of income and expenditure in an economy.
- The circular flow model illustrates the flow of goods, services, and payments among firms and households.

section 2.3

The Production Possibilities Curve

- What is a production possibilities curve?
- What is efficiency?
- How is opportunity cost measured?
- What is the law of increasing opportunity costs?

WHAT IS A PRODUCTION POSSIBILITIES CURVE?

production possibilities curve
the potential total output combinations of any two goods for an economy, given the inputs and technology available

The economic concepts of scarcity, choice, and trade-offs can be shown with a simple graph called a *production possibilities curve.* The **production possibilities curve** represents the potential total output combinations of any two goods for an economy, given the inputs and technology available to the economy. That is, it illustrates an economy's potential for allocating its limited resources in producing various combinations of goods, in a given time period.

A Straight-Line Production Possibilities Curve—Grades in Economics and Accounting

What would the production possibilities curve look like if you were "producing" grades in two of your classes—say, economics and accounting? In Exhibit 1, we draw a hypothetical production possibilities curve for your expected grade in economics on the vertical axis and your expected grade in accounting on the horizontal axis. Assume, because of a part-time restaurant job, you choose to study ten hours a week and that you like both courses and are equally adept at studying for both courses.

We see in Exhibit 1 that the production possibilities curve is a straight line. For example, if all ten hours are spent studying economics, the expected grade in economics is 85 percent (an A) and the expected grade in accounting is 45 percent (an F). Moving down the production possibilities curve, we see that as you spend more of your time studying accounting and less on economics, you can raise your expected grade in accounting but only at the expense of lowering your expected grade in economics. Specifically, moving down along the straight-line production possibilities curve, the trade-off is one letter-grade lower in economics for one higher letter-grade in accounting.

Of course, if you increased your study time it would be possible to expect higher grades in both courses. But that would be on a new production possibilities curve; along this production possibilities curve we are assuming that technology and the number of study hours are given. In the next section, the coverage is expanded to cover the more realistic case of a bowed production possibilities curve.

section 2.3
Exhibit 1

Production Possibilities Curve: "Producing" Grades in Economics and Accounting

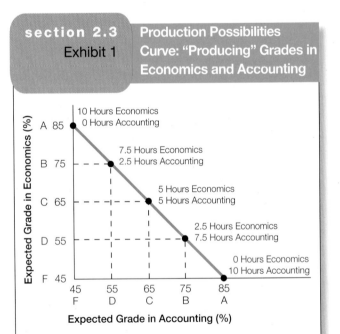

The production possibilities curve highlights the concept of trade-offs. Assuming you choose to study a total of ten hours a week, moving down the production possibilities curve shows that if you use your time to study accounting instead of economics you can raise your expected grade in accounting but only at the expense of lowering your expected grade in economics. With a straight-line production possibilities curve, the opportunity costs are constant.

Production Alternatives On the Bowed Production Possibilities Curve

To more clearly illustrate the production possibilities curve, imagine an economy that produces just two goods: food and shelter. The fact that we have many goods in the real world makes actual decision making more complicated, but it does not alter the basic principles being illustrated. Each point on the production possibilities curve shown in Exhibit 2 represents the potential amounts of food and shelter that can be produced in a given time period, given the quantity and quality of resources available in the economy for production.

Note in Exhibit 2 that if we devoted all of our resources to making shelters, we could produce 10 units of shelter, but no food (point A). If, on the other hand, we chose to devote all of our resources to food, we could produce 80 units of food, but no shelter (point E).

In reality, nations would rarely opt for production possibility A or E, preferring instead to produce a mixture of goods. For example, the economy in question might produce 9 units of shelter and 20 units of food (point B), or perhaps 7 units of shelter and 40 units of food (point C). Still other combinations along the curve, such as point D, are possible.

Production Alternatives Off the Production Possibilities Curve

The economy cannot operate at point N (not attainable) during the given time period because there are presently not enough resources to produce that level of output. However, it is possible the economy can operate inside the production possibilities curve, at point I (inefficient). If the economy is operating at point I, or at any other point inside the production possibilities curve, it is not at full capacity and is operating inefficiently.

section 2.3
Exhibit 2
Production Possibilities Curve:
The Trade-Off between Shelter and Food

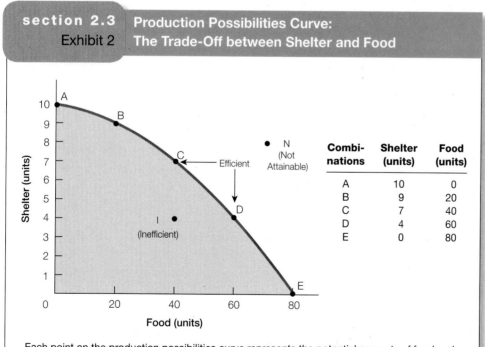

Combinations	Shelter (units)	Food (units)
A	10	0
B	9	20
C	7	40
D	4	60
E	0	80

Each point on the production possibilities curve represents the potential amounts of food and shelter that can be produced in a given time period, given the quantity and quality of resources available in the economy to use for production. All the points on the production possibility curve are efficient. Any points in the shaded area, like point I, are inefficient. Any point outside the production possibilites curve, like point N, is not attainable at the present time.

In short, the economy is not using all of its scarce resources efficiently; as a result, actual output is less than potential output.

WHAT IS EFFICIENCY?

Most modern economies have resources that are idle, at least for some period of time—like during periods of high unemployment. If those resources were not idle, people would have more scarce goods and services available for their use. Unemployed resources create a serious problem. For example, consider an unemployed fisherman who is unable to find work at a "reasonable" wage, or those unemployed in depressed times when factories are already operating below capacity. Clearly, the resources of these individuals are not being used efficiently.

The fact that factories can operate below capacity suggests that it is not just labour resources that should be most effectively used. Rather, all resources entering into production must be used effectively. However, for several reasons, social concern focuses on labour. First, labour costs are the largest share of production costs. Also, unemployed or underemployed labourers (whose resources are not being used to their full potential) may have mouths to feed at home, whereas an unemployed machine does not (although the owner of the unemployed machine may).

Inefficiency and Efficiency

Suppose for some reason there is widespread unemployment or resources are not being put to their best use. The economy would then be operating at a point, such as I, inside the production possibilities curve where the economy is operating inefficiently. At point I, 4 units of shelter and 40 units of food are being produced. By putting unemployed resources to work or by putting already employed resources to better use, we could expand the output of shelter by 3 units (moving to point C) without giving up any units of food. Alternatively, we could boost food output by 20 units (moving to point D) without reducing shelter output. We could even get more of both food and shelter moving to a point on the curve between C and D. Increasing or improving the utilization of resources, then, can lead to greater output of all goods. An efficient use of our resources means more of everything we want can be available for our use. Thus, efficiency requires society to use its resources to the fullest extent—getting the most from our scarce resources; that is, there are no wasted resources. If resources are being used efficiently, that is, at some point along a production possibilities curve, then more of one good or service requires the sacrifice of another good or service. Efficiency does not tell us which point along the production possibilites curve is *best,* but it does tell us that points inside the curve cannot be best because some resources are wasted.

HOW IS OPPORTUNITY COST MEASURED?

When an economy is operating efficiently, the decision to increase the production of one good or service will carry with it a related opportunity cost. Within the framework of the production possibility model, the determination of opportunity cost is greatly simplified since the next best alternative is the only alternative—therefore, in our example, the opportunity cost of increasing the production of shelter would be measured in corresponding forgone units of food, and the opportunity cost of expanding food production would be measured in units of forgone shelter.

Note in Exhibit 2 that if the economy is currently operating at point D (producing 4 units of shelter and 60 units of food), the decision to increase the amount of shelter it produces to 7 units will have an opportunity cost of 20 units of food—as this is the amount of food that the economy must give up to gain the additional units of shelter. In the diagram, this gain of shelter and related opportunity cost would involve the movement along the production possibilities curve from point D to point C.

WHAT IS THE LAW OF INCREASING OPPORTUNITY COSTS?

Note that in Exhibits 2 and 3, the production possibilities curve is not a straight line like that in Exhibit 1. It is concave from below (i.e., bowed outward from the origin). Looking at the figures, you can see that at very low food output, an increase in the amount of food produced will lead to only a small reduction in the units of shelter produced. For example, increasing food output from 0 to 20 (moving from point A to point B on the curve) requires the use of resources capable of producing 1 unit of shelter. This means that for the first 20 units of food, 1 unit of shelter must be given up. When food output is higher, however, more units of shelter must be given up when switching additional resources from the production of shelter to food. Moving from point D to point E, for example, an increase in food output of 20 (from 60 to 80) reduces the production of shelter from 4 to 0. At this point, then, the cost of those 20 additional units of food is 4 units of shelter, considerably more than the 1 unit of shelter required in the earlier scenario. This difference shows us that opportunity costs have not remained constant, but have risen, as more units of food and fewer units of shelter are produced.

The **law of increasing opportunity cost** refers to the concept that, as more of one item is produced by an economy, the opportunity cost of additional units of that product rises. It is this increasing opportunity cost, then, that is represented by the bowed production possibilities curve.

law of increasing opportunity cost
as more of one item is produced by an economy, the opportunity cost of additional units of that product rises

The Reason for the Law of Increasing Opportunity Cost

The basic reason for the law of increasing opportunity cost is that some resources and skills cannot be easily adapted from their current uses to alternative uses. For example, at low levels of food output, additional increases in food output can be obtained easily by

section 2.3
Exhibit 3 — **Increasing Opportunity Cost and the Production Possibilities Curve**

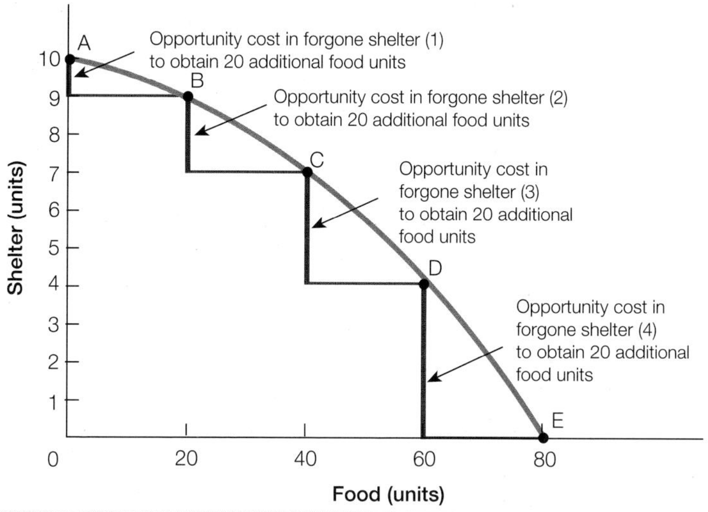

The production possibilities curve also illustrates the opportunity cost of producing more of a given product. For example, if we were to increase food output from 40 units to 60 units (moving from point C to point D), we must produce 3 fewer units of shelter. The opportunity cost of those 20 additional units of food is the 3 units of shelter we must forgo. We can see that moving down the curve from A to E, each additional 20 units of food costs society more and more shelter—the law of increasing opportunity cost.

switching relatively low-skilled carpenters from making shelter to producing food. However, to get even more food output, workers that are less well suited or appropriate for producing food (i.e., they are better adapted to making shelter) must be released from shelter making in order to increase food output. For example, a skilled carpenter may be an expert at making shelter but a very bad farmer, because he lacks the training and skills necessary in that occupation. So, using the skilled carpenter to farm results in a relatively greater opportunity cost than using the poor carpenter to farm. Hence, the production of additional units of food becomes increasingly costly as progressively even lower-skilled farmers (but good carpenters) convert to farming.

SECTION CHECK

- The production possibilities curve represents the potential total output combinations of two goods available to a society given its resources and existing technology.
- Efficiency requires society to use its resources to the fullest extent—no wasted resources. If the economy is operating within the production possibilities curve, the economy is operating inefficiently.
- The cost of altering production within the production possibilities curve framework, at efficiency, is measured in forgone units of the sole alternative.
- A bowed production possibilities curve means that the opportunity costs of producing additional units of a good rise as society produces more of that good (the law of increasing opportunity costs).

section 2.4

Economic Growth and the Production Possibilities Curve

- How do we show economic growth on the production possibilities curve?
- How can we summarize the production possibilities curve?

HOW DO WE SHOW ECONOMIC GROWTH ON THE PRODUCTION POSSIBILITIES CURVE?

How have some nations been able to rapidly expand their output of goods and services over time, whereas others have been unable to increase their standards of living at all?

The economy can grow only with qualitative or quantitative changes in the factors of production—land, labour, capital, and entrepreneurship. Advancement in technology, improvements in labour productivity, or new sources of natural resources (such as previously undiscovered oil) could all lead to outward shifts of the production possibilities curve.

This idea can be clearly illustrated by using the production possibilities curve (Exhibit 1). In terms of the production possibilities curve, economic growth means an outward shift in the possible combinations of goods and services produced. With growth comes the possibility to have more of both goods than were previously available. Suppose we were producing at point C (7 units of shelter, 40 units of food) on our original production possibilities curve. Additional resources and/or new methods of using them (technological progress) can lead to new production possibilities creating the potential for more of all goods (or more of some with no less of others). These increases would push the production possibilities curve outward. For example, if you invest in human capital, such as training the workers making the shelter, it will increase the productivity of those workers. As a result, they will produce more units of shelter. This means, ultimately, that fewer resources will be used to make shelter, freeing them to be used for farming—resulting in more units of food. Notice that at point F (future) on the new curve, it is possible to produce 9 units of shelter and 70 units of food, more of both goods than was previously produced, at point C.

Growth Doesn't Eliminate Scarcity

With all of this discussion of growth, it is important to remember that growth, or increases in a society's output, does not make scarcity disappear. Even when output has grown more rapidly than the population so that people are made better off, they still face trade-offs: At any point along the production possibilities curve, in order to get more of one thing, you must give up something else. There are no free lunches on the production possibilities curve.

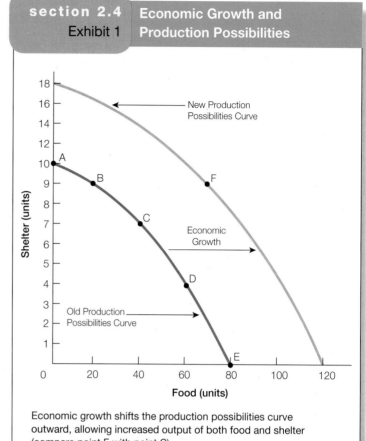

section 2.4 **Economic Growth and**
Exhibit 1 **Production Possibilities**

Economic growth shifts the production possibilities curve outward, allowing increased output of both food and shelter (compare point F with point C).

Capital Goods versus Consumption Goods

Economies that choose to invest more of their resources for the future will grow faster than those that don't. To generate economic growth, a society must produce fewer consumer goods—like pizza, DVD players, cellphones, cars, and so on—in the present and produce more capital goods. The society that devotes a larger share of its productive capacity to capital goods (machines, factories, tools, and education), rather than consumption goods (video games, pizza, and vacations), will experience greater economic growth. It must sacrifice some present consumption of consumer goods and services in order to experience growth in the future. Why? Investing in capital goods, like computers and other new technological equipment, as well as upgrading skills and knowledge, expands the ability to produce in the future. It shifts the economy's production possibilities outward, increasing the future production capacity of the economy. That is, the economy that invests more now (consumes less now) will be able to produce, and therefore consume, more in the future. In Exhibit 2, we see that Economy A invests more in capital goods than Economy B. Consequently, Economy A's production possibilities curve shifts out farther than Economy B's over time.

To better understand the significance of these two production alternatives, it may help to apply the distinction to the Canadian economy. Which type of economy is Canada, Economy A or Economy B? In Canada, consumption expenditure is nearly three times that of investment. As a result, the Canadian economy is best represented by the Economy B illustration.

section 2.4
Exhibit 2   Increasing Opportunity Cost and the Production Possibilities Curve

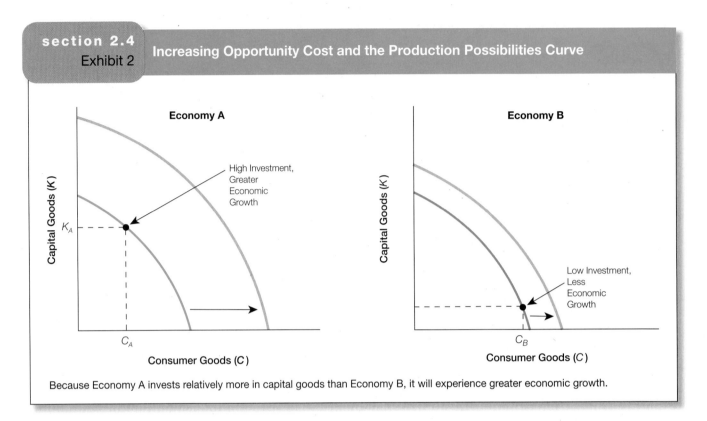

Because Economy A invests relatively more in capital goods than Economy B, it will experience greater economic growth.

The Effects of a Technological Change on the Production Possibilities Curve

In Exhibit 3, we see that a technological advance does not have to impact all sectors of the economy equally: There is a technological advance in food production but not in housing production. The technological advance in agriculture causes the production possibilities curve to extend out farther on the horizontal axis, which measures food production. We can move to any point on the new production possibilities curve. For example, the move from point A on the original curve to point B on the new curve would result in 150 more units of food (500 – 350) and the same amount of housing—200 units. Or, we could move from point A to point C, which would allow us to produce more units of both food and housing. How do we produce more housing, when the technological advance occurred in agriculture? The answer is that the technological advance in agriculture allows us to produce more from a given quantity of resources. That is, it allows us to shift some resources out of agriculture into housing. This is actually an ongoing story in Canadian economic history. In colonial days, almost all of the Canadian population made a living in agriculture. Today, it is less than 3 percent.

HOW CAN WE SUMMARIZE THE PRODUCTION POSSIBILITIES CURVE?

The production possibilities curve shown in Exhibit 4 illustrates the choices faced by an economy that makes military goods and consumer goods. How are the economic concepts of scarcity, choice, opportunity costs, efficiency, and economic growth illustrated in this production possibilities curve framework? In Exhibit 4, we can show scarcity because resource combinations outside the initial production possibilities curve, like point D, are unattainable without economic growth. If the economy is operating efficiently, we are somewhere on that production possibilities curve, like point B or point C. However, if the economy is operating inefficiently, we are operating inside that production possibilities curve, like point A. We can also see in this graph that to get more military goods you must give up consumer goods—that is, there is an opportunity cost. Finally, we see that over time, with economic growth, the whole production possibilities curve can shift outward, making point D now attainable.

section 2.4
Exhibit 3
The Effects of Change on the Production Possibilities Curve

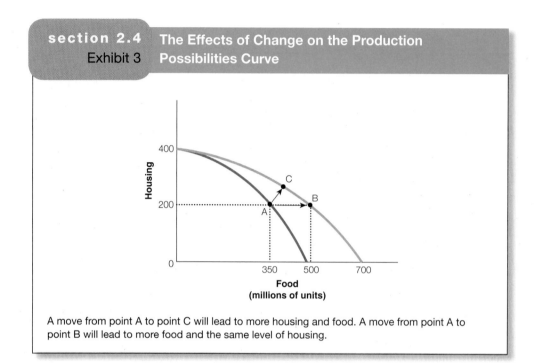

A move from point A to point C will lead to more housing and food. A move from point A to point B will lead to more food and the same level of housing.

section 2.4
Exhibit 4
Production Possibilities Curve

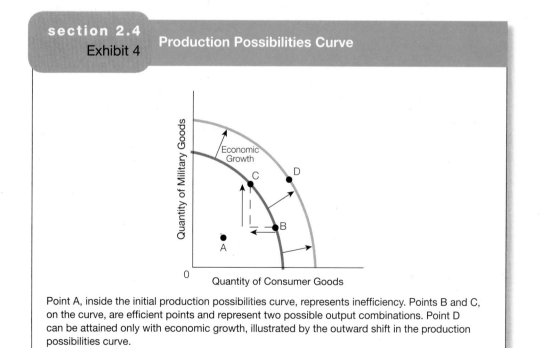

Point A, inside the initial production possibilities curve, represents inefficiency. Points B and C, on the curve, are efficient points and represent two possible output combinations. Point D can be attained only with economic growth, illustrated by the outward shift in the production possibilities curve.

DEBATE

CAN ECONOMIC GROWTH BE SUSTAINED OVER THE LONG TERM?

This is a question that confronts the world's economists and politicians alike. We rarely think about this question, as our own experience has generally been in a period of economic growth. Even with very little formal economic knowledge, you are probably able to defend or negate this proposition based on your own biases and beliefs. While you progress through the course, see if your position changes or solidifies as you learn new ways to think about the how we manage our lives and environment.

Pro:

Since the beginning of mankind (or for that matter, the beginning of life), economic growth has been the norm, albeit at different rates of growth. Mankind has adapted to challenging times, thus always attaining long-term economic growth. If capital was scarce, we turned to labour to meet our needs. If labour was scarce, we used more capital. We are an ingenious species who has always found ways to adapt to new situations, ensuring long-term economic growth and sustainability. Can you think of other arguments that would support the idea of economic growth over the long term?

Con:

Just because mankind has experienced economic growth in the past does not ensure sustainability in the future. We have adapted because we have learned how to use our resources for the benefit of mankind. If we ran short of capital or labour, we substituted one for the other, but we always had the benefits of endless resources to substitute. Long-term economic growth is dependent on the availability of resources, and with the uncertainty of the earth's ability to provide for mankind's increased population, continued economic growth is unsustainable. Think of other reasons why you think mankind cannot sustain long-term economic growth.

SECTION CHECK

- Economic growth is represented by an outward shift of the production possibilities curve, indicating an increase in the possibility of producing more of all goods. Despite this, scarcity inevitably remains a fact of life.
- The production possibilities model is an effective way of illustrating the economic concepts of scarcity, choice, opportunity costs, efficiency, and economic growth.

For Your Review

Section 2.1

1. What are the three basic economic questions? How are decisions made differently in a market economy than in command economies?

2. Recently the American Film Institute selected *Citizen Kane* as the best movie of all time. *Citizen Kane* is a fictional psychological biography of one of the most powerful newspaper publishers in history, William Randolph Hearst. *Titanic,* an epic romance about the sinking of the *Titanic,* has made the most money of any film in history. Unlike *Titanic, Citizen Kane* was not a box office success. Do you think Hollywood will make more movies like *Titanic* or more like *Citizen Kane?* Why?

3. Adam was a university graduate with a double major in economics and art. A few years ago, Adam decided that he wanted to pursue a vocation that utilized both of his talents. In response, he shut himself up in his studio and created a watercolour collection, "Graphs of Famous Recessions." With high hopes, Adam put his collection on display for buyers. After several years of displaying his econ art, however, the only one interested in the collection was his eight-year-old sister, who wanted the picture frames for her room. Recognizing that Adam was having trouble pursuing his chosen occupation, Adam's friend Karl told him that the market had failed. What do you think? Is Karl right?

Section 2.2

4. Identify where the appropriate entries go in the circular flow diagram below.

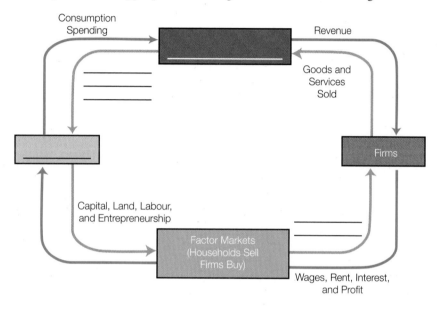

5. Identify whether each of the following transactions takes place in the factor market or the product market.

   a. Billy buys a sofa from Home Time Furniture for his new home.

   b. Home Time Furniture pays its manager her weekly salary.

   c. The manager buys dinner at Billy's Café.

   d. After he pays all of his employees their wages and pays his other bills, the owner of Billy's Café takes his profit.

Section 2.3

6. Assume that the production possibilities for Alberta are the following combinations of kegs of beer and sides of beef.

Beer	Beef
55	0
54	1
52	2
49	3
45	4
40	5
34	6
27	7
19	8
10	9
0	10

a. Construct the production possibilities frontier for beer and beef on the grid below.

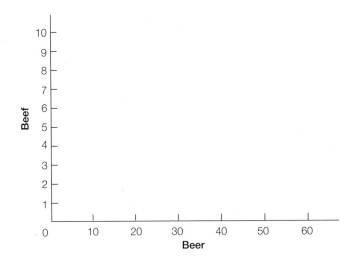

b. Given the information above, what is the opportunity cost of the 55th keg of beer in Alberta? Of the 6th side of beef? Of the 9th side of beef?

c. Suppose Alberta is currently producing 4 sides of beef and 45 kegs of beer. What is the opportunity cost of 5 more sides of beef in Alberta?

d. Would the combination of 40 kegs of beer and 4 sides of beef be efficient? Why or why not?

e. Is the combination of 9 kegs of beer and 10 sides of beef possible for Alberta? Why or why not?

7. Using the table below, answer the questions that follow it.

COMBINATIONS					
	A	**B**	**C**	**D**	**E**
Guns	1	2	3	4	5
Butter	20	18	14	8	0

    a. What are the assumptions for a given production possibilities curve?

    b. What is the opportunity cost of one gun when moving from point B to point C? When moving from point D to point E?

    c. Do these combinations demonstrate constant or increasing opportunity costs?

8. Imagine that you are the sole inhabitant of a small island that produces only two goods: cattle and wheat. About a quarter of the land is not fertile enough for growing wheat, so cattle graze on it. What would happen if you tried to produce more and more wheat, extending your planting even to the less fertile soil?

Sections 2.3 and 2.4

9. How would the following events be shown using a production possibilities curve for shelter and food?

    a. The economy is experiencing double-digit unemployment.

    b. Economic growth is increasing at over 5 percent per year.

    c. Society decides it wants less shelter and more food.

    d. Society decides it wants more shelter and less food.

Section 2.4

10. Given the following production possibilities curve, answer the questions that follow it.

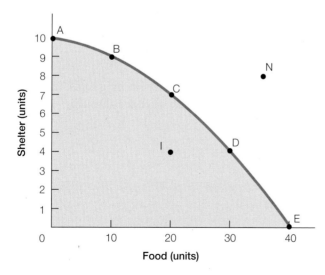

    a. Does this production possibilities curve show increasing opportunity costs? Explain.

    b. What is the opportunity cost of moving from point I to point D? Explain.

    c. What is the opportunity cost of moving from point C to point B?

    d. Which of points A–E is the most efficient? Explain.

    e. Which of the identified production alternatives is currently impossible for this economy to achieve? What must happen in order for this production alternative to become attainable?

    f. Which of the identified production alternatives is currently attainable but inefficient? What must happen in order for this production alternative to become efficient?

11. Economy A produces more capital goods and fewer consumer goods than Economy B. Which economy will grow more rapidly? Draw two production possibilities curves, one for Economy A and one for Economy B. Demonstrate graphically how one economy can grow more rapidly than the other.

12. How does a technological advance that increases the efficiency of shoe production affect the production possibilities curve between shoes and pizza? Is it possible to produce more shoes and pizza or just more shoes? Explain.

13. A politician running for prime minister of Canada promises to build new schools and new prisons if elected, without sacrificing any other goods and services. Using the production possibilities curve between schools and prisons, explain under what conditions the politician would be able to keep her promise.

14. Why one nation experiences economic growth and another does not is a question that has intrigued economists since Adam Smith wrote *An Inquiry into the Nature and Causes of the Wealth of Nations* in 1776. Explain why each of the following would limit economic growth.

    a. The politically connected elite secure a large share of a country's output and put the proceeds into foreign banks.

    b. The national philosophy is "Live for the moment and forget about tomorrow."

    c. The government closes all of the schools so more people will be available for work.

    d. The country fears military invasion and spends half of its income on military goods.

CourseMate

Access an interactive eBook and chapter-specific interactive learning tools, including flashcards, quizzes, a glossary, and more in CourseMate, accessed through **www.sextonmacro3ce.nelson.com**

chapter 3

Supply and Demand

section 3.1

Markets

- What is a market?
- What are the roles of buyers and sellers in a market?

WHAT IS A MARKET?

Although we usually think of a market as a place where some sort of exchange occurs, a market is not really a place at all. A **market** is the process of buyers and sellers exchanging goods and services. This means that supermarkets, the Toronto Stock Exchange, drugstores, roadside stands, garage sales, Internet stores, and restaurants are all markets.

Every market is different. That is, the conditions under which the exchange between buyers and sellers takes place can vary. These differences make it difficult to precisely define a market. After all, an incredible variety of exchange arrangements exists in the real world—organized securities markets, wholesale auction markets, foreign exchange markets, real estate markets, labour markets, and so forth.

Goods being priced and traded in various ways at various locations by various kinds of buyers and sellers further compound the problem of defining a market. For some goods, such as housing, markets are numerous but limited to a geographic area. Homes in Niagara Falls, Ontario, for example (about 130 kilometres from downtown Toronto), do not compete directly with homes in Toronto. Why? Because people who work in Toronto will generally look for homes within commuting distance. Even within cities, there are separate markets for homes, differentiated by amenities such as bigger houses, newer houses, larger lots, and better schools.

In a similar manner, markets are numerous but geographically limited for a good such as cement. Because transportation costs are so high relative to the selling price, the good is not shipped any substantial distance, and buyers are usually in contact only with local producers. Price and output are thus determined in a number of small markets. In other markets, like those for gold or automobiles, markets are global. The important point is not what a market looks like, but what it does—it facilitates trade.

market
the process of buyers and sellers exchanging goods and services

WHAT ARE THE ROLES OF BUYERS AND SELLERS IN A MARKET?

The roles of buyers and sellers in markets are important. The buyers, as a group, determine the demand side of the market. Buyers include the consumers who purchase the goods and services and the firms that buy inputs—labour, capital, and raw materials. Sellers, as a group, determine the supply side of the market. Sellers include the firms that produce and sell goods and services, and the resource owners who sell their inputs to firms—workers who "sell" their labour and resource owners who sell raw materials and capital. It is the interaction of buyers and sellers that determines market prices and output—through the forces of supply and demand.

competitive market
a market in which there are a number of buyers and sellers offering similar products, and no single buyer or seller can influence the market price

In this chapter, we focus on how supply and demand work in a **competitive market.** A competitive market is one in which there are a number of buyers and sellers offering similar products and no single buyer or seller can influence the market price; that is, buyers and sellers have very little market power. Because most markets contain a large degree of competitiveness, the lessons of supply and demand can be applied to many different types of problems.

The supply and demand model is particularly useful in markets like agriculture, finance, labour, construction, services, wholesale, and retail. In short, a model is only as good as it explains and predicts. The model of supply and demand is very good at predicting changes in prices and quantities in many markets, large and small.

SECTION CHECK

- Markets consist of buyers and sellers exchanging goods and services with one another.
- Buyers determine the demand side of the market and sellers determine the supply side of the market.

section 3.2

Demand

- What is the law of demand?
- What is an individual demand schedule and curve?
- What is a market demand curve?

WHAT IS THE LAW OF DEMAND?

Some laws are made to protect us, such as "no speeding" or "no drinking and driving." Other times observed behaviour is so pervasive it is called a law—like the law of demand. According to the **law of demand,** the quantity of a good or service demanded varies inversely (negatively) with its price, *ceteris paribus.* More directly, the law of demand says that, other things being equal, when the price (P) of a good or service falls, the quantity demanded (Q_D) increases, and conversely, if the price of a good or service rises, the quantity demanded decreases.

law of demand
the quantity of a good or service demanded varies inversely (negatively) with its price, ceteris paribus

$$P\uparrow \Rightarrow Q_D\downarrow \text{ or } P\downarrow \Rightarrow Q_D\uparrow$$

The law of demand puts the concept of basic human "needs," at least as an analytical tool, to rest. Needs are those things that you must have at any price. That is, there are no substitutes. There are usually plenty of substitutes available for any good, some better than others. The law of demand, with its inverse relationship between price and quantity demanded, implies that even so-called needs are more or less urgent depending on the circumstances (opportunity costs). Whenever you hear somebody say, "I need a new car," "I need a new CD player," or "I need new clothes," always be sure to ask: What does the person really mean? At what price does that person "need" the good?

Need water? What if the price of water increases significantly? At the new higher price, consumers will still use almost as much water for essentials like drinking and cooking. However, they may no longer "need" to wash their cars as often, water their lawns daily, hose off their sidewalks, run the dishwasher so frequently, take long showers, or flush the toilet as often.

The Negative Relationship between Price and Quantity Demanded

The law of demand describes a negative (inverse) relationship between price and quantity demanded. When price goes up, the quantity demanded goes down, and vice versa. But why is this so? The primary reason for this inverse relationship is the **substitution effect.** At higher prices, buyers increasingly substitute other goods for the good that now has a higher relative price. For example, if the price of orange juice increases, some consumers may substitute out of orange juice into other juices, such as apple or tomato juice, or perhaps water, milk, or coffee. This is what economists call the substitution effect of a price change. Of course, if the relative price of orange juice fell, then consumers would substitute out of other products and increase their quantity of orange juice demanded, because the lower relative price now makes it a more attractive purchase.

Another reason for the inverse relationship between price and quantity demanded is referred to as the **income effect.** In this explanation, higher prices make the buyer feel poorer, causing a lowering of quantity demanded (since they cannot buy the same quantity of goods as they did when prices were lower). When prices decline, this makes buyers feel richer, therefore causing quantity demanded to increase.

substitution effect
at higher prices, buyers increasingly substitute other goods for the good that now has a higher relative price

income effect
at higher prices, buyers feel poorer, causing a lowering of quantity demanded

WHAT IS AN INDIVIDUAL DEMAND SCHEDULE AND CURVE?

The **individual demand schedule** is a table that shows the relationship between the price of the good and the quantity demanded. For example, suppose Elizabeth enjoys eating apples. How many kilograms of apples would Elizabeth be willing and able to buy at various prices during the year? At a price of $3 a kilogram, Elizabeth buys 15 kilograms of apples over the course of a year. If the price is higher, at $4 per kilogram, she might buy only 10 kilograms; if it is lower, say $1 per kilogram, she might buy 25 kilograms of apples during the year. Elizabeth's demand for apples for the year is summarized in the demand schedule in Exhibit 1. Elizabeth might not be consciously aware of the amounts that she would purchase at prices other than the prevailing one, but that does not alter the fact that she has a schedule in the sense that she would have bought various other amounts had other prices prevailed. It must be emphasized that the schedule is a list of alternative possibilities. At any one time, only one of the prices will prevail, and thus a certain quantity will be purchased.

individual demand schedule
a table that shows the relationship between price and quantity demanded

section 3.2 Exhibit 1	Elizabeth's Demand Schedule for Apples

Price (per kilogram)	Quantity Demanded (kilograms per year)
$5	5
4	10
3	15
2	20
1	25

An Individual Demand Curve

individual demand curve
a graphical representation that shows the inverse relationship between price and quantity demanded

An **individual demand curve** is a graphical representation that shows the inverse relationship between price and quantity demanded. By plotting the different prices and corresponding quantities demanded in Elizabeth's demand schedule in Exhibit 1 and then connecting them, we can create an individual demand curve for Elizabeth (Exhibit 2). From the curve, we can see that when the price is higher, the quantity demanded is lower, and when the price is lower, the quantity demanded is higher. The demand curve shows how the quantity demanded of the good changes as its price varies.

section 3.2   **Elizabeth's Demand**
Exhibit 2   **Curve for Apples**

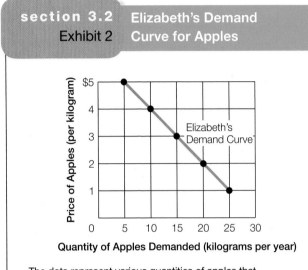

The dots represent various quantities of apples that Elizabeth would be willing and able to buy at different prices in a given time period. The demand curve shows how the quantity demanded varies inversely with the price of the good when we hold everything else constant—*ceteris paribus*. Because of this inverse relationship between price and quantity demanded, the demand curve is downward sloping.

market demand curve
the horizontal summation of individual demand curves

WHAT IS A MARKET DEMAND CURVE?

Although we introduced this concept in terms of the individual, economists usually speak of the demand curve in terms of large groups of people—a whole nation, a community, or a trading area. As you know, every single individual has his or her demand curve for every product. The horizontal summation of individual demand curves is called the **market demand curve.**

Suppose the consumer group comprises Homer, Marge, and the rest of their small community, Springfield, and that the product is still apples. The effect of price on the quantity of apples demanded by Marge, Homer, and the rest of Springfield is given in the demand schedule and demand curves shown in Exhibit 3. At $4 per kilogram, Homer would be willing and able to buy 20 kilograms of apples per year, Marge would be willing and able to buy 10 kilograms, and the rest of Springfield would be willing and able to buy 2970 kilograms. At $3 per kilogram, Homer would be willing and able to buy 25 kilograms of apples per year, Marge would be willing and able to buy 15 kilograms, and the rest of Springfield would be willing and able to buy 4960 kilograms. The market demand curve is simply the (horizontal) sum of the quantities Homer, Marge, and the rest of Springfield demand at each price. That is, at $4, the quantity demanded in the market would be 3000 kilograms of apples (20 + 10 + 2970 = 3000),

What if this house had been on the market for a year at the same price and not sold? Although no one may want this house at the current asking price, a number of people may want it at a lower price—the law of demand.

and at $3, the quantity demanded in the market would be 5000 kilograms of apples (25 + 15 + 4960 = 5000).

In Exhibit 4, we offer a more complete set of prices and quantities from the market demand for apples during the year. Remember, the market demand curve shows the amounts that all the buyers in the market would be willing and able to buy at various

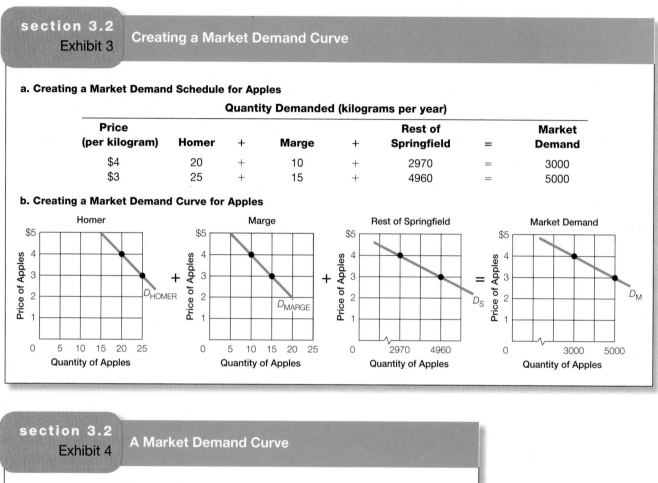

section 3.2
Exhibit 3 Creating a Market Demand Curve

a. Creating a Market Demand Schedule for Apples

	Quantity Demanded (kilograms per year)							
Price (per kilogram)	Homer	+	Marge	+	Rest of Springfield	=	Market Demand
$4	20	+	10	+	2970	=	3000
$3	25	+	15	+	4960	=	5000

b. Creating a Market Demand Curve for Apples

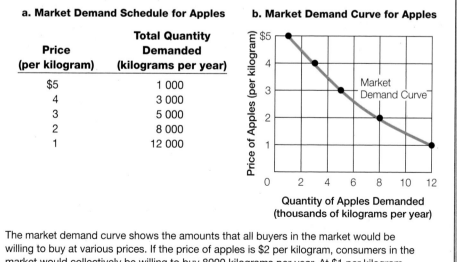

section 3.2
Exhibit 4 A Market Demand Curve

a. Market Demand Schedule for Apples

Price (per kilogram)	Total Quantity Demanded (kilograms per year)
$5	1 000
4	3 000
3	5 000
2	8 000
1	12 000

b. Market Demand Curve for Apples

The market demand curve shows the amounts that all buyers in the market would be willing to buy at various prices. If the price of apples is $2 per kilogram, consumers in the market would collectively be willing to buy 8000 kilograms per year. At $1 per kilogram, the amount demanded would be 12 000 kilograms per year.

prices. For example, if the price of apples is $2 per kilogram, consumers in the market would collectively be willing and able to buy 8000 kilograms per year. At $1 per kilogram, the amount demanded would be 12 000 kilograms per year.

The market demand curve is the negative (inverse) relationship between price and the total quantity demanded, while holding constant all other factors that affect how much consumers are able and willing to pay, *ceteris paribus*. For the most part, we are interested in how the market works, so we will primarily use the market demand curves.

SECTION CHECK

- The law of demand states that when the price of a good falls (rises), the quantity demanded rises (falls), *ceteris paribus*.
- An individual demand curve is a graphical representation of the relationship between the price and the quantity demanded.
- The market demand curve shows the amount of a good that all the buyers in the market would be willing and able to buy at various prices.

section 3.3

Shifts in the Demand Curve

- What is the difference between a change in demand and a change in quantity demanded?
- What are the determinants of demand?
- Can we review the distinction between changes in demand and changes in quantity demanded?

WHAT IS THE DIFFERENCE BETWEEN A CHANGE IN DEMAND AND A CHANGE IN QUANTITY DEMANDED?

Consumers are influenced by the prices of goods when they make their purchasing decisions. At lower prices, people prefer to buy more of a good than at higher prices, holding other factors constant. Why? Primarily, it is because many goods are substitutes for one another. For example, an increase in the price of apples might tempt some buyers to switch from buying apples to buying oranges or peaches.

Understanding this relationship between price and quantity demanded is so important that economists make a clear distinction between it and the various other factors that can influence consumer behaviour. A change in a good's price is said to lead to a **change in quantity demanded.** That is, it "moves you along" a given demand curve. The demand curve is drawn under the assumption that all other things are held constant, except the price of the good. However, economists know that price is not the only thing that affects the quantity of a good that people buy. The other factors that influence the demand curve are called *determinants of demand* and a change in these other factors *shifts the entire demand curve*. These determinants of demand are called demand shifters and they lead to a **change in demand.**

change in quantity demanded
a change in a good's price leads to a change in quantity demanded, a move along a given demand curve

change in demand
a change in a determinant of demand leads to a change in demand, a shift of the entire demand curve

WHAT ARE THE DETERMINANTS OF DEMAND?

An increase in demand shifts the demand curve to the right; a decrease in demand shifts the demand curve to the left, as seen in Exhibit 1. Changes in demand such as these are the result of demand shifters. Some of the possible demand shifters are the prices of related goods, income, number of buyers, tastes, and expectations. We will now look more closely at each of these variables.

The Prices of Related Goods

In deciding how much of a good or service to buy, consumers are influenced by the price of that good or service, a relationship summarized in the law of demand. However, consumers are also influenced by the prices of *related* goods and services—substitutes and complements.

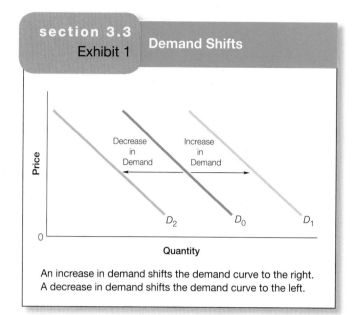

section 3.3
Exhibit 1 — **Demand Shifts**

An increase in demand shifts the demand curve to the right. A decrease in demand shifts the demand curve to the left.

Substitutes   Substitutes are generally goods for which one could be used in place of the other. To many, substitutes would include butter and margarine, domestic and foreign cars, movie tickets and video rentals, jackets and sweaters, Petro Canada and Shell gasoline, and Nikes and Adidas.

Suppose you go into a store to buy a couple of six packs of Coca-Cola and you see that Pepsi is on sale for half its usual price. Is it possible that you might decide to buy Pepsi instead of Coca-Cola? Economists argue that this is the case, and empirical tests have confirmed that people are responsive to both the price of the good in question and the prices of related goods. In this example, Pepsi and Coca-Cola are said to be substitutes. Two goods are **substitutes** if an increase (a decrease) in the price of one good causes an increase (a decrease) in the demand for another good, a direct (or positive) relationship. In Exhibit 2(a), we see that as the price of Coca-Cola increased—a movement up along your demand curve for it—you increased your demand for Pepsi, resulting in a shift in the demand for Pepsi (Exhibit 2[b]).

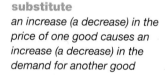

substitute
an increase (a decrease) in the price of one good causes an increase (a decrease) in the demand for another good

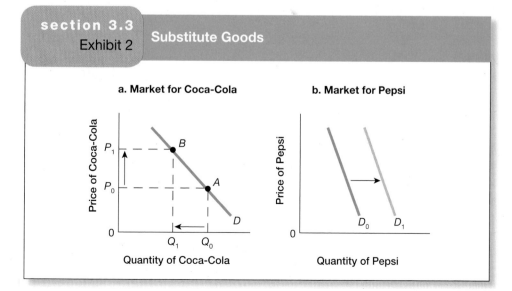

section 3.3
Exhibit 2 — **Substitute Goods**

a. Market for Coca-Cola

b. Market for Pepsi

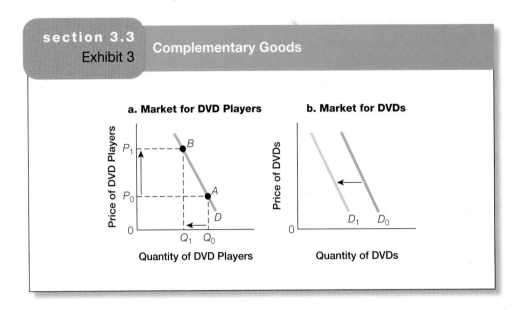

section 3.3
Exhibit 3

Complementary Goods

a. Market for DVD Players

b. Market for DVDs

Quantity of DVD Players

Quantity of DVDs

Complements   Complements are goods that "go together," often consumed and used simultaneously, such as skis and bindings, peanut butter and jam, hot dogs and buns, digital music players and downloadable music, and printers and ink cartridges. If an increase (a decrease) in the price of one good causes a decrease (an increase) in the demand of another good (an inverse or negative relationship), the two goods are called **complements.** For example, in Exhibit 3(a), we see that as the price of DVD players increases, the quantity demanded of DVD players falls (a movement in demand). And with fewer DVD players being purchased, we would expect people to decrease their demand (a leftward shift) for DVDs (Exhibit 3[b]).

complement

an increase (a decrease) in the price of one good causes a decrease (an increase) in the demand of another good

Income

Economists have observed that generally the consumption of goods and services is positively related to the income available to consumers. Empirical studies support the notion that as individuals receive more income they tend to increase their purchases of most goods and services. Other things held equal, rising income usually leads to an increase in the demand for goods (a rightward shift of the demand curve), and decreasing income usually leads to a decrease in the demand for goods (a leftward shift of the demand curve).

normal good

if income increases, the demand for a good increases; if income decreases, the demand for a good decreases

inferior good

if income increases, the demand for a good decreases; if income decreases, the demand for a good increases

Normal and Inferior Goods   If when income increases, the demand for a good increases and decreases when income decreases, the good is called a **normal good.** Most goods are normal goods. Consumers will typically buy more CDs, clothes, pizzas, and trips to the movies as their incomes rise. However, if when income increases, the demand for a good decreases and increases when income decreases, the good is called an **inferior good.** For example, for most people inferior goods might include do-it-yourself haircuts, used cars, thrift-shop and clothing, and macaroni and cheese. The term *inferior* in this sense does not refer to the quality of the good in question but shows that when income changes, demand changes in the opposite direction (inversely).

Consider how an increase in income can affect the market for automobiles and the market for bus rides. Automobiles are generally considered a normal good, so a rise in income will increase the demand for automobiles (Exhibit 4[a]). However, the demand for bus rides may fall, as higher incomes allow consumers to buy automobiles. The demand for bus rides would then be an inferior good (Exhibit 4[b]).

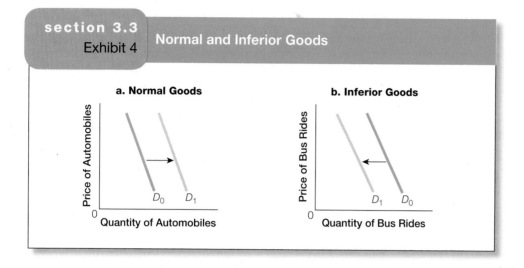

For example, if people's incomes rise and they increase their demand for movie tickets, we say that movie tickets are a normal good. But if people's incomes fall and they increase their demand for bus rides, we say bus rides are an inferior good. Whether goods are normal or inferior, the point here is that income influences demand—usually positively, but sometimes negatively.

Number of Buyers

The demand for a good or service will vary with the size of the potential consumer population. The demand for wheat, for example, rises as population increases because the added population wants to consume wheat products, like bread or cereal. Marketing experts, who closely follow the patterns of consumer behaviour with regards to a particular good or service, are usually vitally concerned with the "demographics" of the product—the vital statistics of the potential consumer population, including size, income, and age characteristics. For example, market researchers for baby-food companies keep a close watch on the birth rate.

For most people, "no name" products are an inferior good. That is, an increase in income will lead to a reduction in the demand for "no name" products.

Tastes

The demand for a good or service may increase or decrease suddenly with changes in fashions or fads. Taste changes may be triggered by advertising or promotion, by a news story, by the behaviour of some popular public figure, and so on. Taste changes are particularly noticeable in apparel. Skirt lengths, coat lapels, shoe styles, and tie sizes change frequently.

Changes in preferences naturally lead to shifts in demand. Much of the predictive power of economic theory, however, stems from the assumption that tastes are relatively stable, at least over a substantial period of time. Tastes *do* change, though. A person may grow tired of one type of recreation or food and try another type. Changes in occupation, number of dependants, state of health, and age also tend to alter preferences. The birth of a baby may cause a family to spend less on recreation and more on food and clothing.

Illness increases the demand for medicine and lessens purchases of other goods. A cold winter increases the demand for natural gas. Changes in customs and traditions also affect preferences, and the development of new products draws consumer preferences away from other goods. Compact discs have replaced record albums, just as in-line skates have replaced traditional roller skates.

Expectations

Sometimes the demand for a good or service in a given time period will dramatically increase or decrease because consumers expect the good to change in price or availability at some future date. For example, in the summer of 2005, many buyers expected oil production in the Gulf of Mexico to be lower because of Hurricane Katrina. As a result of their expectations of higher future gasoline prices, buyers increased their current demand for gasoline. That is, the current demand for gasoline shifted to the right. Other examples, such as waiting to buy a home computer because price reductions may be even greater in the future, are also common. Or, if you expect to earn additional income next month, you may be more willing to dip into your current savings to buy something this month.

CAN WE REVIEW THE DISTINCTION BETWEEN CHANGES IN DEMAND AND CHANGES IN QUANTITY DEMANDED?

Economists put particular emphasis on the impact on consumer behaviour of a change in the price of a good. We are interested in distinguishing between consumer behaviour related to the price of a good itself (movement *along* a demand curve) from behaviour related to other factors changing (shifts of the demand curve).

   As indicated earlier, if the price of a good changes, we say that this leads to a *"change in quantity demanded."* In Exhibit 5, the movement from A to B is called an *increase in quantity demanded,* and the movement from B to A is called a *decrease in quantity demanded.* Economists use the phrase "increase in quantity demanded" or "decrease in quantity demanded" to describe movements along a given demand curve. If one of the

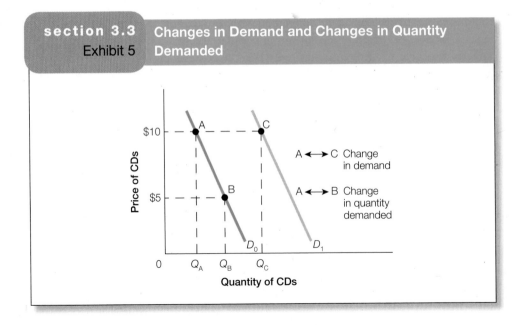

section 3.3 **Changes in Demand and Changes in Quantity**
Exhibit 5 **Demanded**

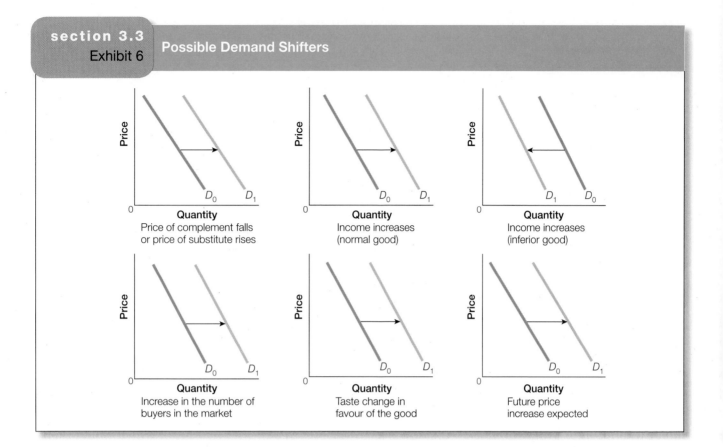

section 3.3
Exhibit 6   **Possible Demand Shifters**

other factors (determinants) influencing consumer behaviour changes, we say there is a *change in demand.* In Exhibit 5, the change from A to C is called an *increase in demand,* and the change from C to A is called a *decrease in demand.* The phrase "increase in demand" or "decrease in demand" is reserved for a shift in the whole curve. So if an individual buys more CDs because the price fell, we say there was an increase in quantity demanded. However, if she buys more CDs even at the current price, say $10, we say there is an increase in demand. The effects of some of the other determinants that cause a change in demand (shifters) are reviewed in Exhibit 6.

SECTION CHECK

■ A change in the quantity demanded describes a movement along a given demand curve in response to a change in the price of the good. A change in demand shifts the entire demand curve in response to a change in some determinant of demand.

■ Some possible determinants of demand (demand shifters) are the prices or related goods, income, number of buyers, tastes, and expectations.

■ The price of a substitute is positively related to the demand curve for the good in question; the price of a complement is inversely related to the demand curve for the good in question; for normal goods, income is positively related to the demand curve for the good in question; for inferior goods, income is inversely related to the demand curve for the good in question; the demand curve will vary according to the number of consumers in the market; taste changes will shift the demand curve; and changes in expected future prices and income can shift the current demand curve.

Supply

- What is the law of supply?
- What is an individual supply curve?
- What is a market supply curve?

WHAT IS THE LAW OF SUPPLY?

In a market, the answer to the fundamental question "What do we produce, and in what quantities?" depends on the interaction of both buyers and sellers. Demand is only half the story. The willingness and ability of suppliers to provide goods are equally important factors that must be weighed by decision makers in all societies. As in the case of demand, factors other than the price of the good are also important to suppliers, such as the cost of inputs or advances in technology. As with demand, the price of the good is an important factor. Although behaviour will vary among individual suppliers, economists expect, other things being equal, that the quantity supplied will vary directly with the price of the good, a relationship called the **law of supply.** According to the law of supply, the higher the price of the good (P), the greater the quantity supplied (Q_S), and the lower the price of the good, the smaller the quantity supplied.

$$P\uparrow \Rightarrow Q_S \uparrow \text{ or } P\downarrow \Rightarrow Q_S \downarrow$$

The relationship described by the law of supply is a direct, or positive, relationship, because the variables move in the same direction.

In order to get more oil, drillers must sometimes drill deeper or go into unexplored areas, and they still may come up with a dry hole. If it costs more to increase oil production, then oil prices would have to rise in order for producers to increase their output.

law of supply
the higher (lower) the price of the good, the greater (smaller) the quantity supplied

A Positive Relationship between Price and Quantity Supplied

Firms supplying goods and services want to increase their profits, and the higher the price per unit, the greater the profitability generated by supplying more of that good. For example, if you were an apple grower, wouldn't you much rather be paid $5 a kilogram than $1 a kilogram, *ceteris paribus*.

WHAT IS AN INDIVIDUAL SUPPLY CURVE?

individual supply curve
a graphical representation that shows the positive relationship between the price and the quantity supplied

To illustrate the concept of an individual supply curve, consider the amount of apples that an individual supplier, John Macintosh, is willing and able to supply in one year. The law of supply can be illustrated, like the law of demand, by a table or graph. John's supply schedule for apples is shown in Exhibit 1(a). The price–quantity supplied combinations were then plotted and joined to create the individual supply curve shown in Exhibit 1(b). The resulting **individual supply curve** is a graphical representation that shows the positive relationship between the price and the quantity supplied. Note that the individual supply curve is upward sloping as you move from left to right. At higher prices, it will be more attractive to increase production. Existing firms, or growers, will produce more at higher prices than at lower prices.

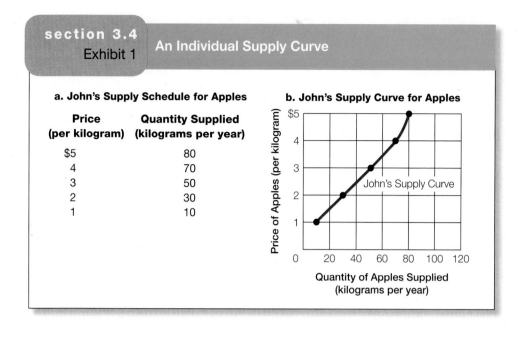

section 3.4
Exhibit 1 An Individual Supply Curve

a. John's Supply Schedule for Apples

Price (per kilogram)	Quantity Supplied (kilograms per year)
$5	80
4	70
3	50
2	30
1	10

b. John's Supply Curve for Apples

WHAT IS A MARKET SUPPLY CURVE?

The **market supply curve** may be thought of as the horizontal summation of individual supply curves. The market supply schedule, which reflects the total quantity supplied at each price by all of the apple producers, is shown in Exhibit 2(a). Exhibit 2(b) illustrates the resulting market supply curve for this group of apple producers.

market supply curve
the horizontal summation of individual supply curves

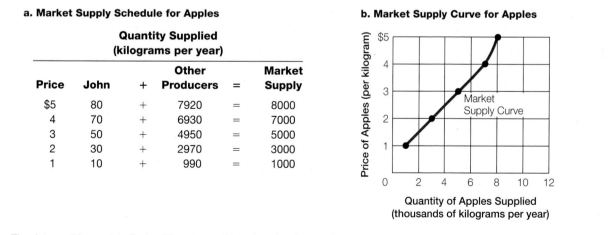

section 3.4
Exhibit 2 A Market Supply Curve

a. Market Supply Schedule for Apples

			Quantity Supplied (kilograms per year)		
Price	John	+	Other Producers	=	Market Supply
$5	80	+	7920	=	8000
4	70	+	6930	=	7000
3	50	+	4950	=	5000
2	30	+	2970	=	3000
1	10	+	990	=	1000

b. Market Supply Curve for Apples

The dots on this graph indicate different quantities of apples that producers would be willing and able to supply at various prices. The line connecting those combinations is the market supply curve.

SECTION CHECK

- The law of supply states that the higher (lower) the price of the good, the greater (smaller) the quantity supplied.
- The individual supply schedule and curve show the positive relationship between the price and quantity supplied of a given good or service.
- The market supply curve is a graphical representation of the amount of goods and services that suppliers are willing and able to supply at various prices. The law of demand states that when the price of a good falls (rises), the quantity demanded rises (falls), *ceteris paribus*.

section 3.5

Shifts in the Supply Curve

- What is the difference between a change in supply and a change in quantity supplied?
- What are the determinants of supply?
- Can we review the distinction between a change in supply and a change in quantity supplied?

WHAT IS THE DIFFERENCE BETWEEN A CHANGE IN SUPPLY AND A CHANGE IN QUANTITY SUPPLIED?

Changes in the price of a good lead to changes in quantity supplied by suppliers, just as changes in the price of a good lead to changes in quantity demanded by buyers. Similarly, a change in supply, whether an increase or a decrease, will occur for reasons other than changes in the price of the product itself, just as changes in demand are due to factors (determinants) other than the price of the good. In other words, a change in the price of the good in question is shown as a movement along a given supply curve, leading to a change in quantity supplied. A change in any other factor that can affect supplier behaviour (input prices, the prices of related products, expectations, number of suppliers, technology, regulation, taxes and subsidies, and weather) results in *a shift in the entire supply curve,* leading to a change in supply.

WHAT ARE THE DETERMINANTS OF SUPPLY?

An increase in supply shifts the supply curve to the right; a decrease in supply shifts the supply curve to the left, as seen in Exhibit 1. We will now look at some of the possible determinants of supply—factors that determine the position of the supply curve—in greater depth.

Input Prices

Suppliers are strongly influenced by the costs of inputs used in the production process, such as steel used for automobiles or microchips used in computers. For

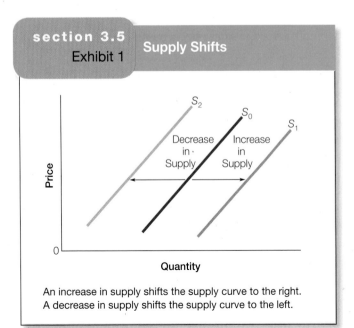

| section 3.5 Exhibit 1 | Supply Shifts |

An increase in supply shifts the supply curve to the right.
A decrease in supply shifts the supply curve to the left.

example, higher labour, materials, energy, or other input costs increase the costs of production, causing the supply curve to shift to the left at each and every price. If input prices fall, this will lower the costs of production, causing the supply curve to shift to the right—more will be supplied at each and every price.

The Prices of Related Products

Suppose you own your own farm, on which you plant wheat and corn. Then, the price of corn falls and farmers reduce the quantity supplied of corn, as seen in Exhibit 2(a). What effect would the lower price of corn have on your wheat production? Easy—it would increase the supply of wheat. You would want to produce relatively less of the crop that had fallen in price (corn) and relatively more of the now more attractive other crop (wheat). Wheat and corn are *substitutes in production* because both goods can be produced using the same resources. This example demonstrates why the price of related products is important as a supply shifter as well as a demand shifter. Producers tend to substitute the production of more profitable products for that of less profitable products. This is desirable from society's perspective as well because more profitable products tend to be those considered more valuable by society, whereas less profitable products are usually considered less valuable. Hence, the lower price in the corn market has caused an increase in supply (a rightward shift) in the wheat market, as seen in Exhibit 2(b).

If the price of corn, a substitute in production, increases, then that crop becomes more profitable. This leads to an increase in the quantity supplied of corn. Consequently, farmers will shift their resources out of the relatively lower-priced crop (wheat); the result is a decrease in supply of wheat.

Other examples of substitutes in production include automobile producers that have to decide between producing sedans or pickup trucks or construction companies that have to choose between single residential houses or commercial buildings.

Some goods are *complements in production*. Producing one good does not prevent the production of the other, but actually enables production of the other. For example, leather and beef are complements in production. Suppose the price of beef rises and as a result, cattle ranchers increase the quantity supplied of beef, moving up the supply curve for beef, as seen in Exhibit 3(a). When cattle ranchers produce more beef, they automatically produce more leather. Thus, when the price of beef increases, the supply of the related good, leather, shifts to the right, as seen in Exhibit 3(b). Suppose the price of beef falls, and as a result, the quantity supplied of beef falls; this leads to a decrease (a leftward shift) in the supply of leather.

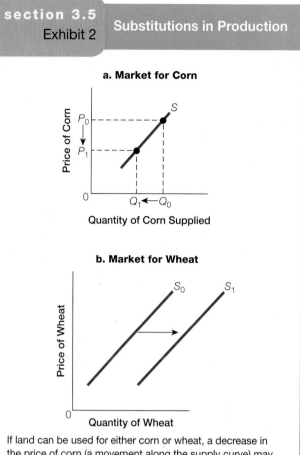

section 3.5 Exhibit 2   Substitutions in Production

a. Market for Corn

b. Market for Wheat

If land can be used for either corn or wheat, a decrease in the price of corn (a movement along the supply curve) may cause some farmers to shift out of the production of corn and into wheat—shifting the wheat supply curve to the right.

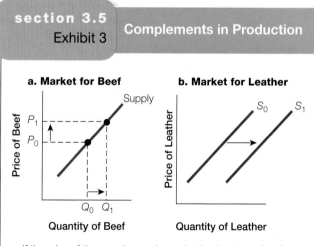

section 3.5 Exhibit 3   Complements in Production

a. Market for Beef

b. Market for Leather

If the price of the complement in production increases (beef), it becomes more profitable and as a result, cattle ranchers increase the quantity supplied of beef, moving up the supply curve for beef, as seen in Exhibit 3(a). When cattle ranchers produce more beef, they also produce more leather. Thus, when the price of beef increases, the supply of the related good, leather, shifts to the right, as seen in Exhibit 3(b).

Business CONNECTION

A DANCE OF DEMAND AND SUPPLY

Much of economics is involved with demand and supply. Economists often speak of an increase in demand or an increase in supply. The shifting back and forth of demand and supply could be considered to be a type of dance between demand and supply.

Successful business operators usually have a practical sense of how demand changes for the specific goods or services they provide. For instance, they understand that an increase in the demand for new condominiums will generally lead to an increase in the demand for new appliances. A significant increase in workers' incomes often supports an increase in the purchase of new clothes. Breaking news that consumption of a particular food or drink might cause undesirable side effects and usually results in a swift decrease in demand for that product. Finally, expectations of an economic recession often lead to fewer trips to the shopping mall. While none of the above developments are particularly surprising, successful businesspeople are more likely to be aware of the speed with which demand is likely to change and the impact that such changes in demand might have on their businesses.

Demand is swift, agile, and responsive to the music of the economy. Those who are able and willing to buy will often react very quickly to changes or expected changes in their personal situation or to changes in the economy.

What about supply? With other factors constant, if the cost of inputs increase (e.g., the ingredients or components for making a product), suppliers might be unwilling or unable to continue to supply that good or service. In fact, faced with increasing costs, many suppliers often choose to close their businesses and leave the industry or switch to another industry, resulting in a decrease in supply. On the other hand, more suppliers entering an industry increase market supply. Also, improvements in technology as well as government deregulation of an industry often leads to increases in supply.

As a dancer, supply is slower to react to changes in demand. Why is this so? To increase supply, firms often need to hire new employees, build new facilities, and install new equipment, and/or develop new processes. These steps can take considerable time to plan and execute. It is only after they are completed that supply increases. In the opposite direction, once a firm decides to reduce supply, it often must provide employees with termination notices, cancel orders for new materials, and give up leases for lands and buildings. These steps also consume much time.

Successful businesspeople understand what determines demand and what determines supply. As well, they understand the swiftness with which demand often increases or decreases and the reality that changes in supply is a slow and difficult process. Yes, as demand and supply dance to the music of the economy, one can expect demand to quickly lead and supply to slowly follow.

Other examples of complements in production where goods are produced simultaneously from the same resource include a lumber mill that produces lumber and sawdust and an oil refinery that can produce gasoline or heating oil from the same resource—crude oil.

Expectations

Another factor shifting supply is suppliers' expectations. If producers expect a higher price in the future, they will supply less now than they otherwise would have, preferring to wait and sell when their goods will be more valuable. For example, if an oil producer expected the future price of oil to be higher next year, he might decide to store some of his current production of oil for next year when the price would be higher. Similarly, if producers expect now that the price will be lower later, they will supply more now.

Number of Suppliers

We are normally interested in market demands and supplies (because together they determine prices and quantities) rather than in the behaviour of individual consumers and firms. As we discussed earlier, the supply curves of individual suppliers can be summed horizontally to create a market supply curve. An increase in the number of suppliers leads to an increase in supply, denoted by a rightward shift in the supply curve. For example, think of the number of smartphones that have entered the market over the last ten years, shifting the supply curve of smartphones to the right. An exodus of suppliers has the opposite impact, a decrease in supply, which is indicated by a leftward shift in the supply curve.

Technology

Most of us think of prices as constantly rising, given the existence of inflation, but, in fact, decreases in costs often occur because of technological progress, and such advances can lower prices. Human creativity works to find new ways to produce goods and services using fewer or less costly inputs of labour, natural resources, or capital. In recent years, despite generally rising prices, the prices of electronic equipment such as computers, cellphones, and DVD players have fallen dramatically. At any given price this year, suppliers are willing to provide many more (of a given quality of) computers than in previous years simply because technology has dramatically reduced the cost of providing them. Graphically, the increase in supply is indicated by a shift to the right in the supply curve.

Regulation

Supply may also change because of changes in the legal and regulatory environment in which firms operate. Government regulations can influence the costs of production to the firm, leading to cost-induced supply changes similar to those just discussed. For example, if new safety or anti-pollution requirements increase labour and capital costs, the increased cost will result, other things equal, in a decrease in supply, shifting the supply curve to the left, or up. An increase in a government-imposed minimum wage may have a similar effect by raising labour costs and decreasing supply in markets that employ many low-wage workers. However, deregulation—the process by which governments reduce or outright eliminate restrictions on individuals or businesses—can shift the supply curve to the right.

Taxes and Subsidies

Certain types of taxes can also increase the costs of production borne by the supplier, causing the supply curve to shift to the left at each price. The opposite of a tax (a subsidy) can lower the firm's costs and shift the supply curve to the right. For example, the government sometimes provides farmers with subsidies to encourage the production of certain agricultural products.

DEBATE

IS IT ETHICAL TO GROW CORN FOR FUEL?

Why do you think the price of gas has risen at the pumps? Is it because of an increase in consumption (more people are driving) or is it due to an increasing scarcity of crude oil? Over the past decade, we have seen the market adjust to the rise in gas prices by blending ethanol into gasoline. This has been a boon for farmers, who now benefit from a new, more lucrative market for their corn. When there are greater revenues to be had for growing corn instead of wheat or soybeans, farmers will adjust their crop plans in favour of corn. However, is this an ethical decision?

Pro:
Farmers are free to choose which markets to participate in, and most will choose to grow the crop that provides the greatest return on their investment. Presently, corn is a very lucrative crop. Corn prices have increased due to the introduction of the secondary market of ethanol, but also because as more hectares are devoted to corn, fewer are used for wheat and soybean crops; this will increase the prices of wheat and soybeans, which benefits the farmers who grow those crops. This is the market in action—there's nothing unethical about it. Are you able to defend the farmers' decisions?

Con:
Growing crops for fuel instead of for food will ultimately mean higher world prices for food, which will hurt the poorest the most. This is unethical, as it's the market that's promoting famine rather than famine brought on by nature. Those who believe that the market should consider ethical issues, not just prices would likely support a less-efficient market. What do you believe: Should we promote growing corn for our transportation needs? Is there a conflict between the wider society's needs and the farmer as an individual?

Weather

In addition, weather can certainly affect the supply of certain commodities, particularly agricultural products and transportation services. A drought or freezing temperatures will almost certainly cause the supply curves for many crops to shift to the left, whereas exceptionally good weather can shift a supply curve to the right. For example, record rains in the Prairies during the summer of 2010 prevented some 4.2 million hectares from being used, as they were too wet to plant.

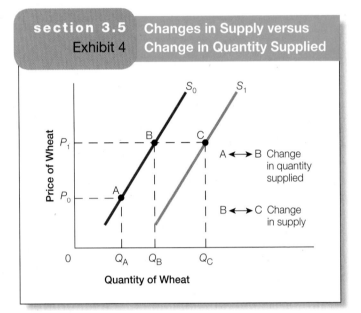

section 3.5
Exhibit 4
Changes in Supply versus Change in Quantity Supplied

CAN WE REVIEW THE DISTINCTION BETWEEN A CHANGE IN SUPPLY AND A CHANGE IN QUANTITY SUPPLIED?

If the price of a good changes, we say this leads to a *change in the quantity supplied.* For example, in Exhibit 4, if the price of wheat rises from P_0 to P_1, the market for wheat experiences a movement from A to B. If one of the other factors influences sellers' behaviour, we say this leads to a *change in supply.* For example, if production costs fall because of a wage decrease or lower fuel costs, other things remaining constant, we would expect an increase in supply—that is, a rightward shift in the supply curve as illustrated by the change from B to C in Exhibit 4. Alternatively, if some variable, like lower input prices, causes the costs of production to fall, the supply curve will shift to the right. Exhibit 5 illustrates the effect of some of the determinants that cause shifts in the supply curve.

section 3.5
Exhibit 5
Possible Supply Shifts

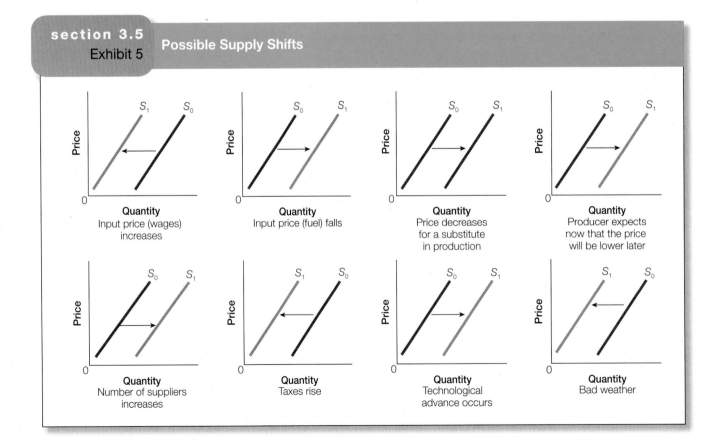

SECTION CHECK

- A movement along a given supply curve is caused by a change in the price of the good in question. As we move along the supply curve, we say there is a change in the quantity supplied. A shift of the entire supply curve is called a *change in supply.*
- Input prices, the prices of related products, expectations, the number of suppliers, technology, regulation, taxes and subsidies, and weather can all lead to changes in supply (shifts in supply).
- Input prices are inversely related to the supply curve for the good in question; the price for a substitute in production is inversely related to the supply curve for the good in question; the price for a complement in production is positively related to the supply curve for the good in question; changes in expected future prices can shift the current supply curve; the supply curve will vary according to the number of suppliers in the market; taxes (subsidies) are inversely (positively) related to the supply curve for the good in question; changes in technology can shift the supply curve for the good in question; and weather will shift the supply curve.

For Your Review

Section 3.1

1. Evaluate the validity of the following statement: "Canadians spend millions of dollars every year shopping online, buying everything from investment products to children's toys. However, due to the virtual nature of these transactions (buyers and sellers do not actually meet in person), these exchanges do not occur in what economists would consider markets."

2. What role do buyers and sellers have in a market?

Section 3.2

3. Assume the following demand schedule information:

Ben		Boris		Bilal	
P	Q_D	P	Q_D	P	Q_D
$5	1	$5	2	$5	3
4	2	4	4	4	6
3	3	3	6	3	9
2	4	2	8	2	12
1	5	1	10	1	15

a. Complete the market demand schedule if Ben and Bilal are the only demanders and graph the market demand curve.

P	Q_D
$5	
4	
3	
2	
1	

b. Complete the market demand schedule if Boris joins Ben and Bilal in the market and graph the market demand curve.

P	Q_D
$5	
4	
3	
2	
1	

c. Complete the market demand schedule if Ben now leaves the market, and only Boris and Bilal remain and graph the market demand curve.

P	Q_D
$5	
4	
3	
2	
1	

4. Sid moves from downtown Toronto, where he lived in a small condominium, to rural Alberta, where he buys a big house on two hectares of land. Using the law of demand, what do you think is true of land prices in downtown Toronto relative to those in rural Alberta?

5. The following table shows Hillary's demand schedule for Cherry Blossom lotion. Graph Hillary's demand curve.

Price (dollars per mL)	Quantity Demanded (mL per week)
15	5
12	10
9	15
6	20
3	25

6. The following table shows Cherry Blossom lotion demand schedules for Hillary's friends, Marita and Jacquie. If Hillary, Marita, and Jacquie constitute the whole market for Cherry Blossom lotion, complete the market demand schedule and graph the market demand curve.

Price (dollars per mL)	Quantity Demanded (mL per week)			
	Hillary	Marita	Jacquie	Market
15	5	0	15	_____
12	10	5	20	_____
9	15	10	25	_____
6	20	15	30	_____
3	25	20	35	_____

Section 3.3

7. What would be the effects of each of the following on the demand for hamburger in Swift Current, Saskatchewan. In each case, identify the responsible determinant of demand.
   a. The price of chicken falls.
   b. The price of hamburger buns doubles.
   c. Scientists find that eating hamburger prolongs life.
   d. The population of Swift Current doubles.

8. What would be the effect of each of the following on the demand for Chevrolets in Canada? In each case, identify the responsible determinant of demand.
   a. The price of Fords plummets.
   b. Consumers believe that the price of Chevrolets will rise next year.
   c. The incomes of Canadians rise.
   d. The price of gasoline falls dramatically.

9. The following graph shows three market demand curves for cantaloupe. Starting at point A, which point represents
   a. an increase in quantity demanded?
   b. an increase in demand?
   c. a decrease in demand?
   d. a decrease in quantity demanded?

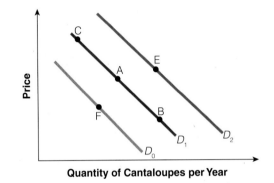

10. Using the demand curve, show the effect of the following events on the market for beef.
    a. Consumer income increases.
    b. The price of beef increases.
    c. An outbreak of mad cow disease occurs.
    d. The price of chicken (a substitute) increases.
    e. The price of barbecue grills (a complement) increases.

11. Draw the demand curves for the following goods. If the price of the first good listed rises, what will happen to the demand for the second good, and why?
    a. hamburger and ketchup
    b. Coca-Cola and Pepsi
    c. camera and film
    d. golf clubs and golf balls
    e. a skateboard and a razor scooter

12. If the price of ice cream increased,
    a. what would be the effect on the demand for ice cream?
    b. what would be the effect on the demand for frozen yogurt?

13. Using the graph on the next page, answer the following questions:
    a. What is the shift from D_0 to D_1 called?
    b. What is the movement from (B) to (A) called?
    c. What is the movement from (A) to (B) called?
    d. What is the shift from D_1 to D_0 called?

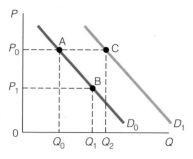

14. Show and describe what would happen to the market demand curve for a good in each of the following cases:

    a. an increase in the price of a substitute and a decrease in the price of a complement

    b. a decrease in the price of a substitute and an increase in the price of a complement

    c. an increase in the number of buyers and an increase in income, for a normal good

    d. a decrease in the number of buyers and an increase in income, for an inferior good

    e. a decrease in expected future prices and a shift in tastes away from the good

Section 3.4

15. Felix is a wheat farmer who has two fields he can use to grow wheat. The first field is right next to his house and the topsoil is rich and thick. The second field is 16 kilometres away in the mountains and the soil is rocky. At current wheat prices, Felix produces only from the field next to his house because the market price for wheat is just high enough to cover his costs of production, including a reasonable profit. What would have to happen to the market price of wheat for Felix to have the incentive to produce from the second field?

16. The following table shows the supply schedule for Rolling Rock Oil Co. Plot Rolling Rock's supply curve on a graph.

Price (dollars per barrel)	Quantity Demanded (barrels per month)
5	10 000
10	15 000
15	20 000
20	25 000
25	30 000

17. The following table shows the supply schedules for Rolling Rock and two other petroleum companies, Armadillo Oil and Pecos Petroleum. Assuming these three companies make up the entire supply side of the oil market, complete the market supply schedule and draw the market supply curve on a graph.

Quantity Supplied (barrels per month)				
Price (dollars per barrel)	Rolling Rock	Armadillo	Pecos	Market
5	10 000	8 000	2 000	_____
10	15 000	10 000	5 000	_____
15	20 000	12 000	8 000	_____
20	25 000	14 000	11 000	_____
25	30 000	16 000	14 000	_____

18. Assume the following supply schedule information.

Sacha		Steve		Sean	
P	*Q*$_S$	*P*	*Q*$_S$	*P*	*Q*$_S$
$5	10	$5	15	$5	5
4	8	4	12	4	4
3	6	3	9	3	3
2	4	2	6	2	2
1	2	1	3	1	1

a. Complete the market supply schedule if Sacha and Steve are the only suppliers and graph the market supply curve.

P	*Q*$_S$
$5	
4	
3	
2	
1	

b. Complete the market supply schedule if Sean joins Sacha and Steve in the market and graph the market supply curve.

P	*Q*$_S$
$5	
4	
3	
2	
1	

c. Complete the market supply schedule if Sacha now leaves the market, and only Steve and Sean remain and graph the market supply curve.

P	Q_S
$5	
4	
3	
2	
1	

Section 3.5

19. Using the graph below, answer the following questions:
    a. What is the shift from S_0 to S_1 called?
    b. What is the movement from (A) to (B) called?
    c. What is the movement from (B) to (A) called?
    d. What is the shift from S_1 to S_0 called?

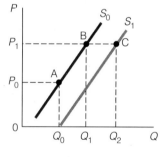

20. Show and describe what would happen to the market supply curve for a good in each of the following cases.
    a. an increase in the number of suppliers and an increase in subsidies
    b. a decrease in the number of suppliers and an increase in taxes
    c. an increase in input prices and increasing costs of regulation
    d. producers expect now that the price will be lower later

21. What would be the effect of each of the following on the supply of ketchup in Canada? In each case, identify the responsible determinant of supply.
    a. Tomato prices skyrocket (ketchup is made from tomatoes).
    b. Parliament places a 26 percent tax on ketchup.
    c. Entrepreneurs invent a new, faster tomato crusher to make ketchup.
    d. Wayne Gretzky, Justin Bieber, and Jim Carrey each introduce a new brand of ketchup.

22. What would be the effects of each of the following on the supply of coffee world-wide? In each case, identify the responsible determinant of supply.

    a. Freezing temperatures wipe out half of Brazil's coffee crop.

    b. The wages of coffee workers in Latin America rise as unionization efforts succeed.

    c. Indonesia offers big subsidies to its coffee producers.

    d. Genetic engineering produces a super coffee bean that grows faster and needs less care.

    e. Coffee suppliers expect prices to be higher in the future.

23. The following graph shows three market supply curves for cantaloupe. Compared to point A, which point represents

    a. an increase in quantity supplied?

    b. an increase in supply?

    c. a decrease in quantity supplied?

    d. a decrease in supply?

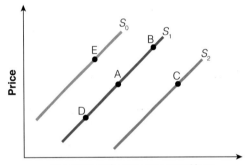

Quantity of Cantaloupes per Year

Sections 3.3 and 3.5

24. Show the impact of each of the following events on the oil market.

    [*Note:* The 12 countries that comprise the Organization of the Petroleum Exporting Countries (OPEC) exert considerable control of the world market for oil.]

    a. OPEC becomes more effective in limiting the supply of oil.

    b. OPEC becomes less effective in limiting the supply of oil.

    c. The price for natural gas (a substitute for heating oil) rises.

    d. New oil discoveries occur in Alberta.

    e. Electric and hybrid cars become subsidized and their prices fall.

CourseMate

Access an interactive eBook and chapter-specific interactive learning tools, including flashcards, quizzes, a glossary, and more in CourseMate, accessed through **www.sextonmacro3ce.nelson.com**

Bringing Supply and Demand Together

Market Equilibrium Price and Quantity

■ What is the equilibrium price and the equilibrium quantity?
■ What is a shortage and what is a surplus?

In the last chapter, we learned about demand and supply separately. We now bring the market supply and market demand together.

WHAT IS THE EQUILIBRIUM PRICE AND THE EQUILIBRIUM QUANTITY?

The **market equilibrium** is found at the point at which the market supply and the market demand curves intersect. It is at market equilibrium that two important values are determined: equilibrium price and equilibrium quantity. The **equilibrium price** is the price at the intersection of the market supply and demand curves. At this price, the quantity demanded equals the quantity supplied; that is, the amount that buyers are willing and able to buy is exactly equal to the amount that sellers are willing and able to produce. The **equilibrium quantity** is the quantity at the intersection of the market supply and demand curves. At this quantity, the quantity demanded equals the quantity supplied.

The equilibrium market solution is best understood with the help of a simple graph. Let's return to the apple example we used in our earlier discussions of supply and demand in Chapter 3. Exhibit 1 combines the market demand curve for apples with the market supply curve. At $3 per kilogram, buyers are willing to buy 5000 kilograms of apples and sellers are willing to supply 5000 kilograms of apples. Neither may be "happy" about the price, because the buyers would like a lower price and the sellers

market equilibrium
the point at which the market supply and the market demand curves intersect

equilibrium price
the price at the intersection of the market supply and demand curves; at this price, the quantity demanded equals the quantity supplied

equilibrium quantity
the quantity at the intersection of the market supply and demand curves; at this quantity, the quantity demanded equals the quantity supplied

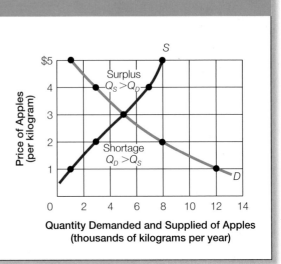

section 4.1
Exhibit 1
A Hypothetical Market Supply and Demand Schedule for Apples

Price	Quantity Supplied	Quantity Demanded	Difference	State of Market
$5	8000	1 000	7 000	Surplus
4	7000	3 000	4 000	Surplus
3	5000	5 000	0	Equilibrium
2	3000	8 000	−5 000	Shortage
1	1000	12 000	−11 000	Shortage

The equilibrium is $3 per kilogram and 5000 kilograms of apples, where quantity demanded and quantity supplied are equal. At higher prices, quantity supplied exceeds quantity demanded, resulting in a surplus. Below $3, quantity demanded exceeds quantity supplied, leading to a shortage.

would like a higher price. But both buyers and sellers are able to carry out their purchase and sales plans at that $3 price. However, at any other price, either suppliers or demanders would be unable to trade as much as they would like.

WHAT IS A SHORTAGE AND WHAT IS A SURPLUS?

surplus
where quantity supplied exceeds quantity demanded

shortage
where quantity demanded exceeds quantity supplied

What happens when the market price is not equal to the equilibrium price? As you can see in Exhibit 1, at $4 per kilogram, the quantity of apples demanded would be 3000 kilograms, but the quantity supplied would be 7000 kilograms. At that price, a **surplus** would exist, where quantity supplied exceeded quantity demanded. That is, at this price, growers would be willing to sell more apples than demanders would be willing to buy. To cut growing inventories, frustrated suppliers would cut their price and cut back on production. And as price falls, consumers buy more, ultimately eliminating the unsold surplus and returning the market to the equilibrium.

What would happen if the price of apples was cut to $1 per kilogram? The yearly quantity demanded of 12 000 kilograms would be greater than the 1000 kilograms that producers would be willing to supply at that low price. So, at $1 per kilogram, a **shortage** would exist, where quantity demanded exceeded quantity supplied. Because of the apple shortage, frustrated buyers would be forced to compete for the existing supply, bidding up the price. The rising price would have two effects: (1) Producers would be willing to increase the quantity supplied; and (2) the higher price would decrease the quantity demanded. Together, these two effects would ultimately eliminate the shortage, returning the market to the equilibrium.

LEARNING THE FIRST LESSON OF SUPPLY *and* DEMAND...

DEBATE

SHOULD A PRODUCT TRADE AT ANY PRICE?

In exploring demand and supply, we find that goods trade at levels where both the consumer and supplier are mutually satisfied, which is an agreed upon price. But not all markets trade at the most efficient levels, and in fact there are markets where people trade that are inefficient or illegal. Take for instance contraband such as drugs or weapons—or even human organs. Some might argue that people should be able to purchase whatever they want without government interference or influence, thereby maximizing personal satisfaction. So the question to debate is "Should all products be made available at any price?"

Pro:

Everything has its price—this would be the pathos used by the pro side. It suggests that trading a product at a price that at least one buyer is willing to pay will maximize both the consumer's and producer's satisfaction, and will ensure that the market trades at the most efficient level. What are other products or reasons you can use to support this position?

Con:

While everything may have its price, there are other considerations to take into account in markets. For instance, is it desirable to trade in human organs? True, there are people who need organs and people who are willing to sell them, but for a product like this, society's best interest is considered and we make the trading of human organs illegal. In this case, the market does not trade at the most efficient level, and we appear comfortable with that inefficiency. What is the basis for this argument? What other arguments could you introduce to support this position?

SECTION CHECK

- The intersection of the supply and demand curve shows the equilibrium price and equilibrium quantity in a market.
- A surplus is where quantity supplied exceeds quantity demanded. A shortage is where quantity demanded exceeds quantity supplied.

Changes in Equilibrium Price and Quantity

- What happens to equilibrium price and equilibrium quantity when the demand curve shifts?
- What happens to equilibrium price and equilibrium quantity when the supply curve shifts?
- What happens when both supply and demand shift in the same time period?

When one of the many determinants of demand or supply changes, the demand and supply curves will shift, leading to changes in the equilibrium price and equilibrium

The Canadian Press(Jacques Boissinot)

quantity. When analyzing a change in demand or supply, it is important to answer three key questions to help ensure that the analysis is complete:

1. Which side of the market is being affected by the event in question, demand or supply?
2. Is the event in question a "shift" or a "movement"?
3. Is the event in question having an expansionary or contractionary impact on the market?

We first consider a change in demand.

WHAT HAPPENS TO EQUILIBRIUM PRICE AND EQUILIBRIUM QUANTITY WHEN THE DEMAND CURVE SHIFTS?

A shift in the demand curve—caused by a change in the price of a related good (a substitute or a complement), income, the number of buyers, tastes, or expectations—results in a change in both equilibrium price and equilibrium quantity. But how and why does this happen? This result can be most clearly explained through the use of an example. What happens in the gasoline market during the summer months when people typically do more travelling?

1. This event has a demand side effect, since we are looking at the impact of consumer behaviour.
2. The event is a shift, since it does not directly involve a change in the price of gasoline.
3. The event is expansionary, since we are looking at how consumers buy more gasoline in the summer months than in the winter months.

Therefore, the demand for gasoline increases during the summer. The greater demand for gasoline during the summer sends prices upward, *ceteris paribus.* As shown in Exhibit 1, the rightward shift of the demand curve results in an increase in both equilibrium price and quantity.

Let's look at a second example, at ski resorts like British Columbia's Whistler, hotel room prices are lower in October (off-season, when there are fewer skiers) than in January and February (in-season, when there are more skiers). Why is this the case?

1. This event has a demand side effect, as it is unlikely that supply is significantly altered between October and January.
2. The event is a shift, since price is being described as the effect and not the cause.
3. The event is contractionary, since we are looking at how *fewer* skiers affect hotel room prices in October than more skiers do in January and February.

Therefore, the demand for Whistler hotel rooms decreases during the off-season in October. The decrease in demand for hotel rooms sends prices downward, *ceteris paribus.* As shown in Exhibit 2, the leftward shift of the demand curve results in a decrease in both equilibrium price and quantity.

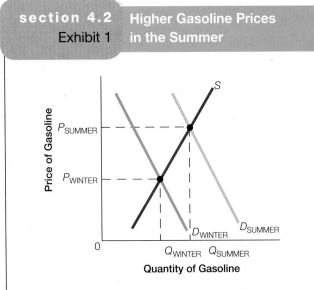

section 4.2
Exhibit 1
Higher Gasoline Prices in the Summer

The demand for gasoline is generally higher in the summer than in the winter. The increase in demand during the summer, coupled with a fixed supply, means a higher price and a greater quantity.

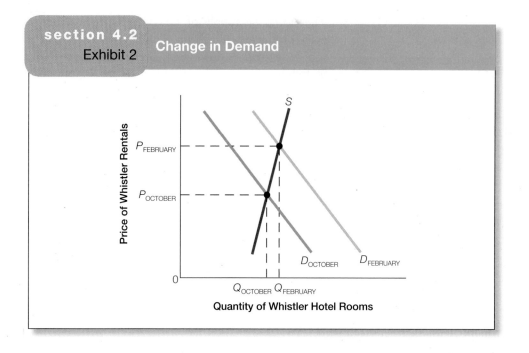

section 4.2
Exhibit 2

Change in Demand

WHAT HAPPENS TO EQUILIBRIUM PRICE AND EQUILIBRIUM QUANTITY WHEN THE SUPPLY CURVE SHIFTS?

Like a shift in demand, a shift in the supply curve also influences both equilibrium price and equilibrium quantity, assuming that demand for the product has not changed. Let's look at another example: Why are strawberries less expensive in summer than in winter (assuming that consumers' tastes and preferences are fairly constant throughout the year)?

1. This event has a supply side effect, since the behaviour of consumers is assumed to be constant.
2. The event is a shift, since it does not directly involve a change in the price of strawberries.
3. The event is expansionary, since producers can make more fresh strawberries available in the summer, when they are in season, than in the winter.

Therefore, as shown in Exhibit 3, this increase in supply shifts the supply curve to the right, resulting in a lower equilibrium price (from P_{WINTER} to P_{SUMMER}) and a greater equilibrium quantity (from Q_{WINTER} to Q_{SUMMER}).

Let's look at a second example of equilibrium price and quantity being impacted by the supply side. When high-definition (HD) televisions were first produced, they were typically very expensive, costing thousands of dollars. However, as the technology became more mainstream, the price of HD televisions fell. Why was this the case?

1. This event has a supply side effect, since we are looking at the production of products.
2. The event is a shift, since price is being described as the effect and not the cause.
3. The event is expansionary, since we are looking at what happens when a product becomes mainstream and more producers begin to make it.

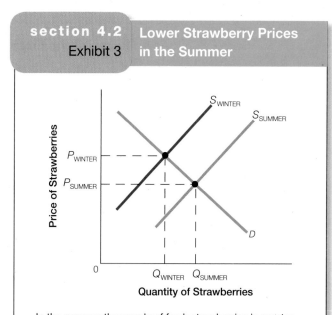

section 4.2
Exhibit 3

Lower Strawberry Prices in the Summer

In the summer the supply of fresh strawberries is greater and this leads to a lower equilibrium price and a greater equilibrium quantity, *ceteris paribus*. In the winter, the supply of fresh strawberries is lower and this leads to a higher equilibrium price and a lower equilibrium quantity, *ceteris paribus*.

section 4.2
Exhibit 4   A Change in Supply

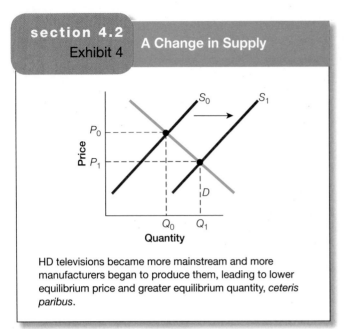

HD televisions became more mainstream and more manufacturers began to produce them, leading to lower equilibrium price and greater equilibrium quantity, *ceteris paribus*.

Therefore, the supply of HD televisions increased as more producers entered the market and the increase in supply sent prices downward, *ceteris paribus*. As shown in Exhibit 4, the rightward shift of the supply curve results in a decrease in equilibrium price and an increase in equilibrium quantity.

WHAT HAPPENS WHEN BOTH SUPPLY AND DEMAND SHIFT IN THE SAME TIME PERIOD?

We have discussed that as part of the continual adjustment process that occurs in the marketplace, supply and demand can each shift in response to many different factors, with the market then adjusting toward the new equilibrium. We have, so far, considered what happens when just one such change occurs at a time. In these cases, we learned that the results of these adjustments in supply and demand on the equilibrium price and quantity are predictable. However, both supply and demand very often will shift in the same time period. Can we predict what will happen to equilibrium prices and equilibrium quantities in these situations?

As you will see, when supply and demand move at the same time, we can predict the change in one variable (price or quantity), but we are unable to predict the direction of the effect on the other variable with any certainty. This change in the second variable, then, is said to be indeterminate because it cannot be determined without additional information about the size of the relative shifts in supply and demand. This concept will become clearer to you as we work through the following example.

An Increase in Supply and a Decrease in Demand

When considering this scenario, it might help you to break it down into its individual parts. As you learned in the last section, an increase in supply (a rightward shift in the supply curve) results in a decrease in the equilibrium price and an increase in the equilibrium quantity. A decrease in demand (a leftward movement of the demand curve), on the other hand, results in a decrease in both the equilibrium price and the equilibrium quantity. These shifts are shown in Exhibit 5(a). Taken together, then, these changes will clearly result in a decrease in the equilibrium price because both the increase in supply and the decrease in demand work to push this price down. This drop in equilibrium price (from P_0 to P_1) is shown in the movement from E_0 to E_1.

The effect of these changes on equilibrium price is clear, but how does the equilibrium quantity change? The impact on equilibrium quantity is indeterminate because the increase in supply increases the equilibrium quantity and the decrease in demand decreases it. In this scenario, the change in the equilibrium quantity will vary depending on the relative changes in supply and demand. If, as shown in Exhibit 5(a), the decrease in demand is greater than the increase in supply, the equilibrium quantity will decrease. If, however, as shown in Exhibit 5(b), the increase in supply is greater than the decrease in demand, the equilibrium quantity will increase.

a. A Little Increase in Supply and a Big Decrease in Demand

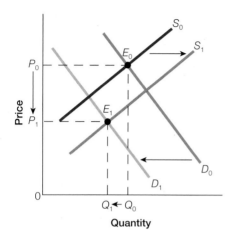

b. A Big Increase in Supply and a Little Decrease in Demand

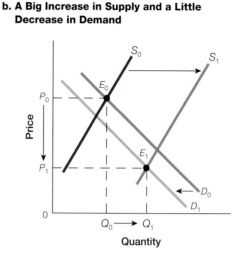

If the decrease in demand (leftward shift) is greater than the increase in supply (rightward shift), the equilibrium price and equilibrium quantity will fall.

If the increase in supply (rightward shift) is greater than the decrease in demand (leftward shift), the equilibrium price will fall and the equilibrium quantity will rise.

Business CONNECTION

WHAT DETERMINES THE PRICE?

Most businesspeople when asked to explain why product prices are at a certain level quickly reply that present price levels are simply a reflection of demand and supply. Strictly speaking, they are correct. The prevailing price of a product in a competitive market is the equilibrium price at the intersection of the market supply and demand curves.

Beyond knowing and understanding the equilibrium price and the equilibrium quantity of products in their industry, businesspeople often attempt to understand what will happen to prices in the future. Will prices drift up or down? Will the quantity demanded drift up or down? These are important questions if one is to prepare a good estimate for future revenues—an essential element in forecasting profitability. Recall that Revenues = Price × Quantity.

First, starting with price: From a microeconomic perspective, what is likely to cause an increase in prices? Generally, increases in market demand for a product, all other factors constant, lead to increases in the equilibrium price, while decreases in market demand lead to decreases in equilibrium price. On the other hand, increases in market supply result in lower equilibrium prices, while decreases in market supply serve to drive increases in equilibrium prices.

While most business operators have some sense of the direction in which demand or supply is changing at any point in time, attempts to determine the net impact on prices in an industry due to simultaneous changes in both market demand and market supply can be extremely difficult and complex. Many questions arise. Will an expanding economy increase market demand for products, leading to higher equilibrium prices? Will higher product prices attract new suppliers to the industry? Will the resulting increase in market supply more than offset the initial increase in demand, ultimately resulting in lower prices?

What about costs? Will new suppliers entering the product market create a shortage of skilled workers in that industry's labour market, leading to higher wages and salaries? Will those companies providing machinery and equipment to the new suppliers also raise their prices? If this is the case, the cost of the inputs (i.e., factors of production) for all suppliers could increase significantly. How might this affect overall profitability for the individual firm, for the industry?

Seeking answers to these questions, companies often construct powerful econometric models to simulate different economic scenarios, often referred to as "what-if" scenarios. In these models, the likely shifts in both market demand and market supply are used to forecast new equilibrium prices, a company's future revenues and costs, and ultimately, its profits over time.

The Combinations of Supply and Demand Shifts

The eight possible changes in demand and/or supply are presented in Exhibit 6, along with the resulting changes in equilibrium quantity and equilibrium price. Although you could memorize the impact of the various possible changes in demand and supply, it would be more worthwhile to draw a graph, as shown in Exhibit 7, whenever a situation of changing demand

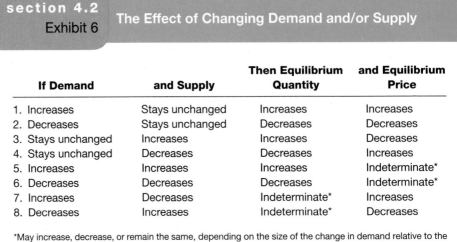

section 4.2
Exhibit 6

The Effect of Changing Demand and/or Supply

If Demand	and Supply	Then Equilibrium Quantity	and Equilibrium Price
1. Increases	Stays unchanged	Increases	Increases
2. Decreases	Stays unchanged	Decreases	Decreases
3. Stays unchanged	Increases	Increases	Decreases
4. Stays unchanged	Decreases	Decreases	Increases
5. Increases	Increases	Increases	Indeterminate*
6. Decreases	Decreases	Decreases	Indeterminate*
7. Increases	Decreases	Indeterminate*	Increases
8. Decreases	Increases	Indeterminate*	Decreases

*May increase, decrease, or remain the same, depending on the size of the change in demand relative to the change in supply.

section 4.2
Exhibit 7

The Combinations of Supply and Demand Shifts

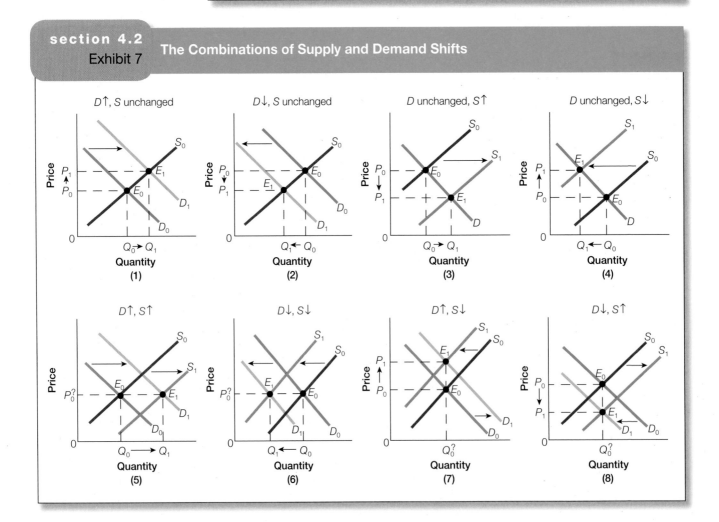

and/or supply arises. Remember that an increase in either demand or supply means a rightward shift in the curve, whereas a decrease in either demand or supply means a leftward shift. Also, when both demand and supply change, one of the two equilibrium values—price or quantity—will change in an indeterminate manner (can increase, decrease, or stay the same) depending on the relative magnitude of the changes in supply and demand.

SECTION CHECK

- Changes in demand will cause a change in the equilibrium price and quantity, *ceteris paribus*.
- Changes in supply will cause a change in the equilibrium price and quantity, *ceteris paribus*.
- When there are simultaneous shifts in both supply and demand curves, either the equilibrium price or the equilibrium quantity will be indeterminate without more information.

section
4.3

Price Controls

- What are price controls?
- What are price ceilings?
- What are price floors?

WHAT ARE PRICE CONTROLS?

Although nonequilibrium prices can occur naturally, reflecting uncertainty, they seldom last for long. Governments, however, may impose nonequilibrium prices for significant time periods. Price controls involve the use of the power of the government to establish prices different from the equilibrium prices that would otherwise prevail. The motivations for price controls vary with the market under consideration. For example, a **price ceiling**—a legally established maximum price—is often set for goods deemed important to low-income households, like housing. Or a **price floor**—a legally established minimum price—may be set on wages because wages are the primary source of income for most people.

Price controls are not always implemented by the federal government. Provincial governments can and do impose local price controls. One fairly well-known example is rent controls, which limit how much landlords can charge for rental housing.

price ceiling
a legally established maximum price

price floor
a legally established minimum price

WHAT ARE PRICE CEILINGS?

Rent controls have been imposed in some provinces. Although the rules may vary, generally the price (or rent) of an apartment remains fixed over the tenure of an occupant, except for allowable annual increases tied to the cost of living or some other price index. When an occupant moves out, the owners can usually, but not always, raise the rent to a near-market level for the next occupant. The controlled rents for existing occupants, however, are generally well below market rental rates.

Results of Rent Controls

Rent controls distort market signals and lead to shortages. In addition, they often do not even help the intended recipients—low-income households. Most people living in rent-controlled apartments have a good deal, one that they would lose by moving as their family circumstances or income changes. Tenants thus are reluctant to give up their governmentally granted right to a below-market-rent apartment. In addition, because the rents received by landlords are constrained and below market levels, the rate of return (roughly, the profit) on housing investments falls compared to that on other forms of real estate not subject to rent controls, like office rents or mortgage payments on condominiums. Hence, the incentive to construct new housing is reduced. Where rent controls are truly effective, there is generally little new construction going on, resulting in a shortage of apartments that persists and grows over time.

Also, when landlords are limited in what rent they can charge, there is little incentive to improve or upgrade apartments, such as by putting in new kitchen appliances or new carpeting, in order to get more rent. In fact, there is some incentive to avoid routine maintenance, thereby lowering the cost of apartment ownership to a figure approximating the controlled rental price, although the quality of the housing stock will deteriorate over time.

Another impact of rent control is that it promotes housing discrimination. Where rent controls do not exist, a prejudiced landlord might willingly rent to someone he believes is undesirable simply because the undesirable family is the only one willing to pay the requested rent (and the landlord is not willing to lower the rent substantially to get a desirable family, since this could translate into the loss of thousands of dollars in income). With rent controls, many families are likely to want to rent the controlled apartment, some desirable and some undesirable as seen by the landlord, simply because the rent is at a below-equilibrium price. The landlord can indulge in his "taste" for discrimination without any additional financial loss beyond that required by the controls.

Consequently, he will be more likely to choose to rent to a desirable family, perhaps a family without children or pets, rather than an undesirable one, perhaps one with a lower income and so a greater risk of nonpayment.

Exhibit 1 shows the impact of rent control. If the price ceiling is set below the market price, the quantity demanded will increase to Q_D from Q^* and the quantity supplied will fall to Q_S from Q^*. The rent control policy will therefore create a shortage, the difference between Q_D and Q_S.

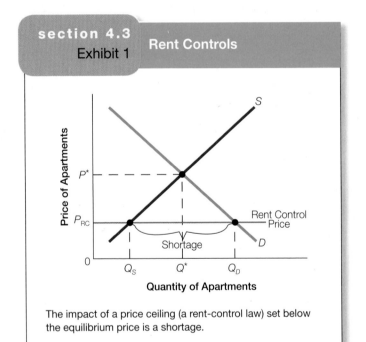

section 4.3
Exhibit 1   **Rent Controls**

The impact of a price ceiling (a rent-control law) set below the equilibrium price is a shortage.

WHAT ARE PRICE FLOORS?

The argument for a minimum wage is simple: Existing wages for workers in some types of labour markets do not allow for a very high standard of living, and a minimum wage allows those workers to live better than before. Provincial and territorial government legislation makes it illegal to pay most workers an amount below the current legislated minimum wage.

Let us examine graphically the impact of a minimum wage on low-skilled workers. In Exhibit 2, suppose the government sets the minimum wage, W_{MIN}, above the market equilibrium wage, W_E. In Exhibit 2, we see that the price floor is binding; that is, there is a surplus of low-skilled workers at W_{MIN} because the quantity of labour supplied is greater than the quantity of labour demanded. The reason for the surplus of low-skilled workers (unemployment) at W_{MIN} is that more people are willing to work than employers are willing and able to hire.

Notice that not everyone loses from a minimum wage. Those workers who continue to hold jobs now have higher incomes (those workers between 0 and Q_D in Exhibit 2). However, many low-skilled workers suffer from a minimum wage—they either lose their jobs or are unable to get them in the first place (those between Q_D and Q_S in Exhibit 2). Although studies disagree somewhat on the precise magnitudes, they largely agree that minimum-wage laws do create some unemployment, and that the unemployment is concentrated among teenagers—the least-experienced and least-skilled members of the labour force.

Most Canadian workers are not affected by the minimum wage because in the market for their skills, they earn wages that exceed the minimum wage. For example, a minimum wage will not affect the unemployment rate for accountants. In Exhibit 3, we see the labour market for skilled and experienced workers. In this market the minimum wage (the price floor) is not binding because these workers are earning wages that far exceed the minimum wage—W_E is much higher than W_{MIN}.

The above analysis does not "prove" minimum-wage laws are "bad" and should be abolished. To begin with, there is the empirical question of how much unemployment is caused by minimum wages. Secondly, some might believe that the cost of unemployment resulting from a minimum wage is a reasonable price to pay for assuring that those with jobs get a "decent" wage. The analysis does point out, however, that there is a cost to having a minimum wage, and the burden of the minimum wage falls not only on low-skilled workers and employers but also on consumers of products made more costly by the minimum wage.

© DOUG MENUEZ/PHOTODISC/GETTY ONE IMAGES

What do you think would happen to the number of low-skilled workers getting jobs if we raised the minimum wage to $20 an hour?

---

section 4.3
Exhibit 2

The Unemployment Effects of a Minimum Wage on Low-Skilled Workers

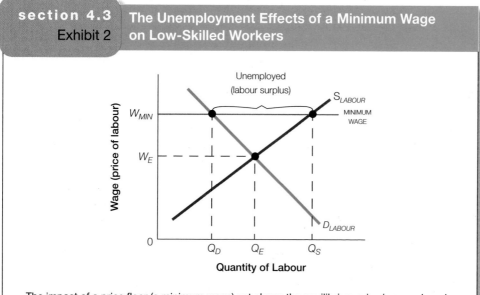

The impact of a price floor (a minimum wage) set above the equilibrium price is a surplus—in this case, a surplus of low-skilled workers.

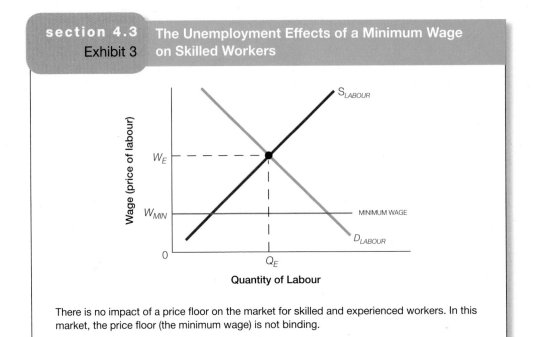

section 4.3   **The Unemployment Effects of a Minimum Wage**
Exhibit 3   **on Skilled Workers**

There is no impact of a price floor on the market for skilled and experienced workers. In this market, the price floor (the minimum wage) is not binding.

Unintended Consequences

unintended consequences

the secondary effects of an action that may occur after the initial effects

When markets are altered for policy reasons, it is wise to remember that actions do not always have the results that were initially intended—**unintended consequences** or secondary effects may occur after the initial effects of actions. As economists, we must always look for the secondary effects of an action that may occur along with the initial effects. For example, the government is often well intentioned when it adopts price controls to help low-skilled workers or tenants in search of affordable housing; however, such policies can also cause unintended consequences, which may completely undermine the intended effects. For example, rent controls may have an immediate effect of lowering rents, but secondary effects may well include very low vacancy rates, discrimination against low-income and large families, and deterioration of the quality of rental units. Similarly, a sizable increase in the minimum-wage rate may help many low-skilled workers or apprentices, but will result in higher unemployment and/or a reduction in fringe benefits, such as vacations and discounts to employees. Society has to make tough decisions, and if the government subsidizes some program or group of people in one area, then something must always be given up somewhere else. The "law of scarcity" cannot be repealed!

SECTION CHECK

- Price controls involve government mandates to keep prices above or below the market-determined equilibrium price.
- Price ceilings are government-imposed maximum prices. When price ceilings are set below the equilibrium price, shortages will result.
- Price floors are government-imposed minimum prices. When price floors are set above the equilibrium price, surpluses will result.

For Your Review

Section 4.1

1. If a price is above the equilibrium price, explain the forces that bring the market back to the equilibrium price and quantity. If a price is below the equilibrium price, explain the forces that bring the market back to the equilibrium price and quantity.

2. The following table shows the hypothetical monthly demand and supply schedules for bottles of maple syrup in Winnipeg.

Price	Quantity Demanded (bottles)	Quantity Supplied (bottles)
$6	700	100
7	600	200
8	500	300
9	400	400
10	300	500

   a. What is the equilibrium price of a bottle of maple syrup in Winnipeg?

   b. At a price of $7 per bottle, is there equilibrium, a surplus, or a shortage? If it is a surplus or shortage, how large is it?

   c. At a price of $10, is there equilibrium, a surplus, or a shortage? If it is a surplus or shortage, how large is it?

Sections 4.1 and 4.2

3. Assume the following information for the demand and supply schedules for Good Z.

Price per Unit	Quantity Demanded	Quantity Supplied
$10	10	55
9	20	50
8	30	45
7	40	40
6	50	35
5	60	30
4	70	25
3	80	20
2	90	15
1	100	10

    a. Draw the corresponding supply and demand curves.

    b. What is the equilibrium price per unit and quantity traded?

    c. If the price was $9, would there be a shortage or a surplus? How large?

    d. If the price was $3, would there be a shortage or a surplus? How large?

    e. If the demand for Z increased by 15 units at every price, what would the new equilibrium price and quantity traded be?

    f. Given the original demand for Z, if the supply of Z was increased by 15 units at every price, what would be the new equilibrium price and quantity traded?

4. The market for baseball tickets at your school's stadium, which seats 2000, is the following:

Price per Ticket	Quantity Demanded	Quantity Supplied
$2	4000	2000
4	2000	2000
6	1000	2000
8	500	2000

    a. What is the equilibrium price?

    b. What is unusual about the supply curve?

    c. At what prices would a shortage occur?

    d. At what prices would a surplus occur?

    e. Suppose that the addition of new students (all big baseball fans) next year will add 1000 to the quantity demanded at each price. What will this increase do to next year's demand curve? What will be the new equilibrium price?

Section 4.2

5. When asked about the reason for a lifeguard shortage that threatened to keep one-third of the city's beaches closed for the summer, the deputy parks commissioner of Vancouver, responded that "Kids seem to want to do work that's more in tune with a career. Maybe they prefer carpal tunnel syndrome to sunburn." What do you think is causing the shortage? What would you advise the deputy parks commissioner to do to alleviate the shortage?

6. Using supply and demand curves, show the effect of each of the following events on the market for wheat.

    a. A major wheat-producing area in Saskatchewan suffers a drought.

    b. The price of corn decreases (assume that many farmers can grow either corn or wheat).

    c. The Prairie provinces have great weather.

    d. The price of fertilizer declines.

    e. More individuals start growing wheat.

7. Beginning from an initial equilibrium, draw the effects of the following changes in terms of the relevant supply and demand curves.

    a. an increase in the price of hot dogs on the hamburger market

    b. a decrease in the number of taxi companies in Toronto on cab trips

    c. the effect of El Niño rainstorms destroying the strawberry crops in Ontario

8. Use supply and demand curves to show the following:

   a. simultaneous increases in supply and demand, with a large increase in supply and a small increase in demand

   b. simultaneous increases in supply and demand, with a small increase in supply and a large increase in demand

   c. simultaneous decreases in supply and demand, with a large decrease in supply and a small decrease in demand

   d. simultaneous decrease in supply and demand, with a small decrease in supply and a large decrease in demand

9. Why do 10 A.M. classes fill up before 8 A.M. classes during class registration? Use supply and demand curves to help explain your answers.

10. What would happen to the equilibrium price and equilibrium quantity in the following cases?

   a. an increase in income for a normal good and a decrease in the price of an input

   b. a technological advance and a decrease in the number of buyers

   c. an increase in the price of a substitute and an increase in the number of suppliers

   d. producers' expectations that prices will soon fall and a reduction in consumer tastes for the good

Section 4.3

11. Refer to the following supply and demand curve diagram.

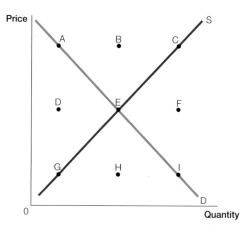

   a. Starting from an initial equilibrium at E, what shift or shifts in supply and/or demand could move the equilibrium price and quantity to each of points A through I?

   b. Starting from an initial equilibrium at E, what would happen if both a decrease in the price of a substitute in production and an increase in income occurred, if it is a normal good?

   c. Starting from an initial equilibrium at E, what would happen if both an increase in the price of an input and an advance in technology occurred?

   d. If a price floor is imposed above the equilibrium price, which of A through I would tend to be the quantity supplied, and which would tend to be the quantity demanded? Which would be the new quantity exchanged?

   e. If a price ceiling is imposed below the equilibrium price, which of A through I would tend to be the quantity supplied, and which would tend to be the quantity demanded? Which would be the new quantity exchanged?

12. Draw a supply and demand curve diagram with a price floor above the equilibrium price, and indicate the quantity supplied and quantity demanded at that price and the resulting surplus.

    a. What happens to the quantity supplied, the quantity demanded, and the surplus if the price floor is raised? If it is lowered?

    b. What happens to the quantity supplied, the quantity demanded, and the surplus if, for a given price floor, the demand curve shifts to the right?

    c. What happens to the quantity supplied, the quantity demanded, and the surplus if, for a given price floor, the supply curve shifts to the right?

13. Draw a supply and demand curve diagram with a price ceiling below the equilibrium price, and indicate the quantity supplied and quantity demanded at that price, and the resulting shortage.

    a. What happens to the quantity supplied, the quantity demanded, and the shortage if the price ceiling is raised? If it is lowered?

    b. What happens to the quantity supplied, the quantity demanded, and the shortage if, for a given price ceiling, the demand curve shifts to the right?

    c. What happens to the quantity supplied, the quantity demanded, and the shortage if, for a given price ceiling, the supply curve shifts to the right?

14. What would be the impact of a rental price ceiling set above the equilibrium rental price for apartments? Below the equilibrium rental price?

15. What would be the impact of a price floor set above the equilibrium price for dairy products? Below the equilibrium price?

16. Giving in to pressure from voters who claim that local theatre owners are gouging their customers with ticket prices as high as $10 per movie, the city council of a local municipality imposes a price ceiling of $2 on all movies. What effect is this likely to have on the market for movies in this particular city? What will happen to the quantity of tickets demanded? What will happen to the quantity supplied? Who gains? Who loses?

CourseMate

Access an interactive eBook and chapter-specific interactive learning tools, including flashcards, quizzes, a glossary, and more in CourseMate, accessed through **www.sextonmacro3ce.nelson.com**

Introduction to the Macroeconomy

section

5.1

Macroeconomic Goals

- What are the three major macroeconomic goals in Canada?
- Are these macroeconomic goals universal?

WHAT ARE THE THREE MAJOR MACROECONOMIC GOALS IN CANADA?

Recall from Chapter 1 that macroeconomics is the study of the whole economy—the study of the forest, not the trees. A macroeconomist may study the changes in the inflation rate or the unemployment rate, the impact of changing monetary policy or fiscal policy on output and inflation, or alternative policies that may contribute to long-term economic growth.

Nearly every society has been interested in three major macroeconomic goals: (1) maintaining employment of human resources at relatively high levels, meaning that jobs are relatively plentiful and financial suffering from lack of work and income is relatively uncommon; (2) maintaining prices at a relatively stable level so that consumers and producers can make better decisions; and (3) achieving a high rate of economic growth, meaning a growth in real output over time. The statistic **real gross domestic product (RGDP)** measures the total value of all final goods and services produced in a given time period, such as a year or a quarter, adjusted for inflation. The word *real* is used to indicate that the output is adjusted for general increases in prices over time. We use real gross domestic product to measure the level of output or production in the entire economy.

Exhibit 1 provides data on Canada's macroeconomic performance since 1991. Economic growth increased sharply after 1995, which helped to lower Canada's unemployment rate from relatively high levels in the early 1990s. For the 2006–2010 period, however, economic growth averaged only 1.2 percent per year. This lower rate of growth is one reason why the unemployment rate has not experienced further substantial declines. Over the 1991–2010 period, the inflation rate remained below 3 percent per year.

real gross domestic product (RGDP)
the total value of all final goods and services produced in a given time period such as a year or a quarter, adjusted for inflation

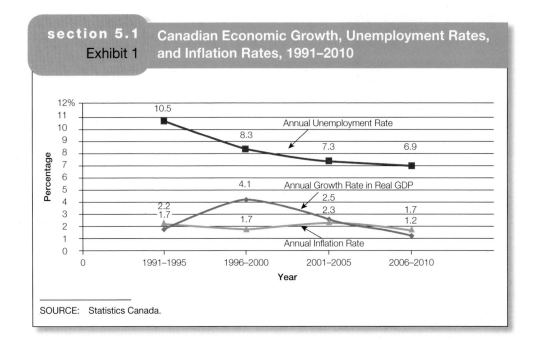

section 5.1
Exhibit 1   Canadian Economic Growth, Unemployment Rates, and Inflation Rates, 1991–2010

SOURCE: Statistics Canada.

ARE THESE MACROECONOMIC GOALS UNIVERSAL?

In addition to these primary goals, concern has been expressed at various times and places about other economic issues, some of which are essentially microeconomic in character. For example, concern about the "quality of life" has prompted some societies to try to reduce "bads" such as pollution and crime, and increase goods and services such as education and health services. Another goal has been "fairness" in the distribution of income or wealth. Still another goal pursued in many nations at one time or another has been self-sufficiency in the production of certain goods or services, such as food and energy.

The Impact of Value Judgments on Economic Goals

In stating that nations have economic goals, we must acknowledge that nations are made up of individuals. Individuals within a society may differ considerably in their evaluation of the relative importance of certain issues, or even whether certain "problems" are really problems after all. For example, economic growth, viewed positively by most persons, is not considered as favourably by others. Although some citizens may think that income distribution is just about right, others might think it provides insufficient incomes to the poorer members of society; still others think it involves taking too much income from the relatively well-to-do and thereby reduces incentives to carry out productive, income-producing activities.

SECTION CHECK

- The three major macroeconomic goals for Canada are full employment, price stability, and economic growth.
- People have their own reasons for valuing certain goals more than others. As a result, there is debate as to what is most important for an economy.

Employment and Unemployment

- What are the consequences of high unemployment?
- What is the unemployment rate?
- Are unemployment statistics accurate reflections of the labour market?
- What are the categories of unemployment?
- What is the labour force participation rate?

WHAT ARE THE CONSEQUENCES OF HIGH UNEMPLOYMENT?

Nearly everyone agrees that it is unfortunate when a person who wants a job cannot find one, and the loss of a job can mean financial insecurity and a great deal of anxiety. High rates of unemployment in a society can increase tensions and despair. A family without income undergoes great suffering; as its savings fade, it wonders where it is going to obtain the means to survive. Society loses some potential output of goods when some of its productive resources—human or nonhuman—remain idle, and potential consumption is also reduced. Clearly, then, there is a loss in efficiency when people willing to work and productive equipment remain idle. That is, other things equal, relatively high rates of unemployment are viewed almost universally as undesirable.

WHAT IS THE UNEMPLOYMENT RATE?

When discussing unemployment, economists and politicians refer to the unemployment rate. In order to calculate the unemployment rate, you must first understand another important concept—the labour force. The **labour force** is the number of persons 15 years of age and over who are employed or are unemployed and seeking work. Exhibit 1 shows the population categories used by Statistics Canada in its analysis of the labour market. First, it calculates the population 15 years of age and over, which

labour force
persons 15 years of age and over who are employed or are unemployed and seeking work

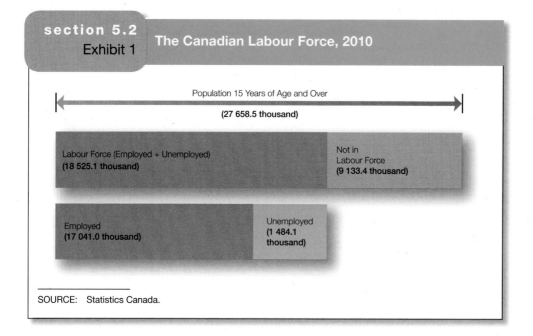

section 5.2
Exhibit 1

The Canadian Labour Force, 2010

Population 15 Years of Age and Over
(27 658.5 thousand)

Labour Force (Employed + Unemployed)
(18 525.1 thousand)

Not in Labour Force
(9 133.4 thousand)

Employed
(17 041.0 thousand)

Unemployed
(1 484.1 thousand)

SOURCE: Statistics Canada.

was 27 658.5 thousand people in 2010. This population is broken down into two categories: those in the labour force and those not in the labour force. Those not in the labour force, 9133.4 thousand people, are people who are not working and are not seeking work. For example, they may be retired persons, full-time homemakers, or full-time students. Those in the labour force, 18 525.1 thousand people, are people who are employed or are unemployed and seeking work.

The **unemployment rate** is defined as the percentage of the people in the labour force who are unemployed. To calculate the unemployment rate, we divide the number of unemployed people by the number of people in the labour force.

Unemployment rate = (Number of unemployed/Labour force) × 100

For 2010, 1484.1 thousand people were unemployed from a labour force of 18 525.1 thousand people.

$$\text{Unemployment rate} = (1484.1 \text{ thousand}/18\,525.1 \text{ thousand}) \times 100$$
$$= 0.080 \times 100$$
$$= 8.0 \text{ percent}$$

The Worst Case of Canadian Unemployment

By far the worst employment downturn in Canadian history was the Great Depression, which began in late 1929 and continued until 1939. Unemployment rose from only 2.9 percent of the labour force in 1929 to more than 19 percent in the early 1930s, and double-digit unemployment persisted through 1939. Some economists would argue that modern macroeconomics, with its emphasis on the determinants of unemployment and its elimination, truly began in the 1930s.

Variations in the Unemployment Rate

Exhibit 2 shows the unemployment rate since 1976. Unemployment has ranged from a high of 11.9 percent in 1983 to a low of 6.0 percent in 2007. Unemployment varies not only over time, it also varies between different segments of the population and by regions of the country. Unemployment tends to be much greater among teenagers, and female unemployment tends to be slightly lower than male unemployment. As Exhibit 3 indicates, the unemployment rate for teenagers (19.9 percent) is three times greater than the unemployment rate for workers aged 45 to 64 (6.4 percent). The difference in unemployment rates for men and women is smaller, with a female unemployment rate of 7.2 percent versus a male unemployment rate of 8.7 percent.

Provincial unemployment rates show considerable variation: from a high of 14.4 percent in Newfoundland and Labrador to a low of 5.2 percent in Saskatchewan. It is also clear from Exhibit 3(b) that, on average, the unemployment rate tends to rise as one moves from west to east across the country.

ARE UNEMPLOYMENT STATISTICS ACCURATE REFLECTIONS OF THE LABOUR MARKET?

In periods of prolonged economic recession and high unemployment, some individuals think that the chances of landing a job are so bleak that they quit looking. People who have left the labour force because they could not find work are called **discouraged workers.** Individuals who have not actively sought work are not counted as unemployed; instead, they fall out of the labour force. Also, people looking for full-time work who grudgingly settle for a part-time job are counted as "fully" employed, yet they are only

section 5.2
Exhibit 2
Unemployment Rate

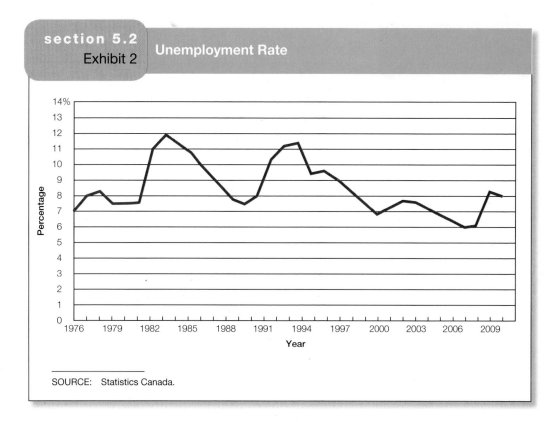

SOURCE: Statistics Canada.

section 5.2
Exhibit 3
Unemployment in Canada by Age, Sex, and Region, 2010

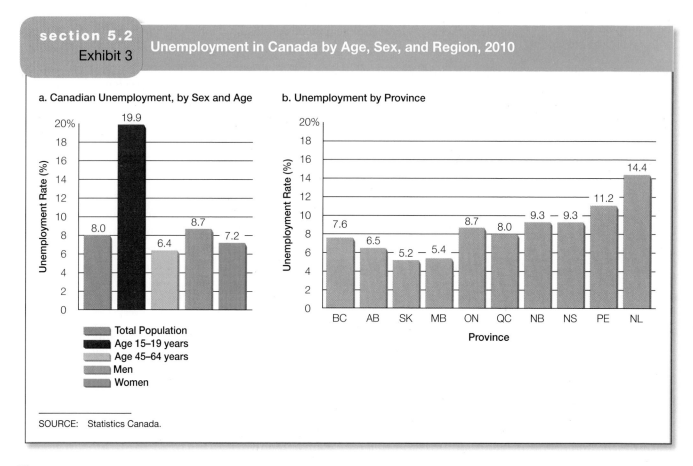

a. Canadian Unemployment, by Sex and Age

b. Unemployment by Province

SOURCE: Statistics Canada.

Teenagers have the highest rates of unemployment. Do you think it would be easier for them to find jobs if they had more experience and higher skill levels?

job loser
an individual who has been laid off or fired

job leaver
a person who quits his or her job

re-entrant
an individual who worked before and is now re-entering the labour force

new entrant
an individual who has not held a job before but is now seeking employment

underemployment
a situation in which workers have skills higher than necessary for a job

"partly" employed. However, at least partially balancing these two biases in official employment statistics are a number of jobs in the underground economy (drugs, prostitution, gambling, and so on) that are not reported at all. In addition, many people may claim they are actually seeking work when, in fact, they may just be going through the motions so that they can continue to collect Employment Insurance or receive other government benefits.

WHAT ARE THE CATEGORIES OF UNEMPLOYMENT?

There are four main categories of unemployed workers: **job losers** (laid off or fired), **job leavers** (quit), **re-entrants** (worked before and are now re-entering the labour force), and **new entrants** (entering the labour force for the first time—primarily teenagers). It is a common misconception that the only reason workers become unemployed is because they have lost their jobs. Although job losers can typically account for 50 to 60 percent of the unemployed, a sizable proportion of unemployment is due to job leavers, new entrants, and re-entrants. Job leavers are typically the smallest source of unemployment.

Reducing Unemployment

Although unemployment is painful to those who have no source of income, reducing unemployment is not costless. In the short run, a reduction in unemployment may come at the expense of a higher rate of inflation, especially if the economy is close to full capacity, where resources are almost fully employed. Also, trying to match employees with jobs quickly may lead to significant inefficiencies because of mismatches between the worker's skill level and the level of skill required for a job. For example, the economy would be wasting resources subsidizing education if people with a Ph.D. in biochemistry were driving taxis or tending bar. That is, situations in which workers have skills higher than necessary for a job are what economists call **underemployment.** Alternatively, employees may be placed in jobs beyond their abilities, which would also lead to inefficiencies.

The Average Duration of Unemployment

The *duration* of unemployment is equally as important as the amount of unemployment. The financial consequences of a head of household being unemployed for four or five weeks are usually not extremely serious, particularly if the individual is covered by Employment Insurance. The impact becomes much more serious if a person is unemployed for many months. Therefore, it is useful to look at the average duration of unemployment to discover what percentage of the labour force is unemployed for more than a certain time period, say, 13 weeks. Canadian data indicate that long-term unemployment (greater than 13 weeks) accounts for approximately 40 to 50 percent of total unemployment.

Exhibit 4 shows the unemployment duration for Canada from 1997–2010. According to the exhibit, the average duration of unemployment has fallen from 26.4 weeks in 1997 to 19.9 weeks in 2010. The duration of unemployment tends to be greater when the amount of unemployment is high, and smaller when the amount of unemployment is low. Unemployment of any duration, of course, means a potential loss of output. This loss of current output is permanent; it is not made up when unemployment starts falling again.

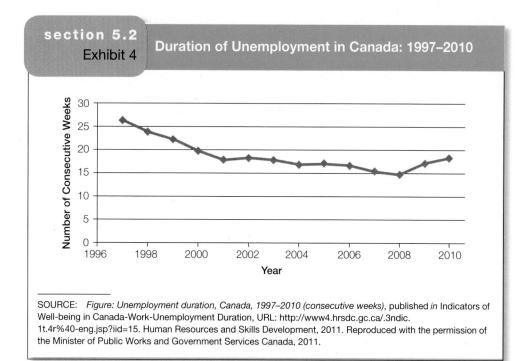

Duration of Unemployment in Canada: 1997–2010

SOURCE: *Figure: Unemployment duration, Canada, 1997–2010 (consecutive weeks),* published *in* Indicators of Well-being in Canada-Work-Unemployment Duration, URL: http://www4.hrsdc.gc.ca/.3ndic. 1t.4r%40-eng.jsp?iid=15. Human Resources and Skills Development, 2011. Reproduced with the permission of the Minister of Public Works and Government Services Canada, 2011.

WHAT IS THE LABOUR FORCE PARTICIPATION RATE?

The percentage of the population aged 15 years and over that is in the labour force is what economists call the **labour force participation rate.** Since 1976, the labour force participation rate has increased from 61.5 to 67.0 percent. The increase in the labour force participation rate can be attributed in large part to the entry of the baby boomers into the labour force and a 17 percentage point increase in the women's labour force participation rate.

Since 1976, the number of women working has shifted dramatically, reflecting the changing role of women in the workforce. In Exhibit 5, we see that in 1976 only 46 percent of women were working or looking for work. Today that figure is roughly 63 percent. In 1976, over 77 percent of men were working or looking for work. Today the labour force participation rate for men has fallen to roughly 72 percent, as many men stay in school longer or opt to retire earlier.

labour force participation rate
the percentage of the population (aged 15 years and over) in the labour force

Labour Force Participation Rates for Men and Women

	1976	1986	1996	2007	2010
Total	61.5%	66.0%	64.7%	67.6%	67.0%
Men	77.6	76.8	72.2	72.7	71.1
Women	45.7	55.5	57.5	62.7	62.4

SOURCE: Statistics Canada.

SECTION CHECK

- The consequences of unemployment to society include a reduction in potential output and consumption—a decrease in efficiency.
- The unemployment rate is found by taking the number of people officially unemployed and dividing by the number in the labour force. Unemployment rates are higher for teenagers, men, and those living in eastern Canada.
- The overall accuracy of the unemployment rate is impacted by factors such as discouraged workers, the treatment of part-time work statistics, and the underground economy.
- There are four main categories of unemployed workers: job losers, job leavers, re-entrants, and new entrants.
- Labour force participation measures the percentage of the adult population that is participating in the labour force. In Canada, women's labour force participation has increased dramatically since 1976.

section
5.3   Different Types of Unemployment

- What is frictional unemployment?
- What is structural unemployment?
- What is cyclical unemployment?
- What is the natural rate of unemployment?

In examining the status of and changes in the unemployment rate, it is important to recognize that there are numerous types of unemployment. In this section, we will examine frictional, structural, and cyclical unemployment and evaluate the relative impact of each on the overall unemployment rate.

WHAT IS FRICTIONAL UNEMPLOYMENT?

frictional unemployment
unemployment from normal turnovers in the economy, such as when individuals change from one job to another

Some unemployment results from normal turnover in the economy, such as when individuals change from one job to another. For example, consider an advertising executive who was laid off in Montreal on March 1 and is now actively looking for similar work in Calgary. This is an example of **frictional unemployment.** Of course, not all unemployed workers were laid off from their jobs; some may have voluntarily quit their jobs. In either case, frictional unemployment is short term and results from the normal turnover in the labour market, such as when people change from one job to another.

Some unemployment occurs because certain types of jobs are seasonal in nature; this type of unemployment is called *seasonal unemployment*. For example, a ski instructor in British Columbia might become seasonally unemployed when the skiing season is over. Or a roofer in Nova Scotia may become seasonally unemployed during the winter months. In agricultural areas, employment increases during the harvest season and falls after harvesting is finished. Even a forest firefighter in a provincial park might be employed only during the months when forest fires are more likely to occur. Because the seasonal unemployment rate is of course higher in the off-season, Statistics Canada also publishes a seasonally adjusted unemployment rate.

Frictional Unemployment—A Sign of Economic Health

Geographic and occupational mobility are considered good for the economy because they generally lead human resources to go from activities of relatively low productivity or value to areas of higher productivity, increasing output in society as well as the wage income of the mover. Hence, frictional unemployment, although not good in itself, is a by-product of a healthy phenomenon, and because it is often short-lived, it is generally not viewed as a serious problem. The amount of frictional unemployment varies somewhat over time; it tends to be greater in periods of low unemployment, when job opportunities are plentiful. This high level of job opportunities stimulates mobility, which, in turn, creates some frictional unemployment.

WHAT IS STRUCTURAL UNEMPLOYMENT?

A second type of unemployment is structural unemployment. Like frictional unemployment, structural unemployment is related to occupational movement or mobility, or in this case, to a lack of mobility. Specifically, **structural unemployment** refers to unemployment that occurs due to a lack of skills necessary for available jobs. For example, if a machine operator in a manufacturing plant loses his job, he could remain unemployed despite the fact that there are openings for computer programmers in his community. The quantity of unemployed workers conceivably could equal the number of job vacancies, but the unemployment persists because the unemployed lack the appropriate skills

structural unemployment *unemployment that occurs due to a lack of skills necessary for available jobs*

for some of the job vacancies. Given the existence of structural unemployment, it is wise to look at both unemployment and job vacancy statistics in assessing labour market conditions. Structural unemployment, like frictional unemployment, reflects the dynamic dimension of a changing economy. Over time, new jobs open up that require new skills, whereas old jobs that required different skills disappear. It is not surprising, then, that many people advocate government-subsidized retraining programs as a means of reducing structural unemployment.

Jules Frazier/Photodisc/Getty One Images

The dimensions of structural unemployment are debatable, in part because of the difficulty in precisely defining the term in an operational sense. Structural unemployment varies considerably—sometimes it is low and at other times, like in the 1970s and 1980s, it is high. To some extent, in this latter period, jobs in the traditional sectors like manufacturing and mining gave way to jobs in the computer and financial services sectors. Consequently, structural unemployment was higher.

Some Unemployment Is Unavoidable

Some unemployment is actually normal and important to the economy. Frictional and structural unemployment are simply unavoidable in a vibrant economy. To a considerable extent, one can view both frictional and structural unemployment as phenomena resulting from imperfections in the labour market. For example, if individuals seeking jobs and employers seeking workers had better information about each other, the amount of frictional unemployment would be considerably lower. It takes time for sup-

What type of unemployment would occur if these miners lost their jobs as a result of a reduction in demand for their output and needed retraining to find other employment? Usually structural unemployment occurs because of a lack of required skills or long-term changes in demand. Consequently, it generally lasts for a longer period of time than frictional unemployment. In this situation, both might come into play.

pliers of labour to find the demanders of labour services, and it takes time and money for labour resources to acquire the necessary skills. But because information is not costless, and because job search also is costly, the bringing of demanders and suppliers of labour services together does not occur instantaneously.

WHAT IS CYCLICAL UNEMPLOYMENT?

cyclical unemployment
unemployment due to short-term cyclical fluctuations in the economy

Often, unemployment is composed of more than just frictional and structural unemployment. In years of relatively low economic activity some unemployment may be due to short-term cyclical fluctuations in the economy. We call this **cyclical unemployment.** Whenever the unemployment rate is greater than the natural rate, or during a recession, there is cyclical unemployment.

The Costs of Cyclical Unemployment

When the unemployment rate is high, numerous economic and social hardships result. The economic costs are the forgone output when the economy is not producing at its potential level. According to Okun's law (really, a rule of thumb), a 1 percent increase in cyclical unemployment reduces output by 2 percent points. Thus, we can actually estimate the economic costs of not producing at our potential output. The costs are particularly high for those groups with the least skills—the poorly educated and teenagers with little work experience.

Reducing Cyclical Unemployment

Most economists believe cyclical unemployment is the most volatile form of unemployment. Given its volatility and dimensions, governments, rightly or wrongly, have viewed unemployment resulting from inadequate demand to be especially correctable through government policies. Most of the attempts to solve the unemployment problem have placed an emphasis on increasing aggregate demand to counter recessions. Attempts to reduce frictional unemployment by providing better labour market information and to reduce structural unemployment through job retraining have also been made, but these efforts have received fewer resources and much less attention from policymakers.

WHAT IS THE NATURAL RATE OF UNEMPLOYMENT?

natural rate of unemployment
the "average" unemployment rate, equal to the sum of frictional and structural unemployment

Looking back at Exhibit 2 in Section 5.2, we see that the unemployment rate averaged around 7.1 percent during the 2006–2010 period. Some economists call this "average" unemployment rate the **natural rate of unemployment** and equate it to the sum of frictional and structural unemployment. When unemployment rises well above 7.1 percent, we have abnormally high unemployment; when it falls below 7.1 percent, we have abnormally low unemployment. When unemployment rises above the natural rate, it reflects the existence of cyclical unemployment. In short, the natural rate of unemployment is the unemployment rate when there is neither a recession nor a boom.

The natural rate of unemployment can change over time as technological, demographic, institutional, and other conditions vary. For example, as baby boomers have aged, the natural rate has fallen because middle-aged workers generally have lower unemployment rates than younger workers. Thus, the natural rate is not fixed because it can change with demographic changes over time. In fact, it is estimated that the natural rate of unemployment was as low as about 5 percent in the 1960s, and then rose to about

8 percent in the 1980s. Today, most economists estimate the natural rate of unemployment to lie in a range between 6 and 7 percent.

Full Employment and Potential Output

When all of the economy's labour resources and other resources like capital are fully employed, the economy is said to be producing its potential level of output: that is, the amount these resources could produce if they were fully employed. Literal full employment of labour means that the economy is providing employment for all who are willing and able to work, with no cyclical unemployment. It also means that capital and land are fully employed. That is, at the natural rate of unemployment, all resources are fully employed and the economy is producing its **potential output** and there is no cyclical unemployment. This does not mean the economy will always be producing at its potential output of resources. For example, when the economy is experiencing cyclical unemployment, the unemployment rate is greater than the natural rate. It is also possible that the economy's output can temporarily exceed the potential output as workers take on overtime or moonlight by taking on extra employment.

potential output
the amount of real output the economy would produce if its labour and other resources were fully employed—that is, at the natural rate of unemployment

Employment Insurance and the Natural Rate of Unemployment

Losing a job can lead to considerable hardship, and Employment Insurance is designed to partially offset the severity of the unemployment problem. The program does not cover those who quit their jobs. To qualify, recipients must have worked a certain length of time. Although the program is intended to ease the pain of unemployment, it also leads to more frictional unemployment, as job seekers stay unemployed for longer periods of time searching for new jobs.

For example, some unemployed people may show little drive in seeking new employment, because Employment Insurance lowers the opportunity cost of being unemployed. For example, a worker making $400 a week when employed receives $220 in compensation when unemployed; as a result, the cost of losing his job is not $400 a week in forgone income, but only $180.

Without Employment Insurance, job seekers would more likely take the first job offered even if did not match their preferences or skill levels. A longer job search might mean a better match but at the expense of lost production and greater amounts of tax dollars.

Technological Change and the Natural Rate of Unemployment

Although many believe that technological advances inevitably result in the displacement of workers, this is not necessarily the case. New inventions are generally cost-saving, and these cost savings will generally generate higher incomes for producers and lower prices and better products for consumers, benefits that will ultimately result in the growth of other industries. If the new equipment is a substitute for labour, then it might displace workers. For example, many fast-food restaurants have substituted self-service beverage bars for workers. However, new capital equipment requires new workers to manufacture and repair the new equipment. The most famous example of this is the computer, which was supposed to displace thousands of workers. Although it did displace workers, the total job growth it generated exceeded the number of lost jobs. The problem is that it is easy to see just the initial effect of technological advances (displaced workers), without recognizing the implications of that invention for the whole economy over time.

© NICK KUODIS/PHOTODISC/GETTY IMAGES

Will new technology in one industry displace workers in the whole economy? No. There may be some job loss of specific jobs or within certain industries. But the overall effect of technological improvements is the release of scarce resources for the expansion of output and employment in other areas and ultimately more economic growth and a higher standard of living.

section 5.4

Inflation

- Why is the overall price level important?
- How is inflation measured using the Consumer Price Index (CPI)?
- Who are the winners and losers during inflation?
- What are the costs of inflation?
- What is the relationship between inflation and interest rates?

WHY IS THE OVERALL PRICE LEVEL IMPORTANT?

price level
the average level of prices in the economy

inflation
a continuous rise in the overall price level

deflation
a decrease in the overall price level

Just as full employment brings about economic security of one kind, stable prices increase another form of security. Most prices in the Canadian economy tend to rise over time and economists use a statistic known as a *price level* to measure this change. A **price level** measures the average level of prices in the economy. A continuous rise in the *overall* price level is called **inflation**. Even when the level of prices is stable, some prices will be rising while others are falling. However, when inflation is present, the goods and services with rising prices will outweigh the goods and services with falling prices. Without stability in the price level, consumers and producers will experience more difficulty in coordinating their plans and decisions. When the *overall* price level is falling, there is **deflation.**

In general, the only thing that can cause a *sustained* increase in the price level is a high rate of growth in money, a topic we will discuss thoroughly in the coming chapters.

HOW IS INFLATION MEASURED USING THE CONSUMER PRICE INDEX (CPI)?

We often use the term *purchasing power* when we discuss how much a dollar can buy of goods and services. In times of inflation, a dollar cannot buy as many goods and services. Thus, the higher the inflation rate, the greater the rate of decline in purchasing power.

relative price
the price of a specific good compared to the prices of other goods

In periods of high and variable inflation, households and firms have a difficult time distinguishing between changes in the **relative price** of individual goods and services (the price of a specific good compared to the prices of other goods) and changes in the general price level of all goods and services. Suppose the price of milk rises by 5 percent between 2010 and 2011, but the overall price level (inflation rate) increases by only 2 percent during that period. Then we could say that between 2010 and 2011, the relative price of milk rose only 3 percent (5 – 2 percent). The next year, the price of milk might increase 5 percent again, but the general inflation rate might be 6 percent. That is, between 2011 and 2012, the relative price of milk might actually fall by 1 percent (5 – 6 percent).

Remember, the relative price is the price of a good relative to all other goods and services. Because of this difficulty in establishing relative prices, inflation distorts the information that flows from price signals. Does the good have a higher price because it has become relatively more scarce and therefore more valuable relative to other goods, or did the price rise along with all other prices because of inflation?

This muddying of price information undermines good decision making, so we need a method to measure inflation. We adjust for the changing purchasing power of the dollar by constructing a price index. Essentially, a **price index** is a measure of the trend in prices for a certain bundle of goods and services over a given time period.

There are many different types of price indices. The best-known price index, the **Consumer Price Index (CPI)** is a measure of the prices of a basket of consumable goods and services that serves to gauge inflation. Constructing the consumer price index is complicated. Since literally thousands of consumer goods and services are involved, attempting to include all of them in the index would be cumbersome and make the index expensive to compute; in addition, it would take a long time to gather the necessary price data. Therefore, Statistics Canada bases the CPI on a basket of over 600 consumer goods and services that are purchased by a typical Canadian household. Each month, the prices of these goods and services are recorded all across Canada. The eight major components of the CPI appear in Exhibit 1. The weight for each component is represented as a proportion of the total expenditures for the CPI basket.

price index
a measure of the trend in prices for a certain bundle of goods and services over a given time period

Consumer Price Index (CPI)
a measure of the prices of a basket of consumable goods and services that serves to gauge inflation

Calculating the CPI—A Simplified Example

Suppose a consumer typically buys 24 loaves of bread and 12 kilograms of oranges in a year. The following table indicates the prices of bread and oranges and the cost of the consumer's typical market basket in the years 2009 to 2011.

Year	Price of Bread	Price of Oranges	Cost of Market Basket
2009	$1.00	$2.00	(24 × $1.00) + (12 × $2.00) = $48.00
2010	1.15	2.10	(24 × 1.15) + (12 × 2.10) = 52.80
2011	1.40	2.20	(24 × 1.40) + (12 × 2.20) = 60.00

We calculate the CPI by comparing the cost of the market basket in the current year to the cost of the market basket in the base year. The base year is arbitrarily chosen; in our example, we will designate 2009 as the base year. The CPI for each year is calculated using the following formula:

$$\text{CPI} = \frac{\text{Cost of market basket in current year}}{\text{Cost of market basket in base year}} \times 100$$

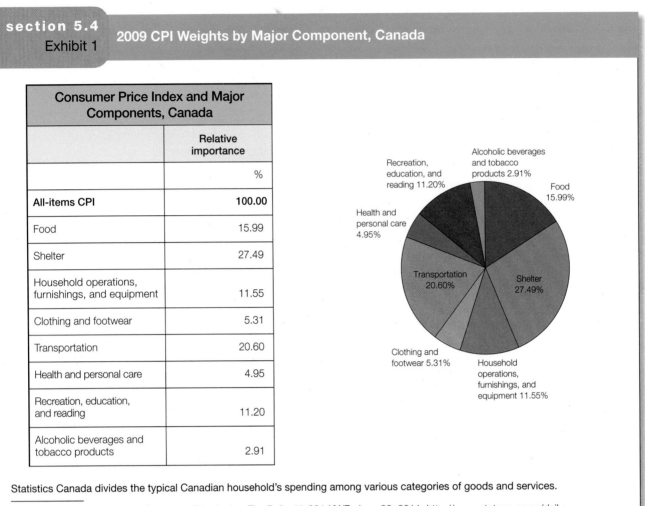

Consumer Price Index and Major Components, Canada	
	Relative importance
	%
All-items CPI	**100.00**
Food	15.99
Shelter	27.49
Household operations, furnishings, and equipment	11.55
Clothing and footwear	5.31
Transportation	20.60
Health and personal care	4.95
Recreation, education, and reading	11.20
Alcoholic beverages and tobacco products	2.91

Statistics Canada divides the typical Canadian household's spending among various categories of goods and services.

SOURCE: Statistics Canada, Consumer Price Indes, *The Daily*, 11-001-XWE, June 29, 2011; http://www.statcan.gc.ca/daily-quotidien/110629/tdq110629-eng.htm

The following table shows the CPI from 2009 to 2011. In 2009, the base year, the CPI equals 100. In 2010 and 2011, the CPI is 110 and 125, respectively, meaning that the average price level has risen in each of these two years.

Year	Consumer Price Index
2009	$48/$48 × 100 = 100.0
2010	$52.80/$48 × 100 = 110.0
2011	$60/$48 × 100 = 125.0

A comparison of the CPI shows that between 2009 and 2010, prices increased an average of 10 percent. Between 2009 and 2011, 25 percent inflation occurred. And between 2010 and 2011, the inflation rate was 13.6 percent, (125 − 110)/110 × 100.

The CPI is not a completely accurate measure of the cost of living since three factors cause the CPI to overestimate changes in the cost of living. First, goods and services change in quality over time but the CIP is not able to adjust for the quality of all products, so the observed price change may, in reality, reflect a quality change in the product rather than a change in the purchasing power of the dollar. A $300 television set today is dramatically bigger and better than a television set in 1950 that cost $499. Second, new products come on the market and occasionally old products disappear. For example, colour TV sets did not exist in 1950 but are a major consumer item now. How do you calculate changes in prices over time when some products did not even exist in the earlier period? Third, the CPI measures the price changes of a fixed basket of goods and services. Thus, the CPI does not capture the fact that consumers are able to keep their cost of living down by substituting those goods whose prices have risen relatively less for those goods whose prices have risen relatively more.

The Price Level Over the Years

Unanticipated and sharp changes in the price level are almost universally considered to be "bad" and to require a policy remedy. What is the historical record of changes in the overall Canadian price level? Exhibit 2 shows changes in the Consumer Price Index (CPI), the standard measure of inflation, from 1915 to 2010. As you can see from the chart, the Canadian economy experienced deflation in the early 1920s and the early 1930s. High rates of inflation, on the other hand, were experienced in the mid-1970s and early 1980s. Notice that since 1992, the annual inflation rate has remained below 3 percent, implying a substantial period of relatively low and stable inflation. Remember, however, that even when the inflation rate is only 3 percent per year, prices on average are rising, and the price level will double in 24 years.

WHO ARE THE WINNERS AND LOSERS DURING INFLATION?

Inflation brings about changes in real incomes of persons, and these changes may be either desirable or undesirable. Suppose you retire on a fixed pension of $3000 per month. Over time, the $3000 will buy less and less if prices generally rise. Your real income—your income adjusted to reflect changes in purchasing power—falls. Inflation lowers income in real terms for people on fixed-dollar incomes. Likewise, inflation can hurt creditors. Suppose you loaned someone $1000 in 2001 and were paid back $1000 plus interest in 2011. The $1000 in principal you were paid back actually is worth less in

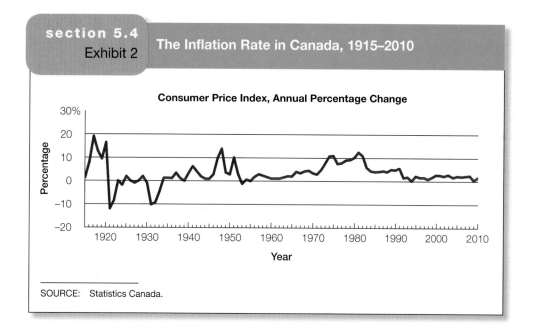

section 5.4
Exhibit 2   The Inflation Rate in Canada, 1915–2010

Consumer Price Index, Annual Percentage Change

SOURCE: Statistics Canada.

2011 than it was in 2001 because inflation has eroded the purchasing power of the dollar. Thus, inflation erodes the real wealth of the creditor. People whose incomes are tied to long-term contracts also sometimes lose as a result of inflation, at least temporarily. If inflation begins shortly after a labour union signs a three-year wage agreement, it may completely eat up the wage gains provided by the contract. The same applies to businesses that agree to sell a quantity of something, say, phone service, for a fixed price for a given number of years.

If some people lose because of changing prices, others must gain. The debtor pays back dollars worth less in purchasing power than those she borrowed. Corporations that can quickly raise the prices on their goods may have revenue gains greater than their increases in costs, providing additional profits. Wage earners sometimes lose as a result of inflation because wages may rise at a slower rate than the price level. The redistributional impact of inflation is not the result of conscious public policy; it just happens.

WHAT ARE THE COSTS OF INFLATION?

The uncertainty that inflation creates can also discourage investment and economic growth. When inflation rates are high, they also tend to vary considerably, which creates a lot of uncertainty. This uncertainty complicates planning for businesses and households, which is vital to capital formation, as well as adding an inflation risk premium to long-term interest rates.

Moreover, inflation can raise one nation's price level relative to that in other countries. In turn, this can make that nation's goods and services less competitive in international markets or can decrease the value of the national currency relative to that of other countries.

Costs of High Inflation

Predictable low rates of inflation, while still a problem, are considerably better than high and variable inflation rates. A slow predictable rate of inflation makes predicting future price increases relatively easy, so setting interest rates will be an easier task and the redistribution effects of inflation will be minimized. High and variable inflation rate make it almost impossible to set long-term contracts, however, because prices and interest rates may be changing by the day or even by the hour in the case of **hyperinflation**—extremely high rates of inflation for a sustained period of time.

hyperinflation
extremely high rates of inflation for a sustained period of time

In its extreme form, inflation can lead to a complete erosion of faith in the value of the pieces of paper we commonly call money. In Germany after both world wars, prices rose so fast that people in some cases finally refused to take paper money, insisting instead on payment in goods or metals, whose prices tend to move predictably with inflation. Unchecked inflation can feed on itself and ultimately can lead to hyperinflation of 300 percent or more per year. We saw these rapid rates of inflation in Argentina in the 1980s and Brazil in the 1990s. Most economists believe we can live quite well in an environment of low, steady inflation, but no economist believes we can prosper with high, variable inflation.

Unanticipated Inflation Distorts Price Signals

In periods of high and variable inflation, households and firms have a difficult time distinguishing between changes in the relative prices of individual goods and services and changes in the general price level of all goods and services. Inflation distorts the information that flows from price signals. Does the good have a higher price because it has become relatively more scarce, and therefore more valuable relative to other goods, or did the price rise along with all other prices because of inflation? This muddying of price information undermines good decision making.

Menu and Shoe-Leather Costs

Another cost of inflation is that incurred by firms as a result of being forced to change prices more frequently. For example, a restaurant may have to print new menus, or a department or mail-order store may have to print new catalogues to reflect changing prices. These costs are called **menu costs**—the costs incurred by a firm as a result of changing its listed prices. In some South American economies in the 1980s, inflation increased at over 300 percent per year, with prices changing on a daily, or even hourly, basis in some cases. Imagine how large the menu costs could be in an economy such as that!

There is also the **shoe-leather cost** of inflation: the cost incurred when individuals reduce their money holdings because of inflation. People want to hold less currency, perhaps going to the ATM once a week rather than twice a month, thus wearing out the leather of their shoes going to and from the ATM. The effects of shoe-leather costs of inflation, like menu costs, are very modest in countries with low inflation rates but can be quite large in countries where inflation is substantial. Also, the higher inflation rates lead to higher nominal interest rates and this may induce more individuals to put money into a savings account at a financial institution rather than allowing it to depreciate in their pockets.

menu costs
the costs incurred by a firm as a result of changing its listed prices

shoe-leather cost
the cost incurred when individuals reduce their money holdings because of inflation

WHAT IS THE RELATIONSHIP BETWEEN INFLATION AND INTEREST RATES?

The interest rate that is usually reported is not adjusted for inflation. This is the **nominal interest rate.** We determine the actual **real interest rate** by taking the nominal rate of interest minus the inflation rate:

$$\text{Real interest rate} = \text{Nominal interest rate} - \text{Inflation rate}$$

For example, if the nominal interest rate was 5 percent and the inflation rate was 3 percent, then the real interest rate would be 2 percent.

If people can correctly anticipate inflation, they will behave in a manner that will largely protect them against loss. Consider the creditor who believes that the overall price level will rise 6 percent a year, based on immediate past experience. Would that creditor lend money to someone at a 5 percent rate of interest? No. A 5 percent rate of interest means that a person borrowing $1000 now will pay back $1050 ($1000 plus 5 percent of $1000) one year from now. But if prices go up 6 percent, it will take $1060 to buy what $1000 does today. (That is, $1060 is 6 percent more than $1000.) Thus, the person who lends at 5 percent will be repaid an amount ($1050) that is less than the purchasing power of the original loan ($1060). The real interest rate, then, would actually be negative. Hence, to protect themselves, lenders will demand a rate of interest large enough to compensate for the deteriorating value of the dollar.

nominal interest rate
the reported interest rate that is not adjusted for inflation

real interest rate
the nominal interest rate minus the inflation rate

Anticipated Inflation and the Nominal Interest Rate

The economic theory behind the behavioural responses of creditors and debtors to anticipated inflation is straightforward and can be expressed in a simple diagram (Exhibit 3). An interest rate is, in effect, the price that one pays for the use of funds. Like other prices, interest rates are determined by the interaction of demand and supply forces. The lower the interest rate (price), the greater the quantity of loanable funds demanded, *ceteris paribus;* the higher the interest rate (price), the greater the quantity of loanable funds supplied by individuals and institutions like banks, *ceteris paribus.* Suppose that in an environment where prices in general are expected to remain stable in the near future, the demand for loanable funds is depicted by D_0 and the supply of such funds is indicated by S_0. In this scenario, the equilibrium price, or interest rate, will be r_0, where the quantity demanded equals the quantity supplied.

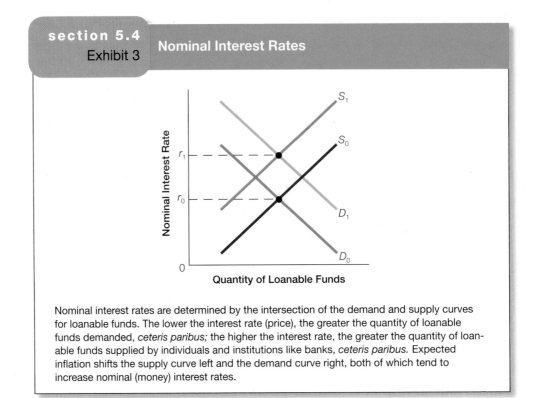

Nominal Interest Rates

Nominal interest rates are determined by the intersection of the demand and supply curves for loanable funds. The lower the interest rate (price), the greater the quantity of loanable funds demanded, *ceteris paribus;* the higher the interest rate, the greater the quantity of loanable funds supplied by individuals and institutions like banks, *ceteris paribus.* Expected inflation shifts the supply curve left and the demand curve right, both of which tend to increase nominal (money) interest rates.

When people start expecting future inflation, creditors such as banks will become less willing to lend funds at any given interest rate because they fear they will be repaid in dollars of lesser value than those they loaned. This is depicted by a leftward shift in the supply curve of loanable funds (a decrease in supply) to S_1. Likewise, demanders of funds (borrowers) are more anxious to borrow because they hope that they will pay their loans back in dollars of lesser purchasing power than the dollars they borrowed. Thus, the demand for funds increases from D_0 to D_1. Both the decrease in supply and the increase in demand push up the interest rate to a new equilibrium, r_1. Whether the equilibrium quantity of loanable funds will increase or decrease depends on the relative sizes of the shifts in the respective curves.

Creditors Don't Always Lose from Inflation

Usually lenders are able to anticipate inflation with reasonable accuracy. For example, in the early 1980s when the inflation rate was over 10 percent a year, nominal interest rates on a three-month Treasury bill were relatively high. Since 2000, with low inflation rates, the nominal interest rate has been relatively low. If the inflation rate is anticipated accurately, new creditors will not lose nor will debtors gain from a change in the inflation rate. However, nominal interest rates and real interest rates do not always run together. For example, in periods of high *unexpected* inflation, the nominal interest rates can be very high whereas the real interest rates may be very low or even negative.

Protecting Ourselves from Inflation

Some groups try to protect themselves from inflation by using cost-of-living clauses in contracts. In labour union contracts with these clauses, workers automatically get wage increases that reflect rising prices. The same is true of some private pension plans that are adjusted for inflation, as well as the government-run Canada Pension Plan. Personal income taxes also are now indexed (adjusted) for inflation. However, some of the tax laws are still not indexed for inflation. This can affect the incentives to work, save, and invest.

Some economists have argued that we should go one step further and index everything, meaning that all contractual arrangements would be adjusted frequently to take changing prices into account. Such an arrangement might reduce the impact of inflation, but it would also entail additional contracting costs. An alternative approach has been to try to stop inflation through various policies relating to the amount of government spending, tax rates, or the amount of money created.

DEBATE

MACROECONOMIC GOALS: SHOULD THE DOMINANT STRATEGY BE TO CONTROL INFLATION?

Governments have a difficult task in relation to economic policy. They have three overriding goals that form the structural foundation of macroeconomic policy. Individually, the goals are to (1) maintain employment rates at relatively high levels, (2) maintain prices at relatively stable levels, and (3) achieve high rates of growth. These are competing forces that act against each other; for example, as growth increases, there is the likelihood that prices (inflation) will increase. Currently, the federal government considers the control of prices to be paramount to the other two goals. Should this be the dominant policy?

Pro:

Stable prices of goods and services, in both the consumer and the factor markets, are of primary importance for a strong economy. Stable prices ensure that investment and interest rates are within manageable levels, which will ensure that growth continues and people are employed. By managing inflation rates, the government benefits in meeting the other goals without having to directly intervene. In an open capitalist economy, the less government intervention, the better. Can you think of other reasons why the government would chose inflation control over the other goals?

Con:

The government's choice to control inflation began in 1991, at a time when rising prices were a concern. The country had undergone a period when high inflation was causing high interest rates and impeded growth. At the time, it was the proper policy. However, under the current economic conditions, there are more important issues, such as helping people to get back to work. Further, if the unemployment rate is too high, growth is impeded and the government will be paying higher costs for social programs.

What is your opinion: Should the government concentrate on employment rates over rising prices? Can you think of other reasons why the government should reconsider its primary target?

SECTION CHECK

- Price level stability is a desirable goal, as it limits inflationary costs.
- A price index allows us to compare prices paid for goods and services over time. The Consumer Price Index (CPI) is the best-known price index.
- Inflation generally hurts creditors and those on fixed incomes and pensions; debtors generally benefit from inflation.
- Unanticipated inflation causes unpredictable transfers of wealth and reduces the efficiency of the market system by distorting price signals.
- The nominal interest rate is the actual amount of interest you pay. The real interest rate is the nominal rate minus the inflation rate. Wage earners attempt to keep pace with inflation by demanding higher wages each year or by indexing their annual wage to inflation.

section 5.5

Economic Fluctuations

- What are short-term economic fluctuations?
- What are the four stages of a business cycle?
- How long does a business cycle last?

WHAT ARE SHORT-TERM ECONOMIC FLUCTUATIONS?

The aggregate amount of economic activity in Canada and most other nations has increased markedly over time, even on a per capita basis, indicating long-term economic growth. Short-term fluctuations in the economy relative to the long-term trend in output are referred to as **business cycles.** Exhibit 1 illustrates the distinction between long-term economic growth and short-term economic fluctuations. Over a long period of time, the line representing economic activity slopes upward, indicating increasing real output. Over short time periods, however, there are downward, as well as upward, output changes. Business cycles are the short-term ups and downs in economic activity, not the long-term trend in output, which in modern times has been upward.

WHAT ARE THE FOUR STAGES OF A BUSINESS CYCLE?

A business cycle has four phases—expansion, peak, contraction, and trough—as illustrated in Exhibit 2. The period of **expansion** occurs when output (real GDP) is rising significantly. Usually during the expansion phase, unemployment is falling and both consumer and business confidence is high. Thus, investment spending by firms is rising, as well as expenditures for expensive durable consumer goods, such as automobiles and

business cycles
short-term fluctuations in the economy relative to the long-term trend in output

expansion
when output (real GDP) is rising significantly—the period between the trough of a recession and the next peak

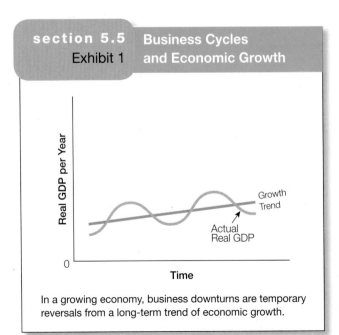

section 5.5　**Business Cycles**
Exhibit 1　**and Economic Growth**

In a growing economy, business downturns are temporary reversals from a long-term trend of economic growth.

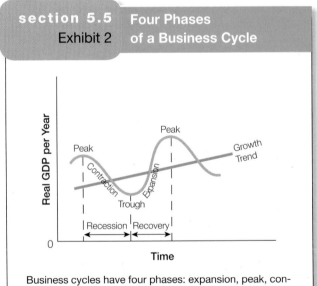

section 5.5　**Four Phases**
Exhibit 2　**of a Business Cycle**

Business cycles have four phases: expansion, peak, contraction, and trough. The expansion phase usually is longer than the contraction, and in a growing economy, output (real GDP) will rise from one business cycle peak to the next.

household appliances. The **peak** is the point in time when the expansion comes to an end, when output is at the highest point in the cycle. The **contraction** is a period of falling real output, and is usually accompanied by rising unemployment and declining business and consumer confidence. The contraction phase is measured from the peak to the trough. Investment spending by firms and expenditures on consumer durable goods fall sharply in a typical contraction. This contraction phase is also called **recession,** a period of significant decline in output and employment (lasting at least six months). The **trough** is the point in time when output stops declining; it is the moment when business activity is at its lowest point in the cycle. Unemployment is relatively high at the trough, although the actual maximum amount of unemployment may not occur exactly at the trough. Often, unemployment remains fairly high well into the expansion phase. The expansion phase is measured from the trough to the peak.

Exhibit 3 shows the growth in Canadian real GDP over the 1962–2010 period. On an annual basis, you can see that there were three major recessions during this period; 1982, 1991, and 2009. In the 1982 recession, the economy declined by 2.9 percent, whereas in 1991, the economy contracted by 2.1 percent. As for the 2009 recession, the Canadian economy experienced a 2.8 percent decline in real GDP. Of the three recessions, the sharp drop in output in 1982 was the deepest recession the economy had experienced since the Great Depression of the 1930s. Both the 1982 and 1991 recessions were accompanied by sharp rises in unemployment, which rose from 7.6 percent (1981) to 12.0 percent (1983), and from 8.1 percent (1990) to 11.4 percent (1993). The 2009 recession, however, was different in that the unemployment rate remained relatively low at around 8.3 percent (2009), the rate being 6.1 percent in 2008.

Another factor you will notice from Exhibit 3 is that the 1991 recession was more prolonged than either the 1982 or 2009 recessions. With the 1991 recession, the economy actually stagnated in 1990, contracted in 1991, and stayed in a state of decline for most of 1992. By comparison, in the years that immediately followed both the 1982 and 2009 recessions, the economy was already exhibiting significant economic growth (2.4 percent and 3.2 percent in 1983 and 2010, respectively). The prolonged nature of

peak
the point in time when the expansion comes to an end, when output is at the highest point in the cycle

contraction
when the economy's output is falling—measured from the peak to the trough

recession
a period of significant decline in output and employment

trough
the point in time when output stops declining; it is the moment when business activity is at its lowest point in the cycle

section 5.5
Exhibit 3 Growth in Canadian Real GDP, 1962–2010

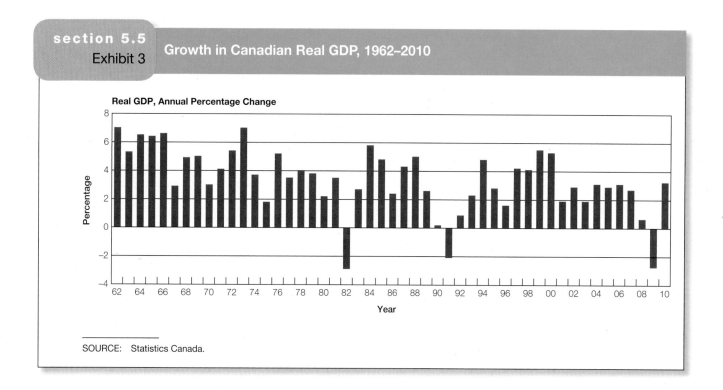

SOURCE: Statistics Canada.

the 1991 recession also impacted unemployment, with the unemployment rate remaining above 10 percent through 1994, even as the economy entered the expansion phase, which is a characteristic of unemployment that we discussed previously.

You will also notice that the expansion phase of the business cycle is characterized by varying rates of economic growth. In 1962 and 1973, for example, the economy grew at a very rapid pace of 7 percent per year. In other years, economic growth can be much more sluggish, as in 1975 and 2003 when the economy grew by less than 2 percent each year.

HOW LONG DOES A BUSINESS CYCLE LAST?

As you can see from Exhibit 3, there is no uniformity to a business cycle's length. This is why economists often call them *economic fluctuations* rather than *business cycles,* since there is not the regularity that the word *cycle* implies. Severe recessions are called **depressions.** Likewise, a prolonged expansion in economic activity is sometimes called a **boom.** For example, during the Great Depression, real GDP contracted for four consecutive years, from 1930 to 1933. An economic boom occurred during the 1960s when real GDP grew by about 6 percent a year on average over that decade.

depression
a severe recession

boom
prolonged expansion in economic activity

Seasonal Fluctuations Affect Economic Activity

The determinants of cyclical fluctuations in the economy are the major thrust of the next several chapters, and some fluctuations in economic activity reflect seasonal patterns. Business activity, whether measured by production or by the sale of goods, tends to be high in the two months before the winter holidays and somewhat lower in the summer, when families often are on vacation. Within individual industries, of course, seasonal fluctuations in output are often extremely pronounced, agriculture being the best example.

Often, key economic statistics, such as unemployment rates, are seasonally adjusted, meaning that the numbers are modified to account for normal seasonal fluctuations. Thus, seasonally adjusted unemployment rates in summer months are below actual unemployment rates, because employment is normally high in the summer due to the inflow of school-aged workers into the labour force.

Forecasting Cyclical Changes

The farmer and the aviator rely heavily on weather forecasters for information on climatic conditions in planning their activities. Similarly, businesses, government agencies, and, to a lesser extent, consumers rely on economic forecasts to learn of forthcoming developments in the business cycle. If it looks like the economy will continue in an expansionary phase, businesses might expand production to meet a perceived forthcoming need; if it looks like contraction is coming, perhaps they will be more cautious.

Forecasting Models   Using theoretical models, which will be discussed in later chapters, economists gather statistics on economic activity in the immediate past, including, for example, consumer expenditures, business inventories, the supply of money, governmental expenditures, and tax revenues. Using past historical relationships between these factors and the overall level of economic activity (which form the basis of economic theories), they formulate *econometric models.* Statistics from the immediate past are plugged into the model and forecasts are made. Because human behaviour changes and we cannot correctly make assumptions about certain future developments, our numbers are imperfect and our econometric models are not always accurate. Like the weather forecasts, although the econometric models are not perfect, they are helpful.

Leading Economic Indicators   One less sophisticated but very useful forecasting tool is watching trends in **leading economic indicators**—factors that typically change before changes in economic activity. Statistics Canada has identified ten such leading indicators: furniture and appliance sales, other durable goods sales, length of average workweek, new orders in manufacturing, shipments-to-inventory ratio, housing starts, business and personal services employment, index of stock prices, money supply, and the U.S. leading indicator. Statistics Canada combines all of these into a composite index of leading indicators. If the index rises sharply for two or three months, it is likely (but not certain) that increases in the overall level of activity will follow.

Although the leading economic indicators do provide a warning of a likely downturn, they do not provide accurate information on the depth or the duration of the downturn.

leading economic indicators
factors that typically change before changes in economic activity

Business CONNECTION

WHAT'S IN MACROECONOMICS FOR BUSINESS?

Macroeconomics deals with the big picture. It examines the economy as a whole, and maintains a focus on increasing economic growth, reducing unemployment, and achieving stable prices. In general, macroeconomics also promotes a better understanding of how to improve our quality of life and how to mitigate or avoid extreme income disparities throughout our society.

From all of this, one might properly conclude that macroeconomics is concerned with the average citizen's standard of living. The standard of living for any country is measured as the real gross domestic product per capita, that is, the real output of goods and services per person. This measure obviously looks at the quality of life of the average citizen from an economic perspective versus a social or psychological perspective. At first glance, the concerns outlined would seem to cover issues more appealing to politicians and ordinary citizens instead of issues that are normally of interest to business with its focus on profitability.

Why should business be concerned with economic growth, that is, real increases in gross domestic product? This question may be answered by recognizing that no real revenue flows into a company unless that company has customers. When an economy grows or expands at a rate in excess of its population, individuals and households will on average receive more income.

These individuals and households with more income have more disposable income. Hence, a growing economy provides businesses with more customers who have more disposable income.

The second focus area of macroeconomics deals with employment levels. There is no debate that there are significant social and psychological benefits to a society when people who want to work are employed. Politicians and social scientists collectively agree that unemployment is undesirable. What about business? Very simply stated, more employed workers result in more customers with the ability and willingness to purchase goods and services. Business is aware of this relationship and supports governments in the goal of reducing unemployment.

Finally, stable prices are of concern to both governments and business. In business, when the rate of price change for the various factors of production, such as labour and materials, and the rate of price change for the goods and services produced are all fairly predictable and modest, business can better forecast the likelihood of making a profit. In this kind of economic environment, business is more likely to expand. Government with its reliance on the taxes collected to pay for the spending services such as schools and hospitals also likes predictability.

Yes, both business and governments have reasons to cheer for stable predictable prices, more employment, and greater economic growth.

SECTION CHECK

- Business cycles (or economic fluctuations) are short-term fluctuations in the amount of economic activity relative to the long-term growth trend in output.
- The four phases of a business cycle are expansion, peak, contraction, and trough.
- Recessions occur during the contraction phase of a business cycle. Severe, long-term recessions are called *depressions,* while prolonged expansions are referred to as *booms.* The economy often goes through short-term contractions even during a long-term growth trend. Overall, the duration of any one business cycle is uncertain.

For Your Review

Section 5.1

1. Visit the Statistics Canada website at www.statscan.gc.ca. Review the links listed under "Latest indicators" (on the right hand side of the page). Based on the most recent information, how is the Canadian economy doing in terms of the macroeconomic goals of maintaining prices, maintaining employment, and achieving a high rate of economic growth?

2. Numerous African nations have targeted food self-sufficiency as their primary economic goal. How can this fact coexist with the three primary economic goals discussed in the chapter?

Section 5.2

3. What would be the labour force participation rate if
   a. The population = 200 million, the labour force = 160 million, and employment = 140 million?
   b. The population = 200 million, the labour force = 140 million, and employment = 120 million?
   c. Starting from the situation in (a), what would happen to the labour force participation rate if 30 million people lost their jobs and all of them exited the labour force?
   d. Starting from the situation in (a), what would happen to the labour force participation rate if employment rose from 140 to 150 million?

4. Answer the following questions about unemployment.
   a. If a country had an adult population (those 15 years of age and over) of 200 million and a labour force of 160 million, and 140 million people were employed, what would be its labour force participation rate and its unemployment rate?
   b. If 10 million new jobs were created in the country and it attracted into the labour force 20 million of the people who were previously not in the labour force, what would its new labour force participation rate and its unemployment rate be?
   c. Beginning from the situation in (a), if 10 million unemployed people became discouraged and stopped looking for work, what would the country's new labour force participation rate and its unemployment rate be?
   d. Beginning from the situation in (a), if 10 million current workers retired but their jobs were filled by others still in the labour force, what would the country's new labour force participation rate and its unemployment rate be?

5. Which of the following individuals would economists consider unemployed?
   a. Sam looked for work for several weeks, but has now given up his search and is going back to university.
   b. A 12-year-old wants to mow lawns for extra cash but is unable to find neighbours willing to hire her.

c. A factory worker is temporarily laid off but expects to be called back to work soon.

d. A receptionist who works only 20 hours per week would like to work 40 hours per week.

e. A high-school graduate spends his days backpacking across the country rather than seeking work.

6. Answer the following questions about reasons for unemployment.

   a. In a severe recession, explain what would tend to happen to the number of people in each of the following categories:

   job losers

   job leavers

   re-entrants

   new entrants

   b. In very good economic times, why might the number of job leavers, re-entrants, and new entrants all increase?

Section 5.3

7. Identify whether each of the following reflects structural, frictional, or cyclical unemployment.

   a. A real estate agent is laid off due to slow business after housing sales fall.

   b. An automotive worker is replaced by robotic equipment on the assembly line.

   c. A salesperson quits a job in Ontario and seeks a new career after moving to Alberta.

   d. An employee is fired for poor job performance and searches the want ads each day for work.

8. Which type of unemployment would be affected with the following changes? Would it go up or down?

   a. increased employment benefits

   b. a heavy snowfall in Saskatchewan

   c. more effective online job search

   d. a large, permanent decrease in the demand for coal

   e. more retraining of people to develop new skills

   f. a sharp fall in demand for goods and services in the economy

9. a. What is the relationship between the natural rate of unemployment and frictional, structural, and cyclical unemployment?

   b. What would happen to both unemployment and the natural rate of unemployment if

      i. cyclical unemployment increases.

      ii. frictional unemployment increases.

      iii. structural unemployment falls and cyclical unemployment rises by the same amount.

      iv. structural unemployment increases and cyclical unemployment decreases by a larger amount.

      v. frictional unemployment decreases and structural unemployment increases by the same amount.

10. Employment insurance benefits in the United States tend to be both less generous and available for shorter periods of time than in Canada. What impact do you think this is likely to have on the unemployment rate in the United States? Why?

11. How can the existence of unions result in higher unemployment rates? How would the results differ for someone who wants to be employed in the union sector than for someone who currently has a job in the union sector?

12. Why isn't it true that technological advances inevitably displace workers?

Section 5.4

13. Answer the following questions about inflation.

    a. What would be the effect of unexpected inflation on each of the following?

       retirees on fixed incomes

       workers

       debtors

       creditors

       shoe-leather costs

       menu costs

    b. How would your answers change if the inflation was expected?

14. Answer the following questions about the nominal and real interest rate.

    a. What would be the real interest rate if the nominal interest rate was 14 percent and the inflation rate was 10 percent? If the nominal interest rate was 8 percent and the inflation rate was 1 percent?

    b. What would happen to the real interest rate if the nominal interest rate went from 9 to 15 percent when the inflation rate went from 4 to 10 percent? If the nominal interest rate went from 11 to 7 percent when the inflation rate went from 8 to 4 percent?

15. You borrow money at a fixed rate of interest to finance your university education. If the rate of inflation unexpectedly slows down between the time you take out the loan and the time you begin paying it back, is there a redistribution of income? What if you already expected the inflation rate to slow at the time you took out the loan? Explain.

16. How does a variable rate mortgage agreement protect lenders against inflation? Who bears the inflation risk?

17. Calculate a price index for 2008, 2009, and 2010 using the following information about prices. Let the market basket consist of one pizza, two sodas, and three video rentals. Let the year 2008 be the base year (with an index value of 100).

Year	Price of a Pizza	Price of a Soda	Price of a Video Rental
2008	$ 9.00	$0.50	$2.00
2009	9.50	0.53	2.24
2010	10.00	0.65	2.90

How much inflation occurred between 2008 and 2009? Between 2008 and 2010? Between 2009 and 2010?

18. Say that the bundle of goods purchased by a typical consumer in the base year consisted of 20 litres of milk at a price of $1 per litre and 15 loaves of bread at a price of $2 per loaf. What would be the price index in a year in which

   a. milk cost $2 per litre and bread cost $1 per loaf?

   b. milk cost $3 per litre and bread cost $2 per loaf?

   c. milk cost $2 per litre and bread cost $4 per loaf?

Section 5.5

19. Suppose the hypothetical economy of Ecoland is characterized by the following economic data. Where along the business cycle would the economy of Ecoland be located?

Variable	Value (%)	Trend
Unemployment rate	8%	Decreasing
Natural rate of unemployment	5	—
Inflation rate	1	Increasing
Real gross domestic product (growth rate)	2	Increasing

20. Evaluate the following statement regarding business cycles: "Typically, unemployment and inflation move in opposite directions as the economy travels through its business cycle."

CourseMate

Access an interactive eBook and chapter-specific interactive learning tools, including flashcards, quizzes, a glossary, and more in CourseMate, accessed through **www.sextonmacro3ce.nelson.com**

chapter 6

Measuring Economic Performance

section 6.1

National Income Accounting: Measuring Economic Performance

- Why do we measure our economy's performance?
- What is gross domestic product (GDP)?

WHY DO WE MEASURE OUR ECONOMY'S PERFORMANCE?

There is a great desire to measure the success, or performance, of our economy. Are we getting "bigger" (and hopefully better) or "smaller" (and worse) over time? Aside from intellectual curiosity, the need to evaluate the magnitude of our economic performance is important to macroeconomic policymakers who want to know how well the economy is performing so that they can set goals and develop policy recommendations.

Measurement of the economy's performance is also important to private businesses because inaccurate measurement can lead to bad decision making. Traders in stocks and bonds are continually checking economic statistics—buying and selling in response to the latest economic data.

National Income Accounting

national income accounting

a uniform means of measuring economic performance

To fulfill the desire for a reliable method of measuring economic performance, **national income accounting**—a uniform means of measuring economic performance—was born early in the twentieth century. The establishment of these accounting rules for economic performance was such an important accomplishment that one of the first Nobel

Prizes in economics was given to the late Simon Kuznets, a pioneer of national income accounting in the United States.

Several measures of aggregate national income and output have been developed, the most important of which is gross domestic product (GDP). We will examine GDP and other indicators of national economic performance in detail later in this chapter.

WHAT IS GROSS DOMESTIC PRODUCT (GDP)?

The measure of aggregate economic performance that receives the most attention in the popular media is **gross domestic product (GDP),** which is defined as the value of all final goods and services produced in a country during a given period of time. By convention, that period of time is almost always one year. But let's examine the rest of this definition. What is meant by "value" and "final goods and services"?

Measuring the Value of Goods and Services

Value is determined by the market prices at which goods and services sell. Underlying the calculations, then, are the various equilibrium prices and quantities for the multitude of goods and services produced.

What Is a Final Good or Service?

The word "final" means that the good is ready for its designated ultimate use. Many goods and services are intermediate goods or services; that is, used in the production of other goods. For example, suppose Magna International produces auto parts that it sells to General Motors for use in making an automobile. If we counted the value of the parts used in making the car as well as the full value of the finished auto in the GDP, we would be engaging in **double counting**—adding the value of a good or service twice by mistakenly counting intermediate goods and services in GDP.

Measuring Gross Domestic Product

Economic output can be calculated primarily by two ways: the expenditure approach and the income approach. Although these methods differ, their result, GDP, is the same, apart from minor "statistical discrepancies." In the following two sections, we will examine each of these approaches in turn.

Production, Income, and the Circular Flow Model

When we calculate GDP in the economy, we are measuring the value of total production—our total expenditures. However, we are also measuring the value of total income because every dollar of spending by some buyer ends up being a dollar of income for some seller. In short, expenditures (spending) must equal income. And this is true whether it is a household, firm, or a government that buys the good or service. The main point in that when we spend (the value of total expenditure) it ends up as someone's income (the value of total income). Buyers have sellers.

In Exhibit 1, we reintroduce the circular flow model to show the flow of money in the economy. For example, households use some of their income to buy domestic goods and services and some to buy foreign goods and services (imports). Households also use some of their income to pay taxes and invest in financial markets (company shares, bonds, saving accounts, and other financial assets). When income flows into the financial system as saving, it makes it possible for consumers, firms, and governments to borrow. This market for saving and borrowing is vital to a well-functioning economy.

gross domestic product (GDP)
the measure of economic performance based on the value of all final goods and services produced in a country during a given period of time

double counting
adding the value of a good or service twice by mistakenly counting intermediate goods and services in GDP

© JANIS CHRISTIE/PHOTODISC/GETTY ONE IMAGES

The paper used in this book is an intermediate good; it is the book, the final good, that is included in the GDP.

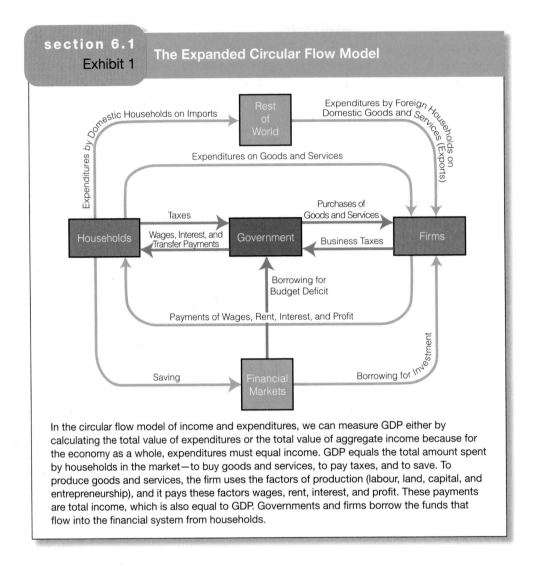

The Expanded Circular Flow Model

In the circular flow model of income and expenditures, we can measure GDP either by calculating the total value of expenditures or the total value of aggregate income because for the economy as a whole, expenditures must equal income. GDP equals the total amount spent by households in the market—to buy goods and services, to pay taxes, and to save. To produce goods and services, the firm uses the factors of production (labour, land, capital, and entrepreneurship), and it pays these factors wages, rent, interest, and profit. These payments are total income, which is also equal to GDP. Governments and firms borrow the funds that flow into the financial system from households.

Firms sell their goods and services to domestic and foreign consumers and foreign firms and governments. Firms use their factors of production (labour, land, capital, and entrepreneurship) to produce goods and services. Firms pay wages to workers, interest for the use of capital, and rent for land. Profits are the return to entrepreneurs for taking the risk of producing the goods and services. Wages, rent, interest, and profit comprise aggregate income in the economy. Governments provide transfer payments such as Employment Insurance payments. Whether we add up the aggregate expenditure on final goods and services, or the value of aggregate income (wages, rent, interest, and profit) we get the same GDP. For an economy as a whole, expenditures and income are the same. Actually, while the two should be exactly the same, there may be a slight variation because of data issues.

SECTION CHECK

- We measure our economy's status in order to see how its performance has changed over time. These economic measurements are important to government officials, private businesses, and investors.
- Gross domestic product (GDP) is the value of all final goods and services produced in a country during a given time period. The two different ways to measure GDP are the expenditure approach and the income approach.

section
6.2

The Expenditure Approach to Measuring GDP

- What is the expenditure approach to measuring GDP?
- What is consumption?
- What is investment
- What are government purchases?
- What are net exports?

WHAT IS THE EXPENDITURE APPROACH TO MEASURING GDP?

One approach to measuring GDP is the **expenditure approach.** With this method, GDP is calculated by adding up how much market participants spend on final goods and services over a period of time. For convenience and for analytical purposes, economists usually categorize spending into four categories: consumption, identified symbolically by the letter C; investment, I; government purchases, G; and net exports, which equals exports (X) minus imports (M), or $(X - M)$. Following the expenditure method, then

$$GDP = C + I + G + (X - M)$$

expenditure approach
calculation of GDP by adding up how much market participants spend on final goods and services over a period of time

WHAT IS CONSUMPTION?

Consumption refers to the purchase of consumer goods and services by households. For most of us, a large percentage of our income in a given year goes for consumer goods and services. The consumption category does not include purchases by business or government. As Exhibit 1 indicates, in 2010 consumption expenditures totalled $941 billion. This figure was 58 percent of GDP.

Consumption spending, in turn, is usually broken down into three subcategories: nondurable goods, durable goods, and services.

consumption
purchases of consumer goods and services by households

section 6.2
Exhibit 1　**2010 Canadian GDP by Type of Spending**

Category	Amount (billions of current dollars)	Percentage of GDP
Gross domestic product	$1625	
Consumption (*C*)	941	57.9%
Investment (*I*)	294	18.1
Government purchases (*G*)	421	25.9
Net exports of goods and services (*X − M*)	−31	−1.9

SOURCE:　Statistics Canada.

Nondurable and Durable Goods

Nondurable goods include tangible consumer items that are typically consumed or used up in a relatively short period of time. Food and pencils are examples, as are drugs, magazines, soap, razor blades, light bulbs, and so on. Nearly everything purchased in a supermarket or drugstore is a nondurable good.

Durable goods include longer-lived consumer goods, the most important single category of which is automobiles. Appliances, consumer electronics like DVD players, and furniture are also included in the durable goods category. On occasion, it is difficult to decide whether a good is durable or nondurable, and the definitions are, therefore, somewhat arbitrary.

The distinction between durables and nondurables is important because consumer buying behaviour is somewhat different for each of these categories of goods. In boom periods, when GDP is rising rapidly, expenditures on durables often increase dramatically, whereas in years of stagnant or falling GDP, sales of durable goods often plummet. By contrast, sales of nondurables like food tend to be more stable over time because purchases of such goods are more difficult to shift from one time period to another. You can "make do" with your car for another year, but not your lettuce.

Services

services
intangible items of value provided to consumers, such as haircuts

Services are intangible items of value provided to consumers, as opposed to physical goods. Legal services, dental services, recreational services, automobile repair, haircuts, airplane transportation—all of these are services. In recent years, service expenditures have been growing faster than spending on goods; the share of total consumption going for services is now over 50 percent. As incomes have risen, service industries such as health, education, financial, and recreation have grown dramatically.

WHAT IS INVESTMENT?

investment
the creation of capital goods to augment future production

Investment, as used by economists, refers to the creation of capital goods to augment future production, that is, inputs like machines and tools whose purpose is to produce other goods. This definition of investment deviates from the popular use of that term. It is common for people to say that they invested in stocks, meaning that they have traded money for a piece of paper, called a stock certificate, that says they own a share in some company. Such transactions are not investment as defined by economists (i.e., an increase in capital goods), even though they might provide the enterprises selling the shares with the resources for new capital goods, which *would* be counted as investment by economists.

There are two categories of investment purchases measured in the expenditures approach: fixed investment and inventory investment.

Fixed Investments

fixed investments
all new spending on capital goods by producers

producer goods
capital goods that increase future production capabilities

Fixed investments include all new spending on capital goods by producers—sometimes called **producer goods**—such as machinery, tools, and factory buildings. All of these goods increase future production capabilities. Residential construction is also included as an investment expenditure in GDP calculations. The construction of a house allows for a valuable consumer service—shelter—to be provided, and is thus considered an investment. Residential construction is the only part of investment that is tied directly to household expenditure decisions.

Inventory Investment

inventory investment
all purchases by businesses that add to the stocks of goods kept by the firm to meet consumer demand

Inventory investment includes all purchases by businesses that add to the stocks of goods kept by firms to meet customer demands. Every business needs inventory and, other things equal, the greater the inventory, the greater the amount of goods and services that can be sold to a consumer in the future. Thus, inventories are considered a form of investment. Consider a grocery store. If the store expands and increases the quantity and variety of goods on its shelves, future sales can rise. An increase in inventory, then, is presumed to increase the firm's future sales, and this is why we say it is an investment.

How Stable Are Investment Expenditures?

In recent years, investment expenditures have generally been around 20 percent of gross domestic product. Investment spending is the most volatile category of GDP, however, and tends to fluctuate considerably with changing business conditions. When the economy is booming, investment purchases tend to increase dramatically. In downturns, the reverse happens. In addition, investment expenditure often increases in advance of an economic recovery, as firms look to position themselves for the return of economic demand. Again, the opposite happens in economic downturns.

WHAT ARE GOVERNMENT PURCHASES?

Expenditures on goods and services are the government purchases that are included in GDP. For example, the government (which includes all four levels of government: federal, provincial/territorial, regional, and municipal) must pay the salaries of its employees, and it must also make payments to the private firms with which it contracts to provide various goods and services, such as highway construction companies and computer companies. All of these payments would be included in GDP. However, transfer payments (such as Employment Insurance benefits and Canada Pension Plan payments) are not included in government purchases because that spending does not go to purchase newly produced goods or services. Transfer payments are merely a transfer of income among that country's citizens (which is why such expenditures are called *transfer payments*). The government purchase proportion of GDP, at 26 percent, has grown over the last 50 years, in part because of rising spending on publicly funded health care.

WHAT ARE NET EXPORTS?

Some of the goods and services that are produced in Canada are exported for use in other countries. The fact that these goods and services were made in Canada means that they should be included in a measure of Canadian production. Thus, we include the value of exports when calculating GDP. At the same time, however, some of our expenditures in other categories (consumption and investment in particular) are for foreign-produced goods and services. These imports must be excluded from GDP in order to obtain an accurate measure of Canadian production. Thus, GDP calculations measure net exports, which equals total exports (X) minus total imports (M).

In 2010, Canada's net exports were $-$31 billion, or $-$2 percent of GDP. However, exports of goods and services themselves were $478 billion, or 29 percent of GDP. Likewise, imports of goods and services were $509 billion, or 31 percent of GDP. These numbers mean that about 29 percent of all Canadian production of goods and services is sold to foreigners, whereas about 31 percent of all Canadian expenditure is on foreign-produced goods and services. These high proportions reflect the fact that Canada is very much an "open" economy; that is, the Canadian economy is highly dependent on foreign

Business CONNECTION

DOES THE GDP HAVE TO BE AN EXACT MEASURE?

In macroeconomics, there is much discussion regarding the measuring of GDP. It is often observed that the existence of an underground economy leads to distortions in achieving more accurate measures of GDP, and how do you capture the value of nonmarket transactions such as homemade meals, housework, and home-grown vegetables and flowers in the measure of GDP? So, GDP may very well be understated. Should business disregard this key economic indicator?

A basic understanding of the composition of the GDP using the expenditure approach indicates four components: (1) the consumer spending of individual and households, (2) the capital spending by businesses, primarily to expand their productive capacity and build up inventory levels, (3) the spending by various levels of government, and (4) the spending by those who purchased goods and services produced by Canadians less the amounts spent by Canadians to purchase goods and services from abroad. While the exact measure of GDP may be in question, much insight may be gained from simply observing the direction and change in each component of GDP over time.

In Canada, spending by consumers accounts for over 55 percent of the GDP measure, using the expenditure approach. Those businesses with a significant reliance on consumer spending will have great interest, if not in the absolute magnitude of the GDP, at least in the change in the direction of this component. If at a point in time, economic growth—essentially increases in GDP—is expected to be fuelled primarily by increases in consumer spending, then businesses with a dependence on consumers can expect growth in demand for the consumer products they sell or produce, presenting an opportunity to increase revenues. At other times, the growth in GDP may be as a result of an increase in demand by foreign buyers for Canadian goods and services, often natural resources such as oil or lumber. When this is the case, those sectors of the economy can expect increases in revenues.

Another component of GDP, government spending, which accounts for some 22 percent of GDP expenditure, is somewhat constrained by government dependence on tax collections. Nevertheless, at times when it appears that economic growth might slow or the economy might dip into a recession (two consecutive periods of negative growth), governments often borrow funds to increase their capacity to spend, thereby mitigating a drop in economic growth. Here again, without contemplating the absolute measure or completeness of the GDP indicator, business operators can gain a sense of the economy's performance and the resulting implications for revenue growth and profits. Hence, the rate of change of GDP may be more significant than its absolute measure.

markets in terms of both buying and selling goods and services. In some years, the value of Canada's exports is greater than the value of its imports, net exports are a positive number, and Canada runs a trade surplus. However, in 2010, the value of imports exceeded the value of exports, net exports were a negative number, and Canada ran a trade deficit.

SECTION CHECK

- The expenditure approach to measuring GDP involves adding up the purchases of final goods and services by market participants. Four categories of spending are used in the GDP calculation: consumption (C), investment (I), government purchases (G), and net exports ($X - M$).
- Consumption includes spending on nondurable consumer goods—tangible items that are usually consumed in a short period of time; durable consumer goods—longer-lived consumer goods; and services—intangible items of value.
- Fixed investment includes all spending on capital goods, such as machinery, tools, and buildings. Inventory investment includes the net expenditures by businesses to increase their inventories.
- Purchases of goods and services are the only part of government spending included in GDP. Transfer payments are not included in these calculations because that spending is not a payment for a newly produced good or service.
- Net exports are calculated by subtracting total imports from total exports.

section
6.3

The Income Approach to Measuring GDP

- What is the income approach to measuring GDP?
- What do personal income and disposable income measure?

WHAT IS THE INCOME APPROACH TO MEASURING GDP?

In the last section, we outlined the expenditure approach to GDP calculation. There is, however, an alternative method called the income approach. The **income approach** is a calculation of GDP based on the summation of incomes received by the owners of resources used in the production of goods and services.

When someone makes an expenditure for a good or service, that spending creates income for someone else. For example, if you spend $10 on groceries at the local supermarket, your $10 of spending creates $10 in income for the grocery store owner. The owner, then, must buy more goods to stock her shelves as a consequence of your consumer purchases; in addition, she must pay her employees, her electricity bill, and so on. Consequently, much of the $10 spent by you will eventually end up in the hands of someone other than the grocer. The basic point, however, is that someone (one person or many) receives the $10 you spent, and that receipt of funds is called *income.* Therefore, by adding up all of the incomes received by producers of goods and services, we can also calculate the gross domestic product, because output creates income of equal value.

income approach
calculation of GDP based on the summation of incomes received by the owners of resources used in the production of goods and services

Factor Payments

Factor payments are the wages (salaries), rent, interest payments, and profits paid to the owners of productive resources; that is, the incomes received by people providing goods and services. Factor payments include wages for labour services; rent for land; payments for the use of capital goods in the form of interest; and profits for entrepreneurs who put labour, land, and capital together. Exhibit 1 presents the income approach to measuring GDP. Wages and salaries are the payment for labour services. They total $850 billion, or 52 percent of GDP. Corporate profits are the profits of corporations before tax. Interest income is the interest that households earn on loans they make minus the interest that households pay on their borrowing. Net income of farm and unincorporated businesses is the earnings of farmers and proprietors from their own businesses. The sum of these four categories of income is called **net domestic income at factor cost,** which totalled $1223 billion in 2010.

We have to make two adjustments to net domestic income at factor cost to arrive at GDP. Net domestic income is the cost of the factor payments, but GDP is the value of the output at market prices. Therefore, the first adjustment we have to make to net domestic income is to add indirect taxes and subtract subsidies. An indirect tax is a tax paid by consumers when they buy goods and services (such as provincial sales taxes, the GST, and excise taxes). Because of indirect taxes, the market price of a product bought by consumers (e.g., $1 plus 7 percent tax = $1.07) is greater than the factor payments to the owners of the resources who produced the good ($1). A subsidy is a payment by the government to producers (such as payments to airplane manufacturers or grain farmers). Because of subsidies, the market price of a product bought by consumers is less than the cost of the factor payments.

factor payments
wages (salaries), rent, interest payments, and profits paid to the owners of productive resources

net domestic income at factor cost
a measure of income earned by the owners of factors of production

2010 Canadian GDP by Type of Income

Category	Amount (billions of current dollars)	Percentage of GDP
Gross domestic product	$1625	
Wages and salaries	850	52.3%
Corporate profits before taxes	196	12.1
Interest income and other investment income	70	4.3
Net income of farm and unincorporated businesses	107	6.6
Indirect taxes less subsidies	173	10.6
Depreciation	229	14.1

SOURCE: Statistics Canada.

The second adjustment to net domestic income is to add depreciation (or capital consumption allowances). When firms purchase capital equipment, the cost of such goods must be allocated over the time that the capital equipment will be used, possibly 10 to 20 years for some types of equipment. The cost allocated, which is called *depreciation,* is an estimate of the amount of the equipment being used up each year in production. Depreciation is a cost of production and is included in the market value of output, but it is not part of any factor's income and is not included in net domestic income.

Adding indirect taxes less subsidies, $173 billion, and depreciation, $229 billion, to net domestic income at factor cost gives us GDP.

WHAT DO PERSONAL INCOME AND DISPOSABLE INCOME MEASURE?

personal income
the amount of income received by households before taxes

disposable income
the personal income available after taxes

Often, we are interested in the income people *receive* rather than the income they *earn,* because the income received reflects the total amount available for spending before taxes. **Personal income** measures the amount of income received by households (including transfer payments) before income taxes. **Disposable income** is the personal income available after taxes. Disposable income can be used by households in two ways: consumption or saving.

SECTION CHECK

- The income approach to measuring GDP involves adding together the incomes received by the producers of goods and services. These payments to the owners of productive resources are also known as *factor payments.* The income approach to GDP adds together wages and salaries, corporate profits, interest income, and net income of farm and unincorporated businesses to get net domestic income at factor cost. Adding indirect taxes less subsidies and depreciation to net domestic income gives us GDP.
- Personal income measures the amount of income received by households (including transfer payments) before taxes. Disposable income is the personal income available after taxes.

Issues with Calculating an Accurate GDP

- What are the problems with GDP in measuring output?
- How is real GDP calculated?
- What is real GDP per capita?

WHAT ARE THE PROBLEMS WITH GDP IN MEASURING OUTPUT?

The primary problem in calculating accurate GDP statistics becomes evident when attempts are made to compare the GDP over time. Between 1971 and 1976, a period of relatively high inflation, GDP in Canada rose over 100 percent. What great progress! Unfortunately, however, the measure used in adding together the values of different products, the Canadian dollar, also changed in value over this time period. A dollar in 1976, for example, would certainly not buy as much as a dollar in 1971, because the *overall* price level for goods and services increased.

One solution to this problem would be to use physical units of output—which, unlike the Canadian dollar, don't change in value from year to year—as our measure of total economic activity. The major problem with this approach is that different products have different units of measurement. How do you add together tonnes of steel, bushels of wheat, kilowatts of electricity, litres of paint, cubic metres of natural gas, kilometres of air passenger travel, number of games of bowling, and number of magazines sold? In order to compare GDP values over time, a common or standardized unit of measure, which only money can provide, must be used in the calculations.

The dollar, then, is the measure of value that we can use to correct the inflation-induced distortion of the GDP. We must adjust for the changing purchasing power of the dollar by constructing a price index. As we discussed in the last chapter, a price index attempts to provide a measure of the trend in prices paid for a certain bundle of goods and services over time. The price index can be used to deflate the nominal or current dollar GDP values to a real GDP expressed in dollars of constant purchasing power.

There are many different types of price indices. In the last chapter, we calculated the Consumer Price Index (CPI), which measures the trend in the prices of certain goods and services purchased for consumption purposes. The CPI may be the most relevant price index to households trying to evaluate their changing financial position over time. Another price index, the **GDP deflator,** corrects GDP statistics for changing prices. The GDP deflator is a price index that measures the average level of prices of all final goods and services produced in the economy.

GDP deflator
a price index that helps to measure the average price level of all final goods and services produced in the economy

HOW IS REAL GDP CALCULATED?

To correct the nominal or current dollar GDP values for inflation, the appropriate price index to use is the GDP deflator. Once the GDP deflator has been calculated, the actual procedure for adjusting nominal, or current dollar, GDP to get real GDP is not complicated. Remember, real GDP gives us a measure of GDP in constant dollars that have been corrected for inflation.

The formula for converting any year's nominal GDP into real GDP (in constant dollars) is as follows:

$$\text{Real GDP} = \frac{\text{Nominal GDP}}{\text{GDP deflator}} \times 100$$

Say, for example, the GDP deflator was expressed in terms of 2002 dollars (2002 = 100), and the GDP deflator for 2012 was 115. This means that prices were 15 percent higher in 2012 than they were in 2002. Now, in order to correct the 2012 nominal GDP, we take the nominal GDP figure for 2012, suppose it is $1000 billion, and divide it by the GDP deflator, 115, which results in a quotient of $8.695 billion. We then multiply this number by 100, giving us $869.5 billion, which is the 2012 GDP in 2002 dollars (that is, 2012 real GDP, in terms of a 2002 base year).

Exhibit 1 presents data on nominal GDP, real GDP, and the GDP deflator for the Canadian economy for the 2002–2010 period. The base year for the GDP deflator is 2002, so real GDP is expressed in billions of 2002 dollars. (You may want to calculate real GDP yourself in order to confirm your understanding of the adjustment process.) Notice that nominal GDP (in current dollars) increased from $1152.9 billion in 2002 to $1624.6 billion in 2010, an increase of 40.9 percent. However, over the same time period, the GDP deflator rose from 100.0 to 122.6, an increase of 22.6 percent. Thus, the average price level of all the final goods and services produced in the economy increased by 23 percent, meaning the economy experienced 23 percent inflation over this eight-year period. This inflation was one of the factors that led to the growth in nominal (current dollar) GDP. The other factor was growth in real GDP, or the economy's actual physical production of final goods and services. As we can see, real GDP (measured in 2002 dollars) increased from $1152.9 billion in 2002 to $1325.0 billion in 2010, an increase of 14.9 percent. This is the economy's "real" economic growth.

When there is inflation, the adjustment of nominal (current dollar) GDP to real GDP (measured in constant dollars) will reduce the growth in GDP suggested by the nominal GDP figures. Thus, it is important when comparing GDP over time that we use real GDP as our measure of the economy's production of final goods and services, as this measure corrects nominal GDP for the distortions caused by inflation.

section 6.4
Exhibit 1   Nominal GDP, Real GDP, and the GDP Deflator

Year	Nominal GDP (billions of current dollars)	GDP Deflator (2002 = 100)	Real GDP (billions of 2002 dollars)
2002	$1152.9	100.00	$1152.9
2003	1213.2	103.29	1174.6
2004	1290.9	106.58	1211.2
2005	1372.6	110.15	1246.1
2006	1450.5	112.90	1284.8
2007	1535.6	116.36	1319.7
2008	1603.4	121.44	1320.3
2009	1529.0	119.11	1283.7
2010	1624.6	122.61	1325.0

SOURCE: Statistics Canada.

WHAT IS REAL GDP PER CAPITA?

The measure of economic well-being, or standard of living, most often used is **real gross domestic product per capita**—real output of goods and services per person. We use a measure of real GDP for reasons already cited. To calculate real GDP per capita, we divide the real GDP by the total population to get the value of real output of final goods and services per person. *Ceteris paribus,* people prefer more goods to fewer, so a higher GDP per capita would seemingly make people better off, improving their standard of living. Economic growth, then, is usually considered to have occurred anytime the real GDP per capita has risen. In Exhibit 2, we see that in Canada, the real gross domestic product per capita more than doubled between 1971 and 2010. However, the growth in real GDP per capita was not steady, as seen by the shaded areas that represent recessions in Exhibit 2. Falling real GDP per capita can bring on many human hardships like rising unemployment, lower profits, stock market losses, and bankruptcies. Note, in particular, the prolonged stagnation in standard of living during the early 1990s, when real GDP per capita was at the same level in 1994 as it was in 1989.

Because one purpose of using GDP is to relate output to human desires, we need to adjust for population change. If we do not take population growth into account, we can

real gross domestic product per capita
real output of goods and services per person

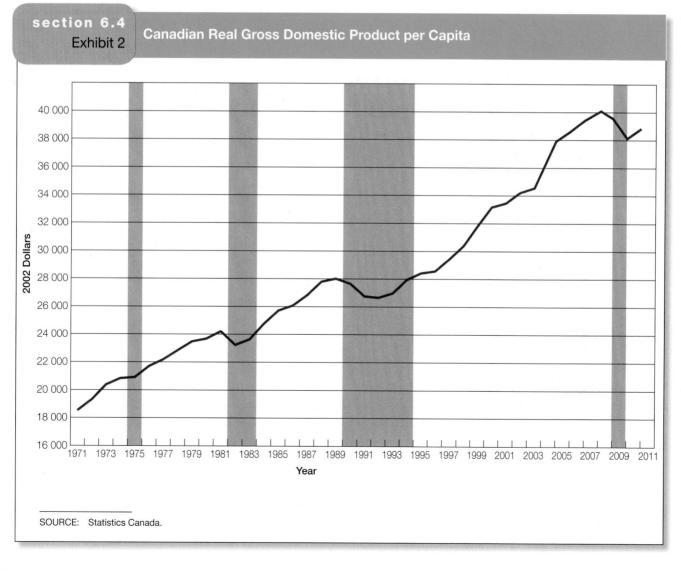

section 6.4
Exhibit 2   **Canadian Real Gross Domestic Product per Capita**

SOURCE: Statistics Canada.

be misled by changes in real GDP values. For example, in some less-developed countries in some time periods, real GDP has risen by perhaps 2 percent a year but the population has grown just as fast. In these cases, the real output of goods and services per person has remained virtually unchanged, but this would not be apparent in an examination of real GDP trends alone.

SECTION CHECK

- It is difficult to compare nominal GDP over time because of the changing value of money over time.
- The GDP deflator is a price index that measures the average level of prices of all final goods and services produced in the economy. It is used to convert nominal measures of GDP into equivalent real measures of GDP.
- Per capita real GDP is the real output of goods and services per person. In some cases, real GDP may increase but per capita real GDP may actually drop as a result of population growth.

section 6.5

Problems with GDP as a Measure of Economic Welfare

- What are some of the deficiencies of GDP as a measure of economic welfare?

WHAT ARE SOME OF THE DEFICIENCIES OF GDP AS A MEASURE OF ECONOMIC WELFARE?

As we have noted earlier, real GDP is often used as a measure of the economic welfare of a nation. The accuracy of this measure for that purpose is, however, questionable because several important factors are excluded from its calculations. These factors include non-market transactions, the underground economy, leisure, externalities, and the quality of the goods purchased.

Nonmarket Transactions

Nonmarket transactions include the provision of goods and services outside of traditional markets for which no money is exchanged. We simply do not have reliable enough information on this output to include it in the GDP. The most important single nonmarket transaction omitted from the GDP is the work of housewives (or househusbands). These services are not sold in any market, so they are not entered into the GDP, but they are nonetheless performed. For example, if a single woman hires a tax accountant, those payments enter into the calculation of GDP. Suppose, though, that the woman marries her tax accountant. Now the woman no longer pays her husband for his accounting services. Reported GDP falls after the marriage, although output does not change.

In less-developed countries, where a significant amount of food and clothing output is produced in the home, the failure to include nonmarket economic activity in GDP is a serious deficiency. Even in Canada, homemade meals, housework, and the vegetables and flowers produced in home gardens are excluded, even though they clearly represent an output of goods and services.

The Underground Economy

It is impossible to know for sure the magnitude of the underground economy, which includes unreported income from both legal and illegal sources. For example, illegal drug dealing and prostitution are not included in the GDP, leading to underreporting of an unknown dimension. The reason these activities are excluded, however, has nothing to do with the morality of the services performed, but rather results from the fact that the payments made for these services are not reported to governmental authorities. Likewise, cash payments made to employees "under the table" slip through the GDP net. The estimates of the size of the underground economy vary from 5 to 15 percent of GDP. It also appears that a good portion of this unreported income comes from legal sources, such as self-employment.

Are her household production efforts included in GDP? If a family hires someone to clean the house, provide child care, mow the lawn, or cook, this is included in GDP; when members of the household provide these services, it is not. Neglecting household production in GDP distorts measurements of economic growth and leads to potential policy problems. Is it time to include household activities in GDP? An estimate of the value of these services could be obtained by calculating the cost to buy these services in the marketplace.

Measuring the Value of Leisure

The value that individuals place on leisure is omitted in calculating GDP. Most of us could probably get a part-time job if we wanted to, earning some additional money by working in the evening or on weekends. Yet we choose not to do so. Why? The opportunity cost is too high—we would have to forgo some leisure. If you work on Saturday nights, you cannot visit your friends, go to parties, see concerts, watch television, or go to the movies. The opportunity cost of the leisure is the income forgone by not working. For example, if people start taking more three-day weekends, GDP will surely fall, but can we necessarily say that the standard of living will fall? GDP will fall but economic well-being may rise.

Leisure, then, has a positive value that does not show up in the GDP accounts. To put leisure in the proper perspective, ask yourself if you would rather live in Country A, which has a per capita GDP of $25 000 a year and a 30-hour work week, or Country B, with a $25 000 per capita GDP and a 50-hour work week. Most would choose Country A. The problem that this omission in GDP poses can be fairly significant in international comparisons, or when one looks at one nation over time.

GDP and Externalities

Economists have observed that side effects can accompany the production of some goods and services. These additional impacts (in the form of either benefits or costs) are referred to as *externalities*. As a result of these positive and negative externalities, the equilibrium prices of goods and services—the figures used in GDP calculations—do not reflect their true value to society (unless the externality has been internalized).

Quality of Goods

GDP calculations can also miss important improvements in the *quality* of goods and services. For example, there is a huge difference between the quality of a computer bought today and one that was bought ten years ago, but it will not lead to an increase in measured GDP. The same is true of many goods, from cellular phones to automobiles to medical care.

DEBATE

SHOULD THE GOVERNMENT WORRY ABOUT THE UNDERGROUND ECONOMY?

The underground economy develops due to high tax rates imposed on citizens by their governments. Left unreported, underground economy activity leads to underestimation of the economic activity taking place in the country, underrepresents employment rates, and represents lost tax revenues for governments. Governments struggle to control the amount of unreported economic activity taking place within their borders, including such measures as the Canadian government's encouragement on its Statistics Canada website for citizens to blow the whistle on underground economy activity.

Some argue that governments should just forget about the underground economy as it is not significant, while others argue that governments ignore these economies at their peril. For the sake of debate, governments have to support the legal economy and do everything possible to eliminate the underground economy.

Pro:

Most well-run economies are based on the trust that citizens have in the system. Those who earn income are expected to pay taxes on those earnings. When citizens believe the system is fair and have an expectation that cheaters will be punished, it provides a solid foundation for a well-run economy. Over the long run, the costs of running the system are less because individuals police themselves. In addition, for those who cheat by not paying taxes, the penalties are stern. What are other reasons why a government needs to restrict the growth of underground economies?

Con:

Underground economies are a fact of life—people will always find ways to avoid paying taxes. The major consideration should not be complete elimination, but controlling such activity to ensure that it doesn't get out of hand. Many would argue that monitoring and enforcement costs outweigh the loss of tax revenue. Further, it is impossible to completely eliminate underground economies simply because they are underground—governments don't know where they exist! Can you think of other reasons why it doesn't make sense for governments to worry about underground economies?

SECTION CHECK

- Several factors make it difficult to use GDP as a welfare indicator, including nonmarket transactions, the underground economy, leisure, and externalities. Nonmarket transactions are the exchanges of goods and services that do not occur in traditional markets, and so no money is exchanged. The underground economy is the unreported production and income that come from legal and illegal activities. The presence of positive and negative externalities also make it difficult to measure GDP accurately.

For Your Review

Section 6.1

1. Which of the following are included in Canadian GDP calculations?
   a. cleaning services performed by a cleaning company
   b. washing your own car
   c. drugs sold illegally on a local street corner
   d. prescription drugs manufactured in Canada and sold at a local pharmacy

e. a rug woven by hand in Turkey

f. air pollution that diminishes the quality of the air you breathe

g. toxic waste cleanup performed by a local company

h. car parts manufactured in Canada for assembly of a car in Mexico

i. a purchase of 1000 shares in a Canadian-owned high-tech company

j. a monthly Canada Pension Plan payment received by a retiree

2. Answer the following questions about GDP.

a. What is the definition of GDP?

b. Why does GDP measure only the final value of goods and services?

c. Why does GDP measure only the value of goods and services produced within a country?

d. How does GDP treat the sales of used goods?

e. How does GDP treat sales of corporate shares from one shareholder to another?

3. Explain how the determination of GDP via the expenditure approach is equivalent to the determination of GDP via the income approach.

4. The expenditures on tires by the Ford Motor Company of Canada are not included directly in GDP statistics, whereas consumer expenditures on replacement tires are included. Why?

Section 6.2

5. To which Canadian GDP expenditure category does each of the following correspond?

a. Ministry of Transportation snow-clearing services

b. automobiles exported to Europe

c. a refrigerator

d. a newly constructed four-bedroom house

e. a restaurant meal

f. additions to inventory at a furniture store

g. purchases of new computers by Statistics Canada

h. a new steel mill

6. Using any relevant information below, calculate GDP via the expenditure approach.

Inventory investment	$ 50 billion
Fixed investment	120 billion
Consumer durables	420 billion
Consumer nondurables	275 billion
Interest	140 billion
Indirect business taxes	45 billion
Government wages and salaries	300 billion
Government purchases of goods and services	110 billion
Imports	80 billion
Exports	40 billion
Profits	320 billion
Consumer services	600 billion

7. Fill in the missing data for the following table (in millions).

Consumption	_____
Consumption of durable goods	$1200
Consumption of nondurable goods	1800
Consumption of services	2400
Investment	_____
Fixed investment	800
Inventory investment	600
Government expenditures on goods and services	1600
Government transfer payments	500
Exports	500
Imports	650
Net exports	_____
GDP	_____

8. Answer these questions about durable goods and GDP:

   a. Do consumer nondurable or durable goods tend to change more over the course of a business cycle?

   b. How are consumer durables like investments?

   c. Can either fixed investment or inventory be negative in a given year?

   d. Why isn't all of government spending part of GDP?

Section 6.3

9. What basic principle proves that the income approach to calculating gross domestic product is valid?

10. Following is a list of national income figures for a given year. All figures are in millions. Using this data, determine GDP by both the expenditure and income approaches. The answer arrived at by each method should be the same.

Government current purchases of goods and services	$ 60
Indirect taxes (less subsidies)	35
Wages, salaries, and supplemental labour income	195
Corporation profits before taxes	62
Exports	10
Net income of nonfarm unincorporated business	16
Gross investment	100
Undistributed corporate profits	12
Interest income and other investment income	15
Capital consumption allowances (depreciation)	32
Net investment	68
Net income of farmers	5
Imports	20
Personal consumption expenditures	210

Section 6.4

11. Nominal GDP in Nowhereland in 2010 and 2011 was as follows:

Nominal GDP 2010	Nominal GDP 2011
$400 billion	$440 billion

Can you say that the production of goods and services in Nowhereland increased between 2010 and 2011? Why or why not?

12. Calculate real GDP for the years 2007 to 2011 using the following information:

Year	Nominal GDP (in billions)	GDP Deflator	Real GDP
2007	$720	100	
2008	750	102	
2009	800	110	
2010	900	114	
2011	960	120	

What was the real economic growth rate in 2011?

13. Fill in the missing data in the following table.

Year	GDP Deflator	Nominal GDP (in billions)	Real GDP (in billions)
2007	90.9	$700	
2008	100.0		$800
2009		1000	800
2010	140.0	1400	
2011	150.0		1200

14. Population and real GDP in Country A are as follows:

Year	Population (in millions)	Real GDP (in millions)
1990	1.25	$4000
2000	1.60	6750
2010	1.80	9000

Calculate real GDP per capita in 1990, 2000, and 2010. Does real output per person increase or decrease over time?

Section 6.5

15. Answer these questions about GDP:

    a. Could next year's real GDP exceed next year's nominal GDP?

    b. Could real GDP grow at the same time that real GDP per capita falls?

    c. Could people's real consumption possibilities expand at the same time that real GDP per capita falls?

    d. How does changing the amount of leisure complicate comparisons of real well-being over time?

16. Evaluate the following statement: "Real GDP in the United States is higher than real GDP in Canada. Therefore, the standard of living in the United States must be higher than in Canada."

CourseMate

Access an interactive eBook and chapter-specific interactive learning tools, including flashcards, quizzes, a glossary, and more in CourseMate, accessed through **www.sextonmacro3ce.nelson.com**

chapter

7

Economic Growth in the Global Economy

Economic Growth

- How does economic growth differ from the business cycle?
- What is economic growth?
- What is the Rule of 70?

HOW DOES ECONOMIC GROWTH DIFFER FROM THE BUSINESS CYCLE?

John Maynard Keynes, one of the most influential economic thinkers of all time, once said that "in the long run, we are all dead." Keynes said this because he was primarily concerned with explaining and reducing short-term fluctuations in the level of business activity. He wanted to smooth out the business cycle, largely because of the implications that cyclical fluctuations had for buyers and sellers in terms of unemployment and price instability. No one would deny that Keynes's concerns were important and legitimate.

At the same time, however, Keynes's flippant remark about the long run ignores the fact that human welfare is greatly influenced by long-term changes in a nation's capacity to produce goods and services. Emphasis on short-run economic fluctuations ignores the longer-term dynamic changes that affect output, leisure, real incomes, and lifestyles.

Economists distinguish between the short-run variations in economic activity that they call *business cycles* and long-run economic growth. In Chapter 5, we discussed the short-run economic fluctuations of business cycles. Here in Chapter 7, our focus will be on the long-run trend rate of growth—that is, economic growth. Exhibit 1 is provided to distinguish between short-run economic fluctuations and long-run economic growth.

section 7.1
Exhibit 1

Short-Run versus Long-Run Economic Growth

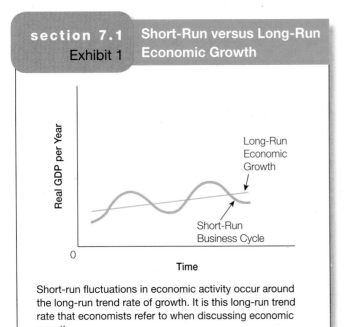

Short-run fluctuations in economic activity occur around the long-run trend rate of growth. It is this long-run trend rate that economists refer to when discussing economic growth.

section 7.1
Exhibit 2

Economic Growth and the Shifting Production Possibilities Curve

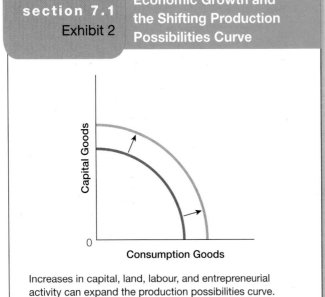

Increases in capital, land, labour, and entrepreneurial activity can expand the production possibilities curve.

economic growth
an upward trend in the real per capita output of goods and services

What are the determinants of long-run economic growth? What are some of the consequences of rapid economic change? Why are some nations rich whereas others are poor? Does growth in output improve our economic welfare? These are a few questions that we need to explore.

WHAT IS ECONOMIC GROWTH?

Economic growth refers to an upward trend in the real per capita output of goods and services (real GDP per capita). In Chapter 2, we introduced the production possibilities curve. Along the production possibilities curve, the economy is producing at its potential output. How much the economy will produce at its potential output, sometimes called its *natural rate of output,* depends on the quantity and quality of an economy's resources, including labour, capital (like factories, machinery, and tools), land (fish, lumber, and so on), and entreprenurial activity. In addition, technology can increase the economy's production capabilities. As shown in Exhibit 2, improvements in and greater stocks of land, labour, capital, and entrepreneurial activity will shift the production possibilities curve outward. Another way of saying that economic growth has shifted the production possibilities curve outward is to say that it has increased potential output.

WHAT IS THE RULE OF 70?

If Nation A and Nation B start off with the same size population and the same level of real GDP but grow at only slightly different rates over a long period of time, will it make much of a difference? Yes. In the first year or two, the differences will be small but even over a decade, the differences will be large and, after 50 to 100 years, the differences will be huge. The final impact will be a much higher standard of living in the nation with the greater economic growth, *ceteris paribus.*

A simple formula, called the *Rule of 70,* shows how long it will take a nation to double its output at various growth rates. If you take a nation's growth rate and divide it into 70, you will have the approximate time it will take to double the income level. For example, if a nation grows at 3.5 percent per year, then the economy will double every 20 years (70/3.5). However, if an economy grows at only 2 percent per year, then the economy will double every 35 years (70/2). And at a 1 percent annual growth rate, it will take 70 years to double income (70/1). So even a small change in the growth rate of a nation will have a large impact over a lengthy period.

Exhibit 3 shows that Canadian real GDP per capita (measured in 2002 dollars) grew from $14 475 in 1961 to $38 846 in 2010. That is, Canadians today, on average, can purchase nearly three times the amount of goods and services purchased 50 years ago.

Due to the differences in growth rates, some countries will become richer than others over time. With relatively slower economic growth, today's richest countries will not be the richest for very long. On the other hand, with even slight improvements in economic growth,

Canadian Real Gross Domestic Product per Capita

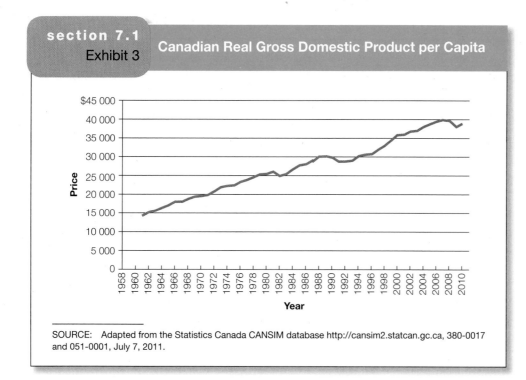

SOURCE: Adapted from the Statistics Canada CANSIM database http://cansim2.statcan.gc.ca, 380-0017 and 051-0001, July 7, 2011.

today's poorest countries will not remain poor for very long. China and India have both experienced spectacular economic growth over the past 20 years. Because of this economic growth, much of the world is now poorer than these two heavily populated countries, although Ireland, once one of the poorest countries in Western Europe, is now one of the richest. Disappointing growth rates over the past 30 years have left Argentina's economy and standard of living unchanged for a quarter of a century.

In Exhibit 4, we see the growth rates in real per capita GDP for selected industrial countries. In Canada's case, our growth rate in the 1989–1998 period was the worst of the seven countries listed; however, our growth rate rebounded in the 1999–2010 period, surpassing that of the United States. In order to close the gap in standard of living with the United States, Canada's growth in real GDP per capita must exceed that of the United States.

Because of past economic growth, the "richest" or "most-developed" countries today have many times the market output per person of the "poorest" or "least-developed" countries. Put differently, the most-developed countries produce and market more output per person per day than the least-developed countries do in a year. The international differences in income, output, and wealth are indeed striking and have caused a great deal of friction between developed and less-developed countries. Canada, the United States, Japan, and the nations of the European Union have had sizable increases in real output over the past two centuries, but even in 1900 most of these nations were better off in terms of real GDP per capita than impoverished countries such as Ethiopia, India, or Nepal are today.

China and India

Both China and India have per capita real GDP levels that are far less than Canada, but the current rate of economic

Growth in Real per Capita GDP, Selected Industrial Countries

	Period Averages	
	1989–1998	**1999–2010**
Canada	0.9%	1.7%
United States	1.8	1.4
Japan	1.7	1.0
Germany	1.8	1.1
France	1.4	1.1
Italy	1.5	0.6
United Kingdom	1.7	1.5

SOURCE: World Economic Outlook, April 2011. International Monetary Fund. Printed by permission from the International Monetary Fund.

growth in these two countries will change things in the future. India experienced an average growth rate of almost 9 percent per year from 2003–2008. While the economic growth rate slowed in 2008–2009 as India felt the effect of the global financial crisis, by 2010 the Indian economy had recorded economic growth of over 10 percent. India has a highly educated English-speaking population and is a major exporter of software workers and software services.

China is growing at about 10 percent per year. Foreign investment in China has helped to spur output of both domestic and export goods. China grew only 9 percent in 2008, its slowest growth rate since 2001. The global financial crisis had a larger impact on China than India because China's economy is more heavily reliant on exports. Exports account for about one-third of China's GDP. Since economic liberalization began in 1978, China's investment and export-led economy has grown 70 times larger and is the fastest-growing major economy in the world. China has the world's third-largest nominal GDP, although its per capita income is still low, surpassed by roughly a hundred other countries. The rapid economic growth in both India and China has pulled millions out of poverty.

SECTION CHECK

- *Economic growth* refers to the long-run trend rate of growth for an economy. *Business cycle* refers to the short-run fluctuation in economic activity around this trend rate of growth.
- Economic growth is usually measured by the annual percentage change in real output of goods and services per capita. Improvements in and greater stocks of land, labour, capital, and entrepreneurial activity will lead to greater economic growth and shift the production possibilities curve outward.
- According to the Rule of 70, if you take a nation's growth rate and divide it into 70, you have the approximate time it will take to double the income level.

section 7.2 Determinants of Economic Growth

- What factors contribute to economic growth?

productivity
the amount of goods and services a worker can produce per hour

Will the standard of living in Canada rise, level off, or even decline over time? The answer depends on productivity growth. **Productivity** is the amount of goods and services a worker can produce per hour. Productivity is especially important because it determines a country's standard of living. For example, slow growth of capital investment can lead to lower labour productivity and, consequently, lower wages. On the other hand, increases in productivity and higher wages can occur as a result of carefully crafted economic policies, such as tax policies that stimulate investment or programs that encourage research and development.

The link between productivity and the standard of living can most easily be understood by recalling our circular flow model in Section 6.1. The circular flow model showed that aggregate expenditures are equal to aggregate income. In other words, the aggregate values of all final goods and services produced in the economy must equal the payments made to the factors of production—the wages and salaries paid to workers, the interest payment to capital, the profits, and so on. That is, the only way an economy can increase its rate of consumption in the long run is if it increases the amount it produces. But why are some countries so much better than others at producing goods and services? We will see the answer in this section as we examine the determinants of productivity—quantity and quality of labour resources, land, physical capital, and technological advances.

WHAT FACTORS CONTRIBUTE TO ECONOMIC GROWTH?

Many explanations of the process of economic growth have been proposed. Which is correct? None of them, by themselves, can completely explain economic growth. However, each of the explanations may be part of a more complicated reality. Economic growth is a complex process involving many important factors, not one of which completely dominates. We can list at least several factors that nearly everyone would agree have contributed to economic growth in some or all countries:

1. The quantity and quality of labour resources (labour and human capital)
2. Increase in the use of inputs provided by the land (natural resources)
3. Physical capital inputs (machines, tools, buildings, inventories)
4. Technological knowledge (new ways of combining given quantities of labour, natural resources, and capital inputs), allowing greater output than previously possible

Labour

We know that labour is needed in all forms of productive activity. But other things being equal, an increase in the quantity of labour inputs does not necessarily increase output per capita. For example, if the increase in the quantity of labour input is due to an increase in population, per capita growth might not occur because the increase in output could be offset by the increase in population. However, if a greater proportion of the population works (i.e., the labour force participation rate rises) or if workers put in longer hours, output per capita will increase—assuming that the additional work activity adds something to output.

Qualitative improvements in workers (learning new skills, for example) can also enhance output. Indeed, it has become popular to view labour skills as **human capital**—the productive knowledge and skill that people receive from education and on-the-job training. Human capital has to be produced like physical capital with teachers, schoolrooms, libraries, computer labs, and time devoted to studying. Human capital may be more important than physical capital as a determinant of economic growth. It certainly can increase labour productivity. Human capital also includes improvements in health. Better health and healthy conditions allow workers to be more productive.

human capital
the productive knowledge and skill people receive from education and on-the-job training

Natural Resources

The abundance of natural resources, like fertile soils, and other raw materials, like lumber and oil, can enhance output. Many scholars have cited the abundance of natural resources in Canada as one reason for its historical economic success. Resources are, however, not the whole story, as is clear with reference to Japan or especially Hong Kong, both of which have had tremendous success with relatively few natural resources. Similarly, Brazil has a large and varied natural resource base yet its income per capita is relatively low compared to many developed countries. It appears that a natural resource base can affect the initial development process but sustained growth is influenced by other factors. However, most economists would agree that a limited resource base does pose an important obstacle to economic growth.

Physical Capital

Recall that physical capital (or just capital) includes goods like tools, machinery, and factories that have already been produced and are now producing other goods and services. Combining workers with more capital makes workers more productive. Thus, capital investment can lead to increases in labour productivity. Even in primitive economies, workers usually have some rudimentary tools to further their productive activity. Take the farmer who needs to dig a ditch to improve drainage in his fields. If he used just his bare hands, it might take years to complete the job. If he used a shovel, he could dig the ditch in hours or days. But with a big earthmoving machine, he could do it in minutes. There is nearly universal agreement that capital formation has played a significant role in the economic development of nations.

Technological Advances

innovation

applications of new knowledge that create new products or improve existing products

Countries that do not keep up with technology will generally be unable to keep up their economic growth and standard of living. If a country is technologically backward, it will lose global competitiveness and often rely on a narrow range of exports that will eventually lose their profitability in the global economy. For example, a country that relies on exporting copper may lose its market as other countries around the world convert their phone and cable lines to fibre optics.

Most economists believe that progress in technology drives productivity, that technology allows workers to produce more. Technological change can lead to better machinery and equipment, increases in capital, and better organization and production methods. Technological advances stem from human ingenuity and creativity in developing new ways of combining the factors of production to enhance the amount of output from a given quantity of resources. The process of technological advance involves invention and innovation. **Innovation** refers to the application of new knowledge that creates new products or improves existing products. For example, the invention and innovation of the combine machine in agriculture, the assembly line in manufacturing, and the railroad were important stimuli to economic growth. New technology, however, must be introduced into productive use by managers or entrepreneurs who must weigh the perceived estimates of benefits of the new technology against estimates of costs. Thus, the entrepreneur is an important economic factor in the growth process.

Technological advance permits us to economize on one or more inputs used in the production process. It can permit savings of labour, such as when a new machine does the work of many workers. When this happens, technology is said to be embodied in capital and to be labour saving. Technology, however, can also be land (natural resource) saving or even capital saving. For example, nuclear fission has permitted us to build power plants that economize on the use of coal, a natural resource. The reduction in transportation time that accompanied the invention of the railroad allowed businesses to reduce the capital they needed for inventories. Because goods could be obtained more quickly, businesses could reduce the stock kept on their shelves.

© LAWRENCE LOWERY/PHOTODISC/GETTY ONE IMAGES

And inventions can come in all sizes. Obviously, the semiconductor chip made a huge impact on productivity and growth, but so did the Post-it Note that was introduced in the early 1980s, the laptop computer, and barcode scanners, which were first introduced in Walmart stores. We have also seen huge advances in communication (the Internet) and medicines.

In short, better methods of organization and production can lead to increases in labour productivity. When fewer workers are needed in a grocery store or a department store due to better methods of organization, or new machinery and equipment, labour productivity rises.

SECTION CHECK

■ The factors that contribute to economic growth are the same factors that determine growth in productivity. They include increased quantity and quality of labour, natural resources, physical capital, and technological advances.

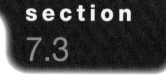

Public Policy and Economic Growth

section 7.3

■ Why is the saving rate so important to economic growth?
■ Why are research and development so important to economic growth?
■ Why are property rights so important to economic growth?
■ What impact will free trade have on economic growth?
■ Why is education so important to economic growth?

Economic growth means more than an increase in the real income (output) of the population. A number of other important changes accompany changes in output. Some have even claimed that economic growth stimulates political freedom or democracy, but the correlation here is far from conclusive. Although there are rich democratic societies and poor authoritarian ones, the opposite also holds. That is, some features of democracy, such as majority voting and special-interest groups, may actually be growth retarding. For example, if the majority decides to vote in large land reforms and wealth transfers, this will lead to higher taxes and market distortions that will reduce incentives for work, investment, and ultimately economic growth. However, there are a number of policies that a nation can pursue to increase economic growth.

WHY IS THE SAVING RATE SO IMPORTANT TO ECONOMIC GROWTH?

One of the most important determinants of economic growth is the saving rate. In order to consume more in the future, we must save more now. Generally speaking, higher levels of saving will lead to higher rates of investment and capital formation and, therefore, to greater economic growth. Individuals can either consume or save their disposable income. If individuals choose to consume all of their disposable income, there will be nothing left for saving, which businesses could use for investment purposes to build new plants or replace worn-out or obsolete equipment. With little investment in capital stock, there will be little economic growth. Capital can also increase as a result of capital injections from abroad (foreign direct investments), but the role of national saving rates in economic growth is of particular importance.

**Saving Rates and GDP Growth during
High-Growth Periods in Selected Economies**

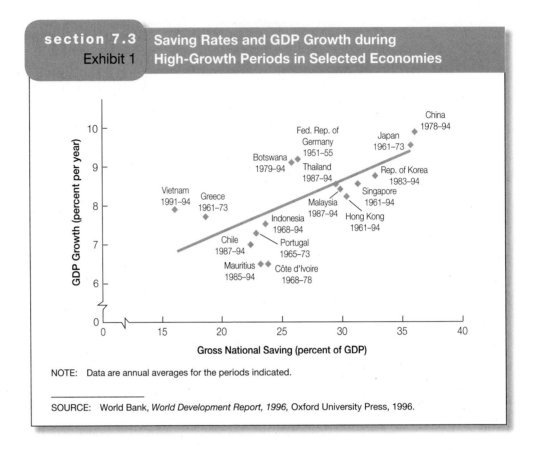

NOTE: Data are annual averages for the periods indicated.

SOURCE: World Bank, *World Development Report, 1996,* Oxford University Press, 1996.

Exhibit 1 clearly shows that sustained rapid economic growth is associated with high rates of saving and investment around the world. However, investment alone does not guarantee economic growth. Economic growth hinges on the quality and the type of investment as well as on investments in human capital and improvements in technology.

WHY ARE RESEARCH AND DEVELOPMENT SO IMPORTANT TO ECONOMIC GROWTH?

Some scholars believe that the importance of research and development is understated. **Research and development (R&D)** are activities that are undertaken to create new products and processes that will lead to technological progress. The concept of R&D is broad indeed—it can include new products, management improvements, production innovations, or simply learning-by-doing. However, it is clear that investing in R&D and rewarding innovators with patents have paid big dividends in the past 50 to 60 years. Some would argue that even larger rewards for research and development would spur even more rapid economic growth. In addition, an important link exists between research and development and capital investment. As already noted, when capital depreciates over time, it is replaced with new equipment that embodies the latest technology. Consequently, R&D may work hand in hand with investment to improve growth and productivity. Lastly, there is the benefit of R&D to foreign countries to consider as they import goods and services from technologically advanced countries. Adoption or adaptation of some of these advances might make their firms more efficient.

**research and
development (R&D)**
*activities undertaken to create
new products and processes
that will lead to technological
progress*

Business CONNECTION

ECONOMIC GROWTH: A LEADING ROLE FOR ENTREPRENEURS

What can an individual business do to contribute to economic growth? If economic growth is considered to be the annual percentage change in the real output of goods and services per capita, then in order to achieve economic growth, a country needs to produce more goods and services per person. In essence it needs to improve its productivity. To do so, it must increase the value of its outputs relative to its inputs.

Entrepreneurship, a very important factor of production, is the input that drives innovation, leading to the development and creation of new goods and services. It is also the factor that determines the mix of the other factors and the processes to be used in creating new and more valuable goods and services. This catalyst for economic growth—entrepreneurship—resides in new and existing business ventures.

Now, while entrepreneurship is a precondition for achieving economic growth, a number of other soft and hard infrastructure supports must also be present. These include the general economic environment in which business is conducted, domestic laws and regulations, institutions such as banks and venture capitalists, intensive research and development efforts, high-quality educational institutions such as universities and colleges, affordable and accessible health-care facilities, and international trade agreements.

To produce goods and services of higher value leading to increases in GDP, entrepreneurs will need the traditional factors of production: capital, labour, and natural resources,

along with information. Regarding capital, countries with relatively high saving rates are able to supply the demand for capital funding at reasonable costs via an infrastructure of banks, venture capital groups, and other financing institutions. Entrepreneurs' demand for labour is reflected in the need to fill high-skill jobs with capable knowledge workers across new and emerging technologies. Along with the challenges of capital labour, and natural resources, entrepreneurs need information resources to understand and respond to markets and to manage the process of transforming the factors of production into highly desirable goods and services.

Accessible health care plays an important role in maintaining a healthy workforce and in reducing worker absenteeism, a negative impact on productivity. As entrepreneurs and other business operators frequently contribute to the cost of maintaining the health-care infrastructure for their workers, they will have concerns about its cost and overall effectiveness. Improvements in technology have consistently led to increases in productivity. Such improvements invariably emerge from a culture of intensive research and development supported by a network of universities and colleges. Finally, international trade agreements that reduce or eliminate quantitative restrictions such as tariffs and quotas allow entrepreneurs access to new, often larger, scalable markets.

Clearly, if countries are to achieve economic growth, a prime macroeconomic goal, entrepreneurs will play an important role.

WHY ARE PROPERTY RIGHTS SO IMPORTANT TO ECONOMIC GROWTH?

Economic growth rates tend to be higher in countries where the government enforces property rights. Property rights give owners the legal right to keep or sell their property—land, labour, or capital. In addition, intellectual property (IP) rights are the legal rights that result from intellectual activity in the industrial, scientific, literary, and artistic fields. IP rights protection can take many forms; patents, copyrights, and trademarks are some examples. Without property and IP rights, life would be a huge free-for-all, where people could take whatever they wanted; in this scenario, protection for private property, such as alarm systems and private security services, would have to be purchased and intellectual property would be fair game for anyone. Economists call the government's ability to protect private property and IP rights and to enforce contracts the *rule of law*.

In most developed countries, property and IP rights are effectively protected by the government. However, in developing countries, this is not usually the case, and if the government is not enforcing these rights, the private sector must respond in costly ways that stifle economic growth. For example, an unreliable judiciary system means that entrepreneurs are often forced to rely on informal agreements that are difficult to enforce. As a result, they may have to pay bribes to get things done, and even then, they may not get the promised

services. Individuals will have to buy private security or pay organized crime for protection against crime and corruption. In addition, landowners and business owners might be fearful of coups or takeovers from a new government, which might confiscate their property altogether. In short, if government is not adequately protecting property and IP rights, the incentive to invest will be hindered, and political instability, corruption, and lower rates of economic growth will be likely.

Free trade and a stable monetary environment are important to economic growth, but governance is important too. The government has to protect private property and individual rights and enforce contracts, otherwise globalization can lead to corruption and violence. Russians have high levels of education, but the failure of the legal system has led to a dismal economic performance.

WHAT IMPACT WILL FREE TRADE HAVE ON ECONOMIC GROWTH?

Allowing free trade can also lead to greater output because of the principle of comparative advantage. Essentially, the principle of comparative advantage suggests that if two nations or individuals with different resource endowments and production capabilities specialize in producing a smaller number of goods and services and engage in trade, both parties will benefit. Total output and consumption will rise. This will be discussed in greater detail in Chapter 14. However, it is important to note that for a country like Canada, which is a significantly open economy that trades considerably with the rest of the world, international trade has played a central role in its economic growth over the last half-century.

WHY IS EDUCATION SO IMPORTANT TO ECONOMIC GROWTH?

Education, an investment in human capital, may be just as important as improvements in physical capital. At any given time, an individual has a choice between current work and investment activities like education that can increase future earning power. People accept reductions in current income to devote current effort to education and training. In turn, a certain return on the investment is expected, because in later years they will earn a higher wage rate (the amount of the increase depending on the nature of the education and training as well as individual natural ability). For example, in Canada, a person

Better education is a relatively inexpensive method to enrich the lives of those in poorer countries. Education allows these countries to produce more advanced goods and services and enjoy the wealth created from trading in the global economy. Taiwan, India, and Korea are now all part of the high-tech global economy, but most of Africa, with the lowest levels of education, has been left behind.

Literacy and Economic Development

Country	GDP Per Capita (US$)	Adult Literacy Rates (%)
United States	$46 653	99.0%
Canada	39 035	99.0
Japan	33 649	99.0
Brazil	10 847	88.6
India	3 354	61.0
Ethiopia	991	35.9
Guinea	1 037	29.5
Niger	667	28.7

NOTE: The literacy rates are based on the ability to read and write at an elementary-school level.

SOURCE: *United Nations Human Development Report 2010.*

with a college or university degree can be expected to earn almost twice as much per year as a high-school graduate.

One argument for government subsidizing education is that this investment can increase the skill level of the population and raise the standard of living. However, even if the individual does not benefit financially from increased education, society may benefit socially and in other respects from having its members highly educated. For example, more education may lead to lower crime rates, new ideas that may benefit the society at large, and more informed voters.

With economic growth, illiteracy rates fall and formal education grows. Exhibit 2 shows the adult literacy rates for selected countries. The correlation between per capita output and the proportion of the population that is able to read or write is striking. Improvements in literacy stimulate economic growth by reducing barriers to the flow of information; when information costs are high, ignorance often results in many resources flowing to or remaining in uses that are rather unproductive. Moreover, education imparts skills that are directly useful in raising labour productivity, whether it is mathematics taught to a salesclerk, engineering techniques taught to a college or university graduate, or just good ideas that facilitate production and design.

Many economists believe that the tremendous growth in East Asia (South Korea, Taiwan, Hong Kong, and Singapore) in the last half of the twentieth century was a result of good basic education for many of their citizens. This reason was one of many factors that contributed to growth, including high rates of saving and a large increase in labour force participation.

However, in developing poor countries, the higher opportunity costs of education present an obstacle. Children in developing countries are an important part of the labour force starting at a young age. But children who are attending school cannot help in the field—planting, harvesting, fence building, and many other tasks that are so important in the rural areas of developing countries. A child's labour contribution to the family is far less important in a developed country. Thus, the higher opportunity cost of an education in developing countries is one of the reasons that school enrollments are lower.

Education may also be a consequence of economic growth, because as incomes rise, people's tendency to consume education increases. People increasingly look to education for more than the acquisition of immediately applicable skills. Education becomes a consumption good as well as a means of investing in human capital.

section 7.4

Population and Economic Growth

- What is the effect of population growth on per capita economic growth?
- What is the Mathusian prediction?

WHAT IS THE EFFECT OF POPULATION GROWTH ON PER CAPITA ECONOMIC GROWTH?

At the beginning of the English Industrial Revolution (c. 1750), the world's population was perhaps 700 million. It took 150 years (to 1900) for that population to slightly more than double to 1.6 billion. Just 64 years later (in 1964), it had doubled again to 3.2 billion.

After another 41 years (in 2005), the population doubled yet again to more than 6.4 billion. At the end of October 2011, the United Nations Population Fund announced that the world's population had reached 7 billion. Economic development occurred amidst all this growth in population, but what role does population play in economic growth?

The effect of population growth on per capita economic growth is far from obvious. If population was to expand faster than output, per capita output would fall; population growth would inhibit growth. With a larger population, however, comes a larger labour force. Also, economies of large-scale production may exist in some forms of production, so larger markets associated with greater populations lead to more efficient-sized production units.

The general feeling, however, is that in many of the developing countries today, rapid population growth threatens the possibility of attaining sustained economic growth. These countries are predominantly agricultural with modest natural resources, especially land. The land–labour ratio is low. Why is population growth a threat in these countries? One answer was provided nearly two centuries ago by an English economist, the Reverend Thomas Malthus.

WHAT IS THE MALTHUSIAN PREDICTION?

Malthus formulated a theoretical model that predicted that per capita economic growth would eventually become negative and that wages would ultimately reach equilibrium at a subsistence level, or just large enough to provide enough income to stay alive. To create this model, Malthus made three assumptions: (1) the economy was agricultural, with goods produced by two inputs, land and labour; (2) the supply of land was fixed; and (3) human sexual desires worked to increase population.

The Law of Diminishing Returns

As population increases, the number of workers increases, and with greater labour inputs available, output also goes up. At some point, however, output will increase by diminishing amounts because of the law of diminishing returns, which states that if you add variable amounts of one input (in this case, labour) to fixed quantities of another input (in this case, land), output will rise but by diminishing amounts (because as the land–labour ratio falls, less land is available per worker). For example, a rapid growth in the labour force might make it more difficult to equip each worker with sufficient capital, and lower amounts of capital per worker lead to lower productivity and a lower real GDP per capita. In short, the increase in the one factor of production, labour, might cause the other factors of production to be spread too thinly.

Avoiding Malthus's Prediction

Fortunately, Malthus's theory proved spectacularly wrong for much of the world. Although the law of diminishing returns is a valid concept, Malthus's other assumptions were unrealistic. The quantity or quality of tillable land is not completely fixed. Irrigation, fertilizer, and conservation techniques effectively increase arable land. More important, Malthus implicitly neglected the potential for technological advances and ignored the real possibility that improved technology, often embodied in capital, could overcome the impact of the law of diminishing returns. Further, the Malthusian assumption that sexual desire would necessarily lead to population increase is not accurate. True, sexual desire will always be with us, but the number of births can be reduced by birth control techniques.

  **DEBATE**

SHOULD CANADA CONTINUE ITS GROWTH TARGETS BASED ON IMMIGRATION GROWTH?

Former Prime Minister Pierre Trudeau recognized that the Canadian economy required substantial rates of immigration to propel the nation into an economic powerhouse. Over the past four decades, the Canadian economy has increased substantially due to the success of this policy. Immigration has ensured that the labour force has increased while the Canadian birth rate declined. However, over the past decade, Canada has been unable to ensure that all immigrants are put to work. Many immigrants come to Canada and are not employed. For this reason, it is argued that the Canadian immigration policy needs to be overhauled so that the economy can grow to the point where all immigrants can be absorbed within the system.

Pro:

While immigration has been good for Canada in the past, the times have changed and the country's economy cannot absorb the current rate of immigration. Many immigrants are coming into the country with skill sets that are not needed and so are working at jobs where their skills are underemployed. This adds to the deadweight loss of the economy. There are a number of other strong arguments to support the suspension of current immigration rates. Can you think of what these arguments might be?

Con:

While the Canadian economy has a number of underemployed immigrants, this is a relatively short-term situation that will work itself out as Canadian workers edge toward retirement. Canadian birthrates cannot produce the number of workers over the long run needed to fund the entitlement (health care, education, and retirement) benefits that Canadians have come to expect. Immigration is Canada's only solution to a declining domestic birthrate. Like the pro side, there are a number of good arguments to continue, and even expand, immigration rates for Canada. What do you think those arguments might be?

As we discussed earlier, some economists believe that population growth can lead to greater economic growth. In some countries, a larger population may lead to more entrepreneurs, engineers, and scientists who will contribute to even greater economic growth through technological progress. These factors turn Malthus's theory on its head; instead of population being the villain, it could actually turn out to be the hero.

Developing Countries and Malthus's Prediction

Unfortunately, however, the Malthusian assumptions don't vary widely from reality for several developing countries today. Some developing nations of the world are having substantial population increases, with a virtually fixed supply of land, slow capital growth, and few technological advances. For example, in some African nations, the population growth rate is 3 percent per year, whereas food output is growing at only 2 percent per year. In these cases, population growth causes a negative effect on per capita output because the added output derived from having more workers on the land is small.

In fact, some developing countries have tried to reduce the rate of population growth to achieve greater economic growth per capita and higher standards of living. For example, China tried to reduce its population growth rate through laws regulating the number of children a family may have. It is true that in many poor countries, the population growth rate is much higher, nearly 3 percent per year, than in richer countries, about 1 percent per year. High population growth rates may be one explanation for lower standards of living, but many non-Malthusian explanations help explain the recurring poverty that exists in developing countries today, such as political instability, the lack of defined and enforceable property rights, and inadequate investment in human capital.

SECTION CHECK

■ Population growth may increase per capita output in resource-rich countries such as Canada, the United States, Australia, and Saudi Arabia, because these countries have more resources for production use by each labourer. Such countries are more likely to be able to take advantage of economies of large-scale production and are also more likely to have rapidly expanding technology.

■ The Malthusian prediction was that, due to limited productive resources and rapid population growth, eventually per capita economic growth would become negative.

For Your Review

Section 7.1

1. Answer the following questions.

    a. According to the Rule of 70, how many years would it take a country to double its output at each of the following annual growth rates?

        0.5 percent: _____ years

        1.0 percent: _____ years

        1.4 percent: _____ years

        2.0 percent: _____ years

        2.8 percent: _____ years

3.5 percent: _____ years

7.0 percent: _____ years

b. If a country had $100 billion of real GDP today, what would its real GDP be in 50 years if it grew at an annual growth rate of

1.4 percent?   _____

2.8 percent?   _____

7.0 percent?   _____

2. Explain how choosing between consumer goods and capital goods in the current period can impact the availability of choices between present and future consumption.

3. Answer the following questions about real GDP per capita:

a. If Country A had four times the initial level of real GDP per capita of Country B and it was growing at 1.4 percent a year, while real GDP was growing at 2.8 percent in Country B, how long would it take before the two countries had the same level of real GDP per capita?

b. If two countries had the same initial level of real GDP per capita and Country A grew at 2.8 percent while Country B grew at 3.5 percent, how would their real per capita GDP levels compare at the end of the century?

4. Suppose that two poor countries experience different growth rates over time. Country A's real GDP per capita grows at a rate of 7 percent per year on average, while Country B's real GDP per capita grows at a rate of only 3 percent per annum. Predict how the standard of living will vary between these two countries over time as a result of divergent growth rates.

5. Which of the following best measures economic growth?

a. the change in nominal GDP

b. the change in real GDP

c. the annual percentage change in nominal GDP per capita

d. the annual percentage change in real GDP per capita

6. Which of the following will shift the Canadian production possibilities curve outward?

a. the discovery of new oil reserves

b. increased immigration of scientists and engineers to Canada

c. a nuclear war that destroys both people and structures

d. producing fewer pizzas in order to produce more tractors

e. producing fewer strawberries in order to produce more corn

Section 7.2

7. Would a shift from investment in capital goods to investment in education increase or decrease the growth rate of real GDP per capita?

8. What is the difference between "labour" and "human capital"? How is human capital increased?

9. Which of the following are likely to improve the productivity of labour and thereby lead to economic growth?

a. on-the-job experience

b. college education

c. a decrease in the amount of capital per worker

d. improvements in management of resources

Sections 7.2 and 7.3

10. Which direction would the following changes alter GDP growth and per capita GDP growth in a country (increase, decrease, or indeterminate), other things being equal?

	Real GDP Growth	Real GDP Growth per Capita
An increase in population	_____	_____
An increase in labour force participation	_____	_____
An increase in population and labour force participation	_____	_____
An increase in current consumption	_____	_____
An increase in technology	_____	_____
An increase in illiteracy	_____	_____
An increase in tax rates	_____	_____
An increase in productivity	_____	_____
An increase in tariffs on imported goods	_____	_____
An earlier retirement age in the country	_____	_____
An increase in technology and a decrease in labour force participation	_____	_____
An earlier retirement age and an increase in the capital stock	_____	_____

Section 7.3

11. What is the implication for an economic system with weak enforcement of patent and copyright laws? Why does weak property right enforcement create an incentive problem?

12. How could permanently lower marginal tax rates increase the capital stock, the level of education, the level of technology, and the amount of developed natural resources over time?

Section 7.4

13. Answer these questions about GDP:

    a. How could real GDP grow, while, over the same period, real GDP per capita falls?

    b. If Country A has a 4 percent annual growth rate of real GDP and a 2 percent annual rate of population growth, while Country B has a 6 percent annual growth rate of real GDP and a 5 percent annual rate of population growth, which country will have a higher growth rate of real GDP per capita?

14. Could a country experience a fall in population and a rise in real GDP at the same time? Could an increase in labour force participation allow that?

CourseMate

Access an interactive eBook and chapter-specific interactive learning tools, including flashcards, quizzes, a glossary, and more in CourseMate, accessed through
www.sextonmacro3ce.nelson.com

chapter

8

Aggregate Demand

section 8.1

The Determinants of Aggregate Demand

- What is aggregate demand?
- What is consumption?
- What is investment?
- What are government purchases?
- What are net exports?

WHAT IS AGGREGATE DEMAND?

Aggregate demand (AD) is the total demand for all final goods and services in the economy. It can also be seen as the quantity of real GDP demanded at different price levels. The four major components of aggregate demand are consumption (C), investment (I), government purchases (G), and net exports ($X - M$). Aggregate demand, then, is equal to $C + I + G + (X - M)$.

aggregate demand (AD)
the total demand for all the final goods and services in the economy

WHAT IS CONSUMPTION?

Consumption (C) is by far the largest component in aggregate demand. Expenditures for consumer goods and services typically absorb almost 60 percent of total economic activity, as measured by GDP. Understanding the determinants of consumption, then, is critical to an understanding of the forces leading to changes in aggregate demand, which in turn, change total output and income.

The Impact of Higher Income on Consumption

The notion that the higher a nation's income, the more it spends on consumer items, has been validated empirically. At the level of individuals, most of us spend more money when we have higher incomes. But what matters most to us is not our total income but

DEBATE

CONSUMPTION EXPENDITURE AND AGGREGATE DEMAND

Consumers have the choice to spend or to save. The more consumers spend, the less they save. In Canada, this is an emerging problem because the amount that people need to save for retirement is far greater than many are actually saving. While Canada has provided tax incentives for people to save (e.g., RRSPs and other tax deferral plans), studies show that these incentives are irrelevant to earners of middle and low incomes, simply because most are unable to save for future needs. In response, some economists advocate a system of "forced savings" using the Canadian Pension Plan (CPP), where money would be withdrawn directly from people's paycheques and deposited into the CPP, where it could be accessed at retirement. Would this be a good way to meet future retirement demands? The less-extreme option of increasing workers' CPP deductions has been suggested. What do you think of that as an alternative?

Pro:

Those who argue for increased CPP deductions state that without such a program, the ability of many Canadians to fund their retirement will be in jeopardy. This will ultimately mean that the state will have to provide higher levels of social programs, which will mean higher future taxes. This transfers the cost of retirement benefits to future generations, which is unfair. Can you think of other problems that might occur when retirement savings are not adequate? What are some possible solutions?

Con:

Increasing CPP deductions is essentially increasing a tax, and increasing taxes reduces the wealth of individuals and firms. Increasing taxes further impacts consumption and investment, thereby limiting the growth of a nation. Many argue that it is up to individuals to look after their own financial future and that the state is not responsible for ensuring the future wealth of individuals. What are other consequences that impact savings, investment, and consumption when a nation's taxes are increased? What are other arguments you could use to defend not increasing the CPP?

our after-tax or *disposable income.* Moreover, other factors might explain consumption. Some consumer goods are "lumpy"; that is, the expenditures for these goods must come in big amounts rather than in small dribbles. Thus, in years in which a consumer buys a new car, takes the family on a European trip, or goes to college or university, consumption may be much greater in relation to income than in years in which the consumer does not buy such high-cost consumer goods or services. Interest rates also affect consumption because they affect savings. At higher real interest rates, people save more and consume less. At lower real interest rates, people save less and consume more.

The Average and Marginal Propensity to Consume

average propensity to consume (APC)
the fraction of total disposable income that households spend on consumption

marginal propensity to consume (MPC)
the additional consumption resulting from an additional dollar of disposable income

Households typically spend a large portion of their disposable income and save the rest. The fraction of their total disposable income that households spend on consumption is called the **average propensity to consume (APC).** For example, a household that consumes $450 out of $500 disposable income has an *APC* of 0.9 ($450/$500). However, households tend to behave differently with additional income than with their income as a whole. How much increased consumption results from an increase in income? That depends on the **marginal propensity to consume (MPC),** which is the additional consumption resulting from an additional dollar of disposable income. If consumption goes from $450 to $600 when disposable income goes from $500 to $700, what is the marginal propensity to consume out of disposable income? First, we calculate the change in consumption: $600 − $450 = $150. Next, we calculate the change in income: $700 − $500 = $200. The marginal propensity to consume, then, equals change in consumption divided by change in disposable income. In this example,

$$MPC = \frac{\text{Change in consumption}}{\text{Change in disposable income}} = \frac{\$150}{\$200} = \frac{3}{4} = 0.75$$

For each additional dollar in after-tax income over this range, this household consumes three-fourths of the addition, or 75 cents.

WHAT IS INVESTMENT?

Because investment (I) spending (purchases of investment goods) is an important component of aggregate demand, which in turn is a determinant of the level of GDP, changes in investment spending are often responsible for changes in the level of economic activity. If consumption is determined largely by the level of disposable income, what determines the level of investment expenditures? As you may recall, investment expenditure is the most unstable category of GDP; it is sensitive to changes in economic, social, and political variables. In 2010, investment was roughly 20 percent of GDP.

If firms expect higher sales and profits, they will increase investment spending on capital goods, such as factories, machinery, and equipment.

Many factors are important in determining the level of investment. Good business conditions "induce" firms to invest because a healthy growth in demand for products in the future is likely based on current experience. In the next section, we will consider the key variables that influence investment spending.

WHAT ARE GOVERNMENT PURCHASES?

Government purchases (G), another component of aggregate demand, are purchases by federal, provincial and territorial, and local governments of new goods and services produced. Government purchases include expenditures on health, education, highways, and police protection. In 2010, government purchases accounted for roughly 25 percent of total spending. Although volatile shifts in government purchases are less frequent than volatile shifts in investment spending, they do occasionally occur, most recently in response to the global financial crisis.

WHAT ARE NET EXPORTS?

The interaction of the Canadian economy with the rest of the world is becoming increasingly important. Models that include international trade effects are called **open economy** models.

open economy
a type of model that includes international trade effects

Remember, exports are Canadian-made goods and services that we sell to foreign customers, like lumber, wheat, and telecommunications equipment; imports are goods and services that we buy from foreign companies, like BMWs, French wine, and Sony TVs. Exports and imports can alter aggregate demand. It makes no difference to Canadian sellers if buyers are in this country or in some other country. A buyer is a buyer, foreign or domestic, so exports (X) must be added to the demand side of our equation. But what about goods and services that are consumed here but not produced by the domestic economy? When Canadian consumers, firms, or the government buy foreign goods and services, there is no direct impact on the total demand for Canadian goods and services, so imports (M) must be subtracted from our equation.

The difference between the value of exports and the value of imports is what we call **net exports** ($X - M$ = Net exports). If exports are greater than imports, we have positive net exports ($X > M$). If imports are greater than exports, net exports are negative ($X < M$).

net exports
the difference between the value of exports and the value of imports

The impact that net exports have on aggregate demand is similar to the impact that government purchases have on aggregate demand. Suppose that Canada has no trade surplus and no trade deficit—zero net exports. Now say that foreign consumers start buying more Canadian goods and services whereas Canadian consumers continue to buy imports at roughly the same rate. This will lead to *positive net exports* ($X > M$) and result in greater demand for Canadian goods and services, a higher level of aggregate demand. From a policy standpoint, this might explain why countries that are currently in a recession might like to run a trade surplus by increasing exports.

Of course, it is also possible that a country could run a trade deficit. Again let us assume that the economy was initially in a position with zero net exports. A trade deficit, or *negative net exports* ($X < M$), *ceteris paribus,* would lower Canadian aggregate demand.

SECTION CHECK

- Aggregate demand is the sum of the demand for all final goods and services in the economy. It can also be seen as the quantity of real GDP demanded at different price levels.
- Consumption—the purchases of consumer goods and services by households— is the largest component of aggregate demand. Empirical evidence suggests that consumption increases directly with any increase in income.
- Investment spending refers to the purchases of investment goods such as machinery and equipment. Changes in investment spending are often responsible for changes in the level of economic activity.
- Government purchases are made up of federal, provincial/territorial, and local purchases of goods and services.
- Net exports are the difference between the value of exports and the value of imports. Trade deficits lower aggregate demand, other things equal; trade surpluses increase aggregate demand, other things equal.

section
8.2

The Investment and Saving Market

- What is the investment demand curve?
- What is the saving supply curve?
- How is equilibrium determined in the investment and saving market?
- What effect do budget surpluses and budget deficits have on the investment and saving market?

Exhibit 1 shows the breakdown of real GDP into its individual components since 2006. While each category of expenditure exhibits some variability from one year to the next, the volatility of investment spending is clearly evident. It is this significant variability along with the sizable contribution of investment spending to total GDP that necessitates we take a closer look at the investment and saving market.

WHAT IS THE INVESTMENT DEMAND CURVE?

If we put the investment demand for the whole economy and national savings together, we can establish the real interest rate in the saving and investment market. We begin by

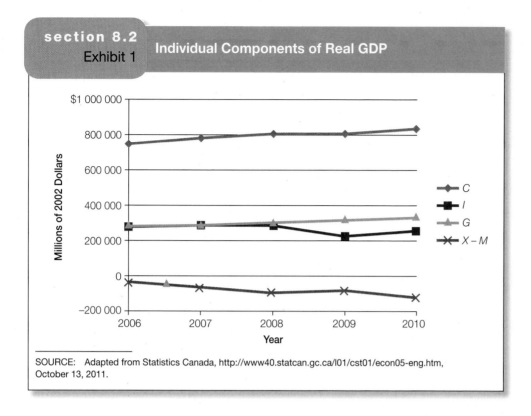

section 8.2
Exhibit 1 **Individual Components of Real GDP**

SOURCE: Adapted from Statistics Canada, http://www40.statcan.gc.ca/l01/cst01/econ05-eng.htm, October 13, 2011.

revisiting investment, and then follow with the introduction of the saving supply curve and equilibrium.

Exhibit 2 shows the investment demand curve for all the firms in the whole economy. The investment demand (*ID*) curve is downward sloping, reflecting the fact that investment spending varies inversely with the real interest rate—the amount borrowers pay for their loans. At high real interest rates, firms will pursue only those few investment activities with even higher expected rates of return. As the real interest rate falls, additional projects with lower expected rates of return become profitable for firms, and the quantity of investment demanded rises. In other words, the investment demand curve shows the dollar amount of investment forthcoming at different real interest rates. Because lower interest rates stimulate the quantity of investment demanded, governments often try to combat recessions by lowering interest rates.

Shifting the Investment Demand Curve

Several other determinants will shift the investment demand curve. If firms expect higher rates of return on their investments, for a given interest rate, the *ID* curve will shift to the right, as seen in Exhibit 3. If firms expect lower rates of return on their investments, for a given interest rate, the *ID* curve will shift to the left, also seen in Exhibit 3. Possible investment demand curve shifters include changes in technology, inventories, expectations, and business taxes.

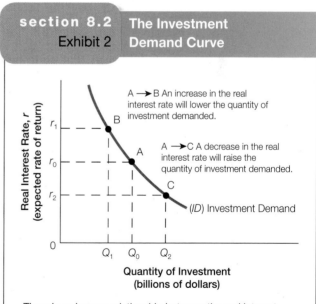

section 8.2
Exhibit 2 **The Investment Demand Curve**

A → B An increase in the real interest rate will lower the quantity of investment demanded.

A → C A decrease in the real interest rate will raise the quantity of investment demanded.

(*ID*) Investment Demand

Quantity of Investment (billions of dollars)

There is an inverse relationship between the real interest rate and the quantity of investment demanded. At higher real interest rates, firms will pursue only those investment activities with the highest expected return and the quantity of investment demanded will fall—a movement from point A to point B. As the real interest rate falls, projects with lower expected returns become potentially profitable for firms and the quantity of investment demanded rises—a movement from point A to point C.

section 8.2
Exhibit 3

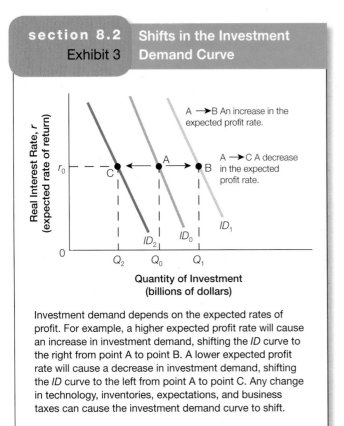

Shifts in the Investment Demand Curve

A →B An increase in the expected profit rate.

A →C A decrease in the expected profit rate.

Investment demand depends on the expected rates of profit. For example, a higher expected profit rate will cause an increase in investment demand, shifting the *ID* curve to the right from point A to point B. A lower expected profit rate will cause a decrease in investment demand, shifting the *ID* curve to the left from point A to point C. Any change in technology, inventories, expectations, and business taxes can cause the investment demand curve to shift.

Technology   Product and process innovation can cause the *ID* curve to shift outward. For example, the development of new machines that can improve the quality and the quantity of products or lower the costs of production will increase the rate of return on investment, independent of the interest rate. The same is true for new products like hand-held computers, the Internet, genetic applications in medicine, or HDTV. Imagine how many different firms increased their investment demand during the computer revolution.

Inventories   When inventories are high and goods are stockpiled in warehouses all over the country, there is a lower expected rate of return on new investment—*ID* shifts to the left. Firms with excess inventories of finished goods have very little incentive to invest in new capital. Alternatively, if inventories are depleted below the levels desired by firms, the expected rate of return on new investment increases, as firms look to replenish their shelves to meet the growing demand—*ID* shifts to the right.

Expectations   If sales and profit rates are expected to be higher in the future, firms will invest more in plant and equipment now, causing the *ID* curve to shift to the right—more investment will be desired at a given interest rate. If lower sales and profits are forecast, the *ID* curve shifts to the left—fewer investments will be desired at a given interest rate.

Business Taxes   If business taxes are lowered—such as with an investment tax credit—potential after-tax profits on investment projects will increase and shift the *ID* curve to the right. Higher business taxes will lead to lower potential after-tax profits on investment projects and shift the *ID* curve to the left.

WHAT IS THE SAVING SUPPLY CURVE?

private saving
the amount of income that households have left over after consumption and taxes

There are two types of saving—private and public. **Private saving** is the amount of income that households have left over after consumption and taxes. So private savings (S_{private}) is equal to the amount of total income (GDP) that remains after people have paid for consumption (C) and taxes (T):

$$S_{\text{private}} = \text{GDP} - C - T$$

public saving
the amount of income that the government has left over after paying for its spending

Public saving is the amount of income the government has left over after paying for its spending. Therefore, public saving (S_{public}) is equal to the amount of tax revenues (T) that the government has left over after paying for government purchases (G):

$$S_{\text{public}} = T - G$$

national saving
the sum of both private and public saving

National saving in an economy is the sum of both private and public saving:

$$S = (\text{GDP} - C - T) + (T - G)$$

Most people are familiar with the idea that households and firms can save but are less familiar with the idea that the government can also save. If the government collects more in taxes than it spends ($T > G$), it runs a surplus and public saving is positive. If the government spends more than it collects in taxes ($G < T$), it runs a deficit and public saving is negative. In the next section, we use the tools of supply and demand to examine how budget surpluses and budget deficits affect the real interest rate, national saving, and investment.

The supply curve of savings is upward sloping, as seen in Exhibit 4. At a higher real interest rate, a greater quantity of savings is supplied. Think of the interest rate as the reward for saving and supplying funds to financial markets. At a lower real interest rate, a lower quantity of savings is supplied.

Shifting the Saving Supply Curve

As with the investment demand curve, there are noninterest determinants of the saving supply curve. Two such saving supply curve shifters are disposable (after-tax) income and future expected earnings.

Disposable Income If taxes are lowered—allowing disposable income to increase—the supply of saving would shift to the right—more saving would occur at any given interest rate. If taxes increased, causing disposable income to decline, there would be less saving at any given interest rate.

Earnings Expectation If you expected lower future earnings, you would tend to save more now at any given interest rate—shifting the saving supply curve to the right. If you expected higher future earnings, you would tend to consume more and save less now, knowing that more income is right around the corner—shifting the saving supply curve to the left.

In Exhibit 5, we see that an increase in disposable income or lower expected future earnings shifts the saving supply curve to the right. A decrease in disposable income or higher expected future earnings will shift the saving supply curve to the left.

HOW IS EQUILIBRIUM DETERMINED IN THE INVESTMENT AND SAVING MARKET?

In equilibrium, desired investment equals desired national saving at the intersection of the investment demand curve and the saving supply curve. The real equilibrium interest rate is shown by the intersection of these two curves, as seen in Exhibit 6. If the real interest rate, r_1, is above the equilibrium real interest rate, r_E, forces within the economy would tend to restore the equilibrium. At a higher-than-real equilibrium

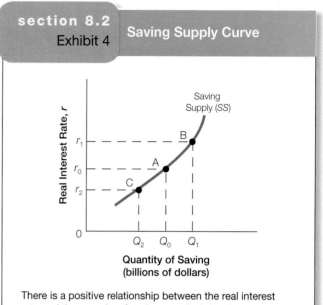

section 8.2
Exhibit 4   **Saving Supply Curve**

There is a positive relationship between the real interest rate and the quantity of saving supplied. At a higher real interest rate, there is a greater quantity of saving supplied— the movement from point A to point B. At a lower real interest rate, there is a lower quantity of saving supplied— the movement from point A to point C.

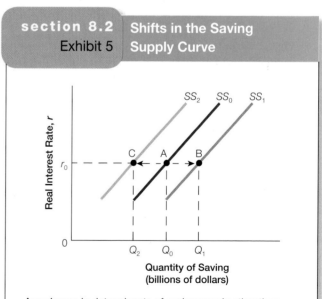

section 8.2
Exhibit 5   **Shifts in the Saving Supply Curve**

Any change in determinants of saving supply other than interest rates, like disposable (after-tax) income or expected future earnings, can cause the saving supply curve to shift. An increase in disposable income or lower expected future earnings shifts the saving supply curve to the right, from point A to point B. A decrease in disposable income and higher expected future earnings will shift the saving supply curve to the left, from point A to point C.

Equilibrium in the Saving and Investment Market

Desired investment equals desired national saving at the intersection of the investment demand curve and the saving supply curve, the equilibrium in the saving and investment market. The intersection of these two curves shows the real equilibrium interest rate. At higher than the real equilibrium interest rate, the quantity of savings supplied would be greater than the quantity of investment demanded; there would be a surplus of savings at this real interest rate. As savers (lenders) compete against each other to attract investment demanders (borrowers), the real interest rate falls. If the real interest rate, r_2, is below the equilibrium real interest rate, r_E, the quantity of investment demanded is greater than the quantity of saving supplied at that interest rate and a shortage of saving occurs. As investment demanders (borrowers) compete against each other for the available saving, the real interest rate is bid up to r_E.

dissaving
consuming more than total available income

interest rate, the quantity of savings supplied would be greater than the quantity of investment demanded—there would be a surplus of savings at this real interest rate. As savers (lenders) compete against each other to attract investment demanders (borrowers), the real interest rate falls. Alternatively if the real interest rate, r_2, is below the equilibrium real interest rate, r_E, the quantity of investment demanded is greater than the quantity of saving supplied at that interest rate—a shortage of saving occurs. As investment demanders (borrowers) compete against each other for the available saving, the real interest rate is bid up to r_E.

WHAT EFFECT DO BUDGET SURPLUSES AND BUDGET DEFICITS HAVE ON THE INVESTMENT AND SAVING MARKET?

First, let's see how a budget surplus affects the real interest rate and the amount of saving and investment. In Exhibit 7, suppose that the government has a balanced budget, the saving supply curve is SS_0, and the investment demand curve is ID_0, resulting in an equilibrium real interest rate equal to r_0 and an equilibrium quantity of saving and investment equal to Q_0. If the government now runs a budget surplus—the government receives more in tax revenues than it spends—there is an increase in public saving, assuming that private saving is unchanged. Because national saving is the sum of private saving and public saving, national saving increases, shifting the saving supply curve from SS_0 to SS_1.

What impact does this budget surplus (government saving) have on the real interest rate, saving, and investment? The increase in the saving supply from SS_0 to SS_1 leads to a decrease in the real interest rate to r_1 and an increase in equilibrium saving and investment from Q_0 to Q_1, as shown in Exhibit 7. The budget surplus leads to an increase in the saving supply, a lower real interest rate, and a larger amount of saving and investment. This increase in capital formation will tend to increase long-term economic growth.

When the government spends more than it receives in tax revenues, it experiences a budget deficit; the government is actually **dissaving**—consuming more than total available income. This negative saving or borrowing will cause national saving to decrease. That is, the budget deficit reduces the national supply of saving, shifting the saving supply curve leftward from SS_0 to SS_1 in Exhibit 8. At the new equilibrium, there is a higher real interest rate and a lower amount of saving and investment.

When the real interest rate rises because of the government budget deficit, private investment decreases. Economists call this the *crowding-out effect,* a topic we will expand on in the chapter entitled "Fiscal Policy." In sum, when the government runs a budget deficit, it reduces national saving, which leads to a higher real interest rate and lower investment. Because investment is critical for capital formation, long-term economic growth is reduced by budget deficits.

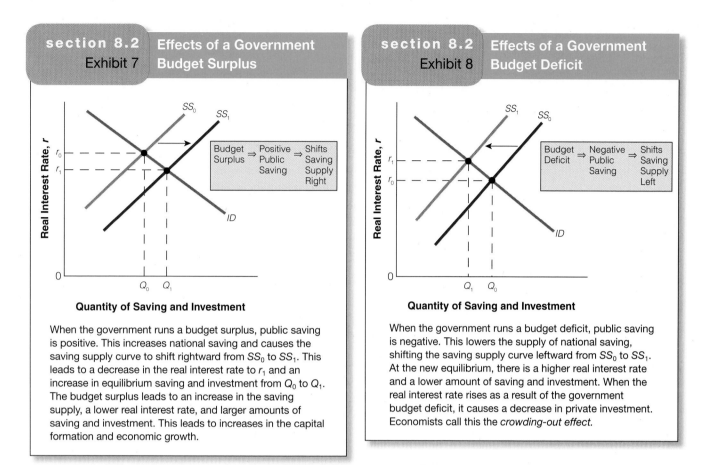

section 8.2
Exhibit 7

Effects of a Government Budget Surplus

section 8.2
Exhibit 8

Effects of a Government Budget Deficit

Exhibit 7 — Effects of a Government Budget Surplus

Budget Surplus $\Rightarrow$ Positive Public Saving $\Rightarrow$ Shifts Saving Supply Right

When the government runs a budget surplus, public saving is positive. This increases national saving and causes the saving supply curve to shift rightward from SS_0 to SS_1. This leads to a decrease in the real interest rate to r_1 and an increase in equilibrium saving and investment from Q_0 to Q_1. The budget surplus leads to an increase in the saving supply, a lower real interest rate, and larger amounts of saving and investment. This leads to increases in the capital formation and economic growth.

Exhibit 8 — Effects of a Government Budget Deficit

Budget Deficit $\Rightarrow$ Negative Public Saving $\Rightarrow$ Shifts Saving Supply Left

When the government runs a budget deficit, public saving is negative. This lowers the supply of national saving, shifting the saving supply curve leftward from SS_0 to SS_1. At the new equilibrium, there is a higher real interest rate and a lower amount of saving and investment. When the real interest rate rises as a result of the government budget deficit, it causes a decrease in private investment. Economists call this the *crowding-out effect*.

SECTION CHECK

- The investment demand curve is downward sloping, reflecting the fact that the quantity of investment demanded varies inversely with the real interest rate. At high real interest rates, firms will pursue only those few investment activities with still higher expected rates of return. At lower real interest rates, projects with lower expected rates of return become profitable for firms, and the quantity of investment demanded rises. Technology, inventories, expectations, and business taxes can shift the investment demand curve at a given real interest rate.

- The supply of national saving is composed of both private saving and public saving. The supply curve of saving is upward sloping. At a higher real interest rate, there is an increase in the quantity of saving supplied. At a lower real interest rate, there is a decrease in the quantity of saving supplied. Two noninterest determinants of the saving supply curve are disposable (after-tax) income and expected future earnings.

- In equilibrium, desired investment equals desired national saving at the intersection of the investment demand curve and the saving supply curve. If the real interest rate is above the equilibrium real interest rate, the quantity of saving supplied is greater than the quantity of investment demanded at that interest rate; lenders will compete against each other to attract borrowers and the real interest rate falls. If the real interest rate is below the equilibrium real interest rate, the quantity of investment demanded is greater than the quantity of saving supplied at that interest rate; borrowers compete with each other for the available saving and drive the real interest rate up.

- Budget surpluses lead to an increase in national saving, a lowering of the real interest rate, and an increase in the quantity of saving and investment. Budget deficits reduce national saving, increase the real interest rate, and lower the quantity of saving and investment.

section 8.3

The Aggregate Demand Curve

- How is the quantity of real GDP demanded affected by the price level?
- Why is the aggregate demand curve negatively sloped?

The aggregate demand curve reflects the total amount of real goods and services that all groups together want to purchase in a given time period. In other words, it indicates the quantities of real gross domestic product (RGDP) demanded at different price levels. Note that this is different from the demand curve for a particular good presented in Chapter 3, which looked at the relationship between the relative price of a good and the quantity demanded.

HOW IS THE QUANTITY OF REAL GDP DEMANDED AFFECTED BY THE PRICE LEVEL?

aggregate demand curve
a graphical representation that shows the inverse relationship between the price level and RGDP demanded

The **aggregate demand curve** is a graphical representation that shows the inverse (or opposite) relationship between the price level and real gross domestic product demanded. Exhibit 1 illustrates this relationship, where the quantity of RGDP demanded is measured on the horizontal axis and the overall price level is measured on the vertical axis. As we move from point A to point B on the aggregate demand curve, we see that an increase in the price level causes RGDP demanded to fall. Conversely, if there is a reduction in the price level, a movement from point B to point A, quantity demanded of RGDP increases. Why do purchasers in the economy demand less real output when the price level rises, and more real output when the price level falls?

section 8.3	The Aggregate
Exhibit 1	Demand Curve

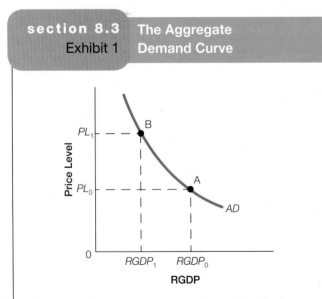

The aggregate demand curve slopes downward, reflecting an inverse relationship between the overall price level and the quantity of real GDP demanded. When the price level increases, the quantity of RGDP demanded decreases; when the price level decreases, the quantity of RGDP demanded increases.

WHY IS THE AGGREGATE DEMAND CURVE NEGATIVELY SLOPED?

Three complementary explanations exist for the negative slope of the aggregate demand curve: the real wealth effect, the interest rate effect, and the open economy effect.

The Real Wealth Effect

Imagine that you are living in a period of high inflation on a fixed pension that is not indexed for the changing price level. As the cost of goods and services rises, your monthly pension cheque remains the same. Therefore, the purchasing power of your pension will continue to decline as long as inflation is occurring. The same would be true of any asset of fixed dollar value, like cash. If you had $1000 in cash stashed under your bed while the economy suffered a serious bout of inflation, the purchasing power of your cash would be eroded by the extent of the inflation. That is, an increase in the price level reduces real wealth and would consequently decrease your planned purchases of goods and services, lowering the quantity of RGDP demanded.

In the event that the price level falls, the reverse would hold true. A falling price level would increase the real value of your cash assets, increasing your purchasing power and increasing RGDP. The connection can be summarized as follows:

$$\uparrow \text{Price level} \Rightarrow \downarrow \text{Real wealth} \Rightarrow \downarrow \text{Purchasing power} \Rightarrow \downarrow \text{RGDP demanded}$$

and

$$\downarrow \text{Price level} \Rightarrow \uparrow \text{Real wealth} \Rightarrow \uparrow \text{Purchasing power} \Rightarrow \uparrow \text{RGDP demanded}$$

The Interest Rate Effect

The effect of the price level on interest rates can also cause the aggregate demand curve to have a negative slope. Suppose the price level increases. As a result, most goods and services will now have a higher price tag. Consequently, consumers will wish to hold more dollars in order to purchase those items that they want to buy, which will increase the demand for money. If the demand for money increases and the Bank of Canada, the controller of the money supply, does not alter the money supply, then interest rates will rise. In other words, if the demand for money increases relative to the supply, then the demanders of dollars will bid up the price of those dollars—the interest rate. At higher interest rates, the opportunity cost of borrowing rises, and fewer interest-sensitive investments will be profitable, reducing the quantity of investment goods demanded. Businesses contemplating replacing worn-out equipment or planning to expand capacity may cancel or delay their investment decisions unless interest rates decline again. Also, at the higher interest rate, many consumers may give up plans to buy new cars, boats, or houses. That is, the higher interest rate also has a consumption link. The net effect of the higher interest rate, then, is that it will result in fewer investment goods demanded and, consequently, a lower RGDP demanded.

On the other hand, if the price level fell and people demanded less money as a result, then interest rates would fall. Lower interest rates would trigger greater investment spending, and a larger real GDP demanded would result. We can summarize this process as follows:

$$\uparrow \text{Price level} \Rightarrow \uparrow \text{Money demand (Money supply unchanged)} \Rightarrow \uparrow \text{Interest rate} \Rightarrow$$
$$\downarrow \text{Investment} \Rightarrow \downarrow \text{RGDP demanded}$$

and

$$\downarrow \text{Price level} \Rightarrow \downarrow \text{Money demand (Money supply unchanged)} \Rightarrow \downarrow \text{Interest rate} \Rightarrow$$
$$\uparrow \text{Investment} \Rightarrow \uparrow \text{RGDP demanded}$$

The Open Economy Effect of Changes in the Price Level

Many goods and services are bought and sold in global markets. If the prices of goods and services in the domestic market rise relative to those in global markets due to a higher domestic price level, consumers and businesses will buy more from foreign producers and less from domestic producers. Because real GDP is a measure of domestic output, the reduction in the willingness of consumers to buy from domestic producers leads to a lower real GDP demanded at the higher domestic price level. And if domestic prices of goods and services fall relative to foreign prices, more domestic products will be bought, increasing real GDP demanded. This relationship can be shown as follows:

$$\uparrow \text{Price level} \Rightarrow \downarrow \text{Demand for domestic goods} \Rightarrow \downarrow \text{RGDP demanded}$$

and

$$\downarrow \text{Price level} \Rightarrow \uparrow \text{Demand for domestic goods} \Rightarrow \uparrow \text{RGDP demanded}$$

SECTION CHECK

- An aggregate demand curve shows the inverse relationship between the amounts of real goods and services (RGDP) that are demanded at each possible price level.
- The aggregate demand curve is downward sloping because of the real wealth effect, the interest rate effect, and the open economy effect.

section 8.4

Shifts in the Aggregate Demand Curve

- What variables cause the aggregate demand curve to shift?
- Can we review the determinants that change aggregate demand?

As with the supply and demand curves in microeconomics (see Chapter 3), there can be both shifts in and movements along the aggregate demand curve. In the previous section, we discussed three factors—the real wealth effect, the interest rate effect, and the open economy effect—that result in the downward slope of the aggregate demand curve. Each of these factors, then, generates a movement *along* the aggregate demand curve because the general price level changed. In this section, we will discuss some of the many factors that can cause the aggregate demand curve to shift to the right or left.

| section 8.4 | Shifts in the Aggregate |
| Exhibit 1 | Demand Curve |

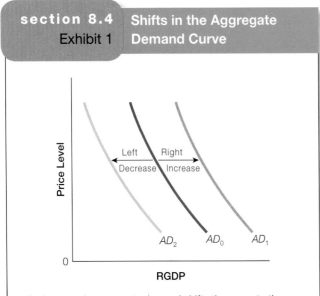

An increase in aggregate demand shifts the curve to the right (from AD_0 to AD_1). A decrease in aggregate demand shifts the curve to the left (from AD_0 to AD_2).

WHAT VARIABLES CAUSE THE AGGREGATE DEMAND CURVE TO SHIFT?

The whole aggregate demand curve can shift to the right or left, as seen in Exhibit 1. Put simply, if some nonprice-level determinant causes total spending to increase, then the aggregate demand curve will shift to the right. If a nonprice-level determinant causes the level of total spending to decline, then the aggregate demand curve will shift to the left. More specifically, an increase in any component of GDP (C, I, G, or $X - M$) can cause the aggregate demand curve to shift rightward. Conversely, decreases in C, I, G, or ($X - M$) will shift aggregate demand leftward. Now let's look at some specific factors that could cause the aggregate demand curve to shift.

Consumption

A whole host of changes could alter consumption (C) patterns. For example, an increase in consumer confidence, an increase in wealth, an increase in transfer payments, or a tax cut each can increase consumption and shift the aggregate demand curve to the right. An increase in population will also increase the aggregate demand because more consumers will be spending more money on goods and services.

Of course, the aggregate demand curve could shift to the left due to decreases in consumption demand. For example, if consumers sensed that the economy was headed for a recession or if the government imposed a tax increase, this would result in a leftward shift of the aggregate demand curve. Because consuming less is saving more, an increase in saving, *ceteris paribus,* will shift aggregate demand to the left. High levels of accumulated consumer debt may also be a reason that some consumers might put off additional spending.

Investment

Investment (I) is also an important determinant of aggregate demand. Increases in the demand for investment goods occur for a variety of reasons. For example, if business confidence increases or real interest rates fall, business investment will increase and aggregate demand will shift to the right. A reduction in business taxes would also shift the aggregate demand curve to the right because businesses would now retain more of their profits to invest. However, if interest rates or business taxes rise, then we would expect to see a leftward shift in aggregate demand.

Business **CONNECTION**

STAYING AHEAD OF CHANGES IN GDP

We know that when the economy is in a broadly based expansionary phase, aggregate demand is increasing. This means that on average, consumers, business, and all levels of government, along with foreign buyers are probably increasing their demand for Canadian goods and services. In expansionary phases, businesses often experience increases in sales revenues and are encouraged to make capital expenditures to increase operating capacity and output.

If business operators want to benefit most from an expansionary phase in the economy, on the monitoring of several leading indicators in such expansions is key to understanding the nature and business implications of the growth. Expansions often start with the consumer sector, which accounts for almost 60 percent of economic growth. A precursor to such growth is often signalled by one or a combination of positive developments, including lower personal taxes, a rise in consumer confidence, greater stock market wealth, a reduction in interest rates, or/and an increase in transfer payments. When these conditions are present, there is every indication that consumer demand will increase, *ceteris paribus*. Failure by businesses to recognize or acknowledge these leading indicators could result in missed opportunities for increased revenues and profits.

To take advantage of the impending growth in consumer demand for goods and services signalled by these indicators, businesses must often expand their capacity by hiring and training workers, acquiring new capital equipment, or implementing new processes. Such changes often take the form of projects requiring considerable time to plan and implement. Businesses serving primarily individuals and households must often complete capacity expansion projects prior to, or coincident with, the predicted growth in consumer spending. Failure to properly time or estimate increases in aggregate demand can result in severe overcapacity, inventory buildups, and higher costs.

Similarly, those industry sectors relying on governments or businesses as customers must watch for certain leading indicators. These include increases in government spending; or in the case of investments, the lowering of interest rates/optimistic business forecasts; or proposed lower business taxes.

While an expanding economy presents opportunities for increases in revenues, a contracting economy invariably presents the challenge of dealing with high and stubborn fixed operating costs in the face of falling production levels, culminating in serious threats to profitability. To avoid such unfavourable developments, businesses must closely follow the leading indicators communicating changes in aggregate demand across all four components of GDP if they are to stay ahead of the curve and maintain profitability.

Government Purchases

Government purchases (G) are also part of total spending and therefore must impact aggregate demand. An increase in government purchases, other things equal, shifts the aggregate demand curve to the right, whereas a reduction shifts aggregate demand to the left.

Net Exports

Global markets are also important in a domestic economy. For example, in 2009, when Canada's major trading partner, the United States, fell into a major recession, U.S. demand for Canadian goods and services fell by nearly 27 percent, causing overall Canadian exports to decline by close to 25 percent. This dramatic reduction in exports was the leading cause of net exports ($X - M$) falling by almost $50 billion in 2009, shifting the aggregate demand curve for Canada to the left. Alternatively, an economic boom in the U.S. economy might lead to an increase in our exports to the United States, causing net exports ($X - M$) to rise and aggregate demand to increase.

Another factor that has an important effect on net exports is the exchange rate. The exchange rate is the price of one unit of a country's currency in terms of another country's currency. For example, if it takes US$0.84 to buy one Canadian dollar (as was the case on October 10, 2008), then the exchange rate is US$0.84 per Canadian dollar. When the Canadian dollar appreciates in value (to, say, US$1.04 per Canadian dollar—as was the case on July 4, 2010), it is more expensive for foreigners to buy Canadian dollars, and therefore more expensive for foreigners to buy Canadian goods and services (which are priced in Canadian dollars). At the same time, it becomes less expensive for Canadians to buy U.S. dollars, and therefore less expensive for Canadians to buy U.S. goods and services (which are priced in U.S. dollars). As a result, Canadian exports decline and Canadian imports increase. Therefore, an appreciation of the Canadian dollar decreases Canadian net exports and shifts the aggregate demand curve to the left. On the other hand, when the Canadian dollar depreciates in value (to, say, US$0.77 per Canadian dollar—as was the case on March 9, 2009), Canadian net exports increase, and the aggregate demand curve shifts to the right.

CAN WE REVIEW THE DETERMINANTS THAT CHANGE AGGREGATE DEMAND?

Any aggregate demand category that has the ability to change total purchases in the economy will shift the aggregate demand curve. That is, changes in consumption purchases, investment purchases, government purchases, or net export purchases shift the aggregate demand curve. Below we list some aggregate demand curve shifters.

An Increase in Aggregate Demand (Rightward Shift)

Consumption (C):
- Lower personal taxes
- A rise in consumer confidence
- Greater stock market wealth
- An increase in transfer payments

Investment (I):
- Lower real interest rates
- Optimistic business forecasts
- Lower business taxes

Government Purchases (*G*):

■ An increase in government purchases

Net Exports (*X* − *M*):

■ Income increases abroad, which will likely increase foreign sales of domestic goods (exports)

■ Exchange rate depreciation

A Decrease in Aggregate Demand (Leftward Shift)

Consumption (*C*):

■ Higher personal taxes

■ A fall in consumer confidence

■ Reduced stock market wealth

■ A reduction in transfer payments

Investment (*I*):

■ Higher real interest rates

■ Pessimistic business forecasts

■ Higher business taxes

Government Purchases (*G*):

■ A reduction in government purchases

Net Exports (*X* − *M*):

■ Income falls abroad, which will likely lead to a reduction in the foreign sales of domestic goods (exports)

■ Exchange rate appreciation

SECTION CHECK

■ A change in the price level causes a movement along the aggregate demand curve, not a shift in the aggregate demand curve. Aggregate demand is made up of total spending, or $C + I + G + (X - M)$. Any change in these factors will cause the aggregate demand curve to shift.

■ Any nonprice-level variable that causes either C, I, G, or X to increase, or M to decrease, will cause the aggregate demand curve to shift to the right. Any non-price-level variable that causes either C, I, G, or X to decrease, or M to increase, will cause the aggregate demand curve to shift to the left.

For Your Review

Section 8.1

1. Assume that Melanie had \$200 000 of disposable income and spent \$180 000 on consumption in 2010, and had \$300 000 of disposable income and spent \$240 000 on consumption in 2011.

a. What was Melanie's average propensity to consume in 2010?

b. What was Melanie's average propensity to consume in 2011?

c. What was Melanie's marginal propensity to consume?

d. If Melanie's income went up to $400 000 in 2012, how much would she be likely to spend on consumption that year? What would be her average propensity to consume?

e. If Melanie's income went down to $100 000 in 2012, how much would she be likely to spend on consumption that year? What would be her average propensity to consume?

2. How can the amount of net exports be positive or negative? How do positive net exports and negative net exports impact aggregate demand?

Section 8.2

3. In the saving and investment market,

a. what happens to the investment demand curve when the real interest rate declines?

b. what happens to the investment demand curve when firms' inventories are rising above what the firms desire?

c. what happens to the investment demand curve when technological advances give rise to popular new products?

d. what happens to the saving supply curve when the real interest rate increases?

e. what happens to the saving supply curve when disposable income increases?

4.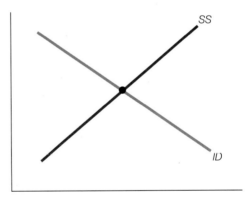

Label the axes for the saving and investment market. Then explain and illustrate what would happen in the saving and investment market if

a. businesses became more optimistic about future business conditions.

b. individuals became less optimistic about their future incomes.

c. business taxes increased.

d. individuals' disposable incomes increased.

5. What would happen to the saving supply curve if there was both an increase in current disposable income and a decrease in new technologies creating investment opportunities?

6. Other things equal, in which direction will an increasing budget deficit change the equilibrium interest rate, the saving supply curve, the level of saving and investment in the economy, and the likely rate of economic growth, other things equal?

Section 8.3

7. Fill in the blanks in the following explanations.

   a. The real wealth effect is described by the following: An increase in the price level leads to a(n) _____ in real wealth, which leads to a(n) _____ in purchasing power, which leads to a(n) _____ in RGDP demanded.

   b. The interest rate effect is described by the following: A decrease in the price level leads to a(n) _____ in money demand, which leads to a(n) _____ in the interest rate, which leads to a(n) _____ in investments, which leads to a(n) _____ in RGDP demanded.

   c. The open economy effect is described by the following: An increase in the domestic price level leads to a(n) _____ in the demand for domestic goods, which leads to a(n) _____ in RGDP demanded.

8. Evaluate the following statement: A higher price level decreases the purchasing power of the dollar and reduces RGDP.

Section 8.4

9. Describe what the effect on aggregate demand would be, other things being equal, if

   a. exports increase.

   b. both imports and exports decrease.

   c. consumption decreases.

   d. investment increases.

   e. investment decreases and government purchases increase.

   f. the price level increases.

   g. the price level decreases.

10. Suppose retailers like Canadian Tire and Zellers find that their inventories are being depleted. What type of change in aggregate demand (a rightward or leftward shift) could be seen as responsible? What are the likely consequences for output and investment of this type of change in aggregate demand?

11. Which of the following both decreases consumption and shifts the aggregate demand curve to the left?

    a. an increase in financial wealth

    b. an increase in taxes

    c. an increase in the price level

    d. a decrease in interest rates

12. Predict how each of the following would impact investment expenditures.

    a. Inventory levels are depleted.

    b. Banks scrutinize borrower credit more carefully and interest rates rise.

    c. Profit rates have decreased over the past few quarters.

    d. Factories operate at 60 percent capacity, down from 80 percent.

13. Identify which expenditure category each of the following will directly impact, and also in which direction the Canadian aggregate demand curve will shift as a result.

    a. Income increases abroad.

    b. There is a decrease in interest rates.

    c. Parliament passes a permanent tax cut.

    d. Firms become more optimistic about the outlook for the economy.

    e. Stocks traded on the Toronto Stock Exchange lose 40 percent of their value in one month's time.

14. Explain how the most recent recession in the United States affected aggregate demand in the Canadian economy.

CourseMate

Access an interactive eBook and chapter-specific interactive learning tools, including flashcards, quizzes, a glossary, and more in CourseMate, accessed through **www.sextonmacro3ce.nelson.com**

**section
9.1**

The Aggregate Supply Curve

- What is the aggregate supply curve?
- Why is the short-run aggregate supply curve positively sloped?
- Why is the long-run aggregate supply curve vertical at the natural rate of output?

WHAT IS THE AGGREGATE SUPPLY CURVE?

The **aggregate supply curve** (*AS*) is a graphical representation that shows the positive relationship between the price level and real gross domestic product supplied. It illustrates the relationship between the overall price level and the total quantity of final goods and services that suppliers are *willing* and *able* to produce. In fact, there are two aggregate supply curves—a short-run aggregate supply curve and a long-run aggregate supply curve. The **short-run aggregate supply curve** (*SRAS*) is the graphical relationship between *RGDP* and the price level when output prices can change but input prices are unable to adjust. For example, nominal wages are assumed to adjust slowly in the short run. The **long-run aggregate supply curve** (*LRAS*) is the graphical relationship between *RGDP* and the price level when output prices and input prices can fully adjust to economic changes.

**aggregate supply
curve (AS)**
*a graphical representation that
shows the positive relationship
between the price level and
real gross domestic product
supplied*

**short-run aggregate
supply curve (SRAS)**
*the graphical relationship
between RGDP and the price
level when output prices can
change but input prices are
unable to adjust*

**long-run aggregate
supply curve (LRAS)**
*the graphical relationship
between RGDP and the price
level when output prices and
input prices can fully adjust to
economic changes*

WHY IS THE SHORT-RUN AGGREGATE SUPPLY CURVE POSITIVELY SLOPED?

In the short run, the aggregate supply curve is upward sloping, as shown in Exhibit 1. This means that at a higher price level, producers are willing to supply more real output, and at lower price levels, they are willing to supply less real output. Why would producers be willing to supply more output just because the price level increases? There are two possible explanations: the profit effect and the misperception effect.

section 9.1
Exhibit 1

The Short-Run Aggregate Supply Curve

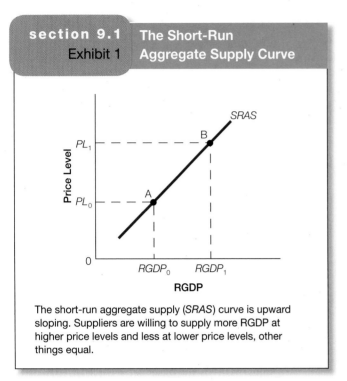

The short-run aggregate supply (SRAS) curve is upward sloping. Suppliers are willing to supply more RGDP at higher price levels and less at lower price levels, other things equal.

The Profit Effect

To many firms, input costs—like wages and rents—are relatively constant in the short run. The slow adjustments of input prices are due to contracts that do not adjust quickly to output price level changes. So when the price level rises, output prices rise relative to input prices (costs), raising producers' short-run profit margins. This is the short-run profit effect. The increased profit margins make it in the producers' self-interest to expand production and sales at higher price levels.

If the price level falls, output prices fall and producers' profits tend to fall. Again, this is because many input costs, such as wages and other contracted costs, are relatively constant in the short run. When output price levels fall, producers find it more difficult to cover their input costs and, consequently, reduce their level of output.

The Misperception Effect

The second explanation of the upward-sloping short-run aggregate supply curve is that producers can be fooled by price changes in the short run. For example, say a wheat farmer sees the price of his wheat rising. If he thinks that the *relative price* of his wheat is rising (i.e., that wheat is becoming more valuable in real terms), he will supply more. Suppose, however, that wheat was not the only thing for which prices were rising. What if the prices of many other goods and services were rising at the same time as a result of an increase in the price level? The relative price of wheat, then, was not actually rising, although it appeared so in the short run. In this case, the producer was fooled into supplying more based on the *short-run misperception* of relative prices. In other words, producers may be fooled into thinking that the relative price of the item they are producing is rising, so they increase production.

WHY IS THE LONG-RUN AGGREGATE SUPPLY CURVE VERTICAL AT THE NATURAL RATE OF OUTPUT?

Along the short-run aggregate supply curve, we assume that wages and other input prices are constant. This is not the case in the long run, which is a period long enough for the price of all inputs to fully adjust to changes in the economy. When we move along the long-run aggregate supply curve, we are then looking at the relationship between RGDP produced and the price level, once input prices have been able to respond to changes in output prices. Along the long-run aggregate supply (*LRAS*) curve, two sets of prices are changing—the price of outputs and the price of inputs. That is, along the *LRAS* curve, a 10 percent increase in the price of goods and services is matched by a 10 percent increase in the price of inputs. The long-run aggregate supply curve, then, is insensitive to the price level. As you can see in Exhibit 2, the *LRAS* curve is drawn as perfectly vertical, reflecting the fact that the level of RGDP producers are willing to supply is not affected by changes in the price level. Note that the vertical long-run aggregate supply curve will always be positioned at the natural rate of output, where all resources are fully employed ($RGDP_{NR}$). That is, in the long run, firms will always produce at the maximum level allowed by their capital, land, labour, and technology, regardless of the price level.

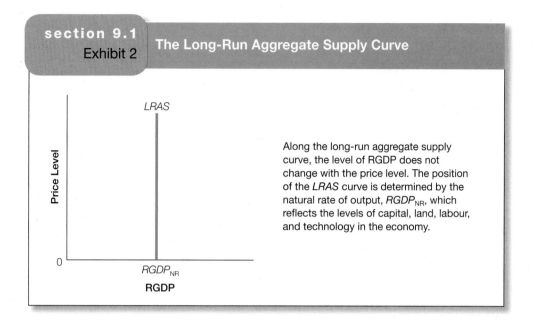

section 9.1
Exhibit 2

The Long-Run Aggregate Supply Curve

Along the long-run aggregate supply curve, the level of RGDP does not change with the price level. The position of the *LRAS* curve is determined by the natural rate of output, $RGDP_{NR}$, which reflects the levels of capital, land, labour, and technology in the economy.

The long-run equilibrium level is where the economy will settle when undisturbed and when all resources are fully employed. Remember that the economy will always be at the intersection of short-run aggregate supply and aggregate demand, but that will not always be at the natural rate of output, $RGDP_{NR}$. Long-run equilibrium will occur only where the short-run aggregate supply and aggregate demand curves intersect along the long-run aggregate supply curve at the natural, or potential, rate of output.

SECTION CHECK

- The aggregate supply curve is the relationship between the overall price level and the total quantity of final goods and services that suppliers are *able* and *willing* to produce.
- The short-run aggregate supply curve measures how much RGDP suppliers are willing to produce at different price levels. In the short run, producers supply more as the price level increases because wages and other input prices tend to change more slowly than output prices. For this reason, producers can make a profit by expanding production when the price level rises. Producers also may be fooled into thinking that the relative price of the item they are producing is rising, so they increase production.
- In the long run, the aggregate supply curve is vertical. In the long run, input prices change proportionally with output prices. The position of the *LRAS* curve is determined by the level of capital, land, labour, and technology at the natural rate of output, $RGDP_{NR}$.

Shifts in the Aggregate Supply Curve

section
9.2

- What factors of production affect the short-run and the long-run aggregate supply curves?
- What factors exclusively shift the short-run aggregate supply curve?
- Can we review the determinants that change aggregate supply?

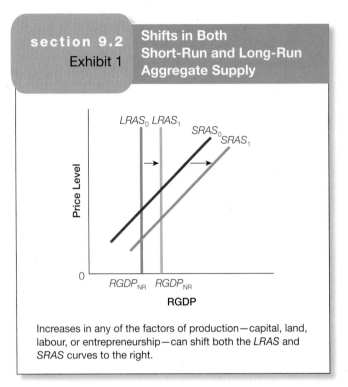

section 9.2
Exhibit 1

**Shifts in Both
Short-Run and Long-Run
Aggregate Supply**

Increases in any of the factors of production—capital, land, labour, or entrepreneurship—can shift both the *LRAS* and *SRAS* curves to the right.

WHAT FACTORS OF PRODUCTION AFFECT THE SHORT-RUN AND LONG-RUN AGGREGATE SUPPLY CURVES?

We will now examine the determinants that can shift the short-run and the long-run aggregate supply curves to the right or left, as shown in Exhibit 1. Any change in the quantity of any factor of production available—capital, land, labour, or entrepreneurship—can cause a shift in both the long-run and short-run aggregate supply curves. We will now see how these factors can change the position of both types of aggregate supply curves.

How Capital Affects Aggregate Supply

Changes in the stock of capital will alter the amount of goods and services the economy can produce. Investing in capital improves the quantity and quality of the capital stock, which lowers the cost of production in the short run. This in turn shifts the short-run aggregate supply curve rightward, and allows output to be permanently greater than before, shifting the long-run aggregate supply curve rightward, *ceteris paribus*.

Changes in human capital can also alter the aggregate supply curve. Investments in human capital may include educational or vocational programs and/or on-the-job training. All of these investments in human capital cause productivity to rise. As a result, the short-run aggregate supply curve shifts to the right because a more skilled workforce lowers the cost of production; in turn, the *LRAS* curve shifts to the right because greater output is achievable on a permanent, or sustainable, basis, *ceteris paribus*.

Land (Natural Resources)

Remember that, in economics, *land* is an all-encompassing definition that includes all natural resources. An increase in natural resources, such as successful oil exploration in Alberta, would presumably lower the costs of production and expand the economy's sustainable rate of output, shifting both the short-run and long-run aggregate supply curves to the right. Likewise, a decrease in natural resources available would result in a leftward shift of both the short-run and long-run aggregate supply curves.

The Labour Force

The addition of workers to the labour force, *ceteris paribus,* can increase aggregate supply. For example, during the 1960s and 1970s, women and baby boomers entered the labour force in large numbers. More recently, however, immigrants have become a major contributor to Canada's labour force—accounting for over 20 percent of Canada's labour force. This increase tended to depress wages and increase short-run aggregate supply, *ceteris paribus*. The expanded labour force also increased the economy's potential output, increasing long-run aggregate supply. Japan's aging population is causing a decrease in the labour force in recent years—a leftward shift in the short-run and long-run aggregate supply curves, *ceteris paribus*.

Entrepreneurship and Technology

The online *Business Dictionary* defines entrepreneurship as "the capacity and willingness to undertake conception, organization, and management of a productive venture with all attendant risks, while seeking profit as a reward." Combining entrepreneurship with the other factors of production (capital, land, and labour) and adding technology can lead to significant rewards, as in the cases of Bill Gates of Microsoft, Ted Rogers of Rogers Communications, and Michael Lazaridis of Research in Motion (RIM). Their innovative technological developments, such as computers and specialized software, have led to many cost savings for all types of businesses—ATMs, bar code scanners, biotechnology, and increased productivity across the board. These activities shift both the short-run and long-run aggregate supply curves outward by lowering costs and expanding real output possibilities.

Government Regulations

Increases in government regulations can increase production costs, resulting in a leftward shift of the short-run aggregate supply curve; a reduction in society's potential output shifts the long-run aggregate supply curve to the left as well. Likewise, a reduction in government regulations on businesses would lower the costs of production and expand potential real output, causing both the *SRAS* and *LRAS* curves to shift to the right.

WHAT FACTORS EXCLUSIVELY SHIFT THE SHORT-RUN AGGREGATE SUPPLY CURVE?

Some factors shift the short-run aggregate supply curve but do not impact the long-run aggregate supply curve. The most important of these factors are changes in wages and other input prices, productivity, and unexpected supply shocks. Exhibit 2 illustrates the impact of these factors on short-run aggregate supply.

Wages and Other Input Prices

The price of factors, or inputs, that go into producing outputs will affect only the short-run aggregate supply curve if they don't reflect permanent changes in the supplies of some factors of production. For example, if wages increase without a corresponding increase in labour productivity, then it will become more costly for suppliers to produce goods and

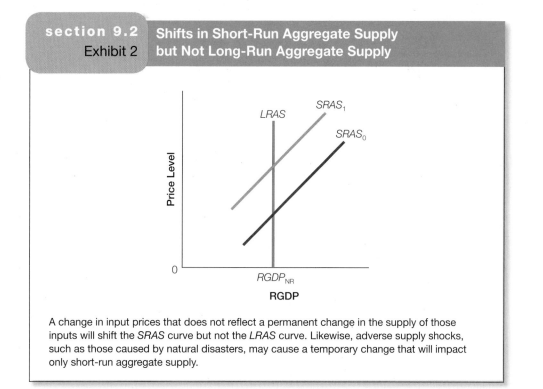

| **section 9.2** | **Shifts in Short-Run Aggregate Supply** |
| **Exhibit 2** | **but Not Long-Run Aggregate Supply** |

A change in input prices that does not reflect a permanent change in the supply of those inputs will shift the *SRAS* curve but not the *LRAS* curve. Likewise, adverse supply shocks, such as those caused by natural disasters, may cause a temporary change that will impact only short-run aggregate supply.

Temporary natural disasters like droughts can destroy crops and leave land parched. This may shift the *SRAS* curve but not the *LRAS* curve.

services at every price level, causing the *SRAS* curve to shift to the left. Long-run aggregate supply will not shift because with the same supply of labour as before, potential output does not change. If the price of steel rises, automobile producers will find it more expensive to do business because their production costs will rise, again resulting in a leftward shift in the short-run aggregate supply curve. The *LRAS* curve will not shift, however, as long as the capacity to make steel has not been reduced.

Temporary Supply Shocks

Supply shocks are unexpected temporary events that can either increase or decrease aggregate supply. For example, major widespread flooding, earthquakes, droughts, and other natural disasters can increase the costs of production, causing the short-run aggregate supply curve to shift to the left, *ceteris paribus*. However, once the temporary effects of these disasters have been felt, no appreciable change in the economy's productive capacity has occurred, so the long-run aggregate supply doesn't shift as a result. Other temporary supply shocks, such as disruptions in trade due to war, electric power blackouts, or labour strikes, will have similar effects on short-run aggregate supply. However, favourable weather conditions or temporary price reductions of imported resources like oil can shift the short-run aggregate supply curve rightward.

CAN WE REVIEW THE DETERMINANTS THAT CHANGE AGGREGATE SUPPLY?

The factors detailed below can shift the short-run aggregate supply curve, the long-run aggregate supply curve, or both, depending on whether the effects are temporary or permanent.

An Increase in Aggregate Supply (Rightward Shift)

Lower costs:
- Lower wages
- Other input prices fall

Government policy:
- Tax cuts
- Deregulation
- Lower trade barriers

Economic growth:
- Improvements in human and physical capital
- Technological advances
- An increase in labour

Favourable weather

A Decrease in Aggregate Supply (Leftward Shift)

Higher costs:
- Higher wages
- Other input prices rise

Government policy:
- Overregulation
- Waste and inefficiency
- Higher trade barriers
- Stagnation
- A decline in labour productivity
- Capital deterioration

Unfavourable weather, natural disasters, and war

section 9.3

Macroeconomic Equilibrium

- How is macroeconomic equilibrium determined?
- What are recessionary and inflationary gaps?
- How can the economy self-correct to a recessionary gap?
- Why can the self-correction to a recessionary gap be slow?
- How can the economy self-correct to an inflationary gap?

HOW IS MACROECONOMIC EQUILIBRIUM DETERMINED?

The intersection of the aggregate demand curve and the short-run aggregate supply curve determines the *short-run* equilibrium level of real output and the price level. When this equilibrium occurs on the long-run aggregate supply curve, as seen in Exhibit 1, the

section 9.3
Exhibit 1   Long-Run Macroeconomic Equilibrium

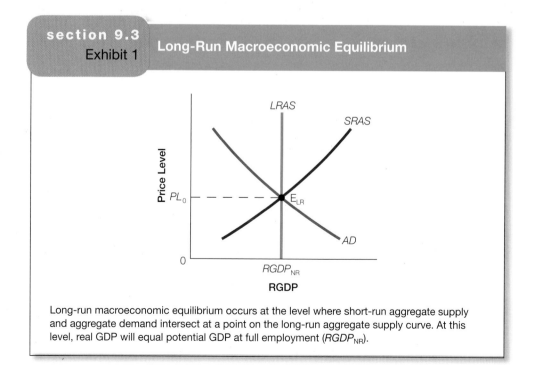

Long-run macroeconomic equilibrium occurs at the level where short-run aggregate supply and aggregate demand intersect at a point on the long-run aggregate supply curve. At this level, real GDP will equal potential GDP at full employment ($RGDP_{NR}$).

long-run equilibrium level of real output and the price level is achieved. At the long-run equilibrium, the economy is operating at its full employment level of RGDP. That is, when the short-run equilibrium occurs on the long-run aggregate supply curve, the economy is at its potential, or natural, rate of output ($RGDP_{NR}$). Only a short-run equilibrium that is at potential output is also a long-run equilibrium.

Short-run equilibrium can change when the aggregate demand curve or the short-run aggregate supply curve shifts rightward or leftward, but the long-run equilibrium level of RGDP changes only when the *LRAS* curve shifts. Sometimes, these supply or demand changes are anticipated; at other times, however, the shifts occur unexpectedly. Economists call these unexpected aggregate supply or aggregate demand changes **shocks.**

shocks

unexpected aggregate supply or aggregate demand changes

WHAT ARE RECESSIONARY AND INFLATIONARY GAPS?

As we just discussed, equilibrium will not always occur at full employment. In fact, equilibrium can occur at less than the potential output of the economy, $RGDP_{NR}$, temporarily beyond $RGDP_{NR}$, or at potential GDP. Exhibit 2 shows these three possibilities. In Exhibit 2(a) we have a recessionary gap at the short-run equilibrium, E_{SR}, at $RGDP_0$. An output gap that occurs when actual output ($RGDP$) is less than potential output ($RGDP_{NR}$) is a **recessionary gap**—aggregate demand is insufficient to fully employ all of society's resources, so unemployment will be above the natural rate. In Exhibit 2(c) we have an inflationary gap at the short-run equilibrium, E_{SR}, at $RGDP_2$. An output gap that occurs when the actual output ($RGDP$) is greater than the potential output ($RGDP_{NR}$) is an **inflationary gap.** In this case, aggregate demand is so high that the economy is temporarily operating beyond full capacity ($RGDP_{NR}$), which will usually lead to inflationary pressure, so unemployment will be below the natural rate. In Exhibit 2(b) the economy is just right, where AD_1 and *SRAS* intersect at $RGDP_{NR}$—the long-run equilibrium position.

recessionary gap

an output gap that occurs when the actual output is less than the potential output

inflationary gap

an output gap that occurs when the actual output is greater than the potential output

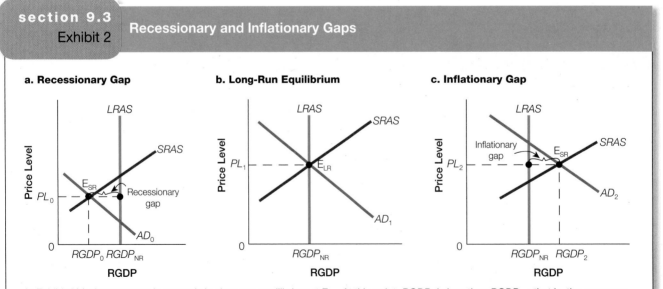

section 9.3
Exhibit 2   Recessionary and Inflationary Gaps

a. Recessionary Gap

b. Long-Run Equilibrium

c. Inflationary Gap

In Exhibit 2(a), the economy is currently in short-run equilibrium at E_{SR}. At this point, $RGDP_0$ is less than $RGDP_{NR}$; that is, the economy is producing less than its potential output and the economy is in a recessionary gap. In Exhibit 2(c), the economy is currently in short-run equilibrium at E_{SR}. At this point $RGDP_2$ is greater than $RGDP_{NR}$. The economy is temporarily producing more than its potential output and we have an inflationary gap. In Exhibit 2(b) the economy is producing its potential output at the $RGDP_{NR}$. At this point the economy is in long-run equilibrium and is not experiencing an inflationary or recessionary gap.

Demand-Pull Inflation

Demand-pull inflation occurs when the price level increases due to an increase in aggregate demand. Consider the case in which an increase in consumer optimism results in a corresponding increase in aggregate demand. Exhibit 3 shows that an increase in aggregate demand causes an increase in the price level and an increase in real output. The movement is along *SRAS* from point E_0 to point E_1. This causes an inflationary gap. Recall that there is an increase in output as a result of the increase in the price level in the short run because firms have an incentive to increase real output when the prices of the goods they are selling are rising faster than the costs of the inputs they use in production.

> **demand-pull inflation**
> *a price level increase due to an increase in aggregate demand*

Note that E_1 in Exhibit 3 is positioned beyond $RGDP_{NR}$—an inflationary gap. It seems peculiar that the economy can operate beyond its potential, but this is possible, temporarily, as firms encourage workers to work overtime, extend the hours of part-time workers, hire recently retired employees, reduce frictional unemployment through more extensive searches for employees, and so on. However, this level of output and employment *cannot* be sustained in the long run.

Cost-Push Inflation

The mid-1970s to early 1980s witnessed a phenomenon known as **stagflation,** a situation in which lower growth and higher prices occurred together. Some economists believe that this was caused by a leftward shift in the short-run aggregate supply curve, as seen in Exhibit 4. If the aggregate demand curve did not increase considerably but the price level increased significantly, then the inflation was caused by supply-side forces. This is called **cost-push inflation**—a price level increase due to a negative supply shock or increase in input prices.

> **stagflation**
> *a situation in which lower growth and higher prices occur together*

> **cost-push inflation**
> *a price level increase due to a negative supply shock or increase in input prices*

The increase in oil prices was the primary culprit responsible for the leftward shift in the aggregate supply curve. As we discussed in the last section, an increase in input prices can cause the short-run aggregate supply curve to shift to the left, and this spelled big trouble for the Canadian economy—higher price levels, lower output, and higher rates of unemployment. The impact of cost-push inflation is illustrated in Exhibit 4.

In Exhibit 4, we see that the economy is initially at full employment equilibrium at point E_0. Now suppose there is a sudden increase in input prices, such as the increase in

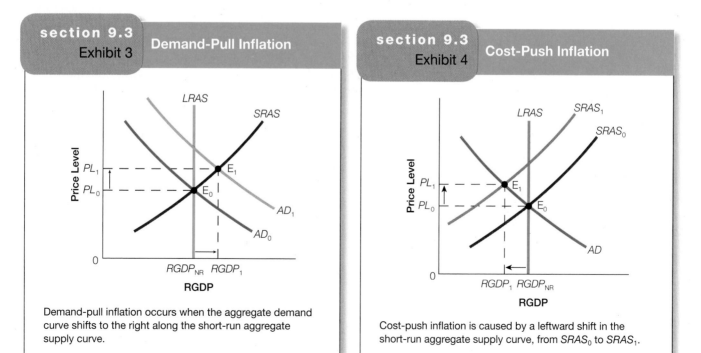

section 9.3 Exhibit 3   Demand-Pull Inflation

Demand-pull inflation occurs when the aggregate demand curve shifts to the right along the short-run aggregate supply curve.

section 9.3 Exhibit 4   Cost-Push Inflation

Cost-push inflation is caused by a leftward shift in the short-run aggregate supply curve, from $SRAS_0$ to $SRAS_1$.

section 9.3
Exhibit 5 **Short-Run Decrease in Aggregate Demand**

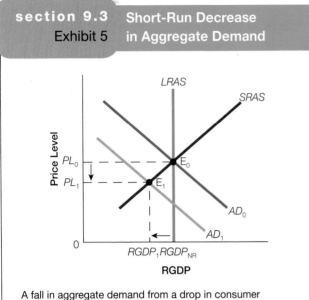

A fall in aggregate demand from a drop in consumer confidence can cause a short-run change in the economy. The decrease in aggregate demand (shown in the movement from point E_0 to E_1) causes lower output and higher unemployment in the short run.

section 9.3
Exhibit 6   **Self-Correcting to a Recessionary Gap**

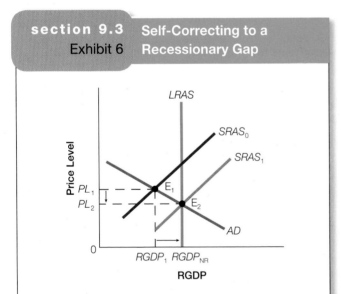

At point E_1, the economy is in a recessionary gap. However, the economy may self-correct as labourers and other input suppliers are now willing to accept lower wages and prices for the use of their resources. This results in a reduction in production costs that shifts the short-run supply curve from $SRAS_0$ to $SRAS_1$. Eventually, the economy returns to a long-run equilibrium at point E_2, at $RGDP_{NR}$, and a lower price level, PL_2. However, if wages and other input prices are sticky, the economy's adjustment mechanism might take many months, or even a few years, to totally self-correct.

the price of oil. This increase would shift the *SRAS* curve to the left—from $SRAS_0$ to $SRAS_1$. As a result of the shift in short-run aggregate supply, the price level rises to PL_1 and real output falls from $RGDP_{NR}$ to $RGDP_1$ (point E_1). Now firms demand fewer workers as a result of the higher input costs that cannot be passed on to the consumers. The result is higher prices, lower real output, and more unemployment—and it leads to a recessionary gap. In Canada, these negative supply shocks have occurred on occasion, the most recent being in 2007–2008 when the prices of many raw materials shot up globally.

A Decrease in Aggregate Demand and Recessions

Just as cost-push inflation can cause a recessionary gap, so can a decrease in aggregate demand. For example, consider the case in which consumer confidence plunges and the stock market crashes. As a result, aggregate demand would fall, shown in Exhibit 5 as the shift from AD_0 to AD_1, and the economy would be in a new short-run equilibrium at point E_1. Now, households are buying fewer goods and services at every price level. In response to this drop in demand, output would fall from $RGDP_{NR}$ to $RGDP_1$, and the price level would fall from PL_0 to PL_1. So in the short run, this fall in aggregate demand causes higher unemployment and a reduction in output—and it too can lead to a recessionary gap.

Most of the post-war recessions have been caused by negative demand shocks. Negative supply shocks have been relatively few but quite severe in terms of unemployment rates. The 2008–2009 recession appears to have been the product of both negative demand and supply shocks. In the chapters on fiscal policy and monetary policy, we will provide more details on the government's role in offsetting shocks to the economy.

HOW CAN THE ECONOMY SELF-CORRECT TO A RECESSIONARY GAP?

Many recoveries from a recessionary gap occur because of increases in aggregate demand—perhaps consumer and business confidence picks up or the government lowers taxes and/or lowers interest rates to stimulate the economy. That is, there is eventually a rightward shift in the aggregate demand curve that takes the economy back to potential output—$RGDP_{NR}$.

However, it is possible that the economy could *self-correct* through declining wages and prices. In Exhibit 6, at point E_1, the intersection of PL_1 and $RGDP_1$, the economy is in a recessionary gap—the economy is producing less than its potential output. At this lower level of output, firms lay off workers to avoid inventory accumulation. In addition, firms may cut prices to increase sales for their products. Unemployed workers and other input suppliers may also bid down wages and prices. That is, labourers and other input suppliers are now willing to accept lower wages and prices for the use of their resources, and the resulting reduction in production costs shifts the short-run supply curve from $SRAS_0$ to $SRAS_1$. Eventually, the economy returns to a long-run equilibrium at E_2 at $RGDP_{NR}$ and a lower price level, PL_2.

WHY CAN THE SELF-CORRECTION TO A RECESSIONARY GAP BE SLOW?

Many economists believe that wages and prices may be very slow to adjust, especially downward. The tendency for prices and wages to only adjust slowly downward to changes in the economy is referred to as **wage and price inflexibility.** The significance of this inflexibility is that it may lead to prolonged periods of a recessionary gap.

For example, in Exhibit 6 we see that the economy is in a recession at E_1 at $RGDP_1$. The economy will eventually self-correct to $RGDP_{NR}$ at E_2, as workers and other input owners accept lower wages and prices for their inputs, shifting the $SRAS$ curve to the right from $SRAS_0$ to $SRAS_1$. However, if wages and other input prices are sticky, the economy's adjustment mechanism might take many months, or even a few years, to totally self-correct.

wage and price inflexibility
the tendency for prices and wages to only adjust slowly downward to changes in the economy

The Causes of Sticky Wages and Prices

Empirical evidence supports several reasons for the downward stickiness of wages and prices. Firms may not be able to legally cut wages because of long-term labour

DEBATE

AGGREGATE SUPPLY AND EQUILIBRIUM

"Economic utopia" occurs when growth, inflation, and employment all fall within acceptable targets. The problem is that the economy is constantly in a state of flux—some caused by human mismanagement (such as the mortgage and credit crisis of 2008), others caused by nature (such as the disruption of the Japanese economy as a result of the tsunami of 2010). Politicians and economists disagree on the degree of economic intervention that should take place: Should governments intervene or should the economy be left alone, for the markets to decide its fate. In Canada, we opt to have greater government intervention, and this is good for our economic well-being.

Pro:
Politicians and economists agree that in Canada, government intervention is highly beneficial to our economy. Those who agree argue that some form of intervention is needed from time to time, for individual as well as social well-being. It is also argued that what's good for the individual in the markets is not necessarily good for the masses, meaning that market decisions may be made at the expense of social goals. Some also argue that not all social goals should be economically based. What are some other reasons why intervention is beneficial and what other intervention tools do you think would work for our economy?

Con:
There are those who believe that any form of intervention has limited benefits, primarily due to the complexity of the economy and the unknown unintended consequences. It is further argued that those who try to value goods or services outside of the market equilibrium will ultimately get it wrong, forcing either shortages or surpluses and definitely causing deadweight losses in the economy. What are other arguments for not intervening in the economy? Why should markets prevail over policies?

contracts (particularly with union workers) or a legal minimum wage. Efficiency wages may also limit a firm's ability to lower wage rates. Menu costs may cause price inflexibility as well.

Efficiency Wages   In economics, it is generally assumed that as productivity rises, wages will rise, and that workers can raise their productivity through investments in human capital like education and on-the-job training. However, some economists believe that in some cases, *higher wages will lead to greater productivity.*

In the efficiency wage model, employers pay their employees more than the equilibrium wage as a means to increase efficiency. Proponents of this theory suggest that higher-than-equilibrium wages may attract the most productive workers, lower job turnover and training costs, and improve morale. Because the efficiency wage rate is greater than the equilibrium wage rate, the quantity of labour that would be willingly supplied is greater than the quantity of labour demanded, resulting in greater amounts of unemployment.

However, aside from creating some additional unemployment, it may also cause wages to be inflexible downward. For example, in the event that there is a decrease in aggregate demand, firms that pay efficiency wages may be reluctant to cut wages in the fear that it could lead to lower morale, greater absenteeism, and general productivity losses. In short, if firms are paying efficiency wages, they may be reluctant to lower wages in a recession, leading to downward wage inflexibility.

Menu Costs   As we explained in Chapter 5, there is a cost to changing prices in an inflationary environment. Thus the higher price level in an inflationary environment is often reflected slowly, as restaurants, mail-order houses, and department stores change their prices gradually so that they incur fewer *menu costs* (the costs of changing posted prices) in printing new catalogues, new mailers, new advertisements, and so on. Since businesses are not likely to change these prices instantly, we can say that some prices are sticky, or slow to change. For example, many outputs, like steel, are inputs in the production of other products, like automobiles. As a result, these prices are slow to change.

Suppose that there was an unexpected reduction in the money supply that led to a decrease in aggregate demand. This could lower the price level. Although some firms may adjust to the change quickly, others may move more slowly because of menu costs. The potential result is that their prices may become too high (above equilibrium); sales and output will fall, causing a potential recession.

If some firms are not responding quickly to changes in demand, there must be a reason, and to some economists, menu costs are at least part of that reason.

HOW CAN THE ECONOMY SELF-CORRECT TO AN INFLATIONARY GAP?

In Exhibit 7, the economy is currently in an inflationary gap at E_1, where $RGDP_0$ is greater than $RGDP_{NR}$. Because

section 9.3 Exhibit 7 Self-Correction to an Inflationary Gap

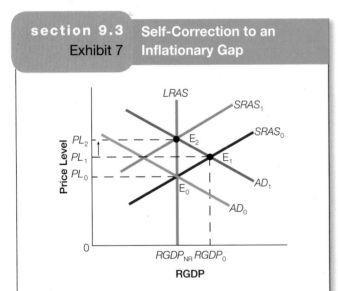

The economy is currently in an inflationary gap at E_1, where $RGDP_0$ is greater than $RGDP_{NR}$. Because the price level is now higher than workers anticipated (i.e., it is PL_1 rather than PL_0), workers become disgruntled with wages that have not yet adjusted to the new price level. Consequently, workers and other suppliers demand higher prices to be willing to supply their inputs. As input prices respond to the higher level of output prices, the short-run aggregate supply curve shifts to the left, from $SRAS_0$ to $SRAS_1$. Suppliers will continually seek higher prices for their inputs until they reach the long-run equilibrium, at point E_2. At point E_2, input suppliers' purchasing power is now restored at the natural rate, $RGDP_{NR}$, at a new higher price level, PL_2.

the price level, PL_1, is now higher than workers anticipated, PL_0, workers become disgruntled with wages that have not yet adjusted to it (if prices have risen, but wages have not risen as much, real wages have fallen). Recall that along the *SRAS* curve, wages and other input prices are assumed to be constant. Therefore, workers' and input suppliers' purchasing power falls as output prices rise. Real (adjusted for inflation) wages have fallen. Consequently, workers and other suppliers demand higher prices, to be willing to supply their inputs. As input prices respond to the higher level of output prices, the short-run aggregate supply curve shifts to the left, from $SRAS_0$ to $SRAS_1$. Suppliers will continually seek higher prices for their inputs until they reach the long-run equilibrium, at point E_2 in Exhibit 7. At point E_2, input suppliers' purchasing power is now restored at the long-run equilibrium, at $RGDP_{NR}$, and a new higher price level, PL_2.

Business **CONNECTION**

INFLATION: RECOGNIZING THE STORM CLOUDS

A business is essentially an organization that transforms factors of production (land, labour, capital, and entrepreneurship) into goods and services, with the goal of generating a profit—the funds remaining after the business subtracts its costs or expenses from its sales revenues. If a business is successful, this residual measure of profit will be a positive number that increases in magnitude over time. Individuals engaging in business face personal and economic risks in attempting to create and provide goods and services. Such efforts are certain to result in costs, but the extent to which the resulting goods or services will generate revenues in excess of these costs is uncertain.

The dynamic play between costs and revenues is further complicated by inflation. Generally, inflation can be regarded as a decline in the purchasing power of money, where purchasing power is the ability of a given amount of money to buy a particular number and quality of goods and services. For instance, if from one year to another, profits increase by 3 percent but inflation increases by 5 percent, the purchasing power of the profits will have declined by 2 percent. For this reason business operators ought to be, and usually are, concerned about inflation.

There are two sources of inflation. Inflation fuelled by aggregate demand, called *demand-pull inflation,* which occurs when the price levels for goods and services in the economy increase because aggregate demand is increasing at a greater rate than aggregate supply. The other source, cost-push inflation, usually occurs due to the increasing costs of some key factors of production, which in turn feed into the costs of a host of basic goods and services. This type of inflation forces suppliers in the affected industries to increase prices or at worst to leave the industry entirely, resulting in a reduction in aggregate supply.

Business operators who can differentiate between these two sources of inflation are often better prepared to anticipate and mitigate the impact of inflation on the profitability of the business or, even better, take steps to exploit inflation to increase profitability. In the early stages, an increase in price levels due to demand-pull inflation is often accompanied by an expanding economy, with opportunities for sharp increases in revenues due to increases in both prices and quantities of consumer end-products sold. On the other hand, cost-push inflation frequently increases the cost of inputs in contracting economies, with few opportunities for producers to pass on these costs to purchasers. Hence, with the onset of demand-pull inflation, a business is more likely to enjoy increases in nominal profits. With cost-push inflation, a business is more likely to see increases in input costs coupled with downward pressures on revenues, with an inability to pass on cost increases to customers. The result is falling margins, leading to lower nominal profits. In business, it pays to read the inflation storm clouds!

SECTION CHECK

- Short-run macroeconomic equilibrium is shown by the intersection of the aggregate demand curve and the short-run aggregate supply curve. A short-run equilibrium is also a long-run equilibrium only if it is at potential output on the long-run aggregate supply curve.
- If short-run equilibrium occurs at less than the potential output of the economy, $RGDP_{NR}$, there is a recessionary gap. If short-run equilibrium temporarily occurs beyond $RGDP_{NR}$, there is an inflationary gap.
- It is possible that the economy could *self-correct* through declining wages and prices. For example, during a recession, labourers and other input suppliers are willing to accept lower wages and prices for the use of their resources, and the resulting reduction in production costs increases the short-run supply curve. Eventually, the economy returns to the long-run equilibrium, at $RGDP_{NR}$, and a lower price level.
- Wages and other input prices may be very slow to adjust, especially downward. This downward wage and price inflexibility may lead to prolonged periods of recession. Firms might not be willing to lower nominal wages in the short run for several reasons, leading to downward wage and price inflexibility or sticky prices. Firms may not be able to legally cut wages because of long-term labour contracts (particularly with union workers) or due to a legal minimum wage. In addition, efficiency wage and menu costs may lead to sticky wages and prices.
- It is possible that the economy could self-correct an inflationary gap by increasing wages and prices. For example, during an inflation, labourers and other input suppliers will experience a loss of purchasing power as output prices rise and input prices remain constant. When production costs eventually do increase, this will decrease the short-run aggregate supply curve, ultimately returning the economy to the long-run level of output, $RGDP_{NR}$, at a higher price level.

For Your Review

Section 9.1

1. You operate a business in which you manufacture furniture. You are able to increase your furniture prices by 5 percent this quarter. You assume that the demand for your furniture has increased and begin increasing furniture production. Only later do you realize that prices in the macroeconomy are rising generally at a rate of 5 percent per quarter. This is an example of what effect? What does it imply about the slope of the short-run aggregate supply curve?

2. Explain why the following statements are false.

   a. The long-run aggregate supply curve is vertical because economic forces do not affect the long run.

   b. If firms adjusted their prices every day, the short-run aggregate supply curve would be horizontal.

Section 9.2

3. How will each of the following changes alter aggregate supply?

Change	Short-Run Aggregate Supply	Long-Run Aggregate Supply
An increase in aggregate demand	_____	_____
A decrease in aggregate demand	_____	_____
An increase in the stock of capital	_____	_____
A reduction in the size of the labour force	_____	_____
An increase in input prices (that does not reflect permanent changes in their supplies)	_____	_____
A decrease in input prices (that does reflect permanent changes in their supplies)	_____	_____
An increase in usable natural resources	_____	_____
A temporary adverse supply shock	_____	_____
Increases in the cost of government regulations	_____	_____

4. What would each of the following do to the short-run aggregate supply curve?
   a. a decrease in wage rates
   b. passage of more stringent environmental and safety regulations affecting businesses
   c. technological progress
   d. an increase in consumer optimism
   e. an electric power blackout in Ontario

5. What would each of the following do to the long-run aggregate supply curve?
   a. advances in medical technologies
   b. increased immigration of skilled workers
   c. an increase in wage rates
   d. an epidemic involving a new strain of the flu kills hundreds of thousands of people

6. Indicate whether the following events affect short-run aggregate supply or long-run aggregate supply. Identify the direction of impact.
   a. Unusually cold weather in Saskatchewan reduces the wheat crop.
   b. A devastating earthquake in British Columbia destroys hundreds of buildings and kills thousands of people.
   c. Economy-wide wage increases are made.
   d. Advances in computers and wireless technologies improve the efficiency of production.

Section 9.3

7. Use the following diagram to answer questions a and b.
   a. On the exhibit provided, illustrate the short-run effects of an increase in aggregate demand. What happens to the price level, real output, employment, and unemployment?
   b. On the exhibit provided, illustrate the long-run effects of an increase in aggregate demand. What happens to the price level, real output, employment, and unemployment?

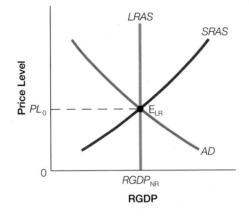

8. Use the following diagram to answer questions a and b.

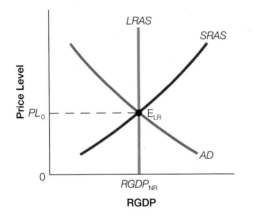

   a. On the exhibit provided, illustrate the short-run effects of a decrease in aggregate demand. What happens to the price level, real output, employment, and unemployment?

   b. On the exhibit provided, illustrate the long-run effects of a decrease in aggregate demand. What happens to the price level, real output, employment, and unemployment?

9. Use the following diagram to answer questions a and b.

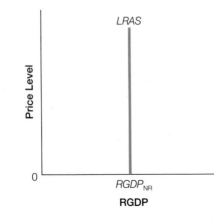

   a. Illustrate a recessionary gap on the diagram provided.

   b. Given the illustration in a, illustrate and explain the eventual long-run equilibrium in this case.

10. Use the following diagram to answer questions a and b.

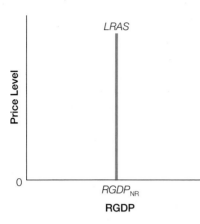

a. Illustrate an inflationary gap on the diagram provided.

b. Given the illustration in a, illustrate and explain the eventual long-run equilibrium in this case.

11. Distinguish cost-push from demand-pull inflation. Provide an example of an event or shock to the economy that would cause each.

12. Is it ever possible for an economy to operate above the full-employment level in the short term? Explain.

13. How does an increase in aggregate demand affect output, unemployment, and the price level in the short run? How does a decrease in short-run aggregate supply affect output, unemployment, and the price level in the short run?

14. Which of the following leads to stagflation, assuming the economy is currently operating at full employment?

a. an increase in government spending on education

b. large nominal wage increases demanded and received by striking workers

c. a decrease in federal spending on national defence

d. a temporary increase in oil production from the Organization of the Petroleum Exporting Countries (OPEC)

e. a temporary decrease in OPEC oil production

Appendix

The Keynesian Aggregate Expenditure Model

THE SIMPLE KEYNESIAN AGGREGATE EXPENDITURE MODEL

The Keynesian aggregate expenditure model is based on the condition that the components of aggregate demand (consumption, investment, government spending, and net exports) must equal total output. Recall from Chapter 7 that Keynes was concerned with explaining and reducing short-term fluctuations in the economy. Keynes believed that total spending was a critical determinant of the overall level of economic activity. When total spending increases, firms increase their output and hire more workers. Even though Keynes ignored an important economic component—aggregate supply—his model still provides a great deal of information about aggregate demand.

Why Do We Assume the Price Level Is Fixed?

In most of this appendix, we will assume that the price level is fixed or constant. If the price level is fixed, then changes in nominal income will be equivalent to changes in real income. That is, when we assume the price level is fixed, we do not have to distinguish real variable changes from nominal variable changes. Keynes believed that prices and wages were rigid or fixed until full employment is reached. But let us begin by looking at the most important aggregate demand determinant—consumption spending.

What Are the Autonomous Factors That Influence Consumption Spending?

Even though income is given for the representative household, other economic factors that influence consumption spending are not. When consumption (or any of the other components of spending, such as investment) does not depend on income, we call it *autonomous* (or independent). Let's look at some of these other autonomous factors and see how they would change consumption spending.

Real Wealth   The larger the value of a household's real wealth (the money value of wealth divided by the price level, which indicates the amount of consumption goods that the wealth could buy), the larger the amount of consumption spending, other things being equal. Thus, in Exhibit 1, an increase in real wealth would raise consumption to C_2, at point D, for a given level of current income. Similarly, something that would lower the value of real wealth, such as a decline in property values or a stock market decline would tend to lower the level of consumption to C_1, at point B in Exhibit 1.

Interest Rate   A higher interest rate tends to make the consumption items that we buy on credit more expensive, which reduces expenditures on those items. An increase in the interest rate increases the monthly payments made to buy such things as automobiles, furniture, and major appliances and reduces our ability to spend out of a given income. This shift is shown as a decrease in consumption from point A to point B in Exhibit 1. Moreover, an increase in the interest rate provides a higher future return from reducing current spending, which motivates increasing savings. Thus, a higher interest rate in the current period would likely motivate an increase in savings today, which would permit households to consume more goods and services at some future date.

Household Debt Remember when that friend of yours ran up his credit card obligations so high that he stopped buying goods except the basic necessities? Well, our average household might find itself in the same situation if its outstanding debt exceeds some reasonable level relative to its income. So, as debt increases, other things being equal, consumption expenditure would fall from point A to point B in Exhibit 1.

Expectations Just as in microeconomics, decisions to spend may be influenced by a person's expectations of future disposable income, employment, or certain world events. Based on monthly surveys conducted that attempt to measure consumer confidence, an increase in consumer confidence generally acts to increase household spending (a movement from point A to point D in Exhibit 1) and a decrease in consumer confidence would act to decrease spending (a movement from point A to point B in Exhibit 1).

Tastes and Preferences Of course, each household is different. Some are young and beginning a working career; some are without children; others have families; still others are older and perhaps retired from the workforce. Some households like to save, putting dollars away for later spending, whereas others spend all their income, or even borrow to spend more than their current disposable income. These saving and spending decisions often vary over a household's life cycle.

appendix Exhibit 1	Autonomous Changes in Consumption Spending

An increase in real wealth would raise consumption spending to C_2, at point D. A decrease in real wealth would tend to lower the level of consumption spending to C_1, at point B. A higher interest rate tends to cause a decrease in consumption spending from point A to point B. As household debt increases, other things equal, consumption spending would fall from point A to point B. In general, an increase in consumer confidence would act to increase household spending (a movement from point A to point D) and a decrease in consumer confidence would act to decrease household spending (a movement from point A to point B).

As you can see, many economic factors affect consumption expenditures. The factors already listed represent some of the most important. All of these factors are considered **autonomous determinants of consumption expenditures;** that is, those expenditures that are not dependent on the level of current disposable income.

autonomous determinants of consumption expenditures
expenditures not dependent on the level of current disposable income

CONSUMPTION IN THE KEYNESIAN MODEL

In our first model, we looked at the economic variables that affected consumption expenditures when disposable income was fixed. This assumption is clearly unrealistic, but it allows us to develop some of the basic building blocks of the Keynesian expenditure model. Now we'll look at a slightly more complicated model in which consumption also depends on disposable income.

If you think about what determines your own current consumption spending, you know that it depends on many factors previously discussed, such as your age, family size, interest rates, expected future disposable income, wealth, and, most importantly, your current disposable income. Recall from earlier chapters, disposable income is your after-tax income. Your personal consumption spending depends primarily on your current disposable income. In fact, empirical studies confirm that most people's consumption spending is closely tied to their disposable income.

Revisiting Marginal Propensity to Consume and Save

What happens to current consumption spending when a person earns some additional disposable income? Most people will spend some of their extra income and save some of it.

marginal propensity to consume (MPC)
the additional consumption resulting from an additional dollar of disposable income

The additional consumption resulting from an additional dollar of disposable income is what economists call your **marginal propensity to consume (MPC).** That is, MPC is equal to the *change* in consumption spending (ΔC) divided by the *change* in disposable income (ΔDY):

$$MPC = \Delta C / \Delta DY$$

For example, suppose you won a lottery prize of $1000. You might decide to spend $750 of your winnings today and save $250. In this example, your marginal propensity to consume is 0.75 (or 75 percent) because out of the extra $1000, you decided to spend 75 percent of it ($0.75 \times \$1000 = \$750$).

The term *marginal propensity to consume* has two parts: (1) *marginal* refers to the fact that you received an extra amount of disposable income—in addition to your income, not your total income; and (2) *propensity to consume* refers to how much you tend to spend on consumer goods and services out of your additional income.

The flip side of the marginal propensity to consume is the **marginal propensity to save (MPS)**—the additional saving that results from an additional dollar of disposable income. That is, MPS is equal to the *change* in savings (ΔS) divided by the change in disposable income (ΔDY):

$$MPS = \Delta S / \Delta DY$$

marginal propensity to save (MPS)
the additional saving that results from an additional dollar of income

In the earlier lottery example, your marginal propensity to save is 0.25, or 25 percent, because you decided to save 25 percent of your additional disposable income ($0.25 \times \$1000 = \$250$). Because your additional disposable income must be either consumed or saved, the marginal propensity to consume plus the marginal propensity to save must add up to 1, or 100 percent.

Let's illustrate the marginal propensity to consume in Exhibit 2. Suppose you estimated that you had to spend $8000 a year, even if you earned no income for the year, for necessities such as food, clothing, and shelter. And suppose for every $1000 of added disposable income you earn, you spend 75 percent of it and save 25 percent of it. So if your disposable income is $0, you spend $8000 (that means you have to borrow or reduce your existing savings just to survive). If your disposable income is $20 000, you'll spend $8000 plus 75 percent of $20 000 (which equals $15 000), for total spending of $23 000. If your disposable income is $40 000, you'll spend $8000 plus 75 percent of $40 000 (which equals $30 000), for total spending of $38 000.

What's your marginal propensity to consume? In this case, if you spend 75 percent of every additional $1000 you earn, your marginal propensity to consume is 0.75 or 75 percent. And if you save 25 percent of every additional $1000 you earn, your marginal propensity to save is 0.25.

In Exhibit 2, the slope of the line represents the marginal propensity to consume. To better understand this concept, look at what happens when your disposable income rises from $18 000 to $20 000. At a disposable income of $18 000, you spend $8000 plus 75 percent of $18 000

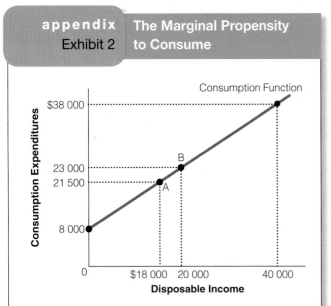

appendix
Exhibit 2   **The Marginal Propensity to Consume**

The slope of the line represents the marginal propensity to consume. At a disposable income of $18 000, you spend $8000 plus 75 percent of $18 000 (which is $13 500), for total spending of $21 500. If your disposable income rises to $20 000, you spend $8000 plus 75 percent of $20 000 (which is $15 000), for total spending of $23 000. So when your disposable income rises by $2000 (from $18 000 to $20 000), your spending goes up by $1500 (from $21 500 to $23 000). Your marginal propensity to consume is $1500 (the increase in spending) divided by $2000 (the increase in disposable income), which equals 0.75, or 75 percent. But notice that this MPC calculation is also the calculation of the slope of the line from point A to point B.

(which is $13 500), for total spending of $21 500. If your disposable income rises to $20 000, you spend $8000 plus 75 percent of $20 000 (which is $15 000), for total spending of $23 000. So when your disposable income rises by $2000 (from $18 000 to $20 000), your spending goes up by $1500 (from $21 500 to $23 000). Your marginal propensity to consume is $1500 (the increase in spending) divided by $2000 (the increase in disposable income), which equals 0.75, or 75 percent. But notice that this calculation is also the calculation of the slope of the line from point A to point B in the exhibit. Recall that the slope of the line is the rise (the change on the vertical axis) over the run (the change on the horizontal axis). In this case, that's $1500 divided by $2000, which makes 0.75 the marginal propensity to consume. So the marginal propensity to consume is the same as the slope of the line in our graph of consumption and disposable income.

Now, let's take this same logic and apply it to the economy as a whole. If we add up, or aggregate, everyone's consumption and everyone's income, we'll get a line that looks like the one in Exhibit 2, but that applies to the entire economy. This line or functional relationship is called a *consumption function*. Let's suppose consumption spending in the economy is $1 billion plus 75 percent of income.

Now, with consumption equal to $1 billion plus 75 percent of income, consumption is partly autonomous (the $1 billion part, which people would spend no matter what their income, which depends on the current interest rate, real wealth, debt, and expectations), and partly *induced,* which means it depends on income. The induced consumption is the portion that's equal to 75 percent of income.

What is the total amount of expenditure in this economy? Because we've assumed that investment, government purchases, and net exports are zero, aggregate expenditure is just equal to the amount of consumption spending represented by our consumption function.

EQUILIBRIUM IN THE KEYNESIAN MODEL

The next part of the Keynesian aggregate expenditure model is to examine what conditions are needed for the economy to be in equilibrium. This discussion also tells us why the Keynesian expenditure model is sometimes called a *Keynesian-cross model.* In order to determine equilibrium, we need to show (1) that income equals output in the economy, and (2) that in equilibrium, aggregate expenditure (or consumption in this example) equals output. First, income equals output because people earn income by producing goods and services. For example, workers earn wages because they produce some product that is then sold on the market, and owners of firms earn profits because the products they sell provide more income than the cost of producing them. So any income that is earned by anyone in the economy arises from the production of output in the economy. From now on, we'll use this idea and say that income equals output; we'll use the terms *income* and *output* interchangeably.

The second condition needed for equilibrium (aggregate expenditure in the economy equals output) is the distinctive feature of the Keynesian expenditure model. Just as income must equal output (because income comes from selling goods and services), aggregate expenditure equals output because people can't earn income until the products they produce are sold to someone. Every good or service that is produced in the economy must be purchased by someone or added to inventories. Exhibit 3 plots aggregate expenditure against output. As you can see, it's a 45-degree line (slope = 1). The 45-degree line shows that the number on the horizontal axis, representing the amount of output in the economy, real GDP (Y), is equal to the number on the vertical axis, representing the amount of real aggregate expenditure (AE) in the economy. If output is $5 billion, then in equilibrium, aggregate expenditure must equal $5 billion. All points of macroeconomic equilibrium lie on the 45-degree line.

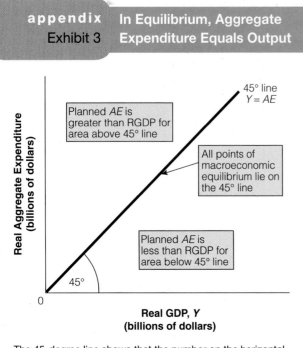

The 45-degree line shows that the number on the horizontal axis, representing the amount of output in the economy, is equal to the number on the vertical axis, representing the amount of aggregate expenditure in the economy. If output is $5 billion, then in equilibrium, aggregate expenditure must equal $5 billion.

DISEQUILIBRIUM IN THE KEYNESIAN MODEL

What would happen if, for some reason, output was lower than its equilibrium level, as would be the case if output was Y_1 in Exhibit 4?

Looking at the vertical dotted line, we see that when output is Y_1, aggregate expenditure (shown by the consumption function) is greater than output (shown by the 45-degree line). This amount is labelled the distance AB on the graph. So, people would be trying to buy more goods and services (A) than were being produced (B), which would cause producers to increase the amount of production, which would increase output in the economy. This process would continue until output reached its equilibrium level, where the two lines intersect. Another way to think about this disequilibrium is that consumers would be buying more than is currently produced, causing a decrease in inventories on shelves and in warehouses from their desired levels. Clearly, profit-seeking businesspeople would increase production to bring their inventory stocks back up to the desired levels. In doing so, they would move production to the equilibrium level.

Similarly, if output was above its equilibrium level, as would occur if output was Y_2 in Exhibit 4, economic forces would act to reduce output. At this point, as you can see by looking at the graph above point Y_2 on the horizontal axis, aggregate expenditure (D) is less than output (C). People wouldn't want to buy all the output that is being produced, so producers would want to reduce their production. They would keep reducing their output until the equilibrium level was reached. Using the inventory adjustment process, inventories would be bulging from shelves and warehouses and firms would reduce output and production until inventory stocks returned to the desired level. More discussion of this inventory adjustment process can be found later in the chapter when the complete model has been developed.

This basic model—in which we've assumed that consumption spending is the only component of aggregate expenditure (i.e., we've ignored investment, government spending, and net exports) and that some consumption spending is autonomous—is quite simple, yet it is the essence of the Keynesian-cross model. From Exhibit 4, you can see where the "cross" part of its name comes from. Equilibrium in this model, and in more complicated versions of the model, always occurs where one line representing aggregate expenditure crosses another line that represents the equilibrium condition where aggregate expenditure equals output (the 45-degree line). The "Keynesian" part of the name reflects the fact that the model is a simple version of John Maynard Keynes' description of the economy from more than 80 years ago.

Now let's put Exhibits 2 and 3 together to find the equilibrium in the economy, shown in Exhibit 4. As you might guess, the point where the two lines cross is the equilibrium point. Why? Because it is only at this point that aggregate expenditure is equal to output. Aggregate expenditure is shown by the flatter line (Aggregate expenditure = Consumption). The equilibrium condition is shown by the 45-degree line ($Y = AE$). The only point for which consumption spending equals aggregate expenditure equals output is the point where those two lines intersect, labelled "Equilibrium." Because these points are on the 45-degree line, equilibrium output equals equilibrium aggregate expenditure.

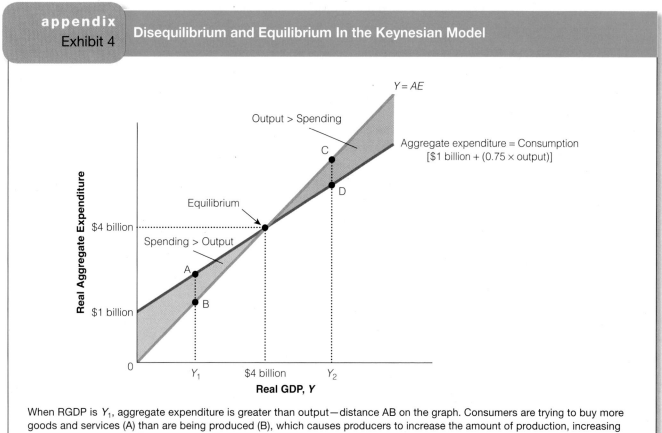

appendix Exhibit 4 Disequilibrium and Equilibrium In the Keynesian Model

$Y = AE$

Output > Spending

Aggregate expenditure = Consumption [$1 billion + (0.75 × output)]

Equilibrium

Spending > Output

Real Aggregate Expenditure

$4 billion

$1 billion

$4 billion

Real GDP, *Y*

When RGDP is Y_1, aggregate expenditure is greater than output—distance AB on the graph. Consumers are trying to buy more goods and services (A) than are being produced (B), which causes producers to increase the amount of production, increasing output in the economy. This process continues until output reaches its equilibrium level, where the two lines intersect. If RGDP is at Y_2, aggregate expenditure (D) is less than output (C). Consumers wouldn't want to buy all the output that is being produced, so producers would want to reduce their production. They would keep reducing their output until the equilibrium level of output was reached. The only point for which consumption spending equals real aggregate planned expenditure equals output is the point where those two lines intersect. Because these points are on the 45-degree line, equilibrium output equals equilibrium aggregate expenditure.

ADDING INVESTMENT, GOVERNMENT PURCHASES, AND NET EXPORTS

Now we can complicate our model in another important way by adding in the other three major components of expenditure in the economy: investment, government purchases, and net exports. We'll add these components to the model but assume that they are autonomous, that is, they don't depend on the level of income or output in the economy.

Suppose that consumption depends on the level of income or output in the economy, but investment, government purchases, and net exports don't; instead, they depend on other things in the economy, such as interest rates, political considerations, or the condition of foreign economies. Now, aggregate expenditure (*AE*) consists of consumption (*C*) plus investment (*I*) plus government purchases (*G*) plus net exports (*NX*):

$$AE \equiv C + I + G + NX$$

This equation is nothing more than a definition (indicated by the $\equiv$ rather than $=$): Aggregate expenditure equals the sum of its components.

When we add up all the components of aggregate expenditure, we'll get an upward-sloping line, as we did in the previous section because consumption increases as income increases. But because we're now allowing for investment, government purchases, and net exports, the autonomous portion of aggregate expenditure is larger. Thus, the intercept of the aggregate expenditure line is higher, as shown in Exhibit 5.

What is the new equilibrium? As before, the equilibrium occurs where the two lines cross, that is, where the aggregate expenditure line intersects the equilibrium line, which is the 45-degree line.

Now that we've added in the other components of spending, especially investment spending, we can begin to discuss some of the more realistic factors related to the business cycle. This discussion of what happens to the economy during business cycles is a major element of Keynesian theory, which was designed to explain what happens in recessions.

If you look at historical economic data, you'll see that investment spending fluctuates much more than overall output in the economy. In recessions, output declines, and a major portion of the decline occurs because investment falls sharply. In expansions, investment is the major contributor to economic growth. The two major explanations for the volatile movement of investment over the business cycle involve planned investment and unplanned investment.

The first explanation for investment's strong business cycle movement is that *planned* investment responds dramatically to perceptions of future changes in economic activity. If business firms think that the economy will be good in the future, they'll build new factories, buy more computers, and hire more workers today, in anticipation of being able to sell more goods in the future. On the other hand, if firms think the economy will be weak in the future, they'll cut back on both investment and hiring. Economists find that planned investment is extremely sensitive to firms' perceptions about the future. And if firms desire to invest more today, it generates ripple effects that make the economy grow even faster.

The second explanation for investment's movement over the business cycle is that businesses encounter *unplanned* changes in investment as well. The idea here is that

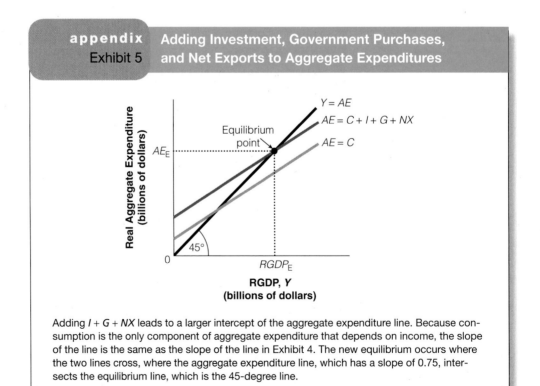

appendix
Exhibit 5

Adding Investment, Government Purchases, and Net Exports to Aggregate Expenditures

Adding $I + G + NX$ leads to a larger intercept of the aggregate expenditure line. Because consumption is the only component of aggregate expenditure that depends on income, the slope of the line is the same as the slope of the line in Exhibit 4. The new equilibrium occurs where the two lines cross, where the aggregate expenditure line, which has a slope of 0.75, intersects the equilibrium line, which is the 45-degree line.

recessions, to some extent, occur as the economy is making a transition, before it reaches equilibrium. We'll use Exhibit 6 to illustrate this idea. In the exhibit, equilibrium occurs at output of Y_0. Now, consider what would happen if, for some reason, firms produced too many goods, bringing the economy to output level Y_1. At output level Y_1, aggregate expenditure is less than output because the aggregate expenditure line is below the 45-degree line at that point. When people aren't buying all the products that firms are producing, unsold goods begin piling up. In the national income accounts, unsold goods in firms' inventories are counted in a subcategory of investment—inventory investment. The firms didn't plan for this to happen, so the piling up of inventories reflects **unplanned inventory investment.** Of course, once firms realize that inventories are rising because they've produced too much, they cut back on production, reducing output below Y_1. This process continues until firms' inventories are restored to normal levels and output returns to Y_0.

Now let's look at what would happen if firms produced too few goods, as occurs when output is at Y_2. At output level Y_2, aggregate expenditure is greater than output because the aggregate expenditure line is above the 45-degree line at that point. People want to buy more goods than firms are producing, so firms' inventories begin to decline or become depleted. Again, this change in inventories shows up in the national income accounts, this time as a decline in firms' inventories and thus a decline in investment. Again, the firms didn't plan for this situation, so once they realize that inventories are declining because they haven't produced enough, they'll increase production beyond Y_2. Equilibrium is reached when firms' inventories are restored to normal levels and output returns to Y_0. So, our Keynesian aggregate expenditure model helps to explain the process of the business cycle, working through investment.

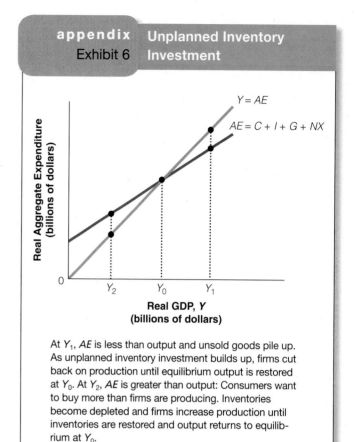

appendix
Exhibit 6

Unplanned Inventory Investment

At Y_1, *AE* is less than output and unsold goods pile up. As unplanned inventory investment builds up, firms cut back on production until equilibrium output is restored at Y_0. At Y_2, *AE* is greater than output: Consumers want to buy more than firms are producing. Inventories become depleted and firms increase production until inventories are restored and output returns to equilibrium at Y_0.

unplanned inventory investment
collection of inventory that results when people do not buy the products firms are producing

CourseMate

Access an interactive eBook and chapter-specific interactive learning tools, including flashcards, quizzes, a glossary, and more in CourseMate, accessed through **www.sextonmacro3ce.nelson.com**

chapter 10

Fiscal Policy

section 10.1

Fiscal Policy

- What is fiscal policy?
- How does fiscal policy affect the government's budget?

WHAT IS FISCAL POLICY?

fiscal policy
use of government spending and/or taxes to alter RGDP and the price level

Fiscal policy is the use of government spending and/or taxes to alter RGDP and the price level. Sometimes it is necessary for the government to use fiscal policy to stimulate the economy during a contraction (or recession) or to try to curb an expansion in order to bring inflation under control. In the early 1980s, the U.S. government implemented large tax cuts, which helped the U.S. economy out of a recession. In 2001 and 2003, tax cuts were again implemented to combat an economic slowdown and promote long-term economic growth. In the 1990s, Japan used large government spending programs to help pull itself out of a recessionary slump.

Beginning in the early 2000s, the federal government in Canada began cutting income taxes to promote long-term economic growth, a policy objective it continued in subsequent budgets. The 2009 budget, however, marked a dramatic departure from the fiscal restraint illustrated in earlier budgets, as the government began to deal with the global economic crisis. This first year of Canada's Economic Action Plan saw the government provide almost $30 billion in support of the Canadian economy. In total, this was equivalent to 1.9 percent of total spending in the Canadian economy in 2009. The 2010 budget confirmed an additional $19 billion in new federal stimulus under year 2 of Canada's Economic Action Plan. To accompany these increases in government spending, the Economic Action Plan also introduced additional tax relief measures to augment the already substantial tax relief provided by the government since 2006. The tax relief provided to individuals and families was estimated to be about $160 billion throughout

2008–2009 and the following five fiscal years. When should the government use such policies? How well do they work? These are just a couple of the questions we will answer in this chapter.

When government spending (for purchases of goods and services and for transfer payments to individuals, like EI benefits) exceeds tax revenues for a given fiscal year, there is a **budget deficit.** When tax revenues are greater than government spending for a given fiscal year, a **budget surplus** exists. A balanced budget, where government expenditures equal tax revenues, may seldom occur unless efforts are made to deliberately balance the budget as a matter of public policy.

HOW DOES FISCAL POLICY AFFECT THE GOVERNMENT'S BUDGET?

When the government wants to stimulate the economy by increasing aggregate demand, it will use **expansionary fiscal policy** and increase government spending on goods and services, lower taxes, or use some combination of these approaches. Any of those options will increase a budget deficit (or reduce a budget surplus). Thus, expansionary fiscal policy is associated with increased government budget deficits. Likewise, if the government wants to dampen a boom in the economy by reducing aggregate demand, it will use **contractionary fiscal policy** and reduce its spending on goods and services, increase taxes, or use some combination of these approaches. Thus, contractionary fiscal policy will tend to increase a budget surplus (or reduce a budget deficit).

budget deficit
government spending exceeds tax revenues for a given fiscal year

budget surplus
tax revenues are greater than government expenditures for a given fiscal year

expansionary fiscal policy
use of fiscal policy tools to foster increased output by increasing government spending and/or lowering taxes

contractionary fiscal policy
use of fiscal policy tools to reduce output by decreasing government spending and/or increasing taxes

SECTION CHECK

■ Fiscal policy is the use of government spending on goods and services and/or taxes to affect aggregate demand and to alter RGDP and the price level.
■ Expansionary fiscal policies will increase a budget deficit (or reduce a budget surplus) through greater government spending, lower taxes, or both. Contractionary fiscal policies will increase a budget surplus (or reduce a budget deficit) through reduced government spending, higher taxes, or both.

Government: Spending and Taxation

section
10.2

■ What are the major categories of government spending?
■ What are the major sources of government revenue?

WHAT ARE THE MAJOR CATEGORIES OF GOVERNMENT SPENDING?

In 2009, the federal government spent $236.5 billion on goods and services and on transfer payments to individuals. The provincial, territorial, and local governments combined spent $418.6 billion on goods and services and on transfer payments to individuals.

Government Expenditures

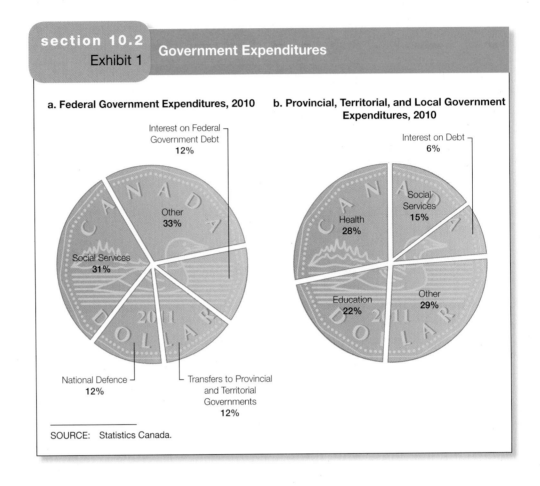

a. Federal Government Expenditures, 2010

b. Provincial, Territorial, and Local Government Expenditures, 2010

SOURCE: Statistics Canada.

Where is all of this money spent? Exhibit 1 illustrates the major categories of government spending as a proportion of total government spending.

Exhibit 1(a) shows that 31 percent of federal government spending in 2009 went to social services, including Employment Insurance and Old Age Security programs. Transfers of money from the federal government to provincial governments (for provincial spending on post-secondary education and health care) amounted to 12 percent of federal government expenditure. Interest payments that the federal government makes on its outstanding debt account for 12 percent of total spending, whereas national defence accounts for 12 percent. The remaining 33 percent of federal government spending includes foreign affairs and international aid, the environment, recreation and culture, resource conservation, and industrial development.

Exhibit 1(b) shows that provincial, territorial, and local government spending is quite different from federal government spending. Health care and education spending, at 28 percent and 22 percent, respectively, account for virtually one-half of all spending by provincial, territorial, and local governments. Social services, such as welfare and social assistance programs, account for 15 percent of total spending. Like the federal government, the provincial, territorial, and local levels of government must also make interest payments on their outstanding debt, accounting for about 6 percent of spending. The remaining 29 percent of provincial, territorial, and local government expenditure involves items such as housing, the environment, police and fire protection, and transportation and communication services.

Business CONNECTION

STABILIZING THE ECONOMY: THE ROLE OF GOVERNMENT IN BUSINESS

There is no argument that one of the primary roles of government is to increase RGDP. Only with increases in economic growth can a country improve its standard of living, characterized and measured by the RGDP per person, called *GDP per capita*. The ability to increase RGDP depends on the traditional four engines of the economy; consumer spending, business investment spending, spending by all levels of government, and net exports (Exports – Imports).

When it appears that RGDP might slip from one period to the next, or that the rate of increase of RGDP might fall due to reductions in consumer spending, business investments, or net exports, or combinations thereof, and when it appears that such changes if left unattended would lead to a stagnation or impairment in standards of living, governments will often intervene, taking a leadership role in spending in an attempt to offset the anticipated drop in spending in the other three engines. There is much debate regarding the extent to which governments should engage in spending to spur economic growth. Notwithstanding such debates, business operators need to understand how such government initiatives might affect revenues, costs, and of course the net profits.

When a business provides goods or services to government or is part of a direct supply chain providing goods or services, the immediate effect of such government intervention will be an increase in government orders. This will in turn lead to the maintenance of or an increase in employment levels in the affected sectors, accompanied by increases in company revenues. Workers with larger incomes or greater security of income are now more likely to make more and perhaps larger purchases. In order to satisfy demand for consumer goods resulting from such purchases, businesses must in turn increase employment levels and make investments. So, in this virtuous circle, business investment spending and consumer spending is revived.

There is a down side, however. A government's ability to spend is constrained by its ability to raise funds. Governments raise funds from taxation or borrowing. In both cases, taxpayers will ultimately pay taxes to fund government spending. In an ideal world, government spending will vary with the health of the economy. When faced with the possibility of a fall in RGDP, astute governments will increase spending, often more than is collected in taxes. When the economy improves with increases in consumer and business investment spending, the same governments will spend less than is collected in taxes. The net effect over a typical business cycle is that deficits in downturns cancel surpluses in expansions. If this is the case, government will have played a key role in maintaining economic stability and economic growth.

WHAT ARE THE MAJOR SOURCES OF GOVERNMENT REVENUE?

Governments have to pay their bills like any person or institution that spends money. But how do they obtain revenue? Two major avenues are open: taxation and borrowing. When the government runs a budget deficit, spending exceeds tax revenue and therefore part of the spending must be financed by borrowing. When the budget is balanced, all spending is financed by tax revenue and there is no necessity to borrow.

Exhibit 2 shows the revenue sources for the federal government and the provincial, territorial, and local governments. At the federal level [Exhibit 2(a)], the majority of revenue, 65 percent, comes in the form of income taxes on individuals and corporations, called *personal income taxes* and *corporate income taxes,* respectively. Consumption taxes, such as the Goods and Services Tax (GST) and federal excise taxes on gasoline, alcohol, and tobacco products, account for 18 percent of federal revenue. Social security contributions, like Employment Insurance premiums paid by both employees and employers, amount to 7 percent of federal government revenue. Other revenue, at 10 percent, comes largely from investment income and sales of goods and services.

A Progressive Tax

One impact of substantial taxes on personal income is that the effective take-home income of Canadians is significantly altered by the tax system. A **progressive tax** is

progressive tax
the amount of an individual's tax rises as a proportion of income, as the person's income rises

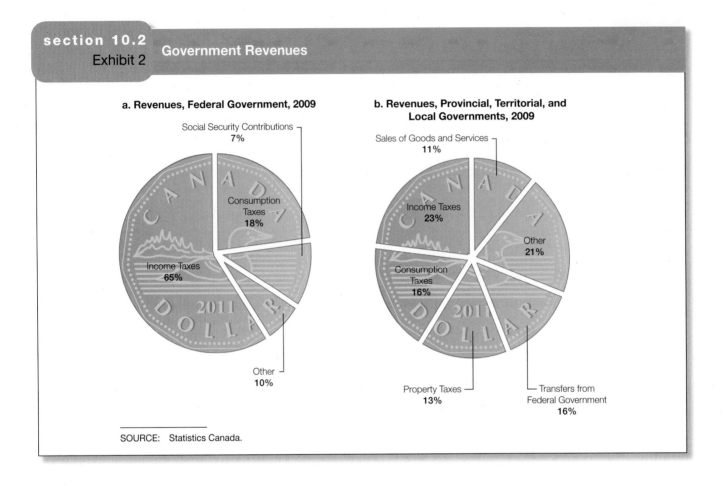

a. Revenues, Federal Government, 2009

Social Security Contributions
7%

Consumption
Taxes
18%

Income Taxes
65%

Other
10%

b. Revenues, Provincial, Territorial, and Local Governments, 2009

Sales of Goods and Services
11%

Income Taxes
23%

Other
21%

Consumption
Taxes
16%

Property Taxes
13%

Transfers from
Federal Government
16%

SOURCE: Statistics Canada.

designed so that the amount of an individual's tax rises as a proportion of income, as the person's income rises. With progressive taxes, of which the federal personal income tax is one example, those with higher incomes pay a greater proportion of their income in taxes. A progressive tax is one tool that the government can use to redistribute income.

A Regressive Tax

excise tax

a sales tax on individual products such as alcohol, tobacco, and gasoline

regressive tax

the amount of an individual's tax falls as a proportion of income, as the person's income rises

Some people consider an **excise tax**—a sales tax on individual products such as alcohol, tobacco, and gasoline—to be the most unfair type of tax because it is generally the most regressive. A **regressive tax** is designed so that the amount of an individual's tax falls as a proportion of income, as the person's income rises. A regressive tax takes a greater proportion of the income of lower-income groups than of higher-income groups. This type of tax on specific items will impose a far greater burden, as a percentage of income, on the poor and middle class than on the wealthy, because low-income families pay a greater proportion of their income on these taxes than do high-income families.

In addition, excise taxes may lead to economic inefficiencies. By isolating a few products and subjecting them to discriminatory taxation, consumption taxes expose economic choices to political manipulation and lead to inefficiency.

Exhibit 2(b) shows that income taxes and consumption taxes accounted for 23 percent and 16 percent, respectively, of total provincial, territorial, and local government revenue, with virtually all that revenue going to provincial governments. Property taxes, however, are the major revenue source for local levels of government, and amount to 13 percent of total provincial, territorial, and local government revenue. Transfers of

DEBATE

FISCAL POLICY: FLAT TAXES

The foundations of fiscal policy are based on government spending and taxation. Over decades of government meddling, the tax system has become complex, arbitrary, and, some would argue, inefficient. The success of the tax system is largely based on trust that individuals and firms have in the system itself.

Each newly elected government comes to power amending the tax system in a manner that it views as equitable to the nation. Many would argue that it is time for "real" tax reform and the idea of a flat tax has been raised. A flat tax is one where all citizens pay the same tax rate, regardless of income. Such a system would be beneficial for the citizens and the federal government.

Pro:

A flat tax system is easy to understand and administer, and has a much lower cost of enforcement for both individuals and firms. Both individuals and firms know in advance, and with surety, what taxes are due. It is also argued that a flat tax return would be less costly and easier to prepare. With these benefits, it is suggested that citizen compliance to the tax system would be better. Proponents of a flat tax argue there are other benefits. Can you think of other reasons why it would make sense for Canada to adopt a flat tax system?

Con:

Opponents of a Canadian flat tax system recognize that the tax system is much more than a method for governments to collect revenues; it is also used to redistribute wealth across various sectors or regions. Opponents also point to the regressive nature and the negative impact of a flat tax. Can you think of other reasons why a flat tax would not be beneficial to the Canadian economy?

money from the federal government are an important source of revenue to lower levels of government, accounting for 16 percent of their revenue. Revenue from the sale of goods and services makes up 11 percent of total revenue. The remaining 21 percent of revenue comes from items such as investment income, health premiums, and other taxes.

SECTION CHECK

- Over 30 percent of federal government spending goes to social services, such as Employment Insurance and Old Age Security programs. Provincial, territorial, and local government spending is much more balanced, with the majority of the expenditure going to health care and education.
- The largest source of federal revenue is income taxes on individuals and corporations. Provincially and territorially, income and consumption taxes are the largest sources of revenue, whereas locally, property taxes represent the major revenue source.

section

10.3

The Multiplier Effect

- What is the multiplier effect?
- What impact does the multiplier effect have on the aggregate demand curve?
- What impact does the multiplier effect have on tax cuts?
- What factors can potentially reduce the size of the multiplier?

The RGDP will change anytime the amount of any one of the four forms of purchases—consumption, investment, government purchases, and net exports—changes. If, for any reason, people generally decide to purchase more in any of these categories out of given income, aggregate demand will shift rightward. If they decide to purchase less, there will be a reduction in aggregate demand.

Any one of the major spending components of aggregate demand (C, I, G, or $X - M$) can initiate changes in aggregate demand, and thus a new short-run equilibrium. Changes in total output are often brought about by alterations in investment plans because investment purchases are a relatively volatile category of expenditures. However, if policymakers are unhappy with the present short-run equilibrium GDP, perhaps because they consider unemployment to be too high, they can deliberately manipulate the level of government purchases in order to obtain a new short-run equilibrium value. Similarly, by changing taxes or transfer payments, they can alter the amount of disposable income of households and thus bring about changes in consumption purchases.

WHAT IS THE MULTIPLIER EFFECT?

multiplier effect
a chain reaction of additional income and purchases that results in total purchases that are greater than the initial increase in purchases

Usually when an initial increase in purchases of goods or services occurs, the ultimate increase in total purchases will tend to be greater than the initial increase; this chain reaction of additional income and purchases that result in total purchases that are greater than the initial increase in purchases is called the **multiplier effect.** But how does this effect work? Suppose the federal government increases its national defence budget by $100 million to buy new search-and-rescue helicopters. When the government purchases the helicopters, not only does it add to the total demand for goods and services directly, it also provides $100 million in added income to the companies that actually construct the helicopters. Those companies will then hire more workers and buy more capital equipment and other inputs in order to produce the new output. The owners of these inputs therefore receive more income because of the increase in government purchases. And what will they do with this additional income? Although behaviour will vary somewhat among individuals, collectively they will probably spend a substantial part of the additional income on additional consumption purchases, pay some additional taxes incurred because of the income, and save a bit of it as well. The marginal propensity to consume (*MPC*) is the fraction of additional disposable income that a household consumes rather than saves.

The Multiplier Effect at Work

Suppose that out of every dollar in *added* disposable income generated by increased government purchases, individuals collectively spend 75 cents on consumption purchases. In other words, the *MPC* is 0.75. The initial $100 million increase in government purchases causes both a $100 million increase in aggregate demand and an income increase of $100 million to suppliers of the inputs used to produce helicopters; the owners of those inputs, in turn, will spend an additional $75 million (75 percent of $100 million) on additional consumption purchases.

As Exhibit 1 illustrates, a chain reaction has been started with each new round of purchases providing income to a new group of people who in turn increase their purchases. As successive changes in consumption purchases occur, the feedback becomes smaller and smaller. The added income generated and the number of resulting consumer purchases get smaller because some of the increase in income goes to savings and tax payments that do not immediately flow into greater investment or government expenditure. For example, as Exhibit 1 indicates, the fifth change in consumption purchases is indeed much smaller than the first change in consumption purchases. What is the total impact of the initial

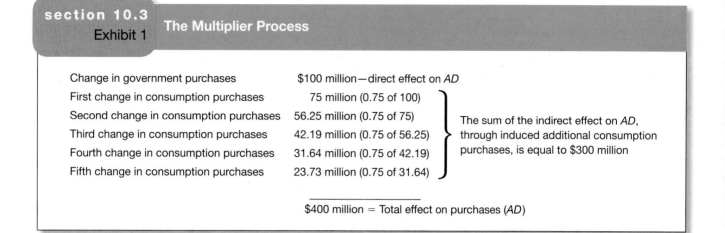

section 10.3
Exhibit 1   **The Multiplier Process**

Change in government purchases	$100 million—direct effect on *AD*	
First change in consumption purchases	75 million (0.75 of 100)	
Second change in consumption purchases	56.25 million (0.75 of 75)	The sum of the indirect effect on *AD*,
Third change in consumption purchases	42.19 million (0.75 of 56.25)	through induced additional consumption
Fourth change in consumption purchases	31.64 million (0.75 of 42.19)	purchases, is equal to $300 million
Fifth change in consumption purchases	23.73 million (0.75 of 31.64)	

$400 million = Total effect on purchases (*AD*)

increase in purchases on additional purchases and income? We can find that out using the multiplier formula, calculated as follows:

$$\text{Multiplier} = \frac{1}{(1 - MPC)}$$

In this case,

$$\text{Multiplier} = 1/(1 - 0.75) = 1/(0.25) = 4$$

An initial increase in purchases of goods or services of $100 million will increase total purchases by $400 million ($100 million × 4), as the initial $100 million in government purchases also generates an additional $300 million in consumption purchases.

Changes in the *MPC* Affect the Multiplier Process

Note that the larger the marginal propensity to consume, the larger the multiplier effect, because relatively more additional consumption purchases out of any given income increase generate relatively larger secondary and tertiary income effects in successive rounds of the process. For example, if the *MPC* is 0.80, the multiplier is 5:

$$\text{Multiplier} = 1/(1 - 0.8) = 1/(0.2) = 5$$

If the *MPC* is only 0.50, however, the multiplier is 2:

$$\text{Multiplier} = 1/(1 - 0.50) = 1/(0.50) = 2$$

WHAT IMPACT DOES THE MULTIPLIER EFFECT HAVE ON THE AGGREGATE DEMAND CURVE?

As we discussed earlier, when the Department of National Defence decides to buy additional helicopters, it affects aggregate demand. It increases the incomes of owners of inputs used to make the helicopters, including profits that go to owners of the firms involved. That is the initial effect. The secondary effect, the greater income that results, will lead to increased consumer purchases. So the initial effect of the government's purchases will tend to have a multiplier effect on the economy. In Exhibit 2, we see that the initial impact of a $100 million additional purchase by the government directly shifts the aggregate demand curve from AD_0 to AD_1. The multiplier effect then causes the aggregate demand

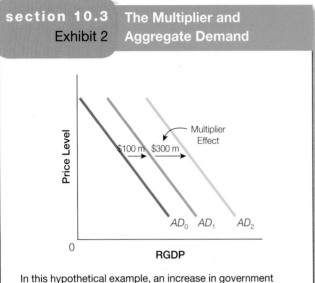

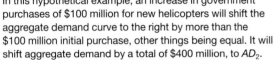

In this hypothetical example, an increase in government purchases of $100 million for new helicopters will shift the aggregate demand curve to the right by more than the $100 million initial purchase, other things being equal. It will shift aggregate demand by a total of $400 million, to AD_2.

to shift out $300 million further, to AD_2. The total effect on aggregate demand of a $100 million increase in government purchases is therefore $400 million, if the marginal propensity to consume equals 0.75.

It is important to note that the multiplier is most effective when it brings idle resources into production. If all resources are already fully employed, the expansion in demand and the multiplier effect will lead to a higher price level, not increases in employment and RGDP.

WHAT IMPACT DOES THE MULTIPLIER EFFECT HAVE ON TAX CUTS?

If the government finds that it needs to use fiscal stimulus to move the economy to the natural rate, increased government spending is only one alternative. The government can also stimulate business and consumer spending through tax cuts. Both Canada (2000, 2003, and again in 2008–2009) and the United States (2001 and 2003) have employed tax cuts to stimulate their economies.

How much of an *AD* shift do we get from a change in taxes? As in the case of government spending, it depends on the marginal propensity to consume. However, the tax multiplier is smaller than the government spending multiplier because government spending has a direct impact on aggregate demand, whereas a tax cut has only an indirect impact on aggregate demand. Why? Because consumers will save some of their income from the tax cut. So if the *MPC* is 0.60, then when their disposable income rises by $1000, households will increase their consumption by $600 ($1000 × 0.60) while saving $400 of the added income.

To compare the multiplier effect of a tax cut with an increase in government purchases, suppose there was a $100 million tax cut and that the *MPC* was 0.75. The initial increase in consumption spending from the tax cut would be 0.75 × 100 million (*MPC* × tax cut) = $75 million. Because in this case people would save 25 percent of their tax-cut income, the effect on aggregate demand of the change in taxes would be smaller than that of a change of equal size in government spending. The cumulative change in spending (the increase in *AD*) due to the $100 million tax cut can be found by plugging the initial effect of the changed consumption spending into our earlier formula: 1/(1 − *MPC*) × $75 million, which is 4 × $75 = $300 million. So the initial tax cut of $100 million leads to a stimulus of $200 million in consumer spending. Although this is less than the $400 million from government spending, it is easy to see why tax cuts and government spending are both attractive policy prescriptions for a slow economy.

An alternative technique for determining the cumulative change in spending due to a tax cut is to use the *tax multiplier* formula, calculated as follows:

$$\text{Tax multiplier} = \frac{MPC}{(1 - MPC)}$$

Returning to our earlier example, if the *MPC* is 0.75, the tax multiplier is 3:

$$\text{Tax multiplier} = \frac{MPC}{(1 - MPC)} = \frac{0.75}{(1 - 0.75)} = \frac{0.75}{0.25} = 3$$

An initial tax cut of $100 million will increase total purchases by $300 million ($100 million × 3).

Taxes and Investment Spending

Taxes can stimulate investment spending. For example, if a cut in corporate-profit taxes leads to expectations of greater after-tax profits, it could fuel additional investment spending. That is, tax cuts designed for consumers and investors can stimulate both the *C* and *I* components of aggregate demand. A number of governments have used this strategy to stimulate aggregate spending and shift the aggregate demand curve to the right: Canada (2003 and 2008–2009), the United States (2000 and 2003), and South Korea (2008).

Spending Cuts and Tax Increases

Spending cuts and tax increases are magnified by the multiplier effect, too. Suppose there was a cutback in the public sector. Not only would it decrease government purchases directly, but civil servants would be laid off and unemployed workers would cut back on their consumption spending; this would have a multiplier effect throughout the economy, leading to an even greater reduction in aggregate demand. Similarly, tax hikes would leave consumers with less disposable income, so they would cut back on their consumption. This would lower aggregate demand and set off the multiplier process, leading to an even larger cumulative effect on aggregate demand.

WHAT FACTORS CAN POTENTIALLY REDUCE THE SIZE OF THE MULTIPLIER?

The multiplier process is not instantaneous. If you get an additional $100 in income today, you may spend two-thirds of that on consumption purchases eventually, but you may wait six months or even longer to do it. Such time lags mean that the ultimate increase in purchases resulting from an initial increase in purchases may not be achieved for a year or more. The extent of the multiplier effect evident within a short time period will be less than the total effect indicated by the multiplier formula. In addition, saving, taxes, and money spent on import goods (which are not part of aggregate demand for domestically produced goods and services) will reduce the size of the multiplier because each of them reduces the fraction of a given increase in income that will go to additional purchases of domestically produced consumption goods.

It is also important to note that the multiplier effect is not restricted to changes in government purchases. The multiplier effect can apply to changes that alter spending in any of the components of aggregate demand: consumption, investment, government purchases, or net exports.

SECTION CHECK

- The multiplier effect is a chain reaction of additional income and purchases that results in a final increase in total purchases that is greater than the initial increase in purchases.
- Initially the *AD* curve shifts rightward by the amount of the original increase in expenditure. The multiplier effect has the effect of shifting the *AD* curve further rightward.
- Because taxes have only an indirect impact on aggregate demand, the tax multiplier is smaller than the government spending multiplier.
- Because of a time lag, the full impact of the multiplier effect on GDP may not be felt until a year or more after the initial purchase. Also, the ultimate size of the multiplier may be reduced by increases in saving rates, taxes, and money spent on imported goods.

section
10.4
Fiscal Policy and the *AD/AS* Model

■ How can fiscal policy alleviate a recessionary gap?
■ How can fiscal policy alleviate an inflationary gap?

HOW CAN FISCAL POLICY ALLEVIATE A RECESSIONARY GAP?

The primary tools of fiscal policy, government spending and taxes, can be presented in the context of the aggregate supply and demand model. In Exhibit 1, we have used the *AD/AS* model to show how the government can use fiscal policy as an expansionary tool to help control the economy.

Budget Deficits and Fiscal Policy

As we discussed earlier, when the government spends more, and/or taxes less, the size of the government's budget deficit will grow, or the size of the budget surplus will fall. Although budget deficits are often thought to be bad, a case can be made for using budget deficits to stimulate the economy when it is operating at less than full capacity. Such expansionary fiscal policy may have the potential to move an economy out of a contraction (or a recession) and closer to full employment.

Expansionary Fiscal Policy at Less Than Full Employment If the government decides to spend more and/or cut taxes, other things constant, total purchases will rise. That is, increased government spending and tax cuts can increase consumption, investment, and government purchases, shifting the aggregate demand curve to the right. The effect of this increase in aggregate demand depends on the position of the macroeconomic equilibrium prior to the government stimulus. For example, in Exhibit 1, the initial equilibrium is at E_0, a recession scenario, with real output below potential RGDP. Starting at this point and moving along the short-run aggregate supply curve, an increase in government spending and/or a tax cut would increase the size of the budget deficit and lead to an increase in aggregate demand, ideally from AD_0 to AD_2. The result of such a change would be an increase in the price level, from PL_0 to PL_2, and an increase in RGDP, from $RGDP_0$ to $RGDP_{NR}$. We must remember, of course, that some of this increase in aggregate demand is caused by the multiplier process (from AD_1 to AD_2), so the magnitude of the change in aggregate demand will be larger than the magnitude of the stimulus package of tax cuts and/or government spending (from AD_0 to AD_1). If the policy change is of the right magnitude and timed appropriately, the expansionary fiscal policy might stimulate the economy, pull it out of the contraction and/or recession, and result in full employment at $RGDP_{NR}$.

---

section 10.4
Exhibit 1

Expansionary Fiscal Policy in a Recessionary Gap

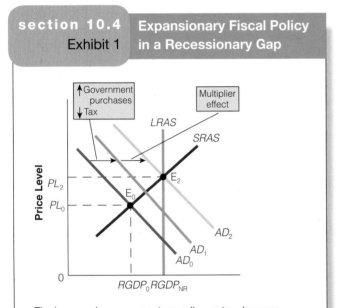

The increase in government spending or tax decrease causes an increase in aggregate demand from AD_0 to AD_1. This triggers the multiplier effect (AD_1 to AD_2) and the result is a new equilibrium at E_2, reflecting a higher price level and a higher RGDP. Because this result is on the *LRAS* curve, it is a long-run, sustainable equilibrium.

The 2008-2009 Recession   The 2008–2009 recession, while not the worst recession in Canadian history, did trigger a massive fiscal expansion. In January 2009, the federal government introduced Canada's Economic Action Plan in response to the global financial crisis. Among other stimulus measures, the plan contained significant tax relief—$20 billion in personal income tax relief over 2008–2009 and the next five fiscal years—in addition to unprecedented government spending initiatives—$12 billion in new infrastructure stimulus funding over two years. Many other countries around the world, most notably the United States, also increased the size of their budget deficits by cutting taxes and increasing government spending in response to the financial crisis.

In terms of the *AD/AS* model, the impact of this type of expansionary fiscal policy is clear: a rightward shift of the aggregate demand curve from AD_0 to AD_1 as shown in Exhibit 1. There is, however, debate among economists as to the effectiveness of fiscal policy to stimulate the economy, and much of that debate depends on the size of the multiplier. A multiplier of 1 means that an increase in government purchases of $100 million would increase aggregate demand and lead to an increase of $100 million in RGDP. The economy could now have new highways, bridges, public arenas, and fighter jets without sacrificing other components of aggregate demand, like private consumption and investment. How is this possible? The answer is that these are idle resources that are now being put to use. If a multiplier is greater than 1, it is even more magical: RGDP rises by more than the increase in government spending.

Despite a lack of uniform agreement on the size of the expenditure multiplier, economists do agree that the multiplier is very small—close to zero—when the economy is at or near full employment and that the effectiveness of fiscal policy depends on the type of action taken. For example, the short-run effect of government spending on infrastructure like highways and bridges tends to be greater than, say, that of a tax cut where individuals will save a large portion of their tax windfall. Tax cuts for poorer people may be more effective than those for richer people, because the poor tend to spend a larger proportion of their additional (marginal) incomes. Economists also agree that tax multipliers are much higher when taxes are permanent than when they are temporary and that fiscal multipliers will be lower in heavily indebted economies than in prudent ones.

HOW CAN FISCAL POLICY ALLEVIATE AN INFLATIONARY GAP?

When the government spends less and/or taxes more, the size of the government's budget deficit will fall or the size of the budget surplus will rise, other things being equal. Sometimes such a change in fiscal policy may help "cool off" the economy when it has overheated and inflation has become a serious problem. Then, contractionary fiscal policy has the potential to offset an overheated, inflationary boom.

Contractionary Fiscal Policy beyond Full Employment

Suppose that the price level is at PL_0 and that short-run equilibrium is at E_0, as shown in Exhibit 2. Say that the government decides to reduce its spending and increase taxes. A government spending change may directly affect aggregate demand. A tax increase on consumers will reduce households' disposable incomes, thus reducing

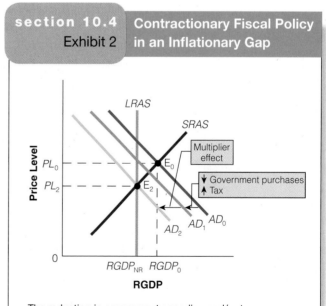

section 10.4
Exhibit 2
Contractionary Fiscal Policy in an Inflationary Gap

The reduction in government spending and/or tax increases, coupled with the multiplier effect, leads to a leftward shift in aggregate demand and a change in the short-run equilibrium from E_0 to E_2, reflecting a lower price level and a return to full-employment RGDP ($RGDP_{NR}$).

purchases of consumption goods and services, and higher business taxes will reduce investment purchases. The reductions in consumption, investment, and/or government spending will shift the aggregate demand curve leftward, ideally from AD_0 to AD_2. This lowers the price level from PL_0 to PL_2 and brings RGDP back to the full-employment level at $RGDP_{NR}$, resulting in a new short- and long-run equilibrium at E_2.

SECTION CHECK

- A government decision to spend more and/or cut taxes would increase total purchases and shift out the aggregate demand curve. If the correct magnitude of expansionary fiscal policy is used in a recession, it could potentially bring the economy to full employment at a higher price level.
- If the correct magnitude of contractionary fiscal policy is used in an inflationary boom, it could potentially bring the economy back to full employment at a lower price level.

section 10.5

Automatic Stabilizers

- What are automatic stabilizers?
- How does the tax system stabilize the economy?

WHAT ARE AUTOMATIC STABILIZERS?

automatic stabilizers
changes in government spending or tax collections that automatically help counter business cycle fluctuations

Some changes in government spending and taxes take place automatically as business cycle conditions change, without deliberations in Parliament. Changes in government spending or tax collections that automatically help counter business cycle fluctuations are called **automatic stabilizers.**

HOW DOES THE TAX SYSTEM STABILIZE THE ECONOMY?

The most important automatic stabilizer is the tax system. For example, with the personal income tax, as incomes rise, tax liabilities also increase automatically. Progressive personal income taxes vary directly in amount with income and, in fact, rise or fall by greater percentage terms than income itself. Big increases and big decreases in GDP are both lessened by automatic changes in income tax receipts. In addition, there is the corporate profit tax. Because incomes, earnings, and profits all fall during a recession, the government collects less in taxes. This reduced tax burden partially offsets the magnitude of the recession.

Beyond this, the Employment Insurance program is another example of an automatic stabilizer. During recessions, unemployment is usually high and Employment Insurance benefits increase, providing income that will be consumed by recipients. During boom

Automatic stabilizers work without legislative action. The stabilizers serve as a shock absorber to the economy. But the key is that they do it quickly.

BRIGITTE BOUVIER, PMO

periods, such benefit payments will fall as the number of unemployed declines. The system of social assistance (welfare) payments tends to be another important automatic stabilizer because the number of low-income persons eligible for some form of social assistance grows during recessions (stimulating aggregate demand) and declines during booms (reducing aggregate demand).

SECTION CHECK

- Automatic stabilizers are changes in government transfer payments or tax collections that happen automatically and with effects that vary inversely with business cycles.
- The tax system is the most important automatic stabilizer; it has the greatest ability to smooth out swings in GDP during business cycles. Other automatic stabilizers are Employment Insurance and social assistance payments.

Possible Obstacles to Effective Fiscal Policy

- How does the crowding-out effect limit the economic impact of expansionary fiscal policy?
- How do time lags in fiscal policy implementation affect policy effectiveness?

HOW DOES THE CROWDING-OUT EFFECT LIMIT THE ECONOMIC IMPACT OF EXPANSIONARY FISCAL POLICY?

The multiplier effect of an increase in government purchases implies that the increase in aggregate demand will tend to be greater than the initial fiscal stimulus, other things being equal. However, this may not be true, because all other things will not tend to stay equal in this case. For example, when an increase in government purchases stimulates aggregate demand, it also drives the interest rate up. In particular, when the federal government's borrowing competes with private borrowers for available savings, it drives up interest rates. As a result of the higher interest rate, consumers may decide against buying a car, a home, or other interest-sensitive good, and businesses may cancel or scale back plans to expand or buy new capital equipment. In short, the higher interest rate will choke off private investment spending, and as a result, the impact of the increase in government purchases may be smaller than we first assumed. Economists call the theory that government borrowing drives up the interest rate, lowering consumption by households and investment spending by firms, the **crowding-out effect.** The crowding-out effect happened in Canada in the late 1980s and early 1990s, when record levels of government borrowing contributed, in part, to interest rates rising above 12 percent.

In Exhibit 1, suppose there was an initial $100 million increase in government purchases. This by itself would shift aggregate demand right by $100 million times the multiplier, from AD_0 to AD_1. However, when the government borrows in the money market to pay for increases in government purchases, the interest rate increases. The higher interest rate

crowding-out effect
theory that government borrowing drives up the interest rate, lowering consumption by households and investment spending by firms

section 10.6
Exhibit 1   The Crowding-Out
Effect

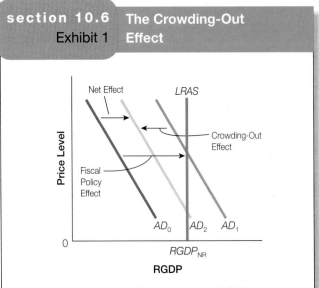

Government borrowing to finance a budget deficit leads to a higher interest rate and lower levels of private investment spending. The lower levels of private spending can crowd out the fiscal policy effect, shifting aggregate demand to the left from AD_1 to AD_2; the net effect of the fiscal policy is AD_0 to AD_2, not the larger increase, AD_0 to AD_1.

crowds out investment spending. This causes the aggregate demand curve to shift left, from AD_1 to AD_2. Because both of these processes are taking place at the same time, the net effect is an increase in aggregate demand from AD_0 to AD_2 rather than AD_0 to AD_1.

Critics of the Crowding-Out Effect

Critics of the crowding-out effect argue that the increase in government spending, particularly if the economy is in a severe recession, could actually improve consumer and business expectations and actually encourage private investment spending. It is also possible that the monetary authorities could actually increase the money supply to offset the higher interest rates from the crowding-out effect.

The Crowding-Out Effect in the Open Economy

Another form of crowding out can take place in international markets. For example, when the government increases purchases, it tends to drive up interest rates (assuming the money supply is unchanged). This is the basic crowding-out effect. However, the higher Canadian interest rate will attract funds from abroad. In order to invest in the Canadian economy, foreigners will have to first convert their currencies into Canadian dollars. The increase in the demand for dollars relative to other currencies will cause the dollar to appreciate in value. This will cause net exports $(X - M)$ to fall for two reasons. One, because of the higher relative price of the Canadian dollar, imports become cheaper for those in Canada, and imports will increase. Two, because of the higher relative price of the dollar, Canadian-made goods become more expensive to foreigners, so exports fall. The increase in imports and the decrease in exports causes a reduction in net exports and a fall in aggregate demand. The net effect is that to the extent net exports are crowded out, fiscal policy has a smaller effect on aggregate demand than it would otherwise.

HOW DO TIME LAGS IN FISCAL POLICY IMPLEMENTATION AFFECT POLICY EFFECTIVENESS?

It is important to recognize that in a democratic country, fiscal policy is implemented through the political process, and that process takes time. Often, the lag between the time that a fiscal response is desired and the time an appropriate policy is implemented and its effects felt is considerable. Sometimes a fiscal policy designed to deal with a contracting economy may actually take effect during a period of economic expansion, or vice versa, resulting in a stabilization policy that actually destabilizes the economy.

The Recognition Lag

Suppose the economy is beginning a downturn. It may take from three to six months before enough data are gathered to indicate the actual presence of a downturn. This is called the *recognition lag*. Sometimes a future downturn can be forecast through econometric models or by looking at the index of leading indicators, but usually decision makers are hesitant to plan policy on the basis of forecasts that are not always accurate.

The Implementation Lag

At some point, however, policymakers may decide that some policy change is necessary. If, for example, a tax cut is recommended, what form should the cut take and how large should it be? Across-the-board income tax reductions? Reductions in corporate taxes? More generous exemptions and deductions from the income tax (e.g., for child care, education)? In other words, who should get the benefits of lower taxes? Likewise, if the decision is made to increase government expenditures, which programs should be expanded or initiated and by how much? These are questions with profound political consequences, so reaching a decision is not always easy and usually involves much compromise and a great deal of time.

Finally, once the budget is formulated by the staff at the Department of Finance, the finance minister presents the budget to Parliament, which must eventually give approval to the budget. This is all part of what is called the *implementation lag*.

In recognition of this lag, the federal government, through Canada's Economic Action Plan, streamlined the federal approval processes so that more provincial, territorial, and municipal projects under the Building Canada Plan could start in 2009 and 2010. Prior to these changes, the infrastructure approval process was subject to significant duplication and administrative inefficiencies, leading to unnecessary project delays. With changes now in place, the time needed to provide federal approvals for major projects was shortened by up to 12 months, allowing construction to begin more quickly.

The Impact Lag

Even after legislation is passed, it takes time to bring about the actual fiscal stimulus desired. If the legislation provides for a reduction in income taxes, for example, it might take a few months before the changes actually show up in workers' paycheques. With respect to changes in government purchases, the delay is usually much longer. If the government increases spending for public works projects like sewer systems, new highways, or urban transit systems, it takes time to draw up plans and get permissions, to advertise for bids from contractors, to get contracts, and then to begin work. And there may be further delays because of government regulations. For example, an environmental impact assessment must be completed before most public works projects can begin, a process that often takes many months or even years. This is called the *impact lag*.

Timing Is Critical

The timing of fiscal policy is crucial. Because of the significant lags before the fiscal policy has its impact, the increase in aggregate demand may occur at the wrong time. For example, imagine that we are initially at E_0 in Exhibit 2. The economy is currently suffering from low levels of output and high rates of unemployment. In response, policymakers decide to increase government purchases and implement a tax cut. But from the time when the policymakers recognized the problem to the time when the policies had a chance to work themselves through the economy, business and consumer confidence increased, shifting the aggregate demand curve rightward from AD_0 to AD_1—increasing RGDP and employment. Now when the fiscal policy takes effect, the

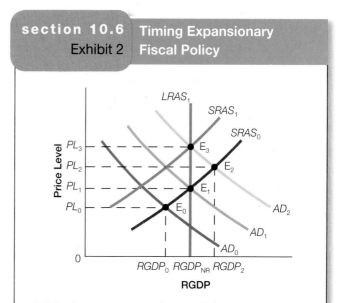

section 10.6
Exhibit 2
Timing Expansionary Fiscal Policy

Initially, the macroeconomy is at equilibrium at point E_0. With high unemployment (at $RGDP_0$), the government decides to increase government purchases and cut taxes to stimulate the economy. This shifts aggregate demand from AD_0 to AD_1 over time, perhaps 12 to 16 months. In the meantime, if consumer confidence increases, the aggregate demand curve might shift to AD_2, leading to much higher prices (PL_3) in the long run, rather than at the target level, E_1, at price level PL_1.

policies will have the undesired effect of causing inflation, with little permanent effect on output and employment. This is seen in Exhibit 2, as the aggregate demand curve shifts from AD_1 to AD_2. At E_2, input owners will require higher input prices, shifting the *SRAS* leftward from $SRAS_0$ to $SRAS_1$ to the new long-run equilibrium at E_3.

SECTION CHECK

- The crowding-out effect states that as the government borrows to finance the budget deficit, it drives up the interest rates and crowds out private investment spending. If crowding out causes a higher Canadian interest rate, it will attract foreign funds. In order to invest in the Canadian economy, foreigners will have to first convert their currencies into Canadian dollars. The increase in the demand for dollars relative to other currencies will cause the dollar to appreciate in value, making imports relatively cheaper in Canada and Canadian exports relatively more expensive in other countries. This will cause net exports $(X - M)$ to fall. This is the crowding-out effect in the open economy.
- The lag time between when a fiscal policy may be needed and when it eventually affects the economy is considerable. Time lags are generally grouped in three classifications: recognition lags, implementation lags, and impact lags.

section 10.7

The Federal Government Debt

- How is the budget deficit financed?
- What has happened to the federal budget balance?
- What is the impact of reducing a budget deficit?
- How much is the burden of government debt in Canada?

HOW IS THE BUDGET DEFICIT FINANCED?

For many years, the Canadian government ran budget deficits and built up a large federal debt. How did it finance those budget deficits? After all, it has to have some means of paying out the funds necessary to support government expenditures that are in excess of the funds derived from tax payments. One thing the federal government can do is simply print money. However, printing money to finance activities is highly inflationary and also undermines confidence in the government. Typically, the budget deficit is financed by issuing debt. The federal government in effect borrows an amount necessary to cover the deficit by issuing bonds, or IOUs, payable typically at some maturity date. The sum total of the values of all bonds outstanding constitutes the federal government debt.

WHAT HAS HAPPENED TO THE FEDERAL BUDGET BALANCE?

Exhibit 1 shows the improvement in the federal budget balance since the early 1990s as a result of economic growth, increased tax revenue, and the efforts of the federal government to control the growth of government spending. Indeed, the improvement in federal government finances is quite remarkable. The yearly budget deficit increased steadily from 1989 to 1994, reaching a record $40 billion in both 1993 and 1994. In 1998, however, the government ran its first budget surplus in almost 25 years, and has succeeded in posting annual budget surpluses for 12 consecutive years, to 2009.

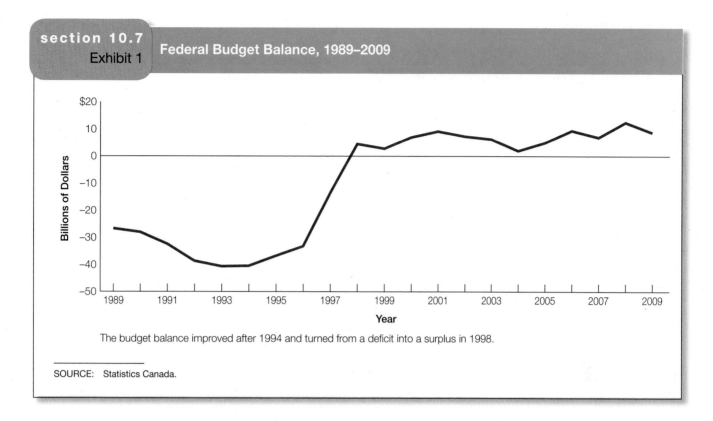

section 10.7
Exhibit 1

Federal Budget Balance, 1989–2009

The budget balance improved after 1994 and turned from a deficit into a surplus in 1998.

SOURCE: Statistics Canada.

WHAT IS THE IMPACT OF REDUCING A BUDGET DEFICIT?

Budget deficits can be important because they provide the federal government with the flexibility to respond appropriately to changing economic circumstances. For example, the government may run deficits in times of special emergencies like military involvement, earthquakes, fires, or floods. The government may also use a budget deficit to avert an economic downturn.

Historically the largest budget deficits and a growing government debt occur during war years when defence spending escalates and taxes typically do not rise as rapidly as spending. For example, during World War II, the federal government debt increased by over 300 percent between 1940 and 1946. The federal government will also typically run budget deficits during recessions as tax revenue falls and government spending increases. However, in the late 1980s, deficits and debt soared in a relatively peaceful and prosperous time. The result was huge budget deficits and a growing federal government debt that continued through the early 1990s, as seen in Exhibit 1.

Recall that when the government borrows to finance a budget deficit, it causes the interest rate to rise. The higher interest rate will crowd out private investment by households and firms. But we know that higher private investment and increases in capital formation are critical in a growing economy. So what would happen if the government reduced the budget deficit? In the short run, deficit reduction is the same as running contractionary fiscal policy; either tax increases and/or a reduction in government purchases will shift the aggregate demand curve to the left from AD_0 to AD_1, as seen in Exhibit 2. Unless this is offset by expansionary monetary policy (see Chapter 13), this will lead to a lower price level and lower RGDP. That is, in the short run an aggressive program of deficit reduction can lead to a recession.

In the long run, however, the story is different. Lowering the budget deficit, or running a larger budget surplus, leads to lower interest rates, which increase private investment and stimulate higher growth in capital formation and economic growth. In fact, this is what

section 10.7
Exhibit 2

Reducing a Budget Deficit—The Short-Run Effects

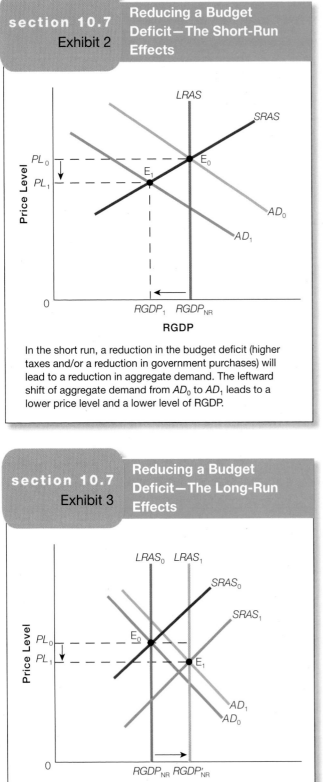

In the short run, a reduction in the budget deficit (higher taxes and/or a reduction in government purchases) will lead to a reduction in aggregate demand. The leftward shift of aggregate demand from AD_0 to AD_1 leads to a lower price level and a lower level of RGDP.

section 10.7
Exhibit 3

Reducing a Budget Deficit—The Long-Run Effects

A smaller budget deficit, or a larger budget surplus, lowers the interest rate and stimulates private investment and capital formation, leading to an increase in RGDP from $RGDP_{NR}$ to $RGDP'_{NR}$. Even with an increase in aggregate demand, the price level would be lower than it would have been without the shift in the *SRAS* and *LRAS* curves.

happened in the late 1990s as the budget deficit was reduced and finally turned into a budget surplus. The reduction in the deficit increased the natural rate of output, shifting the *SRAS* and *LRAS* curves rightward in Exhibit 3. The final effect was a higher RGDP and a lower price level than would have otherwise prevailed. Both investment and RGDP grew as the budget deficit shrank. The long-run effects of the deficit reduction are greater economic growth and a lower price level, *ceteris paribus*. The short-run recessionary effects of a budget deficit reduction can be avoided through the appropriate monetary policy, as we will explore in Chapter 13.

What to Do with a Budget Surplus

When Canada has a budget surplus, policymakers have to decide what to do with it. Some favour paying down the government debt, arguing this might drive interest rates down further and stimulate private investment and economic growth. Others think that we should cut taxes since economic theory indicates that taxes can lead to a misallocation of resources. Still others believe the surplus should be used for improvements in education, health care, and research and development that will lead to greater economic growth.

HOW MUCH IS THE BURDEN OF GOVERNMENT DEBT IN CANADA?

The burden of the federal government debt is a topic that has long interested economists, particularly whether the debt falls on present or future generations. Exhibit 4 shows the level of the outstanding federal government debt and the debt expressed as a percentage of GDP from 1930 to 2009. The debt–GDP ratio measures the size of the debt in relation to the size of our national income. The lower the debt–GDP ratio, the smaller the burden of the debt, because less of our national income goes to the federal government in taxes so that the government can service the debt (i.e., make interest payments to the bondholders). Conversely, the higher the debt–GDP ratio, the greater the burden of the debt, because more of our national income goes to the federal government in taxes so that the government can service the debt.

It is interesting to note that between 1930 and 1950, the debt–GDP ratio increased sharply from 39 to 63 percent, as the growth in the debt (caused largely by the Great Depression in the 1930s and World War II in the 1940s) far exceeded the growth in GDP. Although the debt continued to rise to $73 billion in 1980, the debt–GDP ratio fell to 23 percent as strong economic growth reduced the debt in relation to the size of the economy. Between 1980 and 2000, large budget deficits added almost $500 billion in additional debt, bringing the debt to $572 billion and the debt–GDP ratio up to a burdensome 54 percent. The debt–GDP ratio peaked, in fact, in 1996 at 69 percent.

On a more positive note, the budget surpluses that the federal government was able to post between 2000 and 2008 were, at least in part, used to pay down some of the debt. This in combination with good economic growth over this same period of time enabled the government to lower the debt-GDP ratio to 33 percent by 2008. This trend has since reversed as the Canadian economy struggles to recover from the recent global economic crisis. The most recent data show Canada's debt–GDP ratio at 38 percent.

Arguments can be made that the generation of taxpayers living at the time that the debt is issued shoulders the true cost of the debt, because the debt permits the government to take command of resources that might be available for other, private uses. In a sense, the resources it takes to purchase government bonds might take away from private activities, such as private investment financed by private debt. There is no denying, however, that the issuance of debt does involve some intergenerational transfer of incomes. Long after federal debt is issued, a new generation of taxpayers is making interest payments to people of the generation that bought the bonds issued to finance that debt. If public debt is created intelligently, however, the burden of the debt should be less than the benefits derived from the resources acquired as a result; this is particularly true when the debt allows for an expansion in real economic activity or for the development of vital infrastructure for the future. The opportunity cost of expanded public activity may be very small in terms of private activity that must be forgone to finance the public activity, if unemployed resources are put to work. The real issue of importance is whether the government's activities have benefits that are greater than costs; whether taxes are raised, money is printed, or deficits are run are for the most part financing issues.

Parents can offset some of the intergenerational debt by leaving larger bequests. In addition, if the parents save now to bear the cost of the burden of future taxes, the reduced consumption and increased savings will lower interest rates or, more precisely, offset the higher interest rate caused by the budget deficit. Many parents might not respond that way, but some might.

It is possible that if the budget deficits led people to believe there would be higher future taxes, a budget surplus might lead them to think there would be lower future taxes—and perhaps they would save less and consume more. So do we pay down the debt or cut taxes? They may be equivalent policy prescriptions since each tends to lead to increases in consumption spending.

A look internationally at federal, or central, government indebtedness shows us that Canada's situation is by no means an exception—see Exhibit 5. The reality of

section 10.7 Exhibit 4	Federal Government Debt, Selected Years	
Year	**Debt (billions of dollars)**	**Debt as a Percentage of GDP**
1930	$ 2.2	39%
1940	3.3	49
1950	11.6	63
1960	12.0	31
1970	18.1	20
1980	72.6	23
1990	362.9	53
2000	571.7	54
2003	551.0	45
2004	549.6	43
2005	437.0	39
2006	523.9	36
2007	516.3	34
2008	525.2	33
2009	582.5	38

SOURCE: Statistics Canada.

section 10.7 Exhibit 5	Central Government Debt: Selected Economies (2010)
Country	**Total Central Government Debt as a Percentage of GDP**
Australia	11.0%
Switzerland	20.2
Norway	26.1
Mexico	27.5
Germany	44.4
Ireland	60.7
United States	61.3
France	67.4
United Kingdom	85.5
Italy	109.0
Greece	147.8

SOURCE: Based on data from *Central Government Debt* under *Finance* from OECD. Stat Extracts, http://stats.oecd.org, accessed on October 1, 2011.

public finances around the world is that all central governments are to some extent in debt; the issue is the *amount* of government debt. The recent global economic crisis has increased the debt–GDP ratios of virtually every economy in the world. The central concern now is that, for those economies that already had significant ratios of debt to GDP, recent events have pushed them dangerously higher.

SECTION CHECK

- The budget deficit is financed by issuing debt.
- Improvement in the federal budget balance since the mid-1990s resulted from economic growth, increased tax revenues, and the efforts of the federal government to control the growth of government spending.
- In the short run, reducing a budget deficit can lead to a recession if not offset by expansionary monetary policy. In the long run, however, deficit reduction increases economic growth and lowers the price level.
- With greater fiscal responsibility and increased economic growth, Canada has managed to lower its debt–GDP ratio (the international measure of debt burden).

For Your Review

Section 10.1

1. Answer the following questions.
   a. If there is currently a budget surplus, what would an increase in government purchases do to it?
   b. What would that increase in government purchases do to aggregate demand?
   c. When would an increase in government purchases be an appropriate fiscal policy?

2. Are increases in both government purchases and net taxes at the same time expansionary or contractionary? Would both changes together increase or decrease the federal government deficit?

3. Answer the following questions.
   a. If there is currently a budget deficit, what would an increase in taxes do to it?
   b. What would that increase in taxes do to aggregate demand?
   c. When would an increase in taxes be an appropriate fiscal policy?

4. What is a recessionary gap? What would be the appropriate fiscal policy to combat or offset one? What is an inflationary gap? What would be the appropriate fiscal policy to combat or offset one?

Section 10.2

5. The bulk of the retail price of cigarettes and alcohol in Canada are excise taxes. Explain how excise taxes such as these are regressive and unfairly target lower-income individuals.

6. How does Canada's federal government make money?

Section 10.3

7. What would the multiplier be if the marginal propensity to consume was 0.25, 0.5, and 0.75? How would the value for the tax multiplier differ?

8. If there was a $2 billion increase in government spending, other things being equal, what would be the resulting change in aggregate demand, and how much of the change would be a change in consumption, if the *MPC* was

    a. 0.20?

    b. 0.5?

    c. 2/3?

    d. 0.75?

    e. 0.8?

9. Could the multiplier be written as 1 divided by the marginal propensity to save (*MPS*)?

10. Why does it take a larger reduction in taxes to create the same increase in *AD* as a given increase in government purchases?

Section 10.4

11. Predict the potential impact on real GDP of each of the following events.

    a. an increase in government spending of $5 billion in order to build new highways

    b. a decrease in federal spending of $1 billion due to peacetime military cutbacks

    c. consumer optimism leading to an $8 billion spending increase

    d. gloomy business forecasts leading to a $12 billion decline in investment spending

12. The economy is experiencing a contractionary gap of $30 billion. If the *MPC* = 0.75, what government spending stimulus would you recommend to move the economy back to full employment? If the *MPC* = 0.66?

13. The economy is experiencing a $25 billion expansionary gap. Absent government intervention, what can you predict will happen to the economy in the long run? (Use aggregate demand–aggregate supply analysis in your answer.) If the government decides to intervene using changes in spending, would you recommend a spending increase or decrease? Of what magnitude?

14. Illustrate the impact of a tax cut using aggregate demand–aggregate supply analysis when the economy is operating above full employment. Is this a wise policy? Why or why not?

15. Use the following diagram to answer questions a–f.

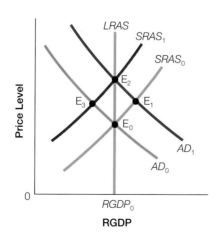

a. At what short-run equilibrium point might expansionary fiscal policy make sense to help stabilize the economy?

b. What would be the result of appropriate fiscal policy in that case?

c. What would be the long-run result if no fiscal policy action was taken in that case?

d. At what short-run equilibrium point might contractionary fiscal policy make sense to help stabilize the economy?

e. What would be the result of appropriate fiscal policy in that case?

f. What would be the long-run result if no fiscal policy action was taken in that case?

Section 10.5

16. How do automatic stabilizers affect budget deficits and surpluses? How would automatic stabilizers be affected by an annually balanced budget rule?

17. Why do automatic stabilizers minimize the lag problems with fiscal policy?

18. What happens to the following variables during an expansion?

a. Employment Insurance benefits

b. welfare payments

c. income tax receipts

d. government budget deficit (surplus)

Section 10.6

19. Can government spending that causes crowding out be detrimental to long-run economic growth? Explain.

20. Answer the following questions:

a. Describe the crowding-out effect of an increase in government purchases.

b. Why does the magnitude of the crowding-out effect depend on how responsive interest rates are to increased government borrowing and how responsive investment is to changes in interest rates?

c. How would the size of the crowding-out effect affect the size of the change in aggregate demand that would result from a given increase in government purchases?

Section 10.7

21. Illustrate diagrammatically the short-run effects of a government budget deficit.

22. Illustrate diagrammatically the long-run effects of a government budget deficit. Describe the mechanism that makes these effects different from the short-run effects described in question 21.

CourseMate

Access an interactive eBook and chapter-specific interactive learning tools, including flashcards, quizzes, a glossary, and more in CourseMate, accessed through **www.sextonmacro3ce.nelson.com**

chapter 11

Money and the Banking System

What Is Money?

- What is money?
- What are the four functions of money?

WHAT IS MONEY?

Money is anything that is generally accepted in exchange for goods or services. Hundreds of years ago, commodities such as tobacco and furs were sometimes used as money. At some times and in some places, even cigarettes and playing cards have been used as money. But commodities have several disadvantages when used as money, the most important of which is that many commodities deteriorate easily after a few trades. Precious metal coins have been used for money for millennia, partly because of their durability.

money
anything generally accepted in exchange for goods or services

WHAT ARE THE FOUR FUNCTIONS OF MONEY?

Money has four important functions in the economy: as a medium of exchange, a store of value, a unit of account, and a means of deferred payment. Let's examine the four important functions of money to see how they are different from the functions of other assets in the economy, such as stocks, bonds, art, real estate, and comic book collections.

Money as a Medium of Exchange

The primary function of money is to serve as a **medium of exchange**, to facilitate transactions, and to lower transactions costs; that is, sellers will accept it as payment in a transaction. However, money is not the only medium of exchange; rather, it is the only medium that is generally accepted for most transactions. How would people trade with one another in the absence of money? They would **barter** for goods and services they desire, that is, transactions would involve the direct exchange of goods and services without the use of money.

medium of exchange
the primary function of money, which is to facilitate transactions and lower transactions costs

barter
direct exchange of goods and services without the use of money

The Barter System Is Inefficient Under a barter system, individuals pay for goods or services by offering other goods and services in exchange. Suppose you are a farmer who needs some salt. You go to the merchant selling salt and offer her 30 kilograms of wheat for 2 kilograms of salt. The wheat that you use to buy the salt is not money, because the salt merchant may not want wheat and therefore may not accept it as payment. That is one of the major disadvantages of barter: The buyer may not have appropriate items of value to the seller. The salt merchant may reluctantly take the wheat that she does not want, later bartering it away to another customer for something that she does want. In any case, barter is inefficient because several trades may be necessary in order to receive the desired goods.

Moreover, barter is extremely expensive over long distances. What would it cost a customer living in Saskatchewan to send wheat to Toronto in return for an item in the Sears catalogue? It is much cheaper to mail a cheque. Finally, barter is time-consuming because of difficulties in evaluating the value of the product that is being offered for barter. For example, the person who is selling the salt may want to inspect the wheat first to make sure that it is pure and not filled with dirt or other unwanted items.

Barter, in short, is expensive, inefficient, and generally prevails only where limited trade is carried out over short distances, which generally means in relatively primitive economies. The more complex the economy (e.g., the higher the real per capita GDP), the greater the economic interactions between people, and consequently, the greater the need for one or more universally accepted assets serving as money. Only in a Robinson Crusoe economy, where people live in isolated settlements and are generally self-sufficient, is the use of money unnecessary.

Money as a Measure of Value

measure of value
money as a common "ruler" of worth allowing for the comparison of diverse goods and services

Besides serving as a medium of exchange, money is also a **measure of value**—a common "ruler" of worth allowing for the comparison of diverse goods and services. With a barter system, one does not know precisely what 30 kilograms of wheat are worth relative to 2 kilograms of salt. With money, a common "ruler" exists so that the values of diverse goods and services can be very precisely compared. Thus, if wheat costs 50 cents a kilogram and salt costs $1 a kilogram, we can say that a kilogram of salt is valued precisely two times as much as a kilogram of wheat ($1 divided by 50 cents = 2). By providing a universally understood measure of value, money serves to lower the information costs involved in making transactions. Without money, a person might not know what a good price for salt is, because so many different commodities can be bartered for it. With money, there is but one price for salt, and that price is readily available as information to the potential consumer.

Money as a Store of Value

store of value
how money provides a means of saving or accumulating purchasing power from the present and transferring it to the future

Money also serves as a **store of value;** that is, money provides a means of saving or accumulating purchasing power from the present and transferring it to the future. The farmer in a barter society who wants to save for retirement might accumulate enormous inventories of wheat, which he would then gradually trade away for other goods in his old age. This is a terribly inefficient way to save. Storage buildings would have to be constructed to hold all of the wheat, and the interest payments that the farmer would earn on the wheat would actually be negative, as rats will eat part of the wheat or it will otherwise deteriorate. Most important, physical goods of value would be tied up in unproductive use for many years. With money, the farmer saves pieces of paper that can be used to purchase goods and services after retirement. It is both cheaper and safer to store paper rather than wheat.

Money as a Means of Deferred Payment

means of deferred payment
the attribute of money that makes it easier to borrow and to repay loans

Finally, the attribute of money that makes it easier to borrow and to repay loans is money is a **means of deferred payment**. With barter, lending is cumbersome and subject to an added problem. What if a wheat farmer borrows some wheat and agrees to pay it back in wheat next year, but the value of wheat soars because of a poor crop resulting from drought? The debt will be paid back in wheat that is far more valuable than that borrowed, causing a problem for the borrower. Of course, fluctuations in the value of money can also occur, and indeed, inflation has been a major problem in our recent past and continues to be a problem in many countries. But the value of money fluctuates far less than the value of many individual commodities, so lending money poses fewer risks to buyers and sellers than lending commodities.

SECTION CHECK

- Money is anything that is generally accepted in exchange for goods or services.
- The four important functions of money are money as a medium of exchange, money as a store of value, money as a unit of account, and money as a means of deferred payment.

Measuring Money

- What is currency?
- What are demand and savings deposits?
- What is liquidity?
- How is the money supply measured?
- What backs the money supply?

WHAT IS CURRENCY?

Currency consists of coins and paper notes that an institution or government has created to be used in the trading of goods and services and the payment of debts. Currency in the form of metal coins is still used as money throughout the world today. But metal currency has a disadvantage: It is bulky. Also, certain types of metals traditionally used in coins, like gold and silver, are not available in sufficient quantities to meet our demands for a monetary instrument. For these reasons, metal coins have been supplemented by paper currency. In Canada, the Bank of Canada issues Bank of Canada notes in various denominations, and this paper currency, along with coins, provides the basis for most transactions of relatively modest size in Canada today.

currency
consists of coins and paper notes that an institution or government has created to be used in the trading of goods and services and the payment of debts

Currency as Legal Tender

In Canada and in most other nations of the world, metal coins and paper currency are the only forms of legal tender. **Legal tender** refers to coins and paper notes officially declared to be acceptable for the settlement of debts incurred in financial transactions. In effect, the government says, "We declare these instruments to be money, and citizens are expected to accept them as a medium of exchange." Legal tender is **fiat money**—a means of exchange that has been established not by custom and tradition or because of the value of the metal in a coin, but by government fiat, or declaration.

legal tender
refers to coins and paper notes officially declared to be acceptable for the settlement of debts incurred in financial transactions

fiat money
a means of exchange established by government declaration

STRABLE/Horizontal/Jutta Klee/2009 Canadian Press Images

Why are financial institution balances that depositors have access to by writing cheques or using debit cards the most popular form of money in Canada, as well as in most other well-developed nations? The answer is simple really: Demand deposits offer all the benefits of coins and paper in terms of liquidity without the danger and inconvenience of having to carry around large sums of money to facilitate daily transactions.

demand deposits

balances in bank accounts that depositors can access on demand

WHAT ARE DEMAND AND SAVINGS DEPOSITS?

Most of the money that we use for day-to-day transactions, however, is not official legal tender. Rather, it is a monetary instrument that has become generally accepted in exchange over the years and has now, by custom and tradition, become money. What is this instrument? It is balances in chequing accounts in financial institutions, more formally called *demand deposits*. **Demand deposits** are defined as balances in financial institution accounts that depositors can access on demand by simply writing a cheque or using a debit card.

The Popularity of Demand Deposits

Demand deposits have replaced paper and metal currency as the major source of money used for larger transactions in Canada and in most other relatively well-developed nations for several reasons, including safety of transactions, lower transaction costs, and transaction records.

Safety of Transactions   Paying for goods and services with a cheque is less risky than paying with paper money. Paper money is readily transferable: If someone takes a $20 bill from you, it is gone, and the thief can use it to buy goods with no difficulty. If, however, someone steals a cheque that you have written to the telephone company to pay a monthly bill, that person probably will have great difficulty using it to buy goods and services, because the individual has to be able to identify himself as a representative of the telephone company. If your chequebook is stolen, a person can use your cheques as money only if she can successfully forge your signature and provide some identification. Hence, transacting business by cheque is much less risky than using legal tender; an element of insurance or safety exists in the use of demand deposits instead of currency.

Lower Transaction Costs   Suppose you decide that you want to buy a compact disc player that costs $81.28 from the current Sears mail-order catalogue. It is much cheaper, easier, and safer for you to send a cheque for $81.28 rather than four $20 bills, a $1 coin, a quarter, and three pennies. Demand deposits are popular precisely because they lower transaction costs compared with the use of metal or paper currency. In very small transactions, the gains in safety and convenience of cheques are outweighed by the time and cost required to write and process them; in these cases, transaction costs are lower with paper and metal currency. For this reason, it is unlikely that the use of paper or metal currency will disappear entirely.

Transaction Record   Another useful feature of demand deposits is that they provide a record of financial transactions. Each month, the financial institution sends the depositor a statement recording the deposit and withdrawal of funds. In an age where detailed records are often necessary for tax purposes, this is a useful feature. Of course, this feature of transaction records could be a negative for some types of business activities, whose participants might prefer that no records exist. In these cases, paper currency transactions could be preferred because they do not leave a paper trail for the government or authorities to follow.

Credit Cards

A credit card is generally acceptable in exchange for goods and services. At the same time, however, a credit card payment is actually a guaranteed loan available on demand to the cardholder, which merely defers the cardholder's payment for a transaction using a demand deposit. Ultimately, an item purchased with a credit card must be paid for with a cheque; monthly payments on a credit card account are required for continued use of the card. A credit card, then, is not money but rather a convenient tool for carrying out transactions that minimize the physical transfer of cheques or currency. In this sense, it is a substitute for the use of money and allows cardholders to use any given amount of money in future exchanges.

Savings Deposits

Coins, paper currency, and demand deposits are certainly forms of money, because all are accepted as direct means of payment for goods and services. Money also includes **savings deposits**, which are financial institution accounts containing funds that cannot be used directly for payment, such as by writing cheques. If these funds cannot be used directly as a means of payment, then why do people hold such accounts? People use these accounts primarily because they generally pay higher interest rates than demand deposits.

savings deposits
financial institution accounts containing funds that cannot be used directly for payment

Stocks and Bonds

Virtually everyone agrees that many other forms of financial assets, such as stocks and bonds, are not money. Suppose you buy 1000 shares of common stock in Microsoft at $30 per share, for a total of $30 000. The stock is traded daily on the Toronto Stock Exchange and elsewhere; you can readily sell the stock and get paid in legal tender or a demand deposit. Why, then, is this stock not considered money? First, it will take a few days for you to receive payment for the sale of stock; you cannot turn the asset into cash as you can a savings deposit in a financial institution. Second, and more importantly, the value of the stock fluctuates over time, and as an owner of the asset, you have no guarantee that you will be able to obtain its original nominal value at any time. Thus, stocks and bonds are not generally considered to be money.

WHAT IS LIQUIDITY?

Money is an asset that we generally use to buy goods or services. In fact, it is so easy to convert money into goods and services that we say it is the most liquid of assets. When we speak of **liquidity** we are speaking about the ease with which one asset can be converted into another asset or into goods and services. For example, to convert a stock or bond into goods and services would prove to be somewhat more difficult—contacting your broker or going online, determining at what price to sell your stock, paying the commission, and waiting for the completion of the transaction. Clearly, stocks and bonds are not as liquid an asset as money. But other assets are even less liquid, like converting your oil paintings or your hockey card collection into other goods and services.

liquidity
the ease with which one asset can be converted into another asset or into goods and services

HOW IS THE MONEY SUPPLY MEASURED?

There is no unique official measure of the Canadian money supply. The most common definition of the money supply is called **M2**, which consists of currency held outside chartered banks plus demand and savings deposits at chartered banks. Exhibit 1 shows that in March 2011, the M2 measure of the money supply in Canada was $1024 billion, comprising $56.7 billion of currency held outside chartered banks plus $967.3 billion of

M2
currency outside chartered banks plus demand and savings deposits at chartered banks

section 11.2
Exhibit 1   Two Definitions of the Money Supply: M2 and M2+

Currency held outside chartered banks	$ 56.7 billion
Demand deposits and savings deposits at chartered banks	967.3 billion
M2	1024.0 billion
Deposits at other financial institutions	342.0 billion
M2+	1366.0 billion

SOURCE: Bank of Canada, March 2011.

M2+

M2 plus demand and savings deposits at trust companies, mortgage loan companies, credit unions, caisses populaires, and other financial institutions

demand deposits and savings deposits at the chartered banks. A broader definition of the money supply is called **M2+**, which consists of M2 plus demand and savings deposits at trust companies, mortgage loan companies, credit unions, caisses populaires, and other financial institutions. M2+ totalled $1366 billion in March 2011. Of these two different definitions of the money supply, it is the M2 measurement that is more commonly used as the official money supply.

WHAT BACKS THE MONEY SUPPLY?

gold standard

defining the dollar as equivalent in value to a certain amount of gold, thereby allowing direct convertibility from currency to gold

Until fairly recently, coins in most nations were largely made from precious metals, usually gold or silver. These metals had considerable intrinsic worth: If the coins were melted down, the metal would be valuable for use in jewellery, industrial applications, dentistry, and so forth. Until 1929, Canada was on an internal **gold standard**, meaning that the dollar was defined as equivalent in value to a certain amount of gold, thereby allowing direct convertibility from currency to gold.

What Backs Our Money Has Changed

Canadian dollars are no longer convertible into gold, so today no meaningful precious metal gives our money value. Why, then, do people accept currency in exchange for goods? After all, a $20 bill is generally a piece of wrinkled paper with virtually no inherent utility or worth. Do we accept these bills because it states on the front of the bills that "This note is legal tender"? Perhaps, but we accept demand deposits without that statement.

The true backing behind money in Canada is faith that people will take it in exchange for goods and services. People accept with great eagerness these small pieces of coloured paper simply because we believe that they will be exchangeable for goods and services with an intrinsic value. If you were to drop two pieces of paper of equal size on the floor in front of 100 students, one a blank piece of paper and the other a $100 bill and then leave the room, the group would probably start fighting for the $100 bill while the blank piece of paper would be ignored. As long as people have confidence in something's convertibility into goods and services, money will exist and no further backing is necessary.

Because governments represent the collective will of the people, they are the institutional force that traditionally defines money in the legal sense. People are willing to accept pieces of paper as money only because of their faith in the government. When people lose faith in the exchangeability of pieces of paper that the government decrees as money, even legal tender loses its status as meaningful money. Something is money only if people will generally accept it. Although governments play a key role in defining money, much of it is actually created by chartered banks. A majority of Canadian money, whether M2 or M2+, is in the form of deposits at privately owned financial institutions.

People who hold money, then, must have faith not only in their government, but also in banks and other financial institutions. If you accept a cheque drawn on a bank, you believe that bank or, for that matter, any financial institution will be willing to convert that cheque into legal tender (currency), enabling you to buy goods or services that you want to have. Thus, you have faith in the bank as well. In short, our money is money because of confidence that we have in private financial institutions as well as in our government.

What makes this paper money valuable? Paper money is valuable if it is acceptable to people who want to sell goods and services. Sellers must be confident that the money they accept is also acceptable at the place where they want to buy goods and services. Imagine if money in Alberta was not accepted as money in Ontario or Nova Scotia. It would certainly make it more difficult to carry out transactions.

SECTION CHECK

- *Currency* refers of the coins and paper notes that are issued by institutions and governments to facilitate the trading of goods and services and the payment of debts. Canadian currency consists of note and coins issued by the Government of Canada, and demand and savings deposits held in various financial institutions.
- While both demand and savings deposits are considered money, only demand deposits can be accessed on demand.
- The ease with which one asset can be converted into another asset or goods and services is called *liquidity*.
- M2 is made up of currency outside chartered banks plus demand and savings deposits at chartered banks. M2+ includes M2 plus demand and savings deposits at trust companies, mortgage loan companies, credit unions, caisses populaires, and other financial institutions.
- Money is backed by our faith that others will accept it from us in exchange for goods and services.

How Banks Create Money

- What types of financial institutions exist in Canada?
- How do banks create money?
- What does a bank balance sheet look like?
- What is a desired reserve ratio?

WHAT TYPES OF FINANCIAL INSTITUTIONS EXIST IN CANADA?

Financial intermediaries in Canada can be classified into three general categories: depository institutions, contractual savings institutions, and investment intermediaries. Each type of institution is unique in terms of where it obtains its funds (primary liability) and how it uses those funds (primary asset). For example, customer deposits are a depository institution's largest liability (source of funds), while the loans and mortgages it grants to its customers are its largest asset (source of funds). Alternatively, consider pension plans that are established by an employer for the purpose of organizing employee retirement contributions (source of funds). Since most companies do not administer their own pension plans, financial institutions receive this money and invest it in corporate stocks and bonds (use of funds).

Exhibit 1 shows the relative size of the major types of financial institutions in Canada in terms of total financial assets. *Deposit-taking institutions,* a category that includes chartered banks, controls over 80 percent of all financial assets in Canada.

Canada's Banking System

chartered banks
financial institutions that accept deposits and make loans

Canada's banking system is widely considered to be the most efficient and safest in the world. The biggest players in the Canadian banking industry are its six large **chartered banks**, financial institutions that accept deposits and make loans. The "Big Six" includes RBC Financial Group, Canadian Imperial Bank of Commerce, BMO Financial Group, Scotiabank, TD Bank Financial Group, and National Bank of Canada. These banks hold over 90 percent of the financial assets in the banking industry and approximately 70 percent of the total domestic assets held by the financial services sector. While chartered banks dominate the financial landscape, there are thousands of other financial institutions offering a variety of financial services in Canada.

By comparison, the structure of Canada's banking industry is dramatically different than that used in the United States. While Canada had a total of 77 banks as of August 2011, the United States had over 7000 commercial banks, far more than any other country in the world. In addition to the extraordinary number of banks, another distinguishing feature of the U.S. banking industry is the fact that the majority of the banks are small: 40 percent of its commercial banks have less than US$100 million in assets.

The Functions of Banks

Banks offer a large number of financial functions. For example, they often will pay an individual's monthly bills by automatic withdrawals, provide financial planning services, rent safe-deposit boxes, and so on. Most important, though, they accept demand deposits

---

section 11.3
Exhibit 1   **Relative Shares of Financial Institutions in Canada—2010**

Type of Institution	Number	Total Assets (in billions)	Percentage (%)
Deposit-taking institutions	150	$3196	80.9
Life insurance companies	101	508	12.9
Property and casualty companies	187	124	3.1
Federally regulated private pension plans	1398	123	3.1
Total	**1836**	**$3951**	**100.0**

SOURCE: *Federally Regulated Financial Institutions and Private Pension Plans*, Figure 1, the Office of the Superintendent of Financial Institutions Canada (OSFI), Annual Report 2009–2010. Reproduced with permission of the Minister of Public Works and Government Services, 2011.

and savings deposits from individuals and firms. They can create money by making loans. In making loans, financial institutions act as intermediaries (the middle persons) between savers, who supply funds, and borrowers, who demand funds.

HOW DO BANKS CREATE MONEY?

As we have already learned, most money, narrowly defined, is in the form of demand deposits, assets that can be directly used to buy goods and services. But how did the balance in, say, a chequing account get there in the first place? Perhaps it was through a loan made by a chartered bank. When a bank lends to a person, it does not typically give the borrower cash (paper and metal currency). Rather, it gives the person the funds by a cheque or by adding funds to an existing chequing account of the borrower. If you go into a bank and borrow $1000, the bank probably will simply add $1000 to your chequing account at the bank. In doing so, a new demand deposit—money—is created.

Bank Profits

Banks make loans and create demand deposits in order to make a profit. How do they make their profit? By collecting higher interest payments on the loans they make than the interest they pay their depositors for those funds. If you borrow $1000 from Loans R Us National Bank, the interest payment you make, less the expenses the bank incurs in making the loan, including its costs of acquiring the funds, represents profit to the bank.

Fractional Reserve System

Because the way to make more profit is to make more loans, banks want to make a large volume of loans. Shareholders, or owners, of banks want the largest profits possible, so what keeps banks from making nearly infinite quantities of loans? A prudent bank would put some limit on its loan (and therefore deposit) volume. For people to accept demand deposits as money, the cheques written must be generally accepted in exchange for goods and services. People will accept cheques only if they know that they are quickly convertible at par (face value) into legal tender. For this reason, banks must have adequate cash reserves on hand to meet the needs of customers who wish to convert their demand deposits into currency.

Our banking system is sometimes called a **fractional reserve system** because banks hold reserves equal to some fraction of their demand deposits. If a bank were to create $100 in demand deposits for every $1 in cash reserves that it had, the bank might well find itself in difficulty before too long. Why? Consider a bank with $10 000 000 in demand deposits and $100 000 in cash reserves. Suppose a couple of large companies with big accounts decide to withdraw $120 000 in cash on the same day. The bank would be unable to convert into legal tender all of the funds requested. The word would then spread that the bank's deposits are not convertible into lawful money. This would cause a so-called "run on the bank." The bank would have to quickly convert some of its other assets into currency, or it would be unable to meet its obligations to convert its demand deposits into currency, and it would have to close.

Therefore, few banks would risk maintaining fewer reserves on hand than they thought prudent for their amount of deposits (particularly demand deposits). Although banks must maintain a prudent level of reserves, they do not want to keep any more of their funds as additional reserves than necessary for safety, because cash reserves do not earn any interest for the bank.

fractional reserve system
a system where banks hold reserves equal to some fraction of their demand deposits

In Canada, if a financial intermediary should fail, depositors are insured against financial loss by the federal government. The Canadian Deposit Insurance Corporation (CDIC), a federal Crown corporation, is the most important government agency that provides this type of insurance. Specifically, deposits at member deposit-taking financial institutions are insured up to $100 000 per account. CDIC members are required to make contribution into the CDIC fund, which is then used to reimburse depositors in the case of a member bank's failure. With some exceptions, virtually all deposit-accepting financial institutions in Canada are members of the CDIC.

WHAT DOES A BANK BALANCE SHEET LOOK LIKE?

balance sheet

a financial record that indicates the balance between a bank's assets and its liabilities plus capital

Earlier in this chapter, we learned that money is created when banks make loans. We will now look more closely at the process of bank lending and its impact on the stock of money. In doing so, we will take a closer look at the structure and behaviour of our hypothetical bank, the Loans R Us National Bank. To get a good picture of the size of the bank, what it owns, and what it owes, we look at its **balance sheet**, which is sort of a financial photograph of the bank at a single moment in time. Exhibit 2 presents a balance sheet for the Loans R Us National Bank.

Assets

The assets of a bank are those things of value that the bank owns (e.g., cash reserves, bonds, and its buildings), including contractual obligations of individuals and firms to pay funds to the bank (loans). The largest asset item for most banks is loans. Banks maintain most of their assets in the form of loans because interest payments on loans are the primary means by which they earn revenue. Some assets are kept in the form of non–interest-bearing cash reserves, to meet the cash demands of customers. Banks also keep some assets in the form of bonds (usually Government of Canada bonds) that are quickly convertible into cash if necessary, but also earn interest revenue.

Liabilities

All banks have substantial liabilities, which are financial obligations that the bank has to other people. The predominant liability of virtually all banks is deposits. If you have

section 11.3
Exhibit 2   **Balance Sheet, Loans R Us National Bank**

Assets		Liabilities and Capital	
Cash reserves	$ 900 000	Demand deposits	$ 5 000 000
Loans	7 200 000	Savings deposits	4 000 000
Bonds	1 500 000	Total Liabilities	$ 9 000 000
		Capital	1 000 000
Bank building, equipment, fixtures	400 000		
Total Assets	**$10 000 000**	**Total Liabilities and Capital**	**$10 000 000**

money in a demand deposit account, you have the right to demand cash for that deposit at any time. Basically, the bank owes you the amount in your chequing account. Savings deposits similarly constitute a liability of banks.

Capital

For a bank to be healthy and solvent, its assets, or what it owns, must exceed its liabilities, or what it owes to others. In other words, if the bank was liquidated and all the assets converted into cash and all the obligations to others (liabilities) paid off, there would still be some cash left to distribute to the owners of the bank, its shareholders. This difference between a bank's assets and its liabilities constitutes the bank's capital. Note that this definition of capital differs from the earlier definition, which described capital as goods used to further production of other goods (machines, structures, tools, etc.). As you can see in Exhibit 2, capital is included on the right side of the balance sheet so that both sides (assets and liabilities plus capital) are equal in amount. Anytime the aggregate amount of bank assets changes, the aggregate amount of liabilities and capital also must change by the same amount, by definition.

WHAT IS A DESIRED RESERVE RATIO?

Suppose for simplicity that the Loans R Us National Bank desires to hold cash reserves equal to 10 percent of its deposits. That percentage of deposits that a bank chooses to hold as cash reserves is often called the **desired reserve ratio**. But what does a desired reserve ratio of 10 percent mean? This means that the bank *wants to* keep cash on hand equal to one-tenth (10 percent) of its deposits. For example, if the desired reserve ratio was 10 percent, banks would want to hold $100 000 in reserves for every $1 million in deposits. The remaining 90 percent of cash, the cash reserves that are in excess of desired reserves, is called **excess reserves**.

Reserves in the form of vault cash earn no revenue for the bank; no profit is made from holding vault cash. Whenever excess reserves appear, banks will invest the excess reserves in interest-earning assets, sometimes bonds but usually loans.

desired reserve ratio
the percentage of deposits that a bank chooses to hold as cash reserves

excess reserves
cash reserves that are in excess of desired reserves

Loaning Excess Reserves

Let's see what happens when someone deposits $100 000 at the Loans R Us National Bank. We will continue to assume that the desired reserve ratio is 10 percent. That is, the bank wants to hold $10 000 in reserves for this new deposit of $100 000. The remaining 90 percent, or $90 000, becomes excess reserves, and most of this will likely become available for loans for individuals and businesses. Notice that at this point, the money supply (M2) is unchanged. Demand deposits have increased by $100 000 while currency outside the chartered banks has decreased by $100 000, as the currency is now stored in the bank's vault.

However, this is not the end of the story. Let us say that the bank loans all of its new excess reserves of $90 000 to an individual who is remodelling her home. At the time that the loan is made, the money supply will increase by $90 000. Specifically, no one has less money—the original depositor still has $100 000 and the bank now adds $90 000 to the borrower's chequing account (demand deposit). A new demand deposit, or chequing account, of $90 000 has been created. *Since demand deposits are money, the issuers of the new loan have created money.*

Furthermore, borrowers are not likely to keep the money in their chequing accounts for long, since you usually take out a loan to buy something. If that loan is

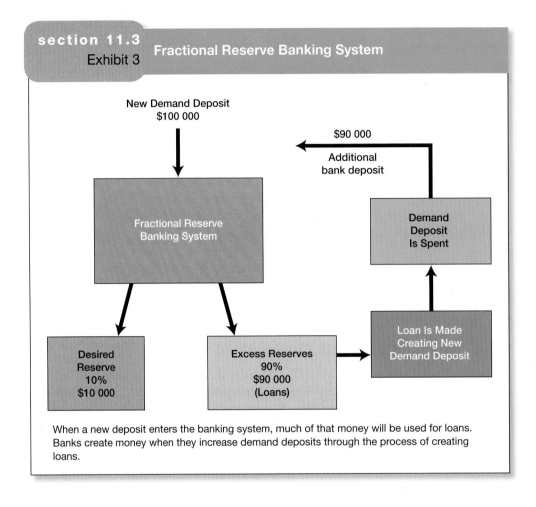

section 11.3
Exhibit 3   **Fractional Reserve Banking System**

New Demand Deposit
$100 000

$90 000

Additional
bank deposit

Fractional Reserve
Banking System

Demand
Deposit
Is Spent

Desired
Reserve
10%
$10 000

Excess Reserves
90%
$90 000
(Loans)

Loan Is Made
Creating New
Demand Deposit

When a new deposit enters the banking system, much of that money will be used for loans. Banks create money when they increase demand deposits through the process of creating loans.

used for remodelling, then the borrower pays the construction company, whose owner will likely deposit the money into his account at another bank to add even more funds for additional money expansion. This whole process is summarized in Exhibit 3.

Money Creation Is Not Wealth Creation

When banks create more money by putting their excess reserves to work, they make the economy more liquid. There is clearly more money in the economy after the loan, but is the borrower any wealthier? The answer is no. Although borrowers have more money to buy goods and services, they are not any richer because the new liability, the loan, has to be repaid.

In short, banks create money when they increase demand deposits through the process of creating loans. However, the process does not stop here. In the next section, we will see how the process of loans and deposits has a multiplying effect throughout the banking industry.

Business **CONNECTION**

WHEN INCREASES IN MONEY SUPPLY LEAD TO INFLATION

Movements in the money supply are associated with changes in inflation and output, variables that are of concern to businesses. Further, the quantity of money supplied in the economy varies with the level of interest rates.

Generally, aggregate supply will experience difficulty increasing and sustaining output beyond the economy's potential if

- the economy is operating at full capacity.
- the broad definition of money supply is increased and sustained.
- such increases finds their way primarily into consumer spending, thereby increasing aggregate demand.

The net effect is an increase in both short-term and long-term price levels, leading to inflation. In this situation the money supply will have increased at a faster rate than the increase in RGDP. Conversely, if the economy is operating at a level of output below its potential, that is, below full employment, increases in aggregate demand led by consumer spending will be responded to by increases in aggregate supply, leading to no long-term increases in price levels or to inflation. As businesses are concerned with increases in inflation, they ought also to be concerned about increases in the money supply, particularly when the economy is or will soon be operating at its potential, as such increases in money supply invariably lead to inflation.

While business is directly responsible for affecting increases in real output, banks are instrumental in affecting movements in money supply. A healthy relationship between these two variables serves as a platform for economic stability. Most developed economies have a central bank, which is a main bank that is under the control of the government and controls all other banks by developing and communicating polices regarding the supplying of money into the economy. At the heart of such policies is the requirement by the central bank that all the other banks hold a specified fraction of their deposits in cash or in accounts with the central bank. This policy requirement serves to regulate the maximum supply of money in the economy.

In situations where there is significant slack in the economy, increasing money supply usually leads to increases in aggregate demand in the short run, with a responding increase in aggregate supply leading to increased output, greater RGDP. If the increases in aggregate demand and aggregate supply are of the same order, there is often no significant change in inflation. However as the economy approaches full capacity, further increases in money supply will invariably lead to increases in price levels, resulting in high and sustained levels of inflation.

While there is much complexity in this area of macroeconomics, business operators with an understanding of the business cycle and who maintain a watchful eye on developments regarding money supply are more likely to better anticipate inflation, and can take steps to mitigate its capacity to erode value and real profits.

SECTION CHECK

- While a variety of financial intermediaries exist in the Canadian financial system, the sector is dominated by deposit-accepting institutions—banks. The Canadian banking industry itself is dominated by six large chartered banks. The "Big Six" hold the majority of the financial assets in the banking industry.
- Money is created when banks make loans. Borrowers receive newly created demand deposits.
- A balance sheet is a financial record that indicates the balance between a bank's assets and its liabilities plus capital. A bank's largest asset is loans and its largest liability is deposits.
- A desired reserve ratio is the percentage of deposits a bank chooses to keep on hand in the form of cash reserves.

The Money Multiplier

■ How does the multiple expansion of the money supply process work?
■ What is the money multiplier?
■ Why is it only "potential" money creation?

HOW DOES THE MULTIPLE EXPANSION OF THE MONEY SUPPLY PROCESS WORK?

We have just learned that banks can create money (demand deposits) by making loans and that the monetary expansion of an individual bank is limited to its excess reserves. Although this is true, it ignores the further effects of a new loan and the accompanying expansion in the money supply. New loans create new money directly, but they also create excess reserves in other banks, which leads to still further increases in both loans and the money supply. There is a multiple expansion effect, where a given volume of bank reserves creates a multiplied amount of money.

New Loans and Multiple Expansions

To see how the process of multiple expansion works, let us extend our earlier example. Say Loans R Us National Bank receives a new cash deposit of $100 000. For convenience, say the bank desires to keep new cash reserves equal to one-tenth (10 percent) of new deposits. With that, Loans R Us chooses to hold $10 000 of the $100 000 deposit for reserves. Thus, Loans R Us now has $90 000 in excess reserves as a consequence of the new cash deposit.

The Loans R Us National Bank, being a profit maximizer, will probably put its newly acquired excess reserves to work in some fashion, earning income in the form of interest. Most likely, it will make one or more new loans totalling $90 000.

When the borrowers from Loans R Us National Bank get their loans, the borrowed money will almost certainly be spent on something—such as new machinery, a new house, a new car, or larger store inventories. The new money will lead to new spending.

The $90 000 spent by people borrowing from Loans R Us National Bank likely will end up in bank accounts in still other banks, such as Bank A shown in Exhibit 1. Bank A now has a new deposit of $90 000 with which to make more loans and create still more money. So Bank A's T-account now looks like this:

Bank A

Assets			Liabilities	
Reserves		$9 000	Chequing deposits	$90 000
Loans		$81 000		

After the deposits, Bank A has liabilities of $90 000. Thus, Bank A creates $81 000 of money. Now if the money deposited in Bank A is made available for a loan and is then deposited in Bank B, the T-account for Bank B will be

Bank B

Assets			Liabilities	
Reserves		$8 100	Chequing deposits	$81 000
Loans		$72 900		

This process continues with Bank C, Bank D, Bank E, and others. Loans R Us National Bank's initial cash deposit, then, has a chain-reaction impact that ultimately involves many banks and a total monetary impact that is far greater than suggested by the size of the original deposit of $100 000; that is, every new loan gives rise to excess reserves, which lead to still further lending and deposit creation. Of course, each round of lending is smaller than the preceding one because some (we are assuming 10 percent) of the new money created will be kept as desired reserves.

WHAT IS THE MONEY MULTIPLIER?

The **money multiplier** measures the potential amount of demand deposit money that the banking system generates with each dollar of reserves. The following formula can be used to measure the potential impact on demand deposits:

Potential money creation = Initial deposit × Money multiplier

To find the size of the money multiplier we simply divide 1 by the desired reserve ratio $(1/R)$. The larger the desired reserve ratio, the smaller the money multiplier. Thus, a desired reserve ratio of 25 percent, or one-fourth, means a money multiplier of four. Likewise, a desired reserve ratio of 10 percent, or one-tenth, means a money multiplier of 10.

In the example in Exhibit 1, where Loans R Us National Bank (with a 10 percent desired reserve ratio) receives a new $100 000 cash deposit, initial deposit equals

money multiplier
measures the potential amount of demand deposit money that the banking system generates with each dollar of reserves

section 11.4 Exhibit 1 — The Multiple Expansion Process

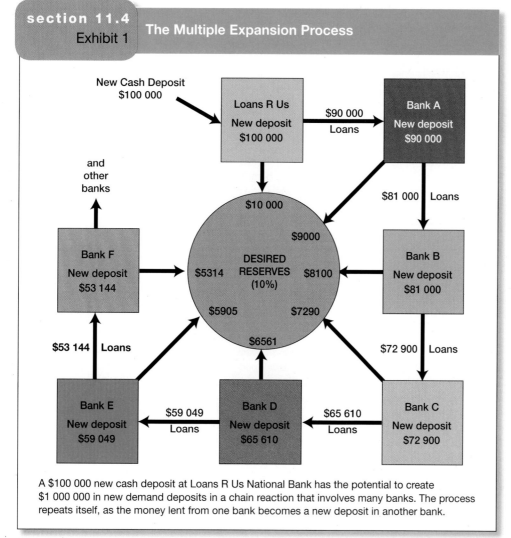

A $100 000 new cash deposit at Loans R Us National Bank has the potential to create $1 000 000 in new demand deposits in a chain reaction that involves many banks. The process repeats itself, as the money lent from one bank becomes a new deposit in another bank.

$100 000. Potential demand deposit creation, then, equals $100 000 (initial deposit) multiplied by 10 (the money multiplier), or $1 000 000. Using the money multiplier, we can calculate that the total potential impact of the initial $100 000 deposit is some $1 000 000 in demand deposit money being created. What is the final impact on the money supply (M2)? Demand deposits at the chartered banks are up by $1 000 000, but currency outside the chartered banks is down by $100 000 (as the initial deposit is in the banks' vaults), so the money supply has increased by $900 000.

WHY IS IT ONLY "POTENTIAL" MONEY CREATION?

Note that the expression "potential" money creation was used in describing the impact of creating loans and deposits out of excess reserves. Why "potential"? Because it is possible that some banks will choose not to lend all of their excess reserves. Some banks may simply be extremely conservative and keep some extra newly acquired cash assets in that form. When that happens, the chain reaction effect is reduced by the amount of excess reserves not loaned out.

Moreover, some borrowers may not spend all of their newly acquired bank deposits, or they may wait a considerable period of time before doing so. Others may choose to keep some of their loans as currency in their pockets. Such leakages and time lags in the bank money expansion process usually mean that the actual monetary impact of an initial deposit created out of excess reserves within a short time period is less than indicated by the money multiplier. Still, the multiplier principle does work, and a multiple expansion of deposits will generally occur in a fractional reserve banking system.

DEBATE

MONEY AND BANKING: FRACTIONAL SYSTEM

One of the Bank of Canada's primary responsibilities is to monitor the supply of money. As you have learned, the definition of money varies depending on what we include as money. One of the most interesting debates emanating from the recession of 2008 is centred on the fractional reserve system and whether deposits should be allowed to expand through the multiplier effect within the fractional system or whether depositors' funds should be protected by hard assets, such as gold. There are benefits to both systems; however, given the recent financial uncertainty caused by the global financial crisis, there are arguments to eliminate fractional reserve banking. Should the fractional system be eliminated?

Pro:

The fractional system creates exponential quantities of money that is loaned and reinvested, thereby expanding GDP. Those who advocate for the elimination of the fractional system point to the recurrence of boom and bust cycles as a result of easy credit and inflation, and assert that with each subsequent boom/bust cycle, the magnitude of the cycles increases significantly. Ultimately, the cycles ensure that bank bailouts will be inevitable, all at the expense of the taxpayer. Are there other consequences that you can think of that would support the elimination of the fractional system and do you think the consequences outweigh the benefits of the system? How do you think the system could be dismantled and what do you think would be the short-term and the long-term consequences?

Con:

Those who are in favour of the system justify it on the basis of the benefits of growth to citizens and firms alike. The fractional system has been integral in generating the exponential growth and wealth of the past half-century, from which most in the developed economies have personally benefitted. While the perils of the system are significant, the impacts are rarely felt over generations and these might be the acceptable "costs" for attaining greater levels of wealth. What other reasons can you think of that would justify the use of the fractional system? Can you think of ways to regulate the system to ensure that it works for society's benefit?

SECTION CHECK

- New loans mean new money (demand deposits), which can increase spending as well as the money supply.
- The money multiplier is equal to one divided by the desired reserve ratio.
- The banking system as a whole can potentially create new money equal to several times the amount of new reserves—as determined by the money multiplier. However, due to various leakages and time lags, the actual monetary impact of an initial deposit created out of excess reserves within a short period of time will be less than that calculated by the money multiplier.

For Your Review

Section 11.1

1. Explain the difficulties that an economics professor might face in purchasing a new car using the barter system.

2. Why do people who live in countries experiencing rapid inflation often prefer to hold another country's currency (e.g., U.S. dollars) rather than their own country's currency? Explain.

Section 11.2

3. Which one of each of the following pairs of assets is most liquid?

   a. Air Canada shares or a savings deposit

   b. a 30-year bond or a six-month Treasury bill

   c. a term deposit or a demand deposit

   d. a savings account or residential real estate

4. Why have ATMs and online banking made savings accounts more liquid than they used to be?

5. What would each of the following changes do to M2 and M2+?

Change	M2	M2+
An increase in currency in circulation		
An increase in demand deposits		
An increase in savings deposits		
A transfer of demand deposit balances from credit unions to chartered banks		

Section 11.3

6. Indicate whether each of the following belong on the asset or liability side of a bank's balance sheet.

   a. loans

   b. holdings of government bonds

  c. demand deposits

  d. vault cash

  e. savings deposits

  f. bank buildings

  g. term deposits

7. Why do you think asking whether money is an asset or a liability is a trick question in economics?

8. If the Bank of Canada paid interest for bank reserves held at the Bank of Canada, would banks still want to avoid holding excess reserves?

Section 11.4

9. Assume there was a new $100 000 deposit into a demand deposit at a bank.

  a. What would be the resulting excess reserves created by that deposit if banks faced a desired reserve ratio of 10 percent, 20 percent, 25 percent, and 50 percent? Display using a T-account.

  b. How many additional dollars could that bank lend out as a result of that deposit if banks faced a desired reserve ratio of 10 percent, 20 percent, 25 percent, and 50 percent? Display using a T-account.

  c. How many additional dollars of demand deposit money could the banking system as a whole create in response to such a new deposit if banks faced a desired reserve ratio of 10 percent, 20 percent, 25 percent, and 50 percent?

10. Answer questions a and b.

  a. If a bank had reserves of $30 000 and demand deposits of $200 000 (and no other deposits), how much could it lend out if had a desired reserve ratio of

   10 percent? _____

   15 percent? _____

   20 percent? _____

  b. If the bank then received a new $40 000 deposit in a customer's demand deposit account, how much could it now lend out (including the amount in question a if it had a desired reserve ratio of

   10 percent? _____

   15 percent? _____

   20 percent? _____

11. Calculate the money multiplier when the desired reserve ratio is

  a. 10 percent.

  b. 2 percent.

  c. 20 percent.

  d. 8 percent.

12. If the desired reserve ratio is 10 percent, calculate the potential change in demand deposits in the banking system under the following circumstances.

  a. You take $5000 from under your mattress and deposit it in your bank.

  b. You withdraw $50 from the bank and leave it in your wallet for emergencies.

  c. You write a cheque for $2500 drawn on your bank (CIBC) to an auto mechanic, who deposits the funds in his bank (TD Bank).

13. Calculate the magnitude of the money multiplier if banks were to hold 100 percent of deposits in reserve. Would banks be able to create money in such a case? Explain.

14. Suppose the simplified balance sheet shown below is for the entire banking system.

Bank Balance Sheet

Assets		Liabilities	
Reserves	$ 500 000	Demand deposits	$2 000 000
Loans	1 600 000		
Buildings	1 200 000	Capital	1 300 000
Total Assets	**$3 300 000**	**Total Liabilities and Capital**	**$3 300 000**

If the desired reserve ratio is 10 percent, how much in excess reserves does the banking system have? If the banking system was to loan out those excess reserves, what is the potential expansion in demand deposits? Redesign the above balance sheet to show how it would look after this amount has been loaned.

15. Suppose the simplified balance sheet shown below is for the entire banking system.

Bank Balance Sheet

Assets		Liabilities	
Reserves	$ 300 000	Demand deposits	$1 500 000
Loans	1 200 000		
Buildings	500 000	Capital	500 000
Total Assets	**$2 000 000**	**Total Liabilities and Capital**	**$2 000 000**

If the desired reserve ratio is 15 percent, how much in excess reserves does the banking system have? If the banking system was to loan out those excess reserves, what is the potential expansion in demand deposits? Redesign the above balance sheet to show how it would look after this amount has been loaned.

16. Suppose the simplified balance sheet shown below is for the entire banking system.

Bank Balance Sheet

Assets		Liabilities	
Reserves	$ 750 000	Demand deposits	$3 500 000
Loans	2 500 000		
Buildings	1 250 000	Capital	1 000 000
Total Assets	**$4 500 000**	**Total Liabilities and Capital**	**$4 500 000**

If the desired reserve ratio is 20 percent, how much in excess reserves does the banking system have? If the banking system was to loan out those excess reserves, what is the potential expansion in demand deposits? Redesign the above balance sheet to show how it would look after this amount has been loaned.

CourseMate

Access an interactive eBook and chapter-specific interactive learning tools, including flashcards, quizzes, a glossary, and more in CourseMate, accessed through **www.sextonmacro3ce.nelson.com**

chapter 12

The Bank of Canada

section 12.1

The Bank of Canada

- What is the Bank of Canada?
- What are the functions of the Bank of Canada?

WHAT IS THE BANK OF CANADA?

In most countries of the world, the job of controlling the supply of money belongs to the central bank. The Bank of Canada is Canada's central bank. It was established in 1935, largely as a result of the economic problems of the Great Depression and the need for better control of the money supply. Chartered banks' goal, remember, is to maximize profits for their shareholders. However, the banks' behaviour can have adverse effects on the nation's money supply. For example, during a period of economic recession, banks may have increasing concerns about the ability of new borrowers to repay their loans, or they may find that their customers are withdrawing more cash due to fears that the banks may fail. As a result, the banks may choose to hold more excess reserves for safety and liquidity, rather than loaning those excess reserves out. Thus, during a period of economic recession there is a tendency for the money supply to decrease, which further destabilizes the economy. A central bank, however, can use certain tools to adjust the money supply in order to help stabilize the economy.

The Bank of Canada is owned by the federal government. It is controlled by a board of directors, which is appointed by the government. The governor of the Bank of Canada, who is the chief executive, is appointed for a seven-year term. The current governor, Mark Carney, was appointed in 2008. Although the government has final responsibility for the Bank of Canada's actions, the governor has considerable independence in the day-to-day operations of the Bank of Canada. This operational independence is important, as studies have shown that central banks with greater degrees of independence appear to have a lower annual inflation rate (see Exhibit 1). If there was a very significant disagreement between the governor and the government, the government could issue a written directive to the governor, forcing him or her to either comply with the directive or resign.

The objectives of the Bank of Canada are outlined in the Bank of Canada Act, which says:

> Whereas it is desirable to establish a central bank in Canada to regulate credit and currency in the best interests of the economic life of the nation, to control and protect the external value of the national monetary unit and to mitigate by its influence fluctuations in the general level of production, trade, prices and employment, so far as may be possible within the scope of monetary action, and generally to promote the economic and financial welfare of Canada.

Inflation control is how the Bank of Canada contributes to improved economic performance. Low inflation allows the economy to function more efficiently, resulting in better economic growth over time and reduced short-run cyclical fluctuations in output and employment. In 1991, the Bank of Canada and the federal government jointly announced inflation targets. The current inflation target aims to keep the annual inflation rate within a target range of 1 to 3 percent.

The Federal Reserve System

In Canada, as in most countries, the central bank is a single bank. In the United States, however, the central bank is 12 institutions, closely tied together and collectively called the *Federal Reserve System*. The Federal Reserve System, or Fed, as it is nicknamed, comprises separate banks in Boston, New York, Philadelphia, Richmond, Atlanta, Dallas, Cleveland, Chicago, St. Louis, Minneapolis–St. Paul, Kansas City, and San Francisco. As Exhibit 2 shows, while these banks and their

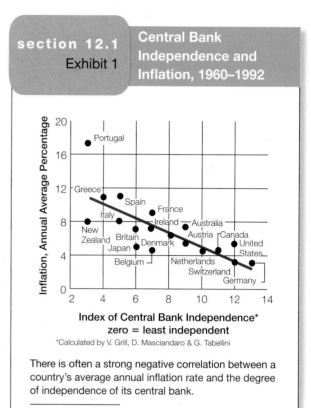

section 12.1
Exhibit 1

Central Bank Independence and Inflation, 1960–1992

There is often a strong negative correlation between a country's average annual inflation rate and the degree of independence of its central bank.

SOURCE: © *The Economist* Newspaper, London (23 September, 1999).

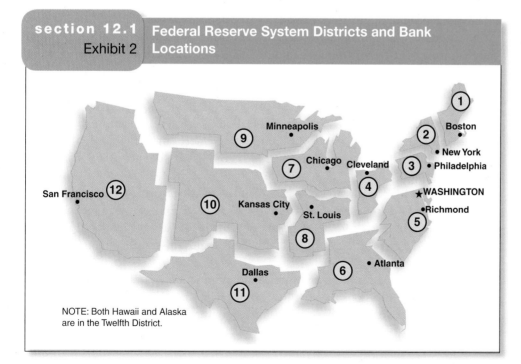

section 12.1
Exhibit 2

Federal Reserve System Districts and Bank Locations

NOTE: Both Hawaii and Alaska are in the Twelfth District.

branches are spread all over the country, they are most heavily concentrated in the eastern states.

Each Federal Reserve bank has its own board of directors and, to a limited extent, can set its own policies. Effectively, however, the 12 banks act in unison on major policy issues, with control of major policy decisions resting with the Board of Governors and the Federal Open Market Committee (FOMC). The chairman of the Federal Reserve Board of Governors, currently Ben Bernanke, is generally regarded as one of the most important and powerful economic policymakers in the United States.

Created in 1913, the Federal Reserve System is privately owned by the banks that "belong" to it. This private ownership, however, is essentially meaningless, as the Federal Reserve Board of Governors, which controls major policy decisions, is appointed by the president of the United States, not by the shareholders.

WHAT ARE THE FUNCTIONS OF THE BANK OF CANADA?

The Bank of Canada has five main functions. The first function is to issue currency for circulation in Canada. The Bank of Canada has monopoly power over issuing legal tender in the form of Bank of Canada notes. The Bank of Canada is responsible for note design, for overseeing the printing and distribution of banknotes, and for replacing worn-out currency.

The second function is to act as a banker to the federal government. The federal government has a demand deposit account at the Bank of Canada and at the chartered banks as well. The Bank of Canada manages the government's bank accounts in these different financial institutions. In addition, the Bank of Canada acts as a fiscal agent to the federal government in managing the government's foreign currency reserves and its bonds.

The third function of the Bank of Canada is to act as a bank to the chartered banks. In Chapter 11, we explained that the chartered banks hold their reserves as currency in their vaults. However, they also hold a small amount of their reserves as a demand deposit at the Bank of Canada. These deposits at the Bank of Canada allow the chartered banks to make payments to each other. For example, let's say you pay your monthly rent by writing a cheque for $800 on your chequing account at the TD Bank. Your landlord deposits the cheque in her chequing account at the Royal Bank. The Royal Bank will credit your landlord's chequing account for $800. But the Royal Bank will want payment of $800 from the TD Bank. Therefore, as the cheque clears, $800 will be deducted from the TD Bank's reserve account at the Bank of Canada and transferred to the Royal Bank's reserve account at the Bank of Canada. Of course, once the cheque clears, the TD Bank will deduct $800 from your chequing account.

The fourth function is to serve as a "lender of last resort." When a bank finds itself in financial distress because it is short of reserves and cannot meet the withdrawal demands of its customers, the Bank of Canada may act as a lender of last resort and lend reserves to the bank in order to help maintain stability in the financial system.

The Bank of Canada's fifth and most important function is controlling the supply of money. The policy decisions that the Bank of Canada makes in controlling the money supply, consistent with its inflation control objective, form the basis of the Bank of Canada's monetary policy.

DEBATE

MONETARY POLICY: INDEPENDENCE

The Bank of Canada is Canada's central bank and it is responsible for controlling the supply of money. Through a variety of tools at its disposal, such as open market operations or setting the overnight interest rate, the Bank can influence the economy in order to meet the country's economic and goals. While fiscal policy uses the government's tools of spending and taxes, monetary policy uses the tools of the Bank of Canada. It has been a tradition to separate the political decisions of fiscal policy from those of the more staid decisions of the Bank. Separation is viewed as a positive and necessary attribute, ensuring a balance between sound policy and self-serving politicians.

Since the economic recession of 2008, there has been a movement advocating the politicizing of monetary policy through intervention of the Bank. Should the Bank of Canada be politicized?

Pro:

The central bank makes decisions that affect all of society, yet answers to only a few, politically nonaccountable individuals. Canadians should expect that those who make such public decisions should be answerable to the public. Further, fiscal policy has to mesh with monetary policy and, without some integration, the two policies can work against each other. What are some other reasons to justify some political influence in central bank policy?

Con:

The Bank of Canada needs to be independent of political influence. Politicians are self-serving as their goal is to get re-elected, which brings their perception of independence into question. Further, in making economic decisions, the Bank employs knowledgeable professionals versed in economics and monetary policy. On the other hand, there is no guarantee that politicians understand the complexities of the decisions that need to be made. Finally, there is merit in keeping politics and monetary policy at arm's length from each other. Can you think of other reasons to leave politics out of the Bank's decision-making process?

SECTION CHECK

- The Bank of Canada is Canada's central bank. It is owned by the federal government, which has the final responsibility for the Bank of Canada's policies. Despite this goal dependence, the governor of the Bank of Canada has considerable independence in formulating the Bank of Canada's monetary policy.
- The Bank has five main functions: currency maintenance, banker of the federal government, bank to the chartered banks, lender of last resort, and money supply management. Of the five main functions of a central bank, the most important is its role in regulating the money supply.

section 12.2

Tools of the Bank of Canada

- What are the tools of the Bank of Canada?
- How does the Bank of Canada influence the money supply?

WHAT ARE THE TOOLS OF THE BANK OF CANADA?

As noted previously, the most important function of the Bank of Canada is to regulate the supply of money. The Bank of Canada decides whether to expand the money supply and, it is hoped, the real level of economic activity, or to contract the money supply, hoping to cool inflationary pressures. How does the Bank of Canada control the money supply, particularly when it is the privately owned chartered banks that actually create and destroy money by making loans, as we discussed earlier?

The Bank of Canada has two methods that it can use to control the supply of money: It can engage in open market operations, or it can set a target for the overnight interest rate.

Open Market Operations

open market operations
purchase and sale of government securities by the Bank of Canada

Open market operations involve the purchase and sale of Government of Canada securities (bonds and Treasury bills) by the Bank of Canada. When the Bank of Canada purchases Government of Canada bonds from the nonbank public, an investment dealer, for example, the Bank of Canada pays for the bonds with a cheque drawn on itself. The investment dealer receiving the payment will likely deposit the cheque in its chequing account at its chartered bank, thereby increasing the money supply in the form of a demand deposit. More important, the chartered bank will collect payment of this cheque from the Bank of Canada. The Bank of Canada will credit the chartered bank's reserve account at the Bank of Canada. Therefore, the chartered bank, in return for crediting the chequing account of the investment dealer with a new deposit, gets a credit in its reserve account at the Bank of Canada.

For example, suppose the Loans R Us National Bank has no excess reserves and that one of its customers, an investment dealer, sells a bond for $10 000 to the Bank of Canada. The customer deposits the cheque from the Bank of Canada for $10 000 in its account, and the Bank of Canada credits the Loans R Us National Bank with $10 000 in reserves. Suppose the desired reserve ratio is 10 percent. The Loans R Us National Bank, then, needs new reserves of only $1000 ($10 000 × 0.10) to support the $10 000 demand deposit, meaning that it has acquired $9000 in new excess reserves ($10 000 new actual reserves minus $1000 in new desired reserves). Loans R Us National Bank can, and probably will, lend out its excess reserves of $9000, creating $9000 in new deposits in the process. The recipients of the loans, in turn, will likely spend the money, leading to still more new deposits and excess reserves in other banks, as discussed in Chapter 11. This series of transactions is illustrated in Exhibit 1.

In other words, the Bank of Canada's purchase of the bond directly creates $10 000 in money in the form of demand deposits, and indirectly permits up to $90 000 in additional money to be created through the multiple expansion in bank deposits. (The money multiplier is 1/0.10, or 10; 10 × $9000 = $90 000.) Thus, if the desired reserve ratio is 10 percent, a potential total of up to $100 000 in new money is created by the purchase of one $10 000 bond by the Bank of Canada.

The process works in reverse when the Bank of Canada sells a bond. The investment dealer purchasing the bond will pay the Bank of Canada by cheque, lowering demand deposits in the banking system. Reserves of the bank where the investment dealer has a bank account will likewise fall. If the bank had zero excess reserves at the beginning of the process, it will now be short of reserves. The bank will likely reduce its volume of loans, which will lead to a further reduction of demand deposits. A multiple contraction of deposits, and money, will begin.

section 12.2
Exhibit 1

Open Market Operations: Bank of Canada Buys Securities from Investment Dealer

a. Investment Dealer (nonbank public)		
Assets		**Liabilities**
Securities	–$10 000	
Demand deposits	+$10 000	

b. Loans R Us Bank		
Assets		**Liabilities**
Reserves	+$10 000	Demand deposits	+$10 000

10 percent desired reserve ratio

c. Bank of Canada		
Assets		**Liabilities**
Securities	+$10 000	Reserves of Loans R Us Bank	+$10 000

d. Loans R Us Bank		
Assets		**Liabilities**
Reserves	$1000	Demand deposits	$10 000
Loans	$9000		

When the Bank of Canada buys securities from the nonbank public in the open market, it creates reserves. The nonbank public exchanges its securities for deposits, as seen in Exhibit 1(a). These additional deposits increase bank reserves, as seen in Exhibit 1(b). The additional bank reserves, along with the original purchase of securities, increase both assets and liabilities at the Bank of Canada, as seen in Exhibit 1(c). The increase in bank reserves will likely trigger additional lending and therefore money creation, as seen in Exhibit 1(d).

The Target for the Overnight Interest Rate

We have seen that chartered banks hold a very small proportion of their deposits as reserves, choosing instead to lend out the vast majority of their deposits as interest-earning loans. The main reason that banks are able to operate with such a low ratio of reserves is that they are able to borrow reserves from the Bank of Canada if they find that their reserves have dropped below the desired level. The interest rate that the Bank of Canada charges chartered banks for the loans it extends to them is called the **bank rate.**

The Bank of Canada sets the bank rate in relation to another important interest rate in the economy called the *overnight interest rate.* The **overnight interest rate** is the interest rate that chartered banks charge each other for one-day loans. The Bank of Canada sets a range for the overnight interest rate by using the bank rate as the upper limit of the range.

bank rate
interest rate that the Bank of Canada charges chartered banks for the loans it extends to them

overnight interest rate
interest rate that chartered banks charge each other for one-day loans

Business CONNECTION

WHEN THE BANK RATE INCREASES, BE VERY CAUTIOUS!

One of the most important functions of the Bank of Canada is controlling the money supply. It uses two methods to do this. First, it buys or sells bonds, which has the effect of increasing or decreasing the money supply, respectively. Second, it can raise or lower its target for the overnight interest rate via changes to the bank rate, which again increases or decreases the money supply, respectively.

The Bank of Canada changes the bank rate primarily to adjust the money supply. A change in the money supply may not readily affect a business; however, a change in the bank rate will often directly and immediately start having a negative effect on the profitability of most businesses, particularly those that have outstanding short-term bank loans or have funds deposited in short-term bank securities. This occurs because the rate that the Canadian chartered banks charge their business customers is tied to an index rate called the *prime rate,* which in turn is tied to the Bank of Canada bank rate.

An increase in a company's bank loan rate is just one of several concerns. When a company experiences an increase in its bank loan rate, the interest expense charges it must pay to the bank will also increase. Without any other changes, increases in loan interest expense will reduce the company's profits. Faced with the reality of higher interest rates, many consumers and businesses that use credit to finance their purchases will refrain from taking out loans and will accordingly reduce their expenditures. The net effect is that for most businesses, revenue growth will be constrained. Also, when the Bank of Canada causes an increase in loan interest rates, there is usually a concern that the economy is overheating and should be restrained. As the Bank of Canada attempts to restrain the economy, the Government of Canada may simultaneously be taking fiscal policy steps to cool the economy. If governments implement fiscal policies resulting in higher tax rates on profit, business will also find that after-tax profits are reduced.

In summary, when the Bank of Canada causes an increase in interest rates, companies must be aware of three developments. First, those with debt will in the first instance see profits eroded due to higher interest expense. Second, revenue growth will come under pressure. Finally, fiscal policies such as higher tax rates will reduce after-tax profits. These three developments can have a significantly negative impact on a company's overall profitability. Therefore, the typical business with some debt cannot afford to be unaware of the actions of the Bank of Canada with respect to its immediate and long-term plans for the overnight interest rate target.

bankers' deposit rate
the interest rate the Bank of Canada pays chartered banks on their reserve deposits at the Bank of Canada

For example, say the Bank of Canada sets a target for the overnight interest rate of 3 percent. That means that chartered banks can borrow funds from each other at an interest rate of 3 percent. To achieve this, the Bank of Canada establishes an operating band around the target overnight interest rate. The operating band is the target overnight interest rate plus or minus one-half of a percentage point. The upper limit of the band (one-half of a percentage point above the target overnight interest rate) is the bank rate and the lower limit (one-half of a percentage point below the target overnight interest rate) is the bankers' deposit rate. The **bankers' deposit rate** is the interest rate the Bank of Canada pays chartered banks on their reserve deposits at the Bank of Canada. In this case, the bank rate would be 3.25 percent and the banker's deposit rate would be 2.75 percent. We can now see that if one chartered bank needed to borrow reserves overnight (because its actual reserves were less than its desired reserves), it would first try to borrow those reserves from a second bank that was then in a position of having some excess reserves. What overnight interest rate might those two banks find it beneficial to agree to?

The actual overnight interest rate will fall somewhere between 2.75 percent and 3.25 percent. The first bank will not borrow reserves from the second bank for more than 3.25 percent, since it can borrow reserves from the Bank of Canada at that interest rate. Likewise, the second bank will not lend reserves to the first bank for less than 2.75 percent, since it can earn that rate of interest by holding its excess reserves at the Bank of Canada. Thus, an overnight interest rate of, say, 3 percent would benefit the chartered bank trying to borrow reserves overnight as well as the chartered bank trying to lend excess reserves overnight.

If the Bank of Canada raises the target for the overnight interest rate, it makes it more costly for banks to borrow funds to increase their reserves. The higher the interest rate banks have to pay on the borrowed funds, the lower the potential profit from any new loans made from borrowed reserves, so fewer new loans will be made and less money created. Thus, if the Bank of Canada wants to contract the money supply, it will raise the target for the overnight interest rate. Conversely, if the Bank of Canada wants to expand the money supply, it will lower the target for the overnight interest rate, making it cheaper for banks to borrow funds. The lower the interest rate that banks have to pay on the borrowed reserves, the higher the potential profit from any new loans made from the reserves, so more new loans will be made and more money created.

HOW DOES THE BANK OF CANADA INFLUENCE THE MONEY SUPPLY?

Reducing the Money Supply

The Bank of Canada can do two things to reduce the money supply or reduce the rate of growth in the money supply: (1) sell bonds or (2) raise the target for the overnight interest rate. Of course, the Bank of Canada could also opt to use some combination of these two tools in its approach.

These moves would tend to decrease aggregate demand, reducing nominal GDP, hopefully through a decrease in price level rather than in the quantity of goods and services produced in a given period. These actions would be the monetary policy equivalent of a fiscal policy of raising taxes, lowering transfer payments, and/or lowering government spending.

Increasing the Money Supply

If the Bank of Canada is concerned about underutilization of resources (e.g., unemployment), it would engage in precisely the opposite policies: (1) buy bonds or (2) lower the target for the overnight interest rate. The Bank of Canada could also use a combination of these two approaches.

These moves would tend to increase aggregate demand, increasing nominal GDP, hopefully through an increase in the quantity of goods and services produced in a given period rather than an increase in the price level. Equivalent expansionary fiscal policy actions would be to reduce taxes, and/or increase government spending.

SECTION CHECK

- The two major tools of the Bank of Canada are open market operations and changing the target for the overnight interest rate.
- If the Bank of Canada wants to stimulate the economy (increase aggregate demand), it will increase the money supply by buying government bonds and/or lowering the target for the overnight interest rate. If the Bank of Canada wants to restrain the economy (decrease aggregate demand), it will lower the money supply by selling bonds and/or raising the target for the overnight interest rate.

Money and Inflation

- What is the equation of exchange?
- What is the quantity theory of money and prices?

For many centuries, scholars have known that there is a positive relationship between the money supply, the price level, the growth in the money supply, and the inflation rate. In the 1500s, a huge influx of gold and silver into Europe followed the Spanish conquest in the New World. The influx of precious metals almost tripled the money supply of Europe—too many coins were chasing what goods were available and prices rose steadily.

One of the major reasons that the control of the money supply is so important is that, in the long run, the amount of money in circulation and the overall price level are closely linked. It is virtually impossible for a country to have sustained inflation without a rapid growth in the money supply. The inflation rate tends to be greater in periods of rapid monetary expansion than in periods of slower growth in the money supply. In Exhibit 1, we see that international data supports the relationship between higher money growth and a higher inflation rate.

section 12.3 Exhibit 1	Money Supply Growth and Inflation Rates in Selected Countries, 1980–2002

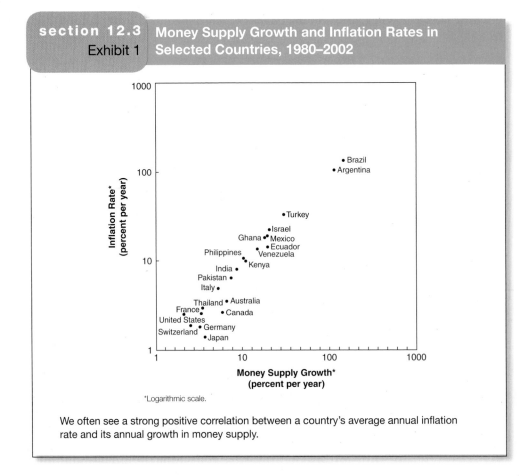

*Logarithmic scale.

We often see a strong positive correlation between a country's average annual inflation rate and its annual growth in money supply.

WHAT IS THE EQUATION OF EXCHANGE?

The role that money plays in determining equilibrium GDP, the level of prices, and real output of goods and services has attracted the attention of economists for generations. There is a useful relationship that helps our understanding of the role of money in the national economy, called the *equation of exchange*. The equation of exchange (or quantity equation) can be presented as follows:

$$M \times V = P \times Q$$

where M is the money supply, however defined (usually M2 or M2+); V is the velocity of money; P is the average level of prices of final goods and services; and Q is the physical quantity of final goods and services produced in a given period (usually one year).

The expression $P \times Q$ represents the dollar value of all final goods and services sold in a country in a given year. Does that sound familiar? It should, because that is the definition of nominal gross domestic product (GDP). Thus, for our purposes, we may consider the average level of prices (P) times the physical quantity of final goods and services in a given time period (Q) to be equal to nominal GDP.

The **velocity of money,** V, represents the average number of times that a dollar is used in purchasing final goods or services in a one-year period. Thus, if individuals are hoarding their money, velocity will be low; if individuals are writing lots of cheques on their chequing accounts and spending currency as fast as they receive it, *velocity* will tend to be high. Velocity is defined as the nominal or current dollar value of output divided by the money supply, or

velocity of money (V)
the average number of times that a dollar is used in purchasing final goods or services in a one-year period

$$V = \frac{P \times Q}{M}$$

Suppose we have a simple economy that produces only frozen yogurt. The economy produces 200 litres of frozen yogurt per year. The frozen yogurt sells for $5 a litre and the quantity of money in the economy is $100. Plugging the number into our equation for velocity, we get

$$V = \frac{P \times Q}{M} = \frac{\$5 \times 200}{\$100} = 10$$

That is, the people in the economy spend $1000 per year on frozen yogurt. If there is only $100 of money in the economy, each dollar must change hands on average 10 times per year. Thus, the velocity is 10.

WHAT IS THE QUANTITY THEORY OF MONEY AND PRICES?

If we make certain assumptions about the variables in the equation of exchange, we can clearly see the relationship between the money supply and the price level. The **quantity theory of money and prices** is a theory of the connection between the money supply and the price level when the velocity of money is constant. If velocity (V) and real GDP (Q) both remain constant, then a 10 percent increase in the money supply will lead to a 10 percent increase in the price level—that is, the money supply and the price level change in the same proportion. We can extend this equation to link the growth rates of

quantity theory of money and prices
a theory of the connection between the money supply and the price level when the velocity of money is constant

these four variables. Using the *growth version of the quantity equation,* we can transform $M \times V = P \times Q$ into

> Growth rate of the money supply + Growth rate of velocity =
> Growth rate of the price level (inflation rate) + Growth rate
> of real output

This makes it easier to see the effects of the money supply on the inflation rate. Suppose money growth is 5 percent per year, the growth of real output is 3 percent per year, and velocity has not changed at all—its growth rate is 0 percent. What is the inflation rate?

> The growth rate of M (5 percent) + The growth rate of V (0 percent) =
>
> The growth rate of P (___ percent) + The growth rate of Q (3 percent)

In this situation, the growth rate of prices (P), the inflation rate, is equal to 2 percent. We can also extend the analysis to predict the inflation rate when real GDP and velocity also vary. For example, if velocity grew at 1 percent annually rather than zero as in our example, the inflation rate would be 3 percent rather than 2 percent.

If velocity remains constant, the growth rate of velocity (the percentage change from one year to the next) will be zero. Then we can simplify our equation once more:

> Inflation rate = Growth rate of the money supply − Growth rate of real GDP

If this is the case, there are three possible scenarios:

1. If the money supply grows at a faster rate than real GDP, then there will be inflation.
2. If the money supply grows at a slower rate than real GDP, then there will be deflation.
3. If the money supply grows at the same rate as real GDP, the price level will be stable.

Economists once expected that they could treat the velocity of money as a given because the determinants of velocity they focused on would change very slowly. We now know that velocity is not constant, but often moves in a fairly predictable pattern. Historically, the velocity of money has been quite stable over a long period of time, particularly when using the M2 definition of money. Thus, the connection between money supply and the price level is still fairly predictable, especially during periods of high inflation.

If an increase in the money supply leads to inflation in the long run, why do countries allow the growth rate of their money supply to increase so rapidly? There are several possible reasons. For instance, due to war or political instability, countries' spending may exceed what they can raise through borrowing from the public or by taxation, so they create more money to pay their bills. The more money these countries create, the larger amount of inflation they will experience.

Hyperinflation

The relationship between the growth rate of the money supply and the inflation rate is particularly strong when there is very rapid inflation, called *hyperinflation*. One of the most famous cases of hyperinflation was in Germany in the 1920s—inflation rose to roughly 300 percent *per month* for over a year. The German government had incurred large amounts of debt as a result of the World War I and could not raise enough money to pay its expenses, so it printed huge amounts of money. The inflation rate became so rapid that store owners would change their prices in the middle of the day, firms had to pay workers several times a week, and many resorted to barter. Recently, Zimbabwe, Brazil, Argentina, and Russia have experienced hyperinflation. The cause of hyperinflation is simply excessive money growth.

SECTION CHECK

- The equation of exchange is expressed as $M \times V = P \times Q$, where M is the money supply, V is the velocity of money, P is the average level of prices of final goods and services, and Q is real GDP in a given year.
- The theory that draws a connection between the money supply and the price level when the velocity of money is constant is referred to as the *quantity theory of money and prices*.

For Your Review

Section 12.1

1. Which of the following are functions of the Bank of Canada?
   a. provide loans to developing economies
   b. supervise banks
   c. back the Canadian dollar with gold
   d. issue currency
   e. regulate the money supply
   f. loan reserves to banks
   g. act as the bank for the Canadian government
   h. set interest rates on mortgages
2. How independent is the Bank of Canada?

Section 12.2

3. If the Bank of Canada purchases from the nonbank public $10 million worth of government bonds in the open market when the desired reserve ratio is 5 percent, what is the potential change in the money supply? If the desired reserve ratio is 25 percent? Using T-accounts, show the impact of this transaction on the nonbank public, the banking system, and the Bank of Canada.
4. Answer question 3 again but this time have the Bank of Canada purchase the bonds directly from a bank within the banking system (as opposed to the nonbank public). Using T-accounts, show the impact of this transaction on the banking system and the Bank of Canada.

5. If the Bank of Canada sells a $10 000 bond to an investor, what is the potential change in the money supply if the desired reserve ratio is 10 percent?

6. The following table shows the balance sheet for the Loans R Us National Bank. If the desired reserve ratio decreases from 10 to 5 percent, what happens to the "reserves" and "excess reserves" on the bank's balance sheet? What is the potential change in the money supply?

Loans R Us National Bank			
Assets		**Liabilities**	
Reserves	$100 000	Demand Deposits	$1 000 000
Excess Reserves	0	Equity Capital	50 000
Loans	700 000		
Securities	250 000		

7. Answer question 6 again for the situation in which the bank increases the desired reserve ratio from 10 to 12.5 percent. Where can the bank acquire the additional funds necessary to cover the desired reserves?

8. In which direction would the money supply change if the Bank of Canada

   a. raised the target on the overnight interest rate?

   b. conducted an open market sale of government bonds?

   c. lowered the target on the overnight interest rate?

   d. conducted an open market sale of government bonds and raised the target on the overnight interest rate?

   e. conducted an open market purchase of government bonds and raised the target on the overnight interest rate?

9. How does an open market purchase by the Bank of Canada increase bank reserves? How does it increase the money supply?

10. Why would the Bank of Canada seldom do an open market purchase of government securities at the same time that it raises the target on the overnight interest rate?

Section 12.3

11. Answer questions a–e.

   a. What is the equation of exchange?

   b. In the equation of exchange, if V doubled, what would happen to nominal GDP as a result?

   c. In the equation of exchange, if V doubled and Q remained unchanged, what would happen to the price level as a result?

   d. In the equation of exchange, if M doubled and V remained unchanged, what would happen to nominal GDP as a result?

   e. In the equation of exchange, if M doubled and V fell by half, what would happen to nominal GDP as a result?

12. Suppose that velocity and the money supply remain constant. If real GDP grows at an annual rate of 5 percent, what can you predict will happen to the price level using the equation of exchange? If real GDP falls by 2 percent?

CourseMate

Access an interactive eBook and chapter-specific interactive learning tools, including flashcards, quizzes, a glossary, and more in CourseMate, accessed through **www.sextonmacro3ce.nelson.com**

chapter

13

Monetary Policy

section

13.1

Money, Interest Rates, and Aggregate Demand

- What determines the money market?
- How does the Bank of Canada affect RGDP in the short run?
- Does the Bank of Canada target the money supply or the interest rate?
- Which interest rate does the Bank of Canada target?
- Does the Bank of Canada influence the real interest rate in the short run?

WHAT DETERMINES THE MONEY MARKET?

The Bank of Canada's policies with respect to the money supply have a direct impact on short-run real interest rates, and accordingly, on the components of aggregate demand. The **money market** is the market in which money demand and money supply determine the equilibrium *nominal* interest rate. When the Bank of Canada acts to change the money supply, it alters the money market equilibrium.

money market
market in which money demand and money supply determine the equilibrium nominal interest rate

The Demand for Money

Money has several functions, but why would people hold money instead of other financial assets? That is, what is responsible for the demand for money? Transaction purposes, precautionary reasons, and asset purposes are at least three determinants of the demand for money.

Transaction Purposes   First, the primary reason that money is demanded is for transaction purposes—to facilitate exchange. The higher one's income, the more transactions a person will make (because consumption is income-related), the greater will be GDP, and the greater the demand for money for transaction purposes, other things being equal.

Precautionary Reasons   Second, people like to have money on hand for precautionary reasons. If unexpected expenses require an unusual outlay of cash, people like to be prepared. The extent to which people demand cash for precautionary reasons depends partly on an individual's income and partly on the opportunity cost of holding money, which is determined by market rates of interest. The higher market interest rates, the higher the opportunity cost of holding money, and people will hold less of their financial wealth as money.

Asset Purposes   Third, money has a trait (liquidity) that makes it a desirable asset. Other things equal, people prefer more-liquid assets to less-liquid assets. That is, they would like to easily convert some of their assets into goods and services. For this reason, most people choose to have some of their portfolio in money form. At higher interest rates on other assets, the amount of money desired for this purpose will be smaller because the opportunity cost of holding money will have risen.

The Demand for Money and the Nominal Interest Rate

The quantity of money demanded varies inversely with the nominal interest rate. When interest rates are higher, the opportunity cost—in terms of the interest income on alternative assets—of holding monetary assets is higher, and people will want to hold less money. At the same time, the demand for money, particularly for transaction purposes, is highly dependent on income levels, because the transaction volume varies directly with income. And lastly, the demand for money depends on the price level. If the price level increases, buyers will need more money to purchase goods and services. Or if the price level falls, buyers will need less money to purchase goods and services.

The demand curve for money is presented in Exhibit 1. At lower interest rates, the quantity of money demanded is greater, a movement from A to B in Exhibit 1. An increase in income will lead to an increase in the demand for money, depicted by a rightward shift in the money demand curve, a movement from A to C in Exhibit 1.

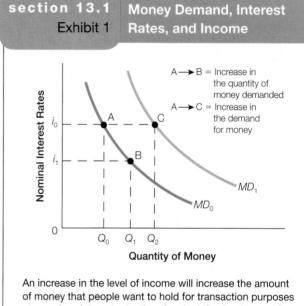

section 13.1
Exhibit 1

Money Demand, Interest Rates, and Income

An increase in the level of income will increase the amount of money that people want to hold for transaction purposes at any given interest rate; therefore it shifts the demand for money to the right, from MD_0 to MD_1. The demand for money curve is downward sloping because at the lower nominal interest rate, the opportunity cost of holding money is lower.

The Supply of Money

The supply of money is largely governed by the monetary policies of the central bank. Whether interest rates are 4 percent or 14 percent, banks seeking to maximize profits will increase lending as long as they have reserves above their desired level. Even a 4 percent return on loans provides more profit than maintaining those excess reserves in noninterest-bearing cash. Given this fact, the money supply is effectively almost perfectly inelastic with respect to interest rates over their plausible range. Therefore, in Exhibit 2, we draw the money supply curve as vertical, other things equal, with changes in Bank of Canada policies acting to shift the money supply curve.

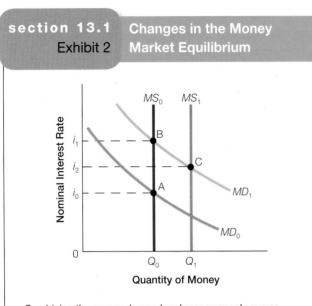

Combining the money demand and money supply curves, money market equilibrium occurs at that nominal interest rate where the quantity of money demanded equals the quantity of money supplied, initially at point A and interest rate i_0. An increase in income will shift the money demand curve to the right, from MD_0 to MD_1, raising the interest rate from i_0 to i_1 and resulting in a new equilibrium at point B. If the economy is presently at point B, an increase in the money supply resulting from expansionary monetary policies (e.g., the Bank of Canada buying bonds or lowering its target for the overnight interest rate) will shift the money supply curve to the right (from MS_0 to MS_1), lowering the nominal interest rate (from i_1 to i_2) and shifting the equilibrium to point C.

Changes in Money Demand and Money Supply and the Nominal Interest Rate

Equilibrium in the money market is found by combining the money demand and money supply curves in Exhibit 2. Money market equilibrium occurs at that *nominal* interest rate, where the quantity of money demanded equals the quantity of money supplied. Initially, the money market is in equilibrium, at point A in Exhibit 2.

For example, rising national income increases the demand for money, shifting the money demand curve to the right from MD_0 to MD_1, and leading to a new higher equilibrium interest rate. If the economy is now at point B, an increase in the money supply (e.g., the Bank of Canada buys bonds) will shift the money supply curve to the right from MS_0 to MS_1, lowering the nominal rate of interest from i_1 to i_2, and shifting the equilibrium to point C.

HOW DOES THE BANK OF CANADA AFFECT RGDP IN THE SHORT RUN?

The Bank of Canada Increases the Money Supply

Suppose the economy is headed for a recession and the Bank of Canada wants to pursue an expansionary monetary policy to increase aggregate demand. It will buy bonds on the open market or it will lower its target for the overnight interest rate. When the Bank of Canada uses either of these tools, the money supply increases. The immediate impact of expansionary monetary policy is to decrease the interest rates, as seen in Exhibit 3(a). The lower interest rate, or the fall in the cost of borrowing money, then leads to an increase in aggregate demand for goods and services at the current price level. The lower interest rate will increase home sales, car sales, business investments, and so on. The increase in the money supply will lead to lower interest rates and an increase in aggregate demand, as seen in Exhibit 3(b).

The Bank of Canada Lowers the Money Supply

Now suppose the Bank of Canada wants to contain an overheated economy—that is, pursue a contractionary monetary policy to reduce aggregate demand. It will sell bonds on the open market or it will raise its target for the overnight interest rate. The use of either of these tools leads to a reduction in the money supply or a leftward shift, as seen in the money market in Exhibit 4(a). The reduction of the money supply leads to an increase in the interest rate in the money market. The higher interest rate, or the rise in the cost of borrowing money, then leads to a reduction in aggregate demand for goods and services, as seen in Exhibit 4(b). That is, the higher interest rate will lead to a decrease in home sales, car sales, business investments, and so on. In sum, lowering of the money supply by the Bank of Canada leads to a higher interest rate and a reduction in aggregate demand, at least in the short run.

The Bank of Canada Increases the Money Supply

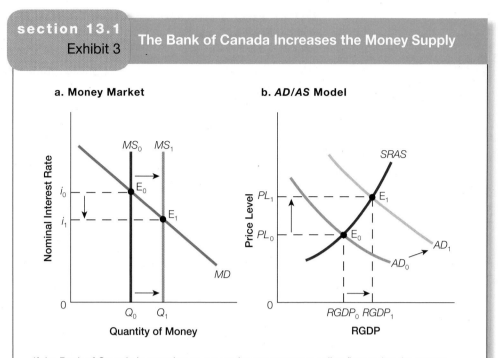

a. Money Market

b. *AD/AS* Model

If the Bank of Canada is pursuing an expansionary monetary policy (increasing the money supply), this will lower the interest rates, as seen in Exhibit 3(a). At lower interest rates, households and businesses will invest more and buy more goods and services, shifting the aggregate demand curve to the right, as seen in Exhibit 3(b).

The Bank of Canada Decreases the Money Supply

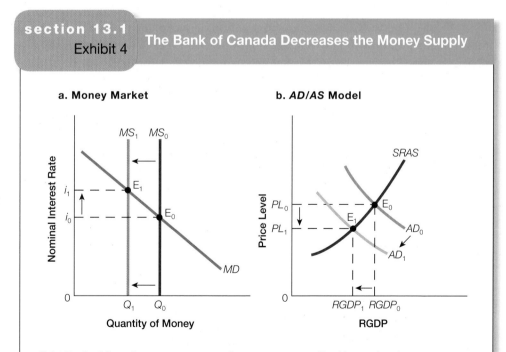

a. Money Market

b. *AD/AS* Model

If the Bank of Canada pursues a contractionary monetary policy (decreasing the money supply), this will lead to a reduction in the money supply or a leftward shift, as seen in the money market in Exhibit 4(a). The reduction of the money supply leads to an increase in the interest rate in the money market. The higher interest rate, or the rise in the cost of borrowing money, then leads to a reduction in aggregate demand for goods and services, as seen in Exhibit 4(b).

section 13.1
Exhibit 5

Bank of Canada Targeting: Money Supply versus the Interest Rate

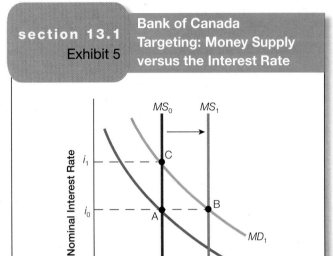

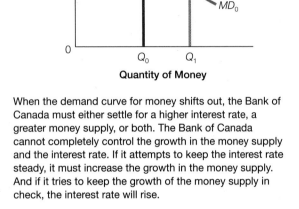

When the demand curve for money shifts out, the Bank of Canada must either settle for a higher interest rate, a greater money supply, or both. The Bank of Canada cannot completely control the growth in the money supply and the interest rate. If it attempts to keep the interest rate steady, it must increase the growth in the money supply. And if it tries to keep the growth of the money supply in check, the interest rate will rise.

DOES THE BANK OF CANADA TARGET THE MONEY SUPPLY OR THE INTEREST RATE?

Some economists believe the Bank of Canada should try to control the money supply. Other economists believe the Bank of Canada should try to control the interest rate. Unfortunately, the Bank of Canada cannot do both—it must pick one or the other.

The economy is initially at point A in Exhibit 5, where the interest rate is i_0 and the quantity of money is at Q_0. Now suppose the demand for money was to increase because of an increase in national income, or an increase in the price level, or overall, people want to hold more money. As a result, the demand curve for money would shift to the right from MD_0 to MD_1. If the Bank of Canada decides it does not want the money supply to increase, it can pursue a no-monetary-growth policy; this will lead to an increase in the interest rate to i_1 at point C in Exhibit 5. The Bank of Canada could also try to keep the interest rate stable at i_0, but it can do so only by increasing the growth in the money supply through expansionary monetary policy. Since the Bank of Canada cannot simultaneously pursue a no-monetary-growth policy and an expansionary monetary policy, it must choose a higher interest rate or a greater money supply or some combination. The Bank of Canada cannot completely control both the growth in the money supply and the interest rate. If it attempts to keep the interest rate steady in the face of increased money demand, it must increase the growth in the money supply. And if it tries to keep the growth of the money supply in check in the face of increased money demand, the interest rate will rise.

The Problem

The problem with targeting the money supply is that the demand for money fluctuates considerably in the short run. Focusing on the growth in the money supply when the demand for money is changing unpredictably will lead to large fluctuations in the interest rate. These erratic changes in the interest rate could seriously disrupt the investment climate.

Keeping interest rates in check would also create problems. For example, when the economy grows, the demand for money also grows, so the Bank of Canada would have to increase the money supply to keep interest rates from rising. And if the economy was in a recession, the Bank of Canada would have to contract the money supply to keep the interest rate from falling. This would lead to the wrong policy prescription—expanding the money supply during a boom would eventually lead to inflation and contracting the money supply during a recession would make the recession even worse.

WHICH INTEREST RATE DOES THE BANK OF CANADA TARGET?

The Bank of Canada targets the overnight interest rate. Remember, the overnight interest rate is the interest rate that chartered banks charge each other for one-day loans. A bank that may be short of reserves might borrow from another bank that has excess reserves. The Bank of Canada has been targeting the overnight interest rate since about 1996. Announcements regarding the overnight interest rate—whether it will be increased, decreased, or made to stay the same—are made by the Bank of Canada on eight prespecified dates during the year.

Monetary policy actions can be conveyed through either the money supply or the interest rate. That is, if the Bank of Canada wants to pursue a contractionary monetary policy, this can be thought of as a reduction in the money supply or a higher interest rate. And, if the Bank of Canada wants to pursue an expansionary monetary policy, this can be thought of as an increase in the money supply or a lower interest rate. So why is the interest rate used? First, as we mentioned earlier, changes in the demand for money can significantly affect money supply targets. Second, many economists believe that the primary effects of monetary policy are felt through the interest rate. Finally, people are more familiar with changes in interest rates than changes in the money supply.

DOES THE BANK OF CANADA INFLUENCE THE REAL INTEREST RATE IN THE SHORT RUN?

In Chapter 8, we saw how the equilibrium real interest rate was found at the intersection of the investment demand curve and the saving supply curve in the saving and investment market. In this chapter, we have seen how the equilibrium nominal interest rate is found at the intersection of the demand for money and the supply of money in the money market. Both are important and the saving and investment market and money markets are interconnected.

Most economists believe that in the short run the Bank of Canada can control the nominal interest rate and the real interest rate. Recall that the *real interest rate is equal to the nominal interest rate minus the expected inflation rate.* So a change in the nominal interest rate tends to change the real interest rate by the same amount because the expected inflation rate is slow to change in the short run. That is, if the expected inflation rate does not change, there is a direct relationship between the nominal and real interest rates; a 1 percent reduction in the nominal interest rate will generally lead to a 1 percent reduction in the real interest rate in the short run. However, in the long run, over several years after the inflation rate has adjusted, the equilibrium real interest rate is found by the intersection of the saving supply curve and investment demand curve.

SECTION CHECK

- The money market is the market where money demand and money supply determine the equilibrium interest rate. Money demand has three possible motives: transaction purposes, precautionary reasons, and asset purposes. The quantity of money demanded varies inversely with interest rates and directly with income. The supply of money is effectively almost perfectly inelastic with respect to interest rates over their plausible range, as controlled by Bank of Canada policies.
- When the Bank of Canada sells bonds to the private sector or raises its target for the overnight interest rate, this leads to a reduction in the money supply, which in turn leads to a higher interest rate and a reduction in aggregate demand, at least in the short run. When the Bank of Canada buys bonds or lowers its target for the overnight interest rate, the money supply increases. The increase in the money supply will lead to lower interest rates and an increase in aggregate demand.
- Since the Bank of Canada cannot completely control both the growth of the money supply and the interest rate, it must choose which target to manage.
- The Bank of Canada signals its intended monetary policy through the overnight interest rate target it sets.
- Since a change in the nominal interest rate tends to change the real interest rate by the same amount in the short run, most economists believe the Bank of Canada can control both the nominal and real interest rates (in the short run).

section 13.2

Expansionary and Contractionary Monetary Policy

- How does expansionary monetary policy work in a recessionary gap?
- How does contractionary monetary policy work in an inflationary gap?
- How does monetary policy work in the open economy?

HOW DOES EXPANSIONARY MONETARY POLICY WORK IN A RECESSIONARY GAP?

Suppose the initial equilibrium is E_0, the point at which AD_0 intersects the short-run aggregate supply curve in Exhibit 1(c). At this point, output is equal to $RGDP_0$ and the price level is PL_0. If the Bank of Canada engages in expansionary monetary policy to combat a recessionary gap, the increase in the money supply will lower the interest rate, as seen in Exhibit 1(a). The lower interest rate leads to an increase in investment demanded, as seen in Exhibit 1(b). For example, business executives invest in new plant and equipment whereas individuals increase their investment in housing at the lower interest rate. In short, lower interest rates lead to greater investment spending. Since investment spending is one of the components of aggregate demand $[C + I + G + (X - M)]$, when interest rates fall, total expenditures rise. That is, as investment expenditures increase, the aggregate demand curve shifts from AD_0 to AD_1, as seen in Exhibit 1(c). The increase in aggregate expenditures then triggers the multiplier effect, which shifts aggregate demand even further, from AD_1 to AD_2. The result is greater RGDP and a higher price level, at E_2. In this case, the Bank of Canada has eliminated the recession and RGDP is equal to the potential level of output at $RGDP_{NR}$.

As seen in Exhibit 2, during 2001, the Bank of Canada aggressively lowered its target for the overnight interest rate to stimulate aggregate demand when faced with a

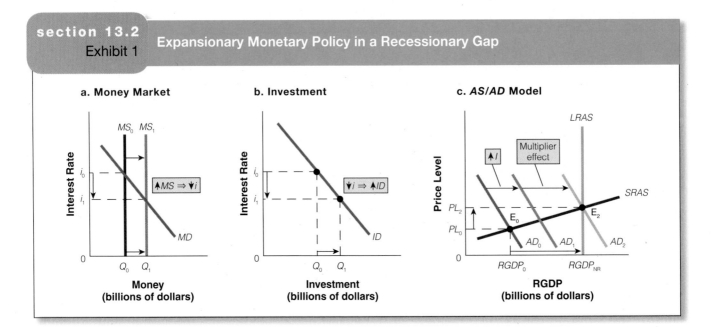

section 13.2

Exhibit 1   Expansionary Monetary Policy in a Recessionary Gap

a. Money Market

b. Investment

c. *AS/AD* Model

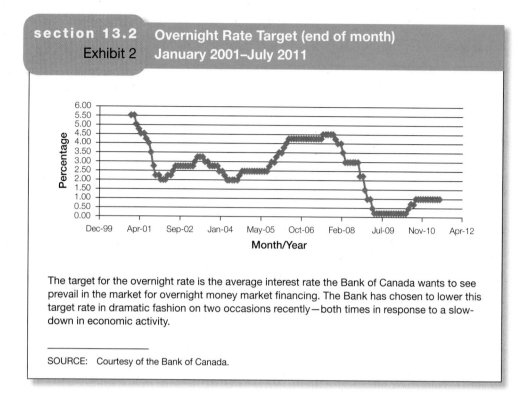

section 13.2   **Overnight Rate Target (end of month)**
Exhibit 2   **January 2001–July 2011**

The target for the overnight rate is the average interest rate the Bank of Canada wants to see prevail in the market for overnight money market financing. The Bank has chosen to lower this target rate in dramatic fashion on two occasions recently—both times in response to a slow-down in economic activity.

SOURCE: Courtesy of the Bank of Canada.

slowing economy. Between January 2001 and January 2002, the Bank of Canada cut its overnight target rate by 3.5 percentage points, from 5.50 percent to 2.00 percent, clearly demonstrating that it was concerned that the economy was dangerously close to falling into a recession.

A similar situation faced the Bank of Canada again in 2007–2008 (Exhibit 2), when it reduced its overnight target rate from a high of 4.50 percent in November 2007 to just 0.25 percent by April 2009. This dramatic reduction was in direct response to the global economic crisis and the recessionary impact it was having on the Canadian economy.

HOW DOES CONTRACTIONARY MONETARY POLICY WORK IN AN INFLATIONARY GAP?

The Bank of Canada may engage in contractionary monetary policy if the economy faces an inflationary gap. Suppose the economy is at initial short-run equilibrium, E_0, in Exhibit 3(c). In order to combat inflation, suppose the Bank of Canada engages in either an open market sale of bonds or an increase in its target for the overnight interest rate. This would lead to a decrease in the money supply, shifting the MS_0 leftward to MS_1, causing the interest rate to rise from i_0 to i_1, as seen in Exhibit 3(a). The higher interest rate leads to a decrease in the quantity of investment demanded, from Q_0 to Q_1, as seen in Exhibit 3(b). Investment expenditures fall as firms find it more costly to invest in plant and equipment and households find it more costly to finance new homes. Since the decrease in investment spending causes a reduction in aggregate expenditures, the aggregate demand curve shifts leftward from AD_0 to AD_1 in Exhibit 3(c). The decrease in aggregate expenditures triggers the multiplier effect that reduces aggregate demand even further, shifting the aggregate demand curve from AD_1 to AD_2. The result is a lower RGDP and a lower price level, at E_2. The economy is now at $RGDP_{NR}$, where RGDP equals the potential level of output.

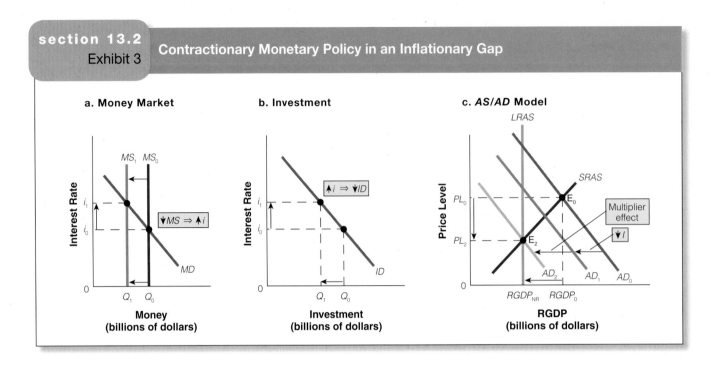

a. Money Market   b. Investment   c. *AS/AD* Model

HOW DOES MONETARY POLICY WORK IN THE OPEN ECONOMY?

For simplicity we have assumed that the global economy does not impact Canadian monetary policy. This is incorrect. Suppose the Bank of Canada decides to pursue an expansionary policy by buying bonds on the open market. As we have seen, if the Bank of Canada buys bonds on the open market or lowers its target for the overnight interest rate, the immediate effect is that the money supply will increase and the interest rate in Canada will fall. As some Canadian investors now seek to invest funds in foreign markets, they will exchange Canadian dollars for foreign currency, leading to a depreciation of the dollar (a decrease in the value of the dollar). The depreciation of the dollar makes Canadian goods and services more attractive to foreign buyers, and foreign goods and services relatively less attractive to Canadian buyers. That is, there is an increase in net exports—fewer imports and more exports—and an increase in RGDP in the short run.

Similarly, if the Bank of Canada reduces the money supply and causes Canadian interest rates to rise, foreign investors will convert their currencies into Canadian dollars to take advantage of the relatively higher interest rates in Canada. This will lead to an appreciation of the dollar (an increase in the value of the dollar). The appreciation of the dollar will make Canadian goods and services relatively more expensive to foreign buyers, and foreign goods and services relatively cheaper to Canadian buyers. This leads to a decrease in net exports and a reduction in RGDP in the short run.

Thus, you can see that in an open economy, like Canada's, monetary policy operates on aggregate demand through two channels: the interest rate and the exchange rate. An expansionary monetary policy causes interest rates to fall and the exchange rate to depreciate, both of which, in turn, cause aggregate demand to increase. Similarly, a contractionary monetary policy causes interest rates to rise and the exchange rate to appreciate, both of which, in turn, cause aggregate demand to decrease.

DEBATE

MONETARY POLICY: QUANTITATIVE EASING

During the "Great Recession" beginning in 2008, various central banks, including those in Canada and the United States, lowered interest rates to stimulate the economy, down to the point where they were close to zero—effectively disabling any benefits derived from classic monetary policy. Coupled with the additional funds injected into the system from fiscal initiatives and the hesitancy of the savings and investment banking systems to free up credit, the economy is poised for a period of stagnant growth. The question to debate: Should the central banks continue to hold interest rates at historical lows or should they inject additional funds into the system [also known as quantitative easing (QE)], bypassing the banks by directly pumping liquidity into the system?

Pro:

The benefits of injecting funds directly into the system allow the central banks to still stimulate the economy during periods when interest rate adjustments are ineffective. This still provides some level of balance between fiscal and monetary policies. Further, the central banks are sending a strong message to the charter banks to loosen credit restraints to assist in getting the economy moving. What are other reasons for supporting the quantitative easing policy?

Con:

Injection of funds directly into the system provides the central banks with opportunities to make fiscal decisions based on which institutions they choose to provide funds to. This may in essence be a political decision for which there are no checks or balances, decisions that are vulnerable to political interference. Opening up the political process within the central banking system makes the system less effective. In addition, with significant funds injected into the system, the central banks make it harder to control inflation as the economy rebounds. Are there other reasons why QE is not good for the economy?

SECTION CHECK

■ An expansionary monetary policy can combat a recessionary gap. By increasing the money supply, the Bank of Canada can lower interest rates, thereby causing an increase in real GDP and the price level.

■ A contractionary monetary policy can close an inflationary gap. By reducing the money supply, the Bank of Canada can raise interest rates, thereby causing a decline in real GDP and the price level.

■ In the open economy, interest rate changes can impact exchange rates. Higher interest rates produced by contractionary monetary policy lead to an appreciation of the Canadian dollar. This appreciation can cause net exports to decline and RGDP to be reduced in the short run. Expansionary monetary policy, having the opposite effect, can increase net exports and expand RGDP in the short run.

Problems in Implementing Monetary and Fiscal Policy

section

13.3

■ What problems exist in implementing monetary and fiscal policy?

WHAT PROBLEMS EXIST IN IMPLEMENTING MONETARY AND FISCAL POLICY?

The lag problem inherent in adopting fiscal policy changes is much less acute for monetary policy, largely because the decisions are not slowed by the same budgetary process. The Bank of Canada, because of its independence, can act very quickly in undertaking open market operations. However, the length and variability of the impact lag before its effects on output and employment are felt are still significant, and the time before the full price level effects are felt is even longer and more variable. The major effects of a change in monetary policy on growth in the overall production of goods and services and on inflation are usually spread over six to eight quarters (18 months to two years).

Chartered Banks and Monetary Policy

One limitation of monetary policy is that it ultimately must be carried out through the banking system. The central bank can change the environment in which banks act, but the banks themselves must take the steps necessary to increase or decrease the money supply. Usually, when the Bank of Canada is trying to constrain monetary expansion, there is no difficulty in getting chartered banks to make appropriate responses. If the Bank of Canada sells bonds and/or raises the bank rate, banks will call in loans that are due for collection, and in the process of collecting loans, they lower the money supply.

When the Bank of Canada wants to induce monetary expansion, however, it can provide banks with excess reserves (by buying government bonds), but it cannot force the banks to make loans, thereby creating new money. Ordinarily, of course, banks want to convert their excess reserves to interest-earning income by making loans. But in a deep recession or depression, banks might be hesitant to make enough loans to put all those reserves to work, fearing that they will not be repaid. Their pessimism might lead them to perceive that the risks of making loans to many normally creditworthy borrowers outweigh any potential interest earnings (particularly at the low real interest rates that are characteristic of depressed times).

Fiscal and Monetary Coordination Problems

Another possible problem that arises out of existing institutional policymaking arrangements is the coordination of fiscal and monetary policy. The Canadian government makes fiscal policy decisions, whereas monetary policy decision making is in the hands of the Bank of Canada. A macroeconomic problem arises if the federal government's fiscal decision makers differ with the Bank of Canada's monetary decision makers on policy objectives or targets. For example, the Bank of Canada may be more concerned about keeping inflation low, whereas fiscal policymakers may be more concerned about keeping unemployment low.

Some people believe that monetary policy should be more directly controlled by the federal government so that all macroeconomic policy will be determined more directly by the political process. Others, however, argue that it is dangerous to turn over control of the nation's money supply to politicians, rather than allowing decisions to be made by an independent central bank, which is more focused on price stability and more insulated from political pressures.

The Shape of the Aggregate Supply Curve and Policy Implications

Many economists argue that the short-run aggregate supply curve is relatively flat at very low levels of real GDP, when the economy has substantial excess capacity, and very steep when the economy is near maximum capacity, as shown in Exhibits 1 and 2.

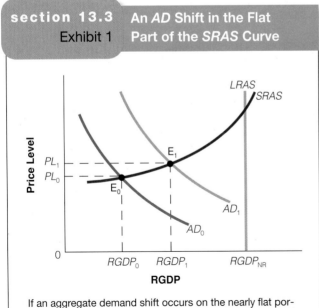

section 13.3   Exhibit 1   **An *AD* Shift in the Flat Part of the *SRAS* Curve**

If an aggregate demand shift occurs on the nearly flat portion of the *SRAS* curve, it causes a large change in RGDP and a small change in the price level.

Why is the *SRAS* curve in Exhibit 1 flat over the range where there is considerable excess capacity? Firms are operating well below their potential output at $RGDP_{NR}$, so the marginal cost of producing more rises little as output expands. Firms can also hire more labour without increasing the wage rate. With many idle resources, producers are willing to sell additional output at current prices because there are few shortages to push prices upward. In addition, many unemployed workers are willing to work at the going wage rate, which diminishes the power of workers to increase wages. In short, when the economy is operating at levels significantly lower than full-employment output, input prices are sticky (relatively inflexible). Empirical evidence for the period 1983–1987, when the Canadian economy was experiencing significant unemployment, appears to confirm that the short-run aggregate supply curve was very flat when the economy was operating with significant excess capacity.

Near the top of the *SRAS* curve, however, the economy is operating close to maximum capacity (and beyond the output level that could be sustained over time). That is, at this level of output, it will be very difficult or impossible for firms to expand output any further—firms may already be running double shifts and paying overtime. At this point, an increase in aggregate demand will be met almost exclusively with a higher price level in the short run.

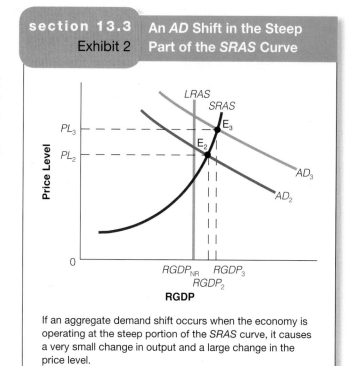

section 13.3
Exhibit 2

An *AD* Shift in the Steep Part of the *SRAS* Curve

If an aggregate demand shift occurs when the economy is operating at the steep portion of the *SRAS* curve, it causes a very small change in output and a large change in the price level.

In short, if the government is using fiscal and/or monetary policy to stimulate aggregate demand, it must carefully assess where it is operating on the *SRAS* curve. As we have seen in Exhibit 1, if the economy is operating on the flat portion of the *SRAS* curve, far from full capacity, an increase in the money supply, a tax cut, or an increase in government spending will result in an increase in output but little change in the price level—a movement from E_0 to E_1 in Exhibit 1. In this case, the expansionary policy works well: higher RGDP and employment with little change in the price level. However, if the shift in aggregate demand occurs when the economy is operating near maximum capacity, the result will be a substantial increase in the price level, with very little change in the output level—a movement from E_2 to E_3 in Exhibit 2. That is, if the economy is operating on the steep portion of the *SRAS* curve, expansionary policy does not work well.

Furthermore, what if the expansionary policy involves an increase in government spending, with no change in the money supply? If the economy is operating in the steep portion of the *SRAS* curve, the increase in *AD* largely causes the price level to rise. The increase in the price level leads to an increase in the demand for money and higher interest rates, which act to crowd out consumer and business investment. This also undermines the effectiveness of the government policy.

It is also easy to see in Exhibits 1 and 2 that contractionary monetary or fiscal policy (a tax increase, a decrease in government spending, and/or a decrease in the money supply) to combat inflation is more effective in the steep region of the *SRAS* curve than in the flat region. In the steep region, contractionary monetary and/or fiscal policy results in a large fall in the price level and a small change in real GDP; in the flat region of the *SRAS* curve, the contractionary policy would result in a large decrease in output and a small change in the price level.

Overall Problems with Monetary and Fiscal Policy

Much of macroeconomic policy in this country is driven by the idea that the federal government can counteract economic fluctuations: stimulating the economy (with increased

Some economists believe that fine-tuning the economy is like driving a car with an unpredictable steering lag on a winding road.

government purchases, tax cuts, transfer payment increases, and easy money) when it is weak, and restraining it when it is overheating. But policymakers must adopt the right policies in the right amounts at the right time for such "stabilization" to do more good than harm. And for this, government policymakers need far more accurate and timely information than experts can give them.

First, economists must know not only which way the economy is heading, but also how rapidly. And the unvarnished truth is that in our incredibly complicated world, no one knows exactly what the economy will do, no matter how sophisticated the econometric models used. It has often been said, and not completely in jest, that the purpose of economic forecasting is to make astrology look respectable.

But let's assume that economists can outperform astrologers at forecasting. Indeed, let's be completely unrealistic and assume that economists can provide completely accurate economic forecasts of what will happen if macroeconomic policies are unchanged. Even then, they could not be certain of how best to promote stable economic growth.

If economists knew, for example, that the economy was going to dip into another recession in six months, they would then need to know exactly how much each possible policy would spur activity in order to keep the economy stable. But such precision is unattainable, given the complex forecasting problems faced. Furthermore, despite assurances to the contrary, economists aren't always sure what effect a policy will have on the economy. Will an increase in government purchases quicken economic growth? It is widely assumed so. But how much? And increasing government purchases increases the budget deficit, which could send a frightening signal to the bond markets. The result can be to drive up interest rates and choke off economic activity. So even when policymakers know which direction to nudge the economy, they can't be sure which policy levers to pull, or how hard to pull them, to fine-tune the economy to stable economic growth.

But let's further assume that policymakers know when the economy will need a boost, and also which policy will provide the right boost. A third crucial consideration is how long it will take a policy before it has its effect on the economy. The trouble is that, even when increased government purchases or expansionary monetary policy does give the economy a boost, no one knows precisely how long it will take to do so. The boost may come very quickly, or many months (or even years) in the future, when it may add inflationary pressures to an economy that is already overheating, rather than helping the economy recover from a recession.

In this way, macroeconomic policymaking is like driving down a twisting road in a car with an unpredictable lag and degree of response in the steering mechanism. If you turn the wheel to the right, the car will eventually veer to the right, but you don't know exactly when or how much. In short, there are severe practical difficulties in trying to fine-tune the economy. Even the best forecasting models and methods are far from perfect. Economists are not exactly sure where the economy is or where or how fast it is going, making it very difficult to prescribe an effective policy. Even if we do know where the economy is headed, we cannot be sure how large a policy's effect will be or when it will take effect.

Unexpected Global and Technological Events   The Bank of Canada must take into account the influences of many different factors that can either offset or reinforce monetary policy. This isn't easy because sometimes these developments occur unexpectedly, and because the size and timing of their effects are difficult to estimate.

For example, during the 1997–1998 currency crisis in East Asia, economic activity in several countries in that region either slowed or declined. This led to a reduction in the aggregate demand for Canadian goods and services. In addition, the foreign exchange value of most of their currencies depreciated, and this made Asian-produced goods less expensive for us to buy and Canadian-produced goods more expensive in Asian countries. Both of these factors would reduce aggregate demand in Canada and lower output and employment. So the Bank of Canada must consider these global events in formulating its monetary policy.

During the late 1990s, the Canadian economy experienced a productivity increase through high-tech and other developments. This "new" economy increased productivity growth, allowing for greater economic growth without creating inflationary pressures. The Bank of Canada was then faced with estimating how fast productivity was increasing and whether those increases were temporary or permanent. Not an easy task.

By 2007, the Canadian economy was facing a new set of global challenges—the Canadian dollar was trading around par with its American counterpart (a reality that had last occurred during the mid-1970s), the U.S. economy was experiencing an economic slowdown, and oil prices had risen to near-record levels. An added complication for the Bank of Canada was the fact that, unlike the 1970s, the high oil prices had not produced strong inflationary expectations for consumers. To successfully navigate this set of challenges, the Bank of Canada would have to carefully consider a wide range of policy options.

By the end of 2007 and into 2008, the Canadian economy had begun to experience the effects of the global economic crisis. The U.S. economy, by this time, was already in the grip of a major recession and global financial markets were experiencing a severe financial crisis. The coordinated response of expansionary fiscal policy and expansionary monetary policy from the Government of Canada and the Bank of Canada is widely believed to have greatly minimized the recessionary effects of the global economic crisis for Canada.

SECTION CHECK

- Monetary policy faces somewhat different implementation problems than fiscal policy. Both face difficult forecasting and lag problems, but the Bank of Canada can take action much more quickly. However, the effectiveness of monetary policy depends largely on the reaction of the private banking system to its policy changes. In Canada, monetary and fiscal policy are carried out by different decision makers, thus requiring cooperation and coordination for effective policy implementation.

section
13.4

The Phillips Curve

- What is the Phillips curve?
- How does the Phillips curve relate to the aggregate supply and demand model?

We usually think of inflation as an evil—higher prices mean lower real incomes for people on fixed incomes, whereas those with the power to raise the prices charged for goods or services they provide may actually benefit. Nevertheless, some economists believe that in the short run, inflation could actually help eliminate unemployment. For example, if output prices rise but money wages do not go up as quickly or as much, real wages fall. At the lower real wage, unemployment is less because the lower wage makes it profitable to hire more, now cheaper, employees than before. The result is real wages that are closer to the full-employment equilibrium wage that clears the labour market. Hence, with increased inflation, one might expect lower unemployment in the short run. In the long run, there is no trade-off between unemployment and inflation. In the long run, output is determined by the *LRAS* curve, and unemployment is at its natural rate.

WHAT IS THE PHILLIPS CURVE?

An inverse short-run relationship between the rate of unemployment and the changing level of prices has been observed in many periods and places in history. Credit for identifying this relationship generally goes to British economist A. H. Phillips, who in the late 1950s published a paper setting forth what has since been called the *Phillips curve*. Phillips and many others since have suggested that at higher rates of inflation, the rate of unemployment is lower, whereas during periods of relatively stable or falling prices, unemployment is substantial. In summary, the cost of lower unemployment appears to be greater inflation, and the cost of greater price stability appears to be higher unemployment, at least in the short run.

Exhibit 1 shows the actual inflation–unemployment relationship for Canada for the 1960s. The points in this graph represent the combination of the inflation rate and the rate of unemployment for the period 1960–1969. The curved line—the Phillips curve—is the smooth line that best fits the data points.

The Slope of the Phillips Curve

In examining Exhibit 1, it is evident that the slope of the Phillips curve is not the same throughout its length. The curve is steeper at higher rates of inflation and lower levels of

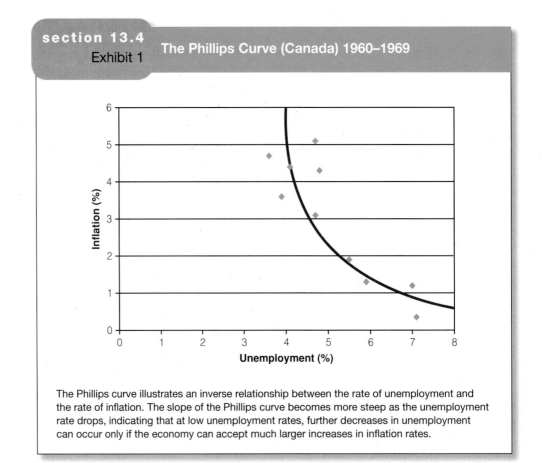

section 13.4
Exhibit 1   **The Phillips Curve (Canada) 1960–1969**

The Phillips curve illustrates an inverse relationship between the rate of unemployment and the rate of inflation. The slope of the Phillips curve becomes more steep as the unemployment rate drops, indicating that at low unemployment rates, further decreases in unemployment can occur only if the economy can accept much larger increases in inflation rates.

unemployment. This relationship suggests that once the economy has relatively low unemployment rates, further reductions in the unemployment rate can occur only if the economy can accept larger increases in the inflation rate. Once the unemployment rate is low, it takes larger and larger doses of inflation to eliminate a given quantity of unemployment. Presumably, at lower unemployment rates, an increased part of the economy is already operating at or near full capacity. Further fiscal or monetary stimulus primarily triggers inflationary pressures in sectors already at capacity, while eliminating decreasing amounts of unemployment in those sectors where some excess capacity and unemployment still exist.

HOW DOES THE PHILLIPS CURVE RELATE TO THE AGGREGATE SUPPLY AND DEMAND MODEL?

In Exhibit 2, we see the relationship between aggregate supply and demand analysis and the Phillips curve. Suppose the economy moved from a 2 percent annual inflation rate to a 4 percent inflation rate, and the unemployment rate simultaneously fell from 5 percent to 4 percent. In the Phillips curve, we see this change as a move up the curve from point A to point B in Exhibit 2(a). We can see a similar relationship in the *AD/AS* model in Exhibit 2(b). Imagine that an increase in aggregate demand occurs. Consequently, the price level increases from PL_0 to PL_1 (the inflation rate rises) and output increases from $RGDP_0$ to $RGDP_1$ (the unemployment rate falls). To increase output, firms employ more workers, so employment increases and unemployment falls—the movement from point A to point B in Exhibit 2(b).

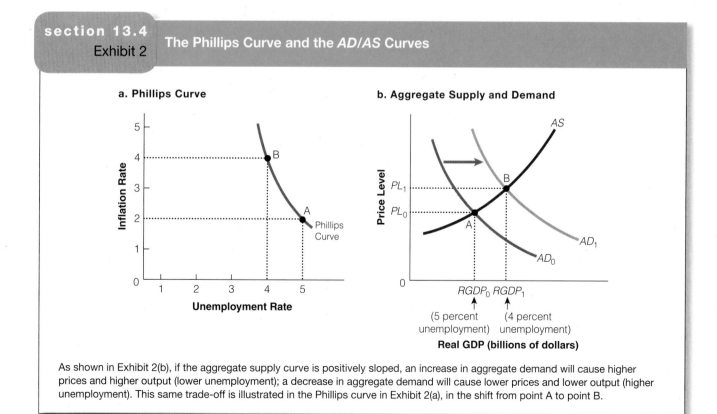

section 13.4
Exhibit 2   The Phillips Curve and the *AD/AS* Curves

a. Phillips Curve

b. Aggregate Supply and Demand

As shown in Exhibit 2(b), if the aggregate supply curve is positively sloped, an increase in aggregate demand will cause higher prices and higher output (lower unemployment); a decrease in aggregate demand will cause lower prices and lower output (higher unemployment). This same trade-off is illustrated in the Phillips curve in Exhibit 2(a), in the shift from point A to point B.

Business CONNECTION

GETTING A JUMP ON INFLATION

Monetary policies are policies whereby the government controls the nation's money supply. In Canada this control is delegated to the Bank of Canada. The Bank of Canada's policies with respect to the money supply have a direct impact on short-run real interest rates, and accordingly on at least two of the components of aggregate demand—consumer expenditure and business investment. Business with an eye on revenues is always concerned about the demand for its goods or services. Many businesses selling big-ticket items such as cars and appliances find revenues extremely sensitive to interest rates, as purchasers often need to finance purchases with borrowed funds.

Sales are also very sensitive to overall demand resulting from the government's fiscal policies. How can business read the road ahead regarding fiscal and monetary policies? The fact is that this area of macroeconomics is fraught with complexity. Policymakers experience great difficulty predicting the impact that various policy initiatives will have on the economy and in forecasting when the expected outcomes will materialize. For businesses, it is almost impossible to gauge the collective impact that government and central bank policy decisions will have on costs of operations, revenue levels, and profitability. Nevertheless, there are some pockets of reliable theory in this area. The Phillips curve is one such theory. Let's examine this theory.

The work of economist A. H. Phillips suggests that there is a trade-off between inflation and unemployment in the short term. Essentially, the cost of lower unemployment appears to be greater inflation, and the cost of greater price stability appears to be higher unemployment. How can firms use this theory to their advantage? Phillips theory maintains that when governments faced with a recessionary gap engage in expansionary monetary policy to reduce unemployment, the result in the near term will be a gradual increase in the rate of inflation. As attempts are made to further reduce unemployment, the rate of inflation is likely to increase more sharply.

Because of this trade-off relationship, where possible, those firms with an awareness of this relationship should seek to enter into long-term contracts for all significant factors of production, labour, land, equipment, and other resources as the economy signals improvement. Ideally, such contracts should be secured early in the business cycle as the cost of the factors are likely to increase sharply as governments attempt to reduce unemployment at the expense of inflation. If the government is successful, the economy will move to a higher level of employment, eventually resulting in scarcity of many factors of production and increased costs for these factors.

Those firms that anticipate such a development will reap benefits on two fronts. First, their unit costs will increase at a rate lower than others in their respective industries. Second, they will have the capacity to enjoy increases in revenue due to increased demand resulting from lower unemployment. All of this should increase a firm's acceleration toward higher profit margins, at least in the short run.

SECTION CHECK

- The inverse relationship between the rate of unemployment and the rate of inflation is called the *Phillips curve*.
- The Phillips curve relationship can also be seen indirectly from the *AD/AS* model.

For Your Review

Section 13.1

1. Why would both the transaction motive and the precautionary motive for holding money tend to vary directly with the price level? Why would the quantity of money people want to hold for both motives tend to vary inversely with interest rates?

2. How does a higher price level affect the money market? How does it affect aggregate demand?

3. Why can't the Bank of Canada target both the money supply and the interest rate at the same time?

4. What is the motive for holding money in each of the following cases (precautionary, transaction, or asset)?

    a. Concerned about the fluctuations of the stock market, you sell stock and keep cash in your brokerage account.

    b. You keep ten $20 bills in your earthquake-preparedness kit.

    c. You go to Vancouver with a large sum of money in order to complete your holiday shopping.

    d. You keep $20 in your glove compartment just in case you run out of gas.

5. Using the following diagram, answer questions a and b.

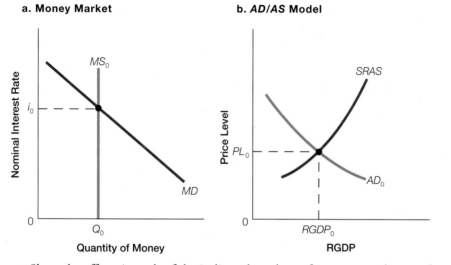

    a. Show the effects in each of the indicated markets of an open market purchase of government bonds by the Bank of Canada.

    b. Show the effects in each of the indicated markets of an open market sale of government bonds by the Bank of Canada.

Section 13.2

6. During the Great Depression in Canada, the price level fell, real GDP fell, and unemployment reached almost 20 percent. Investment fell and the money supply fell. Show the effect of these changes from a vibrant 1929 economy to a battered 1933 economy using the *AD/AS* model? What would have been the appropriate monetary policy response in 1933?

7. Using the following diagram, answer questions a and b.

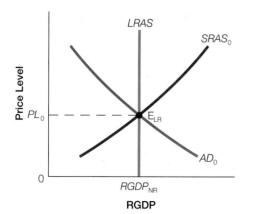

a. On the diagram, illustrate the short-run effects of an increase in aggregate demand caused by expanding the money supply.

b. On the diagram, illustrate the long-run effects of an increase in aggregate demand caused by expanding the money supply.

8. Predict the impact of a decrease in the money supply on the following variables in the short run and in the long run.

a. the inflation rate

b. the unemployment rate

c. real output

d. real wages

Section 13.3

9. Why does the effect of a given increase in aggregate demand have a larger effect on real output in the short run, the more excess capacity exists in the economy?

10. How does the slope of the short-run aggregate supply curve depend on the degree of excess capacity in the economy?

11. How is the coordination or, more correctly, the lack of coordination, between fiscal and monetary policy a potential problem of effective policy implementation?

Section 13.4

12. Suppose the following data represent points along a short-run Phillips curve. Are the data consistent with what you would expect? Why or why not?

	Inflation Rate (%)	Unemployment Rate (%)
A	0%	5.0%
B	1	4.5
C	2	3.75
D	3	2.75
E	4	1.5

13. Why does a movement up and to the left along a Phillips curve correspond to a movement up and to the right along a short-run aggregate supply curve?

14. Why does a movement down and to the right along a Phillips curve correspond to a movement down and to the left along a short-run aggregate supply curve?

CourseMate

Access an interactive eBook and chapter-specific interactive learning tools, including flashcards, quizzes, a glossary, and more in CourseMate, accessed through **www.sextonmacro3ce.nelson.com**

chapter 14

International Trade

section 14.1

Canada's Merchandise Trade

- Who are Canada's trading partners?
- What does Canada import and export?

WHO ARE CANADA'S TRADING PARTNERS?

In its early history, Canadian international trade was largely directed toward Europe and to Great Britain, in particular. Now Canada trades with a vast number of countries. Exhibit 1 shows the country's most important trading partners. The United States is Canada's most important trading partner, accounting for an enormous 73 percent of our exports of goods and 64 percent of our imports of goods. Trade with countries of the European Union (EU) and Japan is also particularly important.

The extent to which the overall health of the Canadian economy is dependent on both exports and imports cannot be understated. However, as Exhibit 2 illustrates, Canada is not alone in its significant involvement in global trade. Several economies (most notably the United States, the European Union, China, Germany, and Japan) trade on a magnitude that is several times greater than that of the Canadian economy.

WHAT DOES CANADA IMPORT AND EXPORT?

Throughout its history, Canada has been a large exporter of natural resource-based products to the rest of the world. Today, as Exhibit 3 shows, Canada's exports of natural resource-based products (including agricultural and fishing products, energy products, forestry products, and industrial goods and materials) total nearly $250 billion, or about

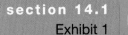

section 14.1
Exhibit 1   Major Canadian Trading Partners

Top Trading Partners—Exports of Goods in 2010				Top Trading Partners—Imports of Goods in 2010		
Rank	**Country**	**% of Total**		**Rank**	**Country**	**% of Total**
1	United States	73.3%		1	United States	62.8%
2	European Union	9.0		2	European Union	9.8
3	Japan	2.4		3	Japan	2.4
4	Other countries	15.3		4	Other countries	25.0

SOURCE: Statistics Canada.

SOURCE: Statistics Canada.

section 14.1
Exhibit 2   Amounts of Merchandise Exports and Imports: Selected Developed Countries, 2010

Exports				Imports		
Rank	**Country**	**Amount (billions of US$)**		**Rank**	**Country**	**Amount (billions of US$)**
1	European Union	$1952		1	United States	$1903
2	China	1506		2	European Union	1690
3	Germany	1337		3	China	1307
4	United States	1270		4	Germany	1120
5	Japan	765		5	Japan	637
6	France	509		6	France	578
7	South Korea	466		7	United Kingdom	547
8	Italy	458		8	Italy	460
9	Netherlands	451		9	Hong Kong	431
10	**Canada**	**407**		10	South Korea	418
				11	Netherlands	408
				12	**Canada**	**406**

SOURCE: CIA, *The World Factbook 2011.*

60 percent of our exports of goods. However, Canada's exports of automotive products, and machinery and equipment total $133 billion, or about 33 percent of our exports of goods.

On the import side, Canada's imports are much more concentrated on finished goods. Imports of machinery and equipment, automotive products, and consumer goods total $114 billion, $69 billion, and $58 billion, respectively, and account for 58 percent of our imports of goods.

Canada's Exports and Imports by Category of Good, 2010

	Exports (billions of dollars)	% of Total	Imports (billions of dollars)	% of Total	Trade Balance (billions of dollars)
Agricultural and fishing products	$ 36.9	9.1%	$ 29.6	7.1%	$ 7.3
Energy products	90.9	22.5	40.6	9.8	50.3
Forestry products	21.9	5.4	2.7	0.6	19.2
Industrial goods and materials	96.5	23.8	86.9	21.0	9.6
Machinery and equipment	76.1	18.8	113.9	27.5	−37.8
Automotive products	56.8	14.0	68.7	16.6	−11.9
Consumer goods	16.4	4.1	57.8	14.0	−41.4
Other transactions and adjustments	9.4	2.3	13.8	3.3	−4.4
Total	404.9	100.0	414.0	100.0	−9.1

SOURCE: Statistics Canada.

Business CONNECTION

WHERE TO GO FROM HERE?

Domestic businesses often find that sales for their products have peaked, the domestic market is saturated with their offerings, or the domestic market has simply matured. Faced with this type of challenge, how does one increase sales? The obvious answer is to go international. If this move is successful, revenues will increase and hopefully, so will profits. However, the decision to go international needs to be properly structured to reduce risk.

In considering the decision to enter international markets, one important factor is the business climate of the host country. Many experienced businesses have encountered cultural, legal, and economic roadblocks in an effort to penetrate foreign markets. Many other key questions also need to be answered prior to making this big leap. For instance, the first and most important question is whether there is indeed a demand for the firm's product in the host country's target market. Until a business is satisfied that there is foreign demand or that they can cultivate such demand, they should avoid venturing into a foreign market.

A second question is whether the firm can customize its products to suit the demands of the foreign customers while achieving attractive profit margins. A third and important question is whether the business climate of the foreign market is favourable for the firm. Is gross domestic product growing?

What is the withholding tax rate? Finally, can the firm obtain the necessary skills and knowledge to actually conduct business in the host country?

If the answer to all of the above questions is "yes," then there is every indication that the attempt to enter foreign markets will be operationally feasible. The next step is to evaluate the likelihood of earning profits. In this area, the firm needs to assess the political and the financial risks. The traditional factors in evaluating broad political risks include the attitude of the local consumers toward the purchasing of foreign-produced or foreign-branded goods, the host government's position toward multinational corporations, currency convertibility, wars or threat of wars, and bureaucratic problems and corruption. In considering the broad financial risk inherent in conducting business, the host country's growth in gross domestic product, prevailing interest rates, exchange rate, rates of unemployment, and rate of inflation need to be taken into account.

The firm then needs to evaluate the operational feasibility and potential profitability of their product specifically. Only after making such assessments is a business reasonably informed and therefore able to make a decision about whether to stay domestic or to go international.

For many domestic businesses the next major opportunity for growth in revenue is to go international. International trade, particularly exports, may indeed be the answer.

When we compare the trade balance (exports of goods minus imports of goods) for the major categories of goods, we can see that the largest trade surpluses exist for energy products ($50.3 billion) and forestry products ($19.2 billion). By far, the largest trade deficit is in the consumer goods category ($41.4 billion).

SECTION CHECK

- Our most important trading partner, the United States, accounts for 73 percent of our exports and 64 percent of our imports. Trade with Japan and the countries of the European Union is also particularly important to Canada.
- Exports of natural resource-based products make up over one-half of our export of goods. Our imports are concentrated in finished goods, like machinery and equipment, automotive products, and consumer goods.

section 14.2
International Trade Agreements

- What has been the impact of international trade on Canada?
- What international trade agreements is Canada involved in?

WHAT HAS BEEN THE IMPACT OF INTERNATIONAL TRADE ON CANADA?

In a typical year, about 15 percent of the world's output is traded in international markets. Of course, the importance of the international sector varies enormously from country to country. Some nations are almost closed economies (no interaction with other economies), with foreign trade equalling only a very small portion (perhaps 5 percent) of total output. The impact of international trade on the Canadian economy is illustrated in Exhibit 1, which shows the current dollar value of Canadian exports and imports of goods and services as a percentage of GDP. As Exhibit 1 shows, the value of both exports and imports has grown from around 20 percent in the 1960s to about 30 percent of GDP for exports and 33 percent of GDP for imports in 2010. In the United States, by contrast, exports were only 13 percent of GDP, whereas imports were 16 percent of GDP, in 2010.

WHAT INTERNATIONAL TRADE AGREEMENTS IS CANADA INVOLVED IN?

International trade agreements have been a positive force in expanding global trade, thereby contributing to economic growth and prosperity in countries covered by such agreements. Government trade policies have contributed to the remarkable rise in international trade for Canada. Listed below are the major trade agreements to which Canada is a participant.

The General Agreement on Tariffs and Trade

Canada and 22 other nations in 1947 signed the General Agreement on Tariffs and Trade (GATT). The objective of GATT was to reduce barriers to international trade, such as tariffs (taxes on imported goods) and quotas (government-imposed restrictions on the quantity

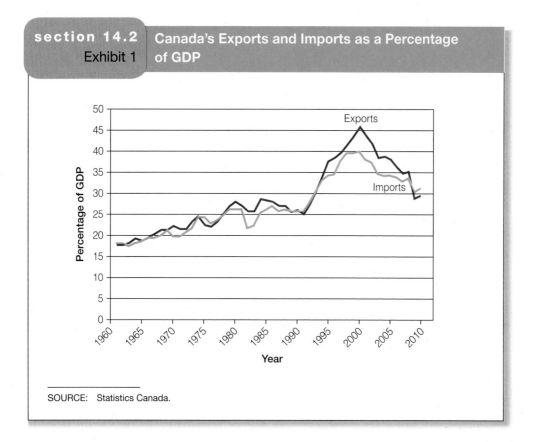

section 14.2
Exhibit 1

Canada's Exports and Imports as a Percentage of GDP

SOURCE: Statistics Canada.

of imports allowed). GATT was based on a few key principles. First, each member nation was to apply any tariffs equally to all countries—that is, in a nondiscriminatory manner. Second, reductions in tariffs were to be the result of multilateral negotiations. And third, quotas were to be eliminated and replaced by tariffs. (We will examine the economic impact of tariffs and quotas later in this chapter.)

Eight rounds of multilateral negotiations took place under GATT, with the last round of negotiations, called the Uruguay Round, taking effect in 1995. That agreement eliminated or reduced trade barriers on a wide range of goods and services. It also gave the world's poorer countries greater access to markets for textiles and garments in developed (richer) nations. On the agricultural side, export subsidies were to be reduced and import quotas on agricultural products were to be replaced by tariffs. Canadian egg and dairy farmers had their trade protection from quotas replaced by high tariffs. Although this has protected Canadian farmers in the short run, as these tariffs are reduced over time, we would expect a higher level of Canadian imports of these products.

The World Trade Organization

In 1995, GATT was replaced by the World Trade Organization (WTO), another multilateral trade organization. The WTO has over 140 nations as members, who negotiate on areas such as liberalizing trade in services, protecting intellectual property rights, and giving fair treatment to foreign investment. Member countries have their international trade disputes resolved by a WTO arbitration board. When the board makes its ruling, the losing country must comply with the ruling. If it does not comply, the winning country can impose trade sanctions on the losing country.

The Doha Development Round, which began in November 2001, is the current negotiation round for the WTO members. The aim of this latest round is "to achieve major reform to the international trade system through the introduction of lower trade barriers and revised trade rules." Unfortunately, as of summer 2011, an agreement has yet to be reached and many fear the round may never conclude. The most significant differences are between developed nations led by the European Union and the United States and the major developing nations led primarily by China and India. Issues of access to domestic markets for manufactured goods and agricultural subsidies are proving the most difficult for WTO members to resolve.

The European Union

In addition to multilateral trade agreements, a large number of regional trade agreements are in effect around the world. The largest such trading bloc is the European Union (EU), consisting of 27 European nations, including France, Germany, Italy, and the United Kingdom. An important aspect of the EU is that it allows for the free movement of labour and capital between member nations. As well, nearly all products are traded freely among member nations, and there is a common system of tariffs for goods from outside the EU.

North American Free Trade Agreement

Canada's first major bilateral trade agreement was the Canada–U.S. Free Trade Agreement (FTA), which came into effect in 1989. It called for the reduction or elimination of tariffs and other barriers to trade, free trade in energy products, freer trade in services, and a reduction in subsidies. As well, it set up a dispute-settlement mechanism to resolve trade disputes between the two countries. This free trade agreement, in particular, has had a significant impact on the volume of exports and imports for Canada. Since 1989, Canadian exports and imports have increased sharply, as shown in Exhibit 1, with virtually all of this rise the result of increased trade with the United States.

In 1994, the Canada–U.S. Free Trade Agreement was replaced by the North American Free Trade Agreement (NAFTA), creating a trading bloc for Canada, the United States, and Mexico. NAFTA's objectives are to eliminate trade barriers among the three countries over a 15-year period, promote fair competition, increase investment opportunities, protect intellectual property rights, and resolve trade disputes.

Since 1994, as expected, Canada's exports and imports with the United States and Mexico have increased substantially. There have been concerns, however, about the impact of free trade with Mexico on Canadian industries and workers. Mexico's lower labour and environmental standards, as well as fears that Canadian businesses would relocate to Mexico to take advantage of the lower wages there, are often discussed. Economists, however, have tried to emphasize the benefits to Canada of freer trade that result from increased specialization and exchange (a topic we look at in the next section). There certainly have been labour market adjustments in Canada since NAFTA, as some Canadian industries have become smaller, resulting in reduced employment in those sectors. At the same time, however, the United States and Mexico represent a combined market of more than 400 million people, providing many Canadian businesses with the opportunity to expand their sales and create additional jobs in Canada.

In addition to NAFTA, Canada has also entered into the following bilateral agreements: Canada–Israel Free Trade Agreement, 1997; Canada–Chile Free Trade Agreement, 1997; Canada–Costa Rica Free Trade Agreement, 2002; Canada–Colombia Free Trade Agreement, 2008; Canada–European Free Trade Agreement, 2008; Canada–Peru Free Trade Agreement, 2009; Canada–Jordan Free Trade Agreement, 2009; Canada–Panama Free Trade Agreement, 2010; and the Canada–Honduras Free Trade Agreement, 2011.

DEBATE

INTERNATIONAL TRADE: BUY CANADA

Canada entered into NAFTA in 1999 with the intent of eliminating trade barriers among its partners, the United States and Mexico. There is no question that Canada has benefited from its participation in NAFTA, but Canada is primarily an exporting country, and not all countries can be exporters. As the agreement has matured, Canada has been exporting low-tech/low-paying jobs to Mexico and the southern United States. There is a growing movement in Canada (and the United States) for consumers to buy domestically—even to the point that U.S. lawmakers have tried to restrict Canadian companies from participating in U.S. public tenders. Maybe it's time to recapture those lost jobs and buy domestic products.

Pro:

Canada is experiencing a growing unemployment rate and it is expected to creep upward as the boomers delay retirement and new workers enter the workforce at the same time as firms are laying off people. Many of the jobs that Canadians have lost have been in the manufacturing sector and many of those workers are not finding replacement jobs, even with retraining. The only way we'll get those workers back to work is for more Canadians to buy Canadian products. We should do what the Americans are doing—promote domestic consumption. How will this policy be good for the Canadian workforce? Or will it?

Con:

Canada is part of the global economy, and being internally focused will ultimately cost Canada jobs. Buying Canadian products that are not competitive in the world markets only delays the inevitable failure of the firms involved and the resulting loss of employment. Consumers will purchase goods and services that have the best value, and Canadian firms that are not meeting global standards need to become more productive and efficient. What are other reasons for buying international products? What are other consequences if we don't buy internationally?

SECTION CHECK

■ The volume of international trade has increased substantially in Canada over the past 50 years. During that time, exports and imports have grown from about 20 percent of GDP to over 30 percent.

■ The numerous trade agreements in which Canada is an active participant range from multilateral global trade agreements (such as GATT/WTO) to regional agreements (such as the Canada–Costa Rica Free Trade Agreement). This substantial involvement is a major reason why Canada has experienced a rise in international trade.

section

14.3

Comparative Advantage and Gains from Trade

■ Why do economies trade?
■ What is the principle of comparative advantage?

WHY DO ECONOMIES TRADE?

Using simple logic, we conclude that the very existence of trade suggests that trade is economically beneficial. This is true if one assumes that people are utility maximizers, are rational and intelligent, and engage in trade on a voluntary basis. Because almost all trade is voluntary, it would seem that trade occurs because the participants feel that they are better off because of the trade. Both participants of an exchange of goods and services anticipate an improvement in their economic welfare. Sometimes, of course, anticipations are not realized (because the world is uncertain), but the motive behind trade remains an expectation of some enhancement in utility or satisfaction by both parties.

Granted, "trade must be good because people do it" is a rather simplistic explanation. The classical economist David Ricardo is usually given most of the credit for developing the economic theory that more precisely explains how trade can be mutually beneficial to both parties, raising output and income levels in the entire trading area.

WHAT IS THE PRINCIPLE OF COMPARATIVE ADVANTAGE?

Ricardo's theory of international trade centres on the concept of comparative advantage. A person, a region, or a country can gain by specializing in the production of the good in which they have a comparative advantage. A **comparative advantage** occurs when a person or a country can produce a good or service at a lower opportunity cost than others can. In other words, a country or a region should specialize in producing and selling those items that it can produce at a lower opportunity cost than other regions or countries.

comparative advantage
occurs when a person or a country can produce a good or service at a lower opportunity cost than others can

Absolute Advantage versus Comparative Advantage

A common point of confusion regarding specialization and trade involves the concepts of absolute advantage and comparative advantage. **Absolute advantage** refers to the ability of a party (nation, region, or individual) to produce more of a good or service while using the same amount of inputs. That is, having an absolute advantage means a nation can produce a good or service more cheaply than other nations. The danger in using the concept of absolute advantage in determining what a nation should specialize in and trade is that a nation could actually lack an absolute advantage in anything. In this case, according to the theory of absolute advantage, the nation would not be involved in trade at all and the case for free trade collapses. By contrast, comparative advantage is never absent; even if a nation is bad at everything, it will still possess a comparative advantage at something.

absolute advantage
the ability of a party (nation, region, or individual) to produce more of a good or service while using the same amount of inputs

To help distinguish between these two important concepts, consider the following example. Canada may be able to produce more clothing per worker than India, but that does not mean Canada should necessarily sell clothing to India. Indeed, Canada has an absolute advantage or productive superiority over India in nearly every good, given the higher levels of output per person in Canada. Yet India's inferiority in producing some goods is much less than for others. In goods where India's productivity is only slightly less than that of Canada, such as perhaps in clothing, it probably has a comparative advantage over Canada. How? For a highly productive nation to produce goods in which it is only marginally more productive than other nations, the nation must take resources from the production of other goods in which its productive abilities are markedly superior. As a result, the opportunity costs in India of making clothing may be less than in Canada. With that, both can gain from trade, despite potential absolute advantages for every good in Canada.

Comparative Advantage and the Production Possibilities Curve

To help illustrate the concepts involved, the principle of comparative advantage can be applied to trading areas. In fact, trade has evolved in large part because different geographic areas have different resources and therefore different production possibilities. In

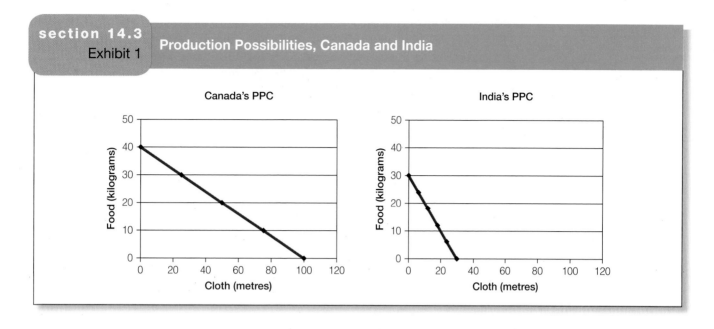

section 14.3
Exhibit 1 **Production Possibilities, Canada and India**

Exhibit 1, we show the production possibilities curves (PPCs) for two trading areas. A "trading area" may be a locality, a region, or (as in this example) a nation. We see that if Canada devotes all of its resources to producing food, it can produce 40 kilograms of food per day; if it devotes all of its resources to producing cloth, it can produce 100 metres of cloth per day. We also see that when India uses all of its resources to produce food, it can produce only 30 kilograms per day, and when it uses all of its resources to produce cloth, it can produce 30 metres per day.

Canada and India have various potential combinations of food and cloth that they can produce. For each region, the cost of producing more food is the output of cloth that must be forgone, and vice versa. We see in Exhibit 1 that Canada can produce more food (40 kilograms per day) and more cloth (100 metres per day) than India can (30 kilograms and 30 metres per day, respectively), perhaps reflecting superior resources (more or better labour, more land, and so on). This means that Canada has an absolute advantage in both products.

Suppose that, before specialization, Canada chooses to produce 75 metres of cloth and 10 kilograms of food per day. Similarly, suppose India decides to produce 12 metres of cloth and 18 kilograms of food per day. Collectively, then, the two areas are producing 87 metres of cloth (75 + 12) and 28 kilograms of food (10 + 18) per day before specialization.

Looking at Exhibit 2, now suppose the two nations specialize. Canada decides to specialize in cloth and devotes all its resources to making that product. As a result, cloth output in Canada rises to 100 metres per day, some of which is sold to India. India, in turn, devotes all its resources to food, producing 30 kilograms of food per day and selling some of it to Canada. Together, the two nations are producing more of both cloth and food than

section 14.3
Exhibit 2 **Specialization and Trade**

Region	Food	Cloth
Canada	(kilograms per day)	(metres per day)
	0	100
	10	75
	20	50
	30	25
	40	0
India	0	30
	6	24
	12	18
	18	12
	24	6
	30	0

Before Specialization

Canada	10	75
India	18	12
Total	28	87

After Specialization

Canada	0	100
India	30	0
Total	30	100

before—100 metres instead of 87 metres of cloth and 30 kilograms instead of 28 kilograms of food per day. Both areas could, as a result, have more of both products than before they began specializing and trading.

How can this happen? In Canada, the opportunity cost of producing food is very high—25 metres of cloth must be forgone to get 10 more kilograms of food. The cost of 1 kilogram of food is 2.5 metres of cloth (25 divided by 10). In India, by contrast, the opportunity cost of producing 6 more kilograms of food is 6 metres of cloth that must be forgone; so the cost of 1 kilogram of food is 1 metre of cloth. In Canada, a kilogram of food costs 2.5 metres of cloth, whereas in India the same amount of food costs only 1 metre of cloth. Food is more costly in Canada in terms of cloth forgone than in India, so India has a comparative advantage in food even though Canada has an absolute advantage in food.

With respect to cloth production, an increase in output by 25 metres, say, from 25 to 50 metres, costs 10 kilograms of food forgone in Canada. The cost of 1 more metre of cloth is 0.4 kilograms of food (10 divided by 25). In India, the cost of 1 metre of cloth is 1 kilogram of food. Cloth is more costly (in terms of opportunity cost) in India and cheaper in Canada, so Canada has a comparative advantage in the production of cloth.

Thus, by specializing in products in which it has a comparative advantage, an area has the potential of consuming more goods and services, assuming it trades the additional output for other desirable goods and services that others can produce at a lower opportunity cost. In the scenario presented here, the people in Canada would specialize in cloth, and the people in India would specialize in food. If Canada exports 20 metres of cloth and imports 11 kilograms of food, it can consume 80 metres of cloth and 11 kilograms of food after trade. Likewise, if India exports 11 kilograms of food and imports 20 metres of cloth, it can consume 20 metres of cloth and 19 kilograms of food after trade. We can see from this example that specialization increases both the division of labour and the interdependence among nations.

SECTION CHECK

- Voluntary trade occurs because the participants feel that they are better off because of the trade.
- A nation, a geographic area, or even a person can gain from trade if the good or service is produced relatively cheaper than anyone else can produce it. That is, an area should specialize in producing and selling those items that it can produce at a lower opportunity cost than others. Through trade and specialization in products in which it has a comparative advantage, a country can enjoy a greater array of goods and services at a lower cost.

section 14.4

Supply and Demand in International Trade

- What are consumer surplus and producer surplus?
- Who benefits and who loses when a country becomes an exporter?
- Who benefits and who loses when a country becomes an importer?

WHAT ARE CONSUMER SURPLUS AND PRODUCER SURPLUS?

The difference between what the consumer is willing and able to pay and what the consumer actually pays for a quantity of a good or service is called **consumer surplus.** The difference between the lowest price at which a supplier is willing and able to supply a good or service and the actual price received for a given quantity of a good or service is called **producer surplus.** With the tools of consumer and producer surplus, we can better analyze the impact of trade. Who gains? Who loses? What happens to net welfare?

The demand curve represents maximum prices that consumers are willing and able to pay for different quantities of a good or service; the supply curve represents minimum prices that suppliers require to be willing to supply different quantities of that good or service. In Exhibit 1, for example, for the first unit of output, the consumer is willing to pay up to $7 and the producer would demand at least $1 for producing that unit. However, the equilibrium price is $4, as indicated by the intersection of the supply and demand curves. It is clear that the two would gain from getting together and trading that unit because the consumer would receive $3 of consumer surplus ($7 − $4) and the producer would receive $3 of producer surplus ($4 − $1). Both would also benefit from trading the second and third units of output—in fact, from every unit up to the equilibrium output. Once the equilibrium output is reached at the equilibrium price, all of the mutually beneficial opportunities from trade between suppliers and demanders will have taken place; the sum of consumer surplus and producer surplus is maximized.

It is important to recognize that the total gains to the economy from trade are the sum of consumer and producer surplus. That is, consumers benefit from additional amounts of consumer surplus and producers benefit from additional amounts of producer surplus.

consumer surplus
the difference between what the consumer is willing and able to pay and what the consumer actually pays for a quantity of a good or service

producer surplus
the difference between the lowest price at which a supplier is willing and able to supply a good or service and the actual price received for a given quantity of a good or service

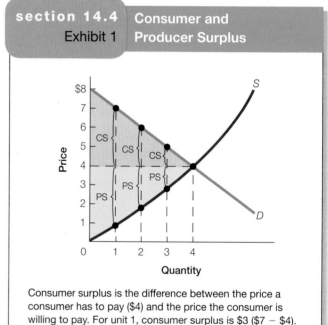

section 14.4 **Consumer and**
Exhibit 1 **Producer Surplus**

Consumer surplus is the difference between the price a consumer has to pay ($4) and the price the consumer is willing to pay. For unit 1, consumer surplus is $3 ($7 − $4). Producer surplus is the difference between the price a seller receives for selling a good or service ($4) and the price at which he is willing to supply that good or service. For unit 1, producer surplus is $3 ($4 − $1).

WHO BENEFITS AND WHO LOSES WHEN A COUNTRY BECOMES AN EXPORTER?

Using the concepts of consumer and producer surplus, we can graphically show the net benefits of free trade. Imagine an economy with no trade, where the equilibrium price, P_{BT}, and the equilibrium quantity, Q_{BT}, of wheat are determined exclusively in the domestic economy, as seen in Exhibit 2. Say that this imaginary economy decides to engage in free trade. You can see that the world price (established in the world market for wheat), P_{WORLD}, is higher than the domestic price before trade, P_{BT}. In other words, the domestic economy has a comparative advantage in wheat because it can produce wheat at a lower relative price than the rest of the world. So this wheat-producing country sells some wheat to the domestic market and some wheat to the world market, all at the going world price.

The price after trade (P_{AT}) is higher than the price before trade (P_{BT}). Because the world market is huge, the demand from the rest of the world at the world price (P_{WORLD}) is assumed to be perfectly elastic. That is, domestic wheat farmers can sell all the wheat they want at the world price. If you were a wheat farmer in Saskatchewan, would you rather sell all of your bushels of wheat at the higher world price or the lower domestic price? As a wheat farmer, you would surely prefer the higher world price. But this is not

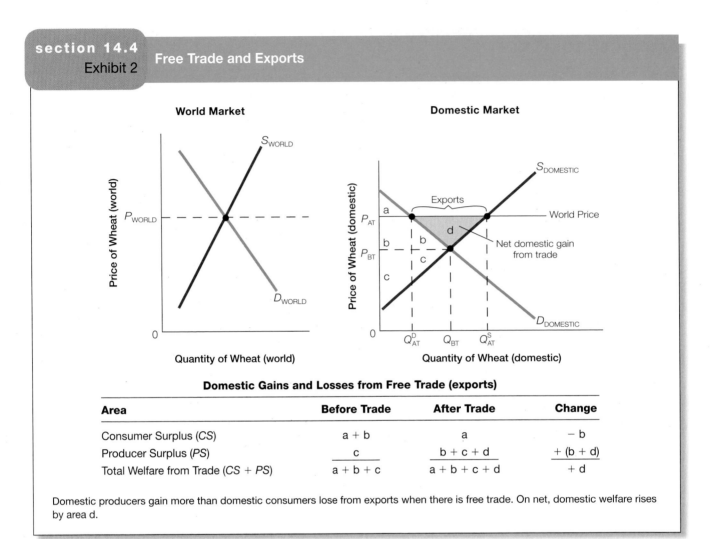

World Market

Domestic Market

Domestic Gains and Losses from Free Trade (exports)

Area	Before Trade	After Trade	Change
Consumer Surplus (*CS*)	a + b	a	− b
Producer Surplus (*PS*)	c	b + c + d	+ (b + d)
Total Welfare from Trade (*CS* + *PS*)	a + b + c	a + b + c + d	+ d

Domestic producers gain more than domestic consumers lose from exports when there is free trade. On net, domestic welfare rises by area d.

good news for domestic cereal and bread eaters, who now have to pay more for products made with wheat, because P_{AT} is greater than P_{BT}.

Graphically, we can see how free trade and exports affect both domestic consumers and domestic producers. At the higher world price, P_{AT}, domestic producers supply Q^S_{AT}, whereas domestic consumers demand Q^D_{AT}. The difference between these two quantities is the amount of wheat exported to the world market. At the higher world price, P_{AT}, domestic wheat producers are receiving larger amounts of producer surplus. Before trade, they received a surplus equal to area c; after trade, they received surplus b + c + d, for a net gain of area b + d. However, part of the domestic producers' gain comes at domestic consumers' expense. Specifically, consumers had a consumer surplus equal to area a + b before the trade (at P_{BT}), but they now have only area a (at P_{AT})—a loss of area b.

Area b reflects a redistribution of income because producers are gaining exactly what consumers are losing. Is that good or bad? We can't say objectively whether consumers or producers are more deserving. However, the net benefits from allowing free trade and exports are clearly visible in area d. Without free trade, no one gets area d. That is, on net, members of the domestic society gain when domestic wheat producers are able to sell their wheat at the higher world price. Although domestic wheat consumers lose from the free trade, those negative effects are more than offset by the positive gains captured by producers. Area d is the net increase in domestic welfare (the welfare gain) from free trade and exports.

In 1993, the North American Free Trade Agreement (NAFTA) was passed. This lowered the trade barriers between Mexico, Canada, and the United States. Proponents of freer trade, especially economists, viewed the agreement as a way to gain greater wealth through specialization and trade for all three countries. Opponents thought the agreement would take away Canadian and U.S. jobs and lower living standards.

WHO BENEFITS AND WHO LOSES WHEN A COUNTRY BECOMES AN IMPORTER?

Now suppose that our economy does not produce shirts as well as other countries of the world. In other words, other countries have a comparative advantage in producing shirts. This means that the domestic price for shirts is above the world price. This scenario is illustrated in Exhibit 3. At the new, lower world price, the domestic producer will supply quantity Q_{AT}^S. However, at the lower world price, the domestic producers will not produce

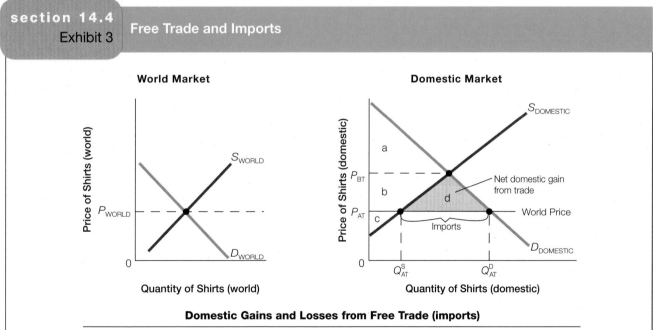

section 14.4
Exhibit 3

Free Trade and Imports

Domestic Gains and Losses from Free Trade (imports)

Area	Before Trade	After Trade	Change
Consumer Surplus (*CS*)	a	a + b + d	+ (b + d)
Producer Surplus (*PS*)	b + c	c	– b
Total Welfare from Trade (*CS* + *PS*)	a + b + c	a + b + c + d	+ d

Domestic consumers gain more than domestic producers lose from imports when there is free trade. On net, domestic welfare rises by area d.

the entire amount demanded by domestic consumers, Q_{AT}^D. At the world price, reflecting the world supply and demand for shirts, the difference between what is domestically supplied and what is domestically demanded is supplied by imports.

At the world price (established in the world market for shirts), we assume the world supply curve to the domestic market is perfectly elastic—that the producers of the world can supply all that domestic consumers are willing to buy at the going price. At the world price, Q_{AT}^S is supplied by domestic producers and the difference between Q_{AT}^D and Q_{AT}^S is imported from other countries.

Who wins and who loses from free trade and imports? Domestic consumers benefit from paying a lower price for shirts. In Exhibit 3, before trade, consumers received only area a in consumer surplus. After trade, the price fell and quantity purchased increased, causing the area of consumer surplus to increase from area a to area a + b + d, a gain of b + d. Domestic producers lose because they are now selling their shirts at the lower world price, P_{AT}. The producer surplus before trade was b + c. After trade, the producer surplus falls to area c, reducing producer surplus by area b. Area b, then, represents a redistribution from producers to consumers, but area d is the net increase in domestic welfare (the welfare gain) from free trade and imports.

SECTION CHECK

- The difference between what a consumer is willing and able to pay and what a consumer actually has to pay is called *consumer surplus*. The difference between what a supplier is willing and able to receive and the price a supplier actually receives for selling a good or service is called *producer surplus*.
- With free trade and exports, domestic producers gain more than domestic consumers lose.
- With free trade and imports, domestic consumers gain more than domestic producers lose.

section 14.5

Tariffs, Import Quotas, and Subsidies

- What is a tariff?
- What is the impact of tariffs on the domestic economy?
- What are some arguments in favour of tariffs?
- What are import quotas?
- What is the impact of import quotas on the domestic economy?
- What is the economic impact of subsidies?

WHAT IS A TARIFF?

tariff
a tax on imported goods

A **tariff** is a tax on imported goods. Tariffs are usually relatively small revenue producers that retard the expansion of trade. They bring about higher prices and revenues to domestic producers, and lower sales and revenues to foreign producers. Moreover, tariffs lead to higher prices for domestic consumers. In fact, the gains to producers are more than offset by the loss to consumers. Let us see how this works graphically.

WHAT IS THE IMPACT OF TARIFFS ON THE DOMESTIC ECONOMY?

The domestic economic impact of tariffs is presented in Exhibit 1, which illustrates the supply and demand curves for domestic consumers and producers of shoes. In a typical international supply and demand illustration, the intersection of the world supply and demand curves would determine the domestic market price. However, with import tariffs, the domestic price of shoes is greater than the world price, as in Exhibit 1. We consider the world supply curve (S_{WORLD}) to domestic consumers to be perfectly elastic; that is, we can buy all we want at the world price (P_{WORLD}). At the world price, domestic producers are willing to provide only quantity Q_S, but domestic consumers are willing to buy quantity Q_D—more than domestic producers are willing to supply. Imports make up the difference.

As you can see in Exhibit 1, the imposition of the tariff shifts up the perfectly elastic supply curve from foreigners to domestic consumers from S_{WORLD} to $S_{WORLD + TARIFF}$, but

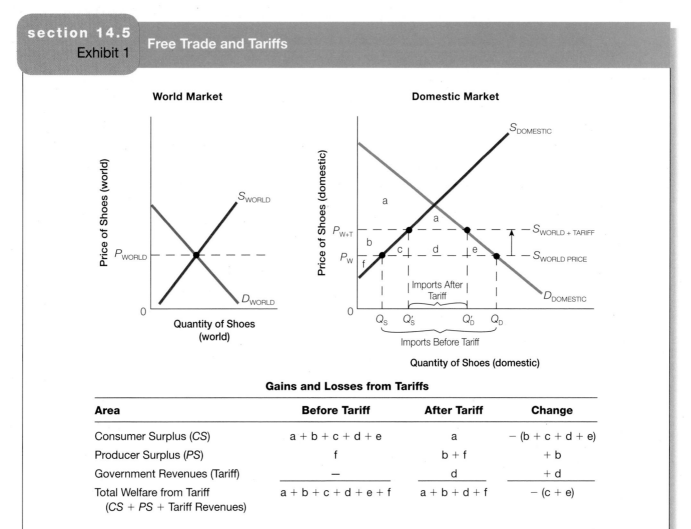

section 14.5
Exhibit 1   **Free Trade and Tariffs**

Gains and Losses from Tariffs

Area	Before Tariff	After Tariff	Change
Consumer Surplus (*CS*)	a + b + c + d + e	a	− (b + c + d + e)
Producer Surplus (*PS*)	f	b + f	+ b
Government Revenues (Tariff)	—	d	+ d
Total Welfare from Tariff (*CS* + *PS* + Tariff Revenues)	a + b + c + d + e + f	a + b + d + f	− (c + e)

In the case of a tariff, we see that consumers lose more than producers and government gain. On net, the deadweight loss associated with the new tariff is represented by area c + e.

it does not alter the domestic supply or demand curve. At the resulting higher domestic price (P_{W+T}), domestic suppliers are willing to supply more, Q'_S, but domestic consumers are willing to buy less, Q'_D, reducing the quantity of imported shoes. Overall, then, tariffs lead to (1) a smaller total quantity sold; (2) a higher price for shoes for domestic consumers; (3) greater sales of shoes at higher prices for domestic producers; and (4) lower sales of foreign shoes.

Although domestic producers do gain more sales and higher earnings, consumers lose much more. The increase in price from the tariff results in a loss in consumer surplus, as shown in Exhibit 1. After the tariff, shoe prices rise to P_{W+T}, and, consequently, consumer surplus falls by area b + c + d + e, representing the welfare loss to consumers from the tariff. Area b in Exhibit 1 shows the gain to domestic producers as a result of the tariff. That is, at the higher price, domestic producers are willing to supply more shoes, representing a welfare gain to producers resulting from the tariff. As a result of the tariff revenues, government gains area d. This is the import tariff—the revenue government collects on imports. However, we see from Exhibit 1 that consumers lose more than producers and government gain from the tariff. That is, on net, the deadweight loss associated with the tariff is represented by area c + e.

WHAT ARE SOME ARGUMENTS IN FAVOUR OF TARIFFS?

Despite the preceding arguments against trade restrictions, they continue to be levied. Some rationale for their existence is necessary. Four common arguments for the use of trade restrictions deserve our critical examination.

Temporary Trade Restrictions Help Infant Industries Grow

A country might argue that a protective tariff will allow a new industry to more quickly reach a scale of operation at which economies of scale and production efficiencies can be realized. That is, temporarily shielding the young industry from competition from foreign firms will allow the infant industry a chance to grow. With the early protection, these firms will eventually be able to compete effectively in the global market. It is presumed that without this protection, the industry could never get on its feet. At first hearing, the argument sounds valid, but there are many problems with it. How do you identify "infant industries" that genuinely have potential economies of scale and will quickly become efficient with protection? We do not know the long-run average total cost curves of industries, a necessary piece of information. Moreover, if firms and governments are truly convinced of the advantages of allowing an industry to reach a large scale, would it not be wise to make massive loans to the industry, allowing it to instantly begin large-scale production rather than slowly and at the expense of consumers? In other words, the goal of allowing the industry to reach its efficient size can be reached without protection. Finally, the history of infant industry tariffs suggests that the tariffs often linger long after the industry is mature and no longer in need of protection.

Tariffs Can Reduce Domestic Unemployment

Exhibit 1 showed how tariffs increase output by domestic producers, thus leading to increased employment and reduced unemployment in industries where tariffs were imposed. Yet the overall employment effects of a tariff imposition are not likely to be positive; the argument is incorrect. Why? First, the imposition of a tariff by Canada on, say, foreign steel is going to be noticed in the countries adversely affected by the tariff. If a new tariff on steel lowers Japanese steel sales to Canada, the Japanese likely will retaliate by imposing tariffs on Canadian exports to Japan, for example, on beef exports. The retaliatory tariff will lower Canadian sales of beef and thus decrease employment in the Canadian beef industry. As a result, the gain in employment in the steel industry will be offset by a loss of employment elsewhere.

Even if the other countries did not retaliate, Canadian employment would likely suffer outside the industry being protected. The way that other countries pay for Canadian goods is by getting Canadian dollars from sales to Canada—imports to us. If new tariffs lead to restrictions on imports, fewer Canadian dollars will be flowing overseas in payment for imports, which means that foreigners will have fewer Canadian dollars available to buy our exports. Other things being equal, this will tend to reduce our exports, thus creating unemployment in the export industries.

Tariffs Are Necessary for National Security Reasons

Sometimes it is argued that tariffs are a means of preventing a nation from becoming too dependent on foreign suppliers of goods vital to national security. That is, by making foreign goods more expensive, we can protect domestic suppliers. For example, if oil is vital to running planes and tanks, a cutoff of foreign supplies of oil during wartime could cripple a nation's defences.

The national security argument is usually not valid. If a nation's own resources are depletable, tariff-imposed reliance on domestic supplies will hasten depletion of domestic reserves, making the country even *more* dependent on imports in the future. If we impose a high tariff on foreign oil to protect domestic producers, we will increase domestic output of oil in the short run, but in the process, we will deplete the stockpile of available reserves. Thus, the defence argument is often of questionable validity. From a defence standpoint, it makes more sense to use foreign oil in peacetime and perhaps stockpile "insurance" supplies so that larger domestic supplies would be available during wars.

Tariffs Are Necessary to Protect against Dumping

Dumping occurs when a foreign country sells its products at prices below the country's costs or below the prices for which the products are sold on the domestic market. For example, the Japanese government has been accused for years of subsidizing Japanese steel producers while they attempt to gain a greater share of the world steel market and greater market power. That is, using this strategy, the short-term losses from selling below cost may be offset by the long-term economic profits. Some have argued that tariffs are needed to protect domestic producers against low-cost dumpers because the tariffs will raise the cost to foreign producers and offset the producers' cost advantage.

Canada has anti-dumping laws; if a Canadian producer suspects that imported goods are being dumped or subsidized, they can file a written complaint with the Canadian Border Services Agency (CBSA). It is then up to the Canadian International Trade Tribunal to establish if the dumping or subsidizing is causing injury to Canadian industry. If the Tribunal finds such evidence, the CBSA is then given the authority to impose anti-dumping or countervailing duties on the dumped or subsidized imports. The duties are designed to raise the price of the foreign goods that are being dumped or subsidized and give Canadian industry an opportunity to compete fairly with the imported goods.

WHAT ARE IMPORT QUOTAS?

An **import quota** is a legal limit on the imported quantity of a good that is produced abroad and can be sold in domestic markets. Like tariffs, import quotas directly restrict imports, leading to reductions in trade and thus preventing nations from fully realizing their comparative advantage. The case for quotas is probably even weaker than the case for tariffs. Suppose that the Japanese have been sending 50 000 cars annually to Canada

import quota
a legal limit on the imported quantity of a good that is produced abroad and can be sold in domestic markets

but now are told that, because of quota restrictions, they can send only 30 000 cars. If the Japanese manufacturers are allowed to determine how the quantity reduction is to occur, they will likely collude, leading to higher prices. Suppose that each producer is simply told to reduce sales by 40 percent. They will substantially raise the price of the cars to Canadians above what the 50 000 original buyers would have paid for them.

The Government Does Not Collect Revenues from Import Quotas

Unlike what occurs with a tariff, the Canadian government does not collect any revenue as a result of the import quota. Despite the higher prices, the loss in consumer surplus, and the loss in government revenue, quotas come about because people often view them as being less "protectionist" than tariffs—the traditional, most maligned form of protection.

Besides the rather blunt means of curtailing imports by using tariffs and quotas, nations have devised still other, more subtle means to restrict international trade. For example, nations sometimes impose product standards, ostensibly to protect consumers against inferior merchandise. Effectively, however, sometimes those standards are simply a means to restrict foreign competition. For example, France might keep certain kinds of wine out of the country on the grounds that the wines were made with allegedly inferior grapes or had an inappropriate alcoholic content. Likewise, Canada might prohibit automobile imports that do not meet certain standards in terms of pollutants, safety, and fuel efficiency. Even if these standards are not intended to restrict foreign competition, the regulations may nonetheless have that impact, restricting consumer choice.

WHAT IS THE IMPACT OF IMPORT QUOTAS ON THE DOMESTIC ECONOMY?

The domestic economic impact of an import quota on autos is presented in Exhibit 2. The introduction of an import quota increases the price from the world price, P_W (established in the world market for autos) to P_{W+Q}. The quota causes the price to rise above the world price. The domestic quantity demanded falls and the domestic quantity supplied rises. Consequently, the number of imports is much smaller than it would be without the import quota. Compared to free trade, domestic producers are better off but domestic consumers are worse off. Specifically, the import quota results in a gain in producer surplus of area b and a loss in consumer surplus of area b + c + d + e. However, unlike the tariff case, where the government gains area d in revenues, the government does not gain any revenues with a quota. Consequently, the deadweight loss is even greater with quotas than with tariffs. That is, on net, the deadweight loss associated with the quota is represented by area c + d + e. Recall that the deadweight loss was only c + e for tariffs.

If tariffs and import quotas hurt importing countries, why do they exist? The reason they exist is that producers can make large profits or "rents" from tariffs and import quotas. Economists call producer efforts to gain profits from government protection **rent seeking.** Because this is money, time, and effort that could have been spent producing something else rather than spent on lobbying efforts, the deadweight loss from tariffs and quotas that we just illustrated will likely understate the true deadweight loss to society.

rent seeking
producer efforts to gain profits from government protections such as tariffs and import quotas

WHAT IS THE ECONOMIC IMPACT OF SUBSIDIES?

Working in the opposite direction to a tariff or import quota, a **subsidy** is a program of financial assistance paid out to producers in a particular industry. As a form of protectionism or trade barrier, subsidies artificially make domestic goods and services competitive

subsidy
a program of financial assistance paid out to producers

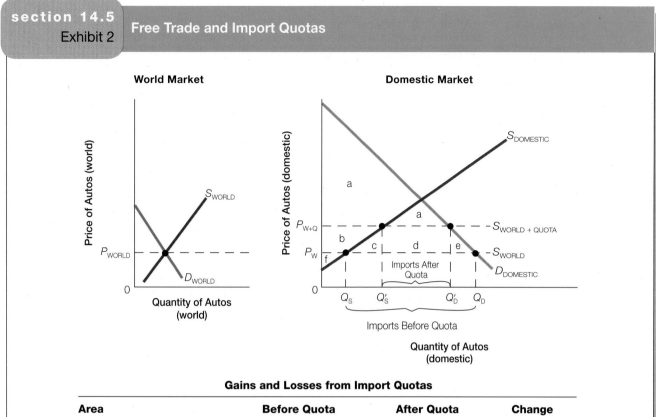

section 14.5
Exhibit 2
Free Trade and Import Quotas

Gains and Losses from Import Quotas

Area	Before Quota	After Quota	Change
Consumer Surplus (*CS*)	a + b + c + d + e	a	− (b + c + d + e)
Producer Surplus (*PS*)	f	b + f	+ b
Total Welfare (*CS* + *PS*) from Quota	a + b + c + d + e + f	a + b + f	− (c + d + e)

With an import quota, the price rises from P_W to P_{W+Q}. Compared to free trade, consumers lose area b + c + d + e and producers gain area b. The deadweight loss from the quota is area c + d + e. Under quotas, consumers lose and producers gain. The difference in deadweight loss between quotas and tariffs is area d that the government is not able to pick up with import quotas.

against imports. Specifically, an export subsidy involves giving revenue to producers for each exported unit of output, therefore encouraging producers to export. Although not a barrier to trade like tariffs and quotas, objections can be raised that subsidies distort trade patterns and lead to inefficiencies. How does this happen? With subsidies, producers will export goods not because their costs are lower than that of a foreign competitor, but because their costs have been artificially reduced by government action, transferring income from taxpayers to the exporter. The subsidy does not reduce the actual labour, raw material, and capital costs of production—society has the same opportunity costs as before. A nation's taxpayers end up subsidizing the output of producers who, relative to producers in other countries, are inefficient. The nation, then, exports products in which it does not have a comparative advantage. Gains from trade in terms of world output are reduced by such subsidies. Thus, subsidies, usually defended as a means of increasing exports and improving a nation's international financial position, are usually of dubious worth to the world economy and even to the economy doing the subsidizing.

Several Canadian subsidy programs have drawn the criticism of other economies. The most controversial of these are the ones provided to our agricultural, forest products, and mining and steel industries.

According to the World Bank and the International Monetary Fund, world trade has benefited enormously from greater trade openness since 1950. Tariffs on goods have fallen from a worldwide average of 26 percent to less than 9 percent today. On average, trade has grown more than twice as fast as output. While tariff use has declined, the incidence of nontariff barriers such as import quotas and export subsidies has risen sharply, indicating that there is still work to be done.

SECTION CHECK

- A tariff is a tax on imported goods.
- Tariffs bring about higher prices and revenues to domestic producers, and lower sales and revenues to foreign producers. Tariffs lead to higher prices and reduce consumer surplus for domestic consumers. Tariffs result in a net loss in welfare because the loss in consumer surplus is greater than the gain to producers and the government.
- Arguments in favour of the use of tariffs include: tariffs help infant industries grow; tariffs can reduce domestic unemployment; tariffs are necessary for national security reasons; and tariffs protect against dumping.
- Import quotas are legal limits on the quantity of an imported good that can be produced abroad and sold in domestic markets.
- Like tariffs, import quotas restrict imports, lowering consumer surplus and preventing countries from fully realizing their comparative advantage. There is a net loss in welfare from quotas, but it is proportionately larger than for a tariff because there are no government revenues.
- Sometimes government tries to encourage production of a certain good by subsidizing its production with taxpayer dollars. Because subsidies stimulate exports, they are not a barrier to trade like tariffs and import quotas. However, they do distort trade patterns and cause overall inefficiencies.

For Your Review

Section 14.1

1. What is the major difference between the nature of Canadian exports and imports?

Section 14.2

2. The North American Free Trade Agreement (NAFTA) is an agreement among Canada, the United States, and Mexico to reduce trade barriers and promote the free flow of goods and services across borders. Some Canadian labour groups were opposed to NAFTA. Can you explain why? Can you predict how NAFTA might affect the nature and production methods of goods and services produced in the participating countries?

Section 14.3

3. Bud and Larry have been shipwrecked on a deserted island. Their economic activity consists of either gathering berries or fishing. We know that Bud can catch four fish in one hour or harvest two buckets of berries. In the same time, Larry can catch two fish or harvest two buckets of berries.

a. Fill in the following table assuming that they *each* spend four hours a day fishing and four hours a day harvesting berries.

	Fish per Day	Buckets of Berries per Day
Bud	_____	_____
Larry	_____	_____
Total	_____	_____

b. If Bud and Larry don't trade with each other, who is better off? Why?

c. Assume that Larry and Bud operate on straight-line production possibilities curves. Fill in the following table:

	Opportunity Cost of a Bucket of Berries	Opportunity Cost of a Fish
Bud	_____	_____
Larry	_____	_____

d. If they trade, who has the comparative advantage in fish? In berries?

e. If Larry and Bud specialize in and trade the good in which they have a comparative advantage, how much of each good will be produced in an eight-hour day? What are the gains from trade?

4. Suppose Canada can produce cars at an opportunity cost of 2 computers for each car it produces. Suppose Mexico can produce cars at an opportunity cost of 8 computers for each car it produces. Indicate how both countries can gain from free trade.

5. The following represents the production possibilities in two countries.

Country A		Country B	
Good X	Good Y	Good X	Good Y
0	32	0	24
4	24	4	18
8	16	8	12
12	8	12	6
16	0	16	0

Which country has a comparative advantage at producing Good X? How can you tell? Which country has a comparative advantage at producing Good Y?

6. Evaluate the following statement: "Canada has an absolute advantage in growing wheat. Therefore, it must have a comparative advantage in growing wheat."

7. Assume that Freeland could produce 8 units of X and no Y, 16 units of Y and no X, or any linear combination in between, and Braveburg could produce 32 units of X and no Y, 48 units of Y and no X, or any linear combination in between.

   a. What is the opportunity cost of producing X in Freeland? In Braveburg?

   b. If Freeland and Braveburg specialize according to comparative advantage, in which directions will traded goods flow?

   c. If trade occurs, what will be the terms of trade between X and Y?

   d. How large would transaction costs, transportation costs, or tariffs have to be to eliminate trade between Freeland and Braveburg?

8. If country A is the lower opportunity cost producer of X and country B is the lowest opportunity cost producer of Y, what happens to their absolute and comparative advantages if country A suddenly becomes three times more productive at producing both X and Y than it was before?

Section 14.4

9. To protect its domestic apple industry, Botswana has for many years prevented international trade in apples. The following graph represents the Botswana domestic market for apples. P_{BT} is the current price, and P_{AT} is the world price.

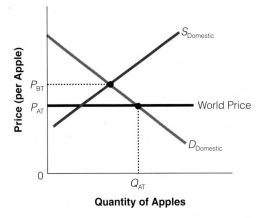

a. If the government allows world trade in apples, what will happen to the price of apples in Botswana? Why?

b. Indicate the amount of apples domestic producers produce after there is trade in apples as QDT. How many apples are imported?

c. Trade in imports causes producer surplus to be reduced by the amount b. Show b on the graph.

d. The gains from trade equal the amount that increased consumer surplus exceeds the loss in producer surplus. Show this gain, g, on the graph.

e. Explain why consumers in Botswana would still be better off if they were required to compensate producers for their lost producer surplus.

10. Using the following graph, illustrate the domestic effects of opening up the domestic market to international trade on the domestic price, the domestic quantity purchased, the domestic quantity produced, imports or exports, consumer surplus, producer surplus, and the total welfare gain from trade.

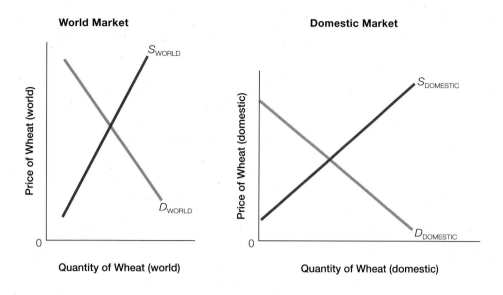

Section 14.5

11. Use the following graph to illustrate the domestic effects of imposing a tariff on imports on the domestic price, the domestic quantity purchased, the domestic quantity produced, the level of imports, consumer surplus, producer surplus, the tariff revenue generated, and the total welfare effect from the tariff.

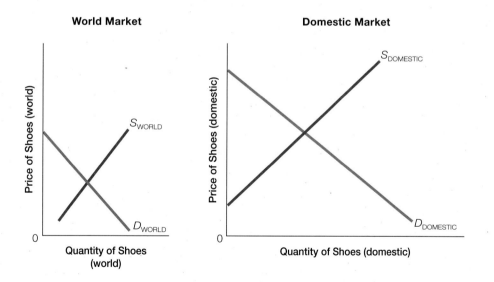

12. Explain why imposing a tariff causes a net welfare loss to the domestic economy.

13. If imposing tariffs and quotas harms consumers, why don't consumers vigorously oppose the implementation of these protectionist policies?

14. Why does rent seeking imply that the traditional measure of deadweight loss from tariffs and quotas will likely understate the true deadweight loss to society?

15. Would you be in favour of freer trade or against it in the following circumstances?

    a. The move to freer trade is in another country and you are an exporter to that country.

    b. The move to freer trade is in your country and you compete with imports from other countries.

    c. The move to freer trade is in your country and you import parts for products you sell domestically.

16. Go through your local newspaper and locate four news items regarding the global economy. Identify the significance of each of these news items to the Canadian economy and whether they are likely to affect international trade.

CourseMate

Access an interactive eBook and chapter-specific interactive learning tools, including flashcards, quizzes, a glossary, and more in CourseMate, accessed through **www.sextonmacro3ce.nelson.com**

chapter 15

International Finance

section 15.1

The Balance of Payments

- What is the balance of payments?
- What is the current account?
- What is the capital account?
- What is the statistical discrepancy?

WHAT IS THE BALANCE OF PAYMENTS?

The record of the international transactions of a nation over a year is called the **balance of payments.** The balance of payments is a statement that records all the exchanges requiring an outflow of funds to foreign nations or an inflow of funds from other nations. Just as an examination of gross domestic product accounts gives us some idea of the economic health and vitality of a nation, the balance of payments provides information about a nation's world trade position. The balance of payments is divided into three main sections: the current account, the capital account, and an "error term" called the *statistical discrepancy*. These are highlighted in Exhibit 1. Let us look at each of these components beginning with the current account, which is largely made up of imports and exports of goods and services.

balance of payments
the record of international transactions of a nation over a year

WHAT IS THE CURRENT ACCOUNT?

Export Goods and the Current Account

The **current account** is a record of a country's imports and exports of goods and services, net investment income, and net transfers. Anytime a foreign buyer purchases a good from a Canadian producer, the foreign buyer must pay the Canadian producer for the good. Usually, the foreigner must pay for the good in Canadian dollars because the seller wants to pay his workers and for other inputs with dollars. This requires the foreign buyer to exchange units of his currency with a foreign exchange dealer for Canadian dollars. Because Canada obtains foreign currency, exports of Canadian goods abroad are considered a credit or plus (+) item in the Canadian balance of payments.

current account
a record of a country's imports and exports of goods and services, net investment income, and net transfers

section 15.1
Exhibit 1
Canadian Balance of Payments, 2010 (billions of dollars)

Type of Transaction

Current Account			Capital Account		
1. Exports of goods	$405		10. Net flow of Canadian assets	$−107	
2. Imports of goods	−414		11. Net flow of Canadian liabilities	151	
3. Merchandise trade balance (lines 1 + 2)		−9	12. Financial account balance (lines 10 + 11)		44
4. Exports of services	71		13. Statistical discrepancy		7
5. Imports of services	−94		14. Net balance (lines 9 + 12 + 13)		$0
6. Services trade balance (lines 4 + 5)		−23			
7. Net investment income		−16			
8. Net transfers		−3			
9. Current account balance (lines 3 + 6 + 7 + 8)		−51			

SOURCE: Adapted from the Statistics Canada website, Canada's balance of international payments (Current account), www40.statcan.ca/101/cst01/econ01a.eng.htm, and Canada's balance of international payments (Capital and financial account), www40.statcan.ca/101/cst01/econ01b.eng.htm, 2010.

Import Goods and the Current Account

When a Canadian consumer buys an imported good, however, the reverse is true: The Canadian importer must pay the foreign producer, usually in that nation's currency. Typically, the Canadian buyer will go to a foreign exchange dealer and exchange Canadian dollars for units of that foreign currency. Imports are thus a debit (−) item in the balance of payments, because Canada loses foreign currency in order to buy imports.

When a foreign tourist visits the CN Tower in Toronto, how does that affect the current account? Tourism provides Canada with foreign currency, which is included in exports.

Services and the Current Account

Although imports and exports of goods are the largest components of the balance of payments, they are not the only ones. Nations import and export services as well. A particularly important service is tourism. When Canadian tourists go abroad, they are buying foreign-produced services. Those services include the use of hotels, sightseeing tours, restaurants, and so forth. In the current account, these services are included in imports. On the other hand, foreign tourism in Canada provides us with foreign currencies, so they are included in exports.

Net Transfers and Net Investment Income

Other items that affect the current account are net transfers, which are largely private and government grants and gifts to and from other countries. When the Canadian government gives foreign aid to another country, this creates a debit in the Canadian balance of payments. Private gifts, such as Canadian individuals receiving money from relatives or friends in foreign countries, show up in the current account as a credit item.

There is also net investment income in the current account—Canadian investors hold foreign assets and foreign investors hold Canadian assets. When Canadian investors hold foreign assets, they earn investment income in the form of interest and dividends, which is a credit item. When foreign investors hold Canadian assets, they earn investment income in the form of interest and dividends, which is a debit item. In Exhibit 1, investment income paid to foreigners on their Canadian assets exceeded the investment income received by Canadians on their foreign assets by $16 billion.

Current Account Balance

The balance on the current account is the net amount of credits or debits after adding up all transactions of goods (merchandise imports and exports), services, investment income, and transfer payments. If the sum of credits exceeds the sum of debits, the nation is said to be running a surplus on the current account. If debits exceed credits, however, the nation is running a deficit on the current account.

The current account balance for 2010 is presented in Exhibit 1. Note that exports and imports of goods were by far the largest credits and debits. Note also that Canadian imports of goods were $9 billion more than Canadian exports of goods. Canada, therefore, experienced a $9 billion deficit in the merchandise trade balance. In addition to this $9 billion merchandise trade deficit was a $23 billion deficit in the services trade balance. When the $16 billion net investment income payment and the $3 billion net transfers payment are also included, the overall current account deficit was $51 billion.

WHAT IS THE CAPITAL ACCOUNT?

How was this deficit on the current account financed? We borrowed from the rest of the world. The current account deficit is reflected by movements of financial, or capital, assets. These transactions are recorded in the *capital account*, so a current account deficit is financed by a capital account surplus. In short, the **capital account** is a record of the foreign purchases or assets in the domestic economy (a monetary inflow) and domestic purchases of assets abroad (a monetary outflow).

capital account
a record of the foreign purchases or assets in the domestic economy (a monetary inflow) and domestic purchases of assets abroad (a monetary outflow)

Capital Account Transactions

Capital account transactions include items such as international bank loans, purchases of corporate stocks and bonds, government bond purchases, and direct investments in foreign subsidiary companies. In Exhibit 1, we see that Canadians purchased an additional $107 billion of foreign assets in 2010, which was a debit because Canada lost foreign currency. On the other hand, foreigners purchased an additional $151 billion of Canadian assets in 2010, which was a credit because it provided Canadians with foreign currency. On balance, then, there was a surplus in the capital account from capital movements of $44 billion, offsetting the $51 billion deficit in the current account.

It is important to highlight one particular capital account transaction: purchases and sales of foreign currencies by the Bank of Canada in the foreign exchange market. The Bank of Canada can intervene in the foreign exchange market to counter disruptive short-term movements in the external value of the Canadian dollar. For example, to moderate a decline in the value of the Canadian dollar, the Bank of Canada can sell foreign currency (usually U.S. dollars) and buy Canadian dollars on the foreign exchange market, thereby putting upward pressure on the Canadian dollar. Similarly, if the Canadian dollar is appreciating too rapidly, the Bank of Canada can buy foreign currency (usually U.S. dollars) and sell Canadian dollars on the foreign exchange market, thereby putting downward pressure on the Canadian dollar. These purchases and sales of foreign currencies by the Bank of Canada affect the level of Canada's official international reserves (the Government of Canada's holdings of foreign currencies), and these transactions are recorded in the capital account of the balance of payments.

WHAT IS THE STATISTICAL DISCREPANCY?

In the final analysis, it is true that the overall balance of payments account must balance so that credits and debits are equal. Why is this so? Because every unit of foreign currency used (debit) must have a source (credit). We can see that the current account deficit ($51 billion debit) does not exactly equal the capital account surplus ($44 billion credit). That is because there are considerable international flows of goods and capital that government authorities are unable to measure and record (e.g., smuggling of goods, or undeclared financial investments). These "errors" are entered into the balance of payments as the statistical discrepancy. In Exhibit 1, the statistical discrepancy was $7 billion (credit). By including the statistical discrepancy with the current account balance and the capital account balance, the overall balance of payments does balance.

Balance of Payments: A Useful Analogy

In concept, the international balance of payments is similar to the personal financial transactions of individuals. Each individual has his or her own "balance of payments," reflecting that person's trading with other economic units: other individuals, corporations, or governments. People earn income or credits by "exporting" their labour service to other economic units, or by receiving investment income (a return on capital services). Against that, they "import" goods from other economic units; we call these imports *consumption*. This debit item is sometimes augmented by payments made to outsiders (e.g., banks) on loans, and so forth. Fund transfers, such as gifts to children or charities, are other debit items (or credit items for recipients of the assistance).

As individuals, if our spending on our consumption ("imports") exceeds our income from our "exports" of our labour and capital services, we have a "deficit" that must be financed by borrowing or selling assets. On the other hand, if we "export" more than we "import," we can make new investments and/or increase our "reserves" (savings and investment holdings). Like nations, individuals who run a deficit in daily transactions must make up for it through accommodating transactions (e.g., borrowing or reducing their savings or investment holdings) to bring about an ultimate balance of credits and debits to their personal account. Likewise, individuals who run a surplus in daily transactions must make new investments and/or increase their savings and investment holdings to bring about a balance of credits and debits.

In summary, the international balance of payments works like this: A country that runs a current account surplus lends that surplus to the rest of the world, creating a capital account deficit; a country that runs a current account deficit finances that deficit by borrowing from the rest of the world, thus creating a capital account surplus.

Exchange Rates

- What are exchange rates?
- How are exchange rates determined?

When Canadian consumers buy goods from people in other countries, the sellers of those goods want to be paid in their own domestic currencies. Canadian consumers, then, must first exchange Canadian dollars for the seller's currency in order to pay for those goods. Canadian importers must, therefore, constantly buy U.S. dollars, yen, euros, pesos, and other currencies in order to finance their purchases. Similarly, people in other countries buying Canadian goods must sell their currencies to obtain Canadian dollars in order to pay for those goods.

WHAT ARE EXCHANGE RATES?

The price of one unit of a country's currency in terms of another country's currency is called the **exchange rate.** If a Canadian importer has agreed to pay euros (the currency of the European Union) to buy a cuckoo clock made in the Black Forest in Germany, she would then have to exchange Canadian dollars for euros. If it takes $2 to buy 1 euro, then the exchange rate is $2 per euro. From the German perspective, the exchange rate is 0.50 euros per Canadian dollar.

exchange rate
the price of one unit of a country's currency in terms of another country's currency

Exhibit 1 shows the exchange rate for the Canadian dollar against the currencies of some of our major trading partners. The exchange rates listed were the average exchange rates for the year 2010. It took 0.9710 U.S. dollars to buy one Canadian dollar (i.e., the exchange rate of the Canadian dollar in terms of the U.S. dollar). Conversely, it took 1.0299 Canadian dollars to buy one U.S. dollar (i.e., the exchange rate of the U.S. dollar in terms of the Canadian dollar). Note carefully that 1.0299 equals 1 divided by 0.9710. Similarly, it took 85.0340 Japanese yen to buy one Canadian dollar, and it took 0.0118 Canadian dollars (1 divided by 85.0340) to buy one Japanese yen.

A review of exchange rates over time will reveal that they are not constant: They can increase and decrease. An increase in the value of a currency is referred to as an **appreciation.** For example, suppose the exchange rate rises from 25 to 30 Russian rubles per Canadian dollar. Since you can now get more Russian rubles for each Canadian dollar, the dollar is said to have appreciated. A decrease in the value of a currency is referred to as **depreciation.** If the exchange rate falls from 15 to 10 Mexican pesos per Canadian dollar, the dollar is said to have depreciated.

appreciation
an increase in the value of a currency

depreciation
a decrease in the value of a currency

section 15.2
Exhibit 1

Exchange Rates for the Canadian Dollar in 2010

Country	Currency	Units of Foreign Currency per Canadian Dollar	Canadian Dollars per Unit of Foreign Currency
Australia	Dollar	1.0560	0.9470
China	Renminbi	6.5746	0.1521
European Monetary Union	Euro	0.7320	1.3661
Hong Kong	Dollar	7.5431	0.1326
India	Rupee	44.3459	0.0226
Japan	Yen	85.0340	0.0118
Mexico	Peso	12.2594	0.0816
New Zealand	Dollar	1.3459	0.7430
Norway	Krone	5.8617	0.1706
Russia	Rouble	29.4811	0.0339
South Korea	Won	1122.3345	0.0009
Sweden	Krona	6.9832	0.1432
Switzerland	Franc	1.0105	0.9896
United Kingdom	Pound	0.6282	1.5918
United States	Dollar	0.9710	1.0299

SOURCE: Bank of Canada.

DEBATE

INTERNATIONAL FINANCE: THE RISING CANADIAN DOLLAR

Canada has long enjoyed a "discounted dollar," providing an artificial competitive advantage for exporters by making their goods appear to have more value, simply because of the lower cost. The low Canadian dollar is good for exporters but bad for migrating "snowbirds."

When our dollar appreciates, it makes our products more expensive to the rest of the world and this causes foreign firms to reduce the amount of goods and services they purchase from Canadian producers. The high dollar is attractive to Canadian consumers, though, as foreign products are more affordable. This is a double hit for Canadian manufacturing firms—foreign firms don't buy as many Canadian goods, and Canadians buy more foreign goods. One of the major issues that any government has to deal with is, Should the Canadian dollar be artificially held to lower levels to assist Canadian firms?

Pro:
Those who trade with Canada want a low Canadian dollar— it keeps the prices of Canadian products down. Trade unions and Canadian manufacturing firms enjoy the benefits of a low dollar, as it provides the illusion of value. Who are the other stakeholders who would benefit from a low dollar, and what would be some other reasons to justify their preference for a discounted dollar?

Con:
The rising Canadian dollar sends a message to the world— that the Canadian economy is strong and that Canadian products are desirable. The improvements in real productivity versus the aura of productivity brought on by a discounted dollar are a boon to those firms that embrace the opportunity to improve. Canadian consumers benefit from the high dollar when they travel and purchase foreign goods. What are other reasons why Canada should embrace the rising dollar and who are the stakeholders who benefit?

Changes in Exchange Rates Affect the Domestic Demand for Foreign Goods

Prices of goods in their currencies combine with exchange rates to determine the domestic price of foreign goods. Suppose the cuckoo clock sells for 100 euros in Germany. What is the price to Canadian consumers? Let us assume that tariffs and other transaction costs are zero. If the exchange rate is $2 = 1 euro, then the equivalent Canadian dollar price of the cuckoo clock is 100 euros times $2 per euro, or $200. If the exchange rate was to change to $3 = 1 euro, fewer clocks would be demanded in Canada. This is because the effective Canadian dollar price of the clocks would rise to $300 (100 euros times $3 per euro). The new higher relative value of a euro compared to the dollar (or equivalently, the lower relative value of a dollar compared to the euro) would lead to a reduction in Canadian demand for German-made clocks.

The Demand for a Foreign Currency

The demand for foreign currencies is an example of what economists call a **derived demand**—a demand for an input derived from consumers' demand for the good or service produced with that input. Specifically, the demand for foreign currency is derived from the demand for foreign goods and services or for foreign assets. The more foreign goods are demanded, the more of that foreign currency will be needed to pay for those goods. Such an increased demand for the currency will push up the exchange rate of that currency relative to other currencies.

The Supply of a Foreign Currency

Similarly, the supply of foreign currency is provided by foreigners who want to buy the exports of another nation. For example, the more that foreigners demand Canadian products, the more of their currencies they will supply in exchange for Canadian dollars, which they use to buy our products.

HOW ARE EXCHANGE RATES DETERMINED?

We know that the demand for foreign currencies is derived in part from the demand for foreign goods, but how does that affect the exchange rate? Just as in the product market, the answer lies with the forces of supply and demand. In this case, it is the supply of and demand for a foreign currency that determine the equilibrium price (exchange rate) of that currency.

The Demand Curve for a Foreign Currency

As Exhibit 2 shows, the demand curve for a foreign currency—the euro, for example—is downward sloping, just as a demand curve is in product markets. In this case, however, the demand curve has a negative slope because as the price of the euro falls relative to the Canadian dollar (i.e., the euro depreciates in value), European products become relatively cheaper to Canadian consumers, who therefore buy more European goods. To do so, the quantity of euros demanded by Canadian consumers will increase to buy more European goods as the price of the euro falls. This is why the demand for foreign currencies is considered to be a derived demand.

The Supply Curve for a Foreign Currency

The supply curve for a foreign currency is upward sloping, just as a supply curve is in product markets. In this case, as the price of the euro increases relative to the Canadian

The euro makes it easy to compare prices for the same goods in different European countries using this currency. For example, if you use mail order or shop on the Internet, it is easier to spot the bargains between countries.

derived demand
the demand for an input derived from consumers' demand for the good or service produced with that input

section 15.2
Exhibit 2   Equilibrium in the Foreign Exchange Market

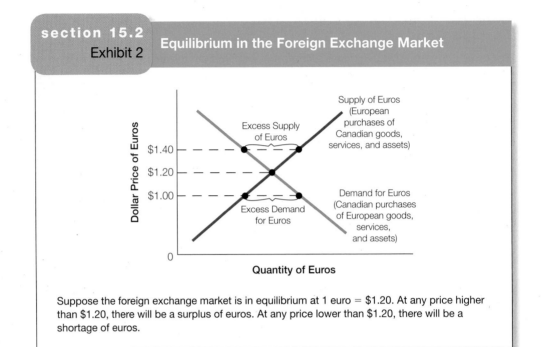

Suppose the foreign exchange market is in equilibrium at 1 euro = $1.20. At any price higher than $1.20, there will be a surplus of euros. At any price lower than $1.20, there will be a shortage of euros.

dollar (i.e., the euro appreciates in value), Canadian products will become relatively cheaper to European buyers and they will increase the quantity of dollars they demand. Europeans will, therefore, increase the quantity of euros supplied to the foreign exchange market by buying more Canadian products. Hence, the supply curve is upward sloping.

Business CONNECTION

MANAGING TRANSACTION EXPOSURE

Companies that engage in international trade incur transaction fees, amounts payable, and amounts receivable that expose the firm's cash flow to fluctuations in exchange rates. The risk is that the amount payable might increase if the foreign currency actually appreciates in value relative to the domestic currency between the time the payable was incurred and the actual date of payment. Similarly, if the international transaction results in an amount receivable, the foreign exchange risk is the risk that the amount to be received might decrease in value if the foreign currency actually depreciates in value relative to the domestic currency between the time the receivable was incurred and the actual date of receipt.

What can businesses do to manage transaction exposure to fluctuations in foreign currencies? First, on an ongoing basis, the business should attempt to measure the net exposure it has to each foreign currency. The net exposure for each currency in a period is the amounts receivable less the amounts payable. Once this net amount is determined for each currency, the firm can manage the exposure using a variety of methods. For example, if the net

amount is payable, a futures or forward contract can be purchased to obtain the currency at a predetermined exchange rate in the future. Alternatively, a currency swap can be arranged through a financial intermediary such as a bank, or a call option on the foreign currency can be a purchased. At times, the firm might want to borrow its home currency and convert the proceeds into the foreign currency that will be needed in the future to pay the net amount payable.

To hedge a net receivable, a futures or forward contract could be sold to sell the currency at a predetermined exchange rate in the future. While futures contracts and forward contracts normally yield similar results, forward contracts are more flexible as they are not standardized. As in the case of payables, a currency swap can be arranged through a financial intermediary such as a bank, or a put option on the foreign currency can be sold. The firm could also consider borrowing the foreign currency and converting the proceeds into its domestic currency, repaying the loan with the net receivable in due course.

With some forward planning, the transaction risk associated with fluctuations in exchange rates can be mitigated.

Equilibrium in the Foreign Exchange Market

Equilibrium is reached where the demand and supply curves for a given currency intersect. In Exhibit 2, the equilibrium price of a euro is $1.20. As in the product market, if the Canadian dollar price of euros is higher than the equilibrium price, an excess quantity of euros will be supplied at that price, or a surplus of euros. Competition among euro sellers will push the price of euros down toward equilibrium. Likewise, if the dollar price of euros is lower than the equilibrium price, an excess quantity of euros will be demanded at that price, or a shortage of euros. Competition among euro buyers will push the price of euros up toward equilibrium.

SECTION CHECK

- The price of a unit of one foreign currency in terms of another currency is called the *exchange rate*.
- The exchange rate for a currency is determined by the supply of and demand for that currency in the foreign exchange market.

<section>

15.3

Equilibrium Changes in the Foreign Exchange Market

- What are the major determinants in the foreign exchange market?

WHAT ARE THE MAJOR DETERMINANTS IN THE FOREIGN EXCHANGE MARKET?

The equilibrium exchange rate of a currency changes many times daily. Sometimes, these changes can be quite significant. Any force that shifts either the demand for or supply of a currency will shift the equilibrium in the foreign exchange market, leading to a new exchange rate. These factors include changes in consumer tastes for goods, changes in income, changes in tariffs, changes in relative interest rates, changes in relative inflation rates, and speculation.

Increased Tastes for Foreign Goods

Because the demand for foreign currencies is derived from the demand for foreign goods, any change in the demand for foreign goods will shift the demand schedule for foreign currency in the same direction. For example, if a cuckoo clock revolution sweeps through Canada, German producers would have reason to celebrate, knowing that many Canadian buyers will turn to Germany for their cuckoo clocks. The Germans, however, will only accept payment in the form of euros, and so Canadian consumers and retailers must convert their dollars into euros before they can purchase their clocks. The increased taste for European goods in Canada would, therefore, lead to an increased

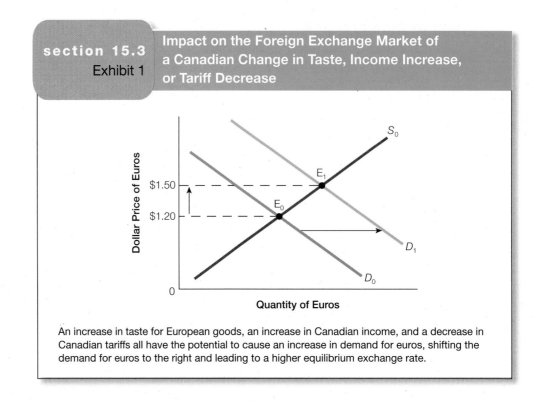

section 15.3
Exhibit 1

Impact on the Foreign Exchange Market of a Canadian Change in Taste, Income Increase, or Tariff Decrease

An increase in taste for European goods, an increase in Canadian income, and a decrease in Canadian tariffs all have the potential to cause an increase in demand for euros, shifting the demand for euros to the right and leading to a higher equilibrium exchange rate.

demand for euros. As shown in Exhibit 1, this increased demand for euros shifts the demand curve to the right, resulting in a new, higher equilibrium dollar price of euros.

What impact will an increase in travel to Paris by Canadian consumers have on the Canadian dollar price of euros? In order for a consumer to buy souvenirs at the Eiffel Tower, she will need to exchange dollars for euros. This would increase the demand for euros and result in a new higher dollar price of euros.

Canadian Income Increases or Reductions in Canadian Tariffs

Any change in the average income of Canadian consumers will also change the equilibrium exchange rate, *ceteris paribus*. If, on the whole, incomes increased in Canada, Canadians would buy more goods, including imported goods, so more European goods would be bought. This increased demand for European goods would lead to an increased demand for euros, resulting in a higher exchange rate for the euro. A decrease in Canadian tariffs on European goods would tend to have the same effect as an increase in incomes by making European goods more affordable. As Exhibit 1 shows, this would again lead to an increased demand for European goods and a higher equilibrium exchange rate for the euro.

Changes in European Income, Tariffs, or Tastes

If European incomes rose, European tariffs on Canadian goods fell, or European tastes for Canadian goods increased, the supply of euros in the foreign exchange market would increase. Any of these changes would cause Europeans to demand more Canadian goods, and therefore more Canadian dollars in order to purchase those goods. To obtain those added dollars, Europeans must exchange more of their euros, increasing the supply of euros on the foreign exchange market. As Exhibit 2 demonstrates, the effect of this would be a rightward shift in the euro supply curve, leading to a new equilibrium at a lower exchange rate for the euro.

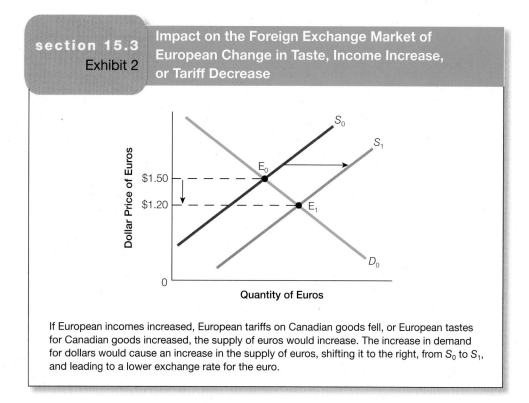

section 15.3
Exhibit 2

Impact on the Foreign Exchange Market of European Change in Taste, Income Increase, or Tariff Decrease

If European incomes increased, European tariffs on Canadian goods fell, or European tastes for Canadian goods increased, the supply of euros would increase. The increase in demand for dollars would cause an increase in the supply of euros, shifting it to the right, from S_0 to S_1, and leading to a lower exchange rate for the euro.

Changes in Relative Interest Rates

If interest rates in Canada were to increase relative to, say, European interest rates, other things equal, the rate of return on Canadian bonds would increase relative to that on European bonds. European investors would thus increase their demand for Canadian bonds, and therefore offer euros for sale to buy dollars to buy Canadian bonds, shifting the supply curve for euros to the right, from S_0 to S_1 in Exhibit 3.

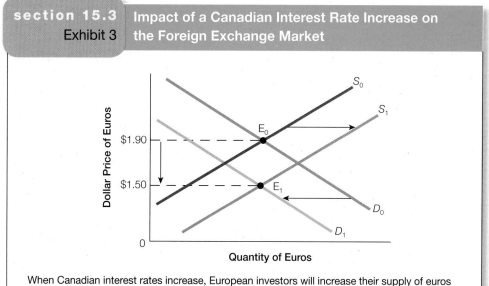

section 15.3
Exhibit 3

Impact of a Canadian Interest Rate Increase on the Foreign Exchange Market

When Canadian interest rates increase, European investors will increase their supply of euros to buy dollars—the supply curve of euros increases from S_0 to S_1. In addition, Canadian investors will also shift their investments away from Europe, decreasing their demand for euros and shifting the demand curve from D_0 to D_1. This will lead to a depreciation of the euro and an appreciation of the dollar.

In this scenario, Canadian investors would also shift their investments away from Europe by decreasing their demand for euros, from D_0 to D_1 in Exhibit 3. A subsequent lower equilibrium exchange rate ($1.50) would result for the euro due to an increase in the Canadian interest rate. That is, the euro would depreciate. In short, the higher Canadian interest rate attracted more investment to Canada and led to a relative appreciation of the dollar and a relative depreciation of the euro.

You may remember this analysis from our discussion of monetary policy in the open economy in Chapter 13. When the Bank of Canada runs a contractionary monetary policy and causes Canadian interest rates to rise, the Canadian dollar appreciates, which leads to a decrease in net exports and a reduction in real GDP in the short run.

Changes in Relative Inflation Rates

If Europe experienced an inflation rate greater than that experienced in Canada, other things being equal, what would happen to the exchange rate? In this case, European products would become relatively more expensive to Canadian consumers. Canadians would decrease the quantity of European goods demanded and, therefore, decrease their demand for euros. The result would be a leftward shift of the demand curve for euros.

On the other side of the Atlantic, Canadian goods would become relatively cheaper to Europeans, leading Europeans to increase the quantity of Canadian goods demanded and, therefore, to demand more Canadian dollars. This increased demand for dollars translates into an increased supply of euros, shifting the supply curve for euros rightward. Exhibit 4 shows the shifts of the supply and demand curves and the new lower equilibrium exchange rate for the euro resulting from the higher European inflation rate.

Expectations and Speculation

Every trading day, billions of Canadian dollars trade hands in the foreign exchange markets. Suppose currency traders believed Canada was going to experience more rapid

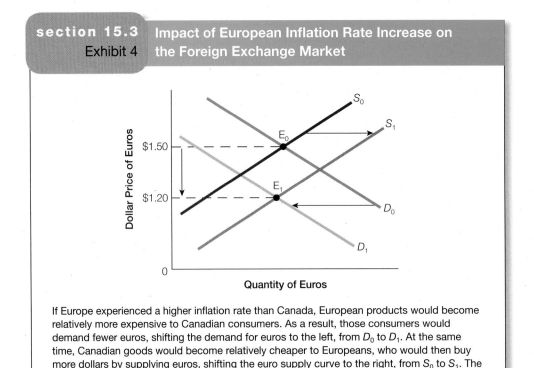

section 15.3 **Exhibit 4**   **Impact of European Inflation Rate Increase on the Foreign Exchange Market**

If Europe experienced a higher inflation rate than Canada, European products would become relatively more expensive to Canadian consumers. As a result, those consumers would demand fewer euros, shifting the demand for euros to the left, from D_0 to D_1. At the same time, Canadian goods would become relatively cheaper to Europeans, who would then buy more dollars by supplying euros, shifting the euro supply curve to the right, from S_0 to S_1. The result: a new lower equilibrium exchange rate for the euro.

inflation in the future than Japan. If currency speculators believe that the value of the dollar will soon be falling because of the anticipated rise in the Canadian inflation rate, those traders that are holding dollars will convert them to yen. This leads to an increase in the demand for yen—the yen appreciates and the dollar depreciates relative to the yen, *ceteris paribus*. In short, if speculators believe that the price of a country's currency is going to rise, they will buy more of that currency, pushing up the price and causing the country's currency to appreciate.

SECTION CHECK

■ Any force that shifts either the demand or supply curves for a foreign currency will shift the equilibrium in the foreign exchange market and lead to a new exchange rate. Changes in tastes, tariffs, income levels, relative interest rates, relative inflation rates, or speculation will cause the demand for and supply of a currency to shift.

Flexible Exchange Rates

■ How are exchange rates determined today?
■ What are the advantages of a flexible exchange rate system?
■ What are the disadvantages of a flexible exchange rate system?

HOW ARE EXCHANGE RATES DETERMINED TODAY?

Since 1973, the world has essentially operated on a system of flexible exchange rates. With flexible exchange rates, currency prices are allowed to fluctuate with changes in supply and demand, without governments stepping in to prevent those changes. Prior to 1973, governments operated under what was called the *Bretton Woods fixed exchange rate system*, in which they would maintain a stable exchange rate by buying or selling currencies or reserves to bring demand and supply for their currencies together at the fixed exchange rate. The present system of flexible exchange rates evolved out of the Bretton Woods fixed-rate system and occurred by accident, not design. Governments were unable to agree on an alternative fixed-rate approach when the Bretton Woods system collapsed, so nations simply let market forces determine currency values.

Government Intervention in the Exchange Rate System

To be sure, governments sensitive to sharp changes in the exchange value of their currencies do still intervene from time to time to prop up their currency's exchange rate if it is considered to be too low or falling too rapidly, or to depress its exchange rate if it is considered to be too high or rising too rapidly. However, present-day fluctuations in exchange rates are not determined solely by market forces. Economists sometimes say that the current exchange rate system is a **dirty float system,** meaning that fluctuations in currency values are partly determined by market forces and partly influenced by government intervention. Over the years, however, such governmental support attempts have been insufficient to dramatically alter exchange rates for long, and currency exchange rates have changed dramatically.

dirty float system
a description of the exchange rate system that means that fluctuations in currency values are partly determined by market forces and partly influenced by government intervention

🍁 CANADA	CAD			
CHINA	CNY			
EURO	EUR			
JAPAN	JPY			
SINGAPORE	SGD			
HONG KONG	HKD			
NEW ZEALAND	NZD			
	MYR			

© ISTOCKPHOTO.COM/DAVID FRANKLIN

The exchange rate is the rate at which one country's currency can be traded for another country's currency. Under a flexible-rate system, the government allows the forces of supply and demand to determine the exchange rate. Changes in exchange rates occur daily or even hourly.

When exchange rates change, they affect not only the currency market but the product markets as well. For example, if Canadian consumers were to receive fewer and fewer British pounds and Japanese yen per Canadian dollar, the effect would be an increasing price for foreign imports, *ceteris paribus*. It would now take a greater number of dollars to buy a given number of yen or pounds, which Canadian consumers use to purchase those foreign products. It would, however, lower the cost of Canadian exports to foreigners. If, however, the dollar increased in value relative to other currencies, then the relative price of foreign goods would decrease, *ceteris paribus*. But foreigners would find that Canadian goods were more expensive in terms of their own currency prices, and, as a result, would import fewer Canadian products.

WHAT ARE THE ADVANTAGES OF A FLEXIBLE EXCHANGE RATE SYSTEM?

As mentioned earlier, the present system of flexible exchange rates was not planned. Indeed, most central bankers thought that a system where rates were not fixed would lead to chaos. What in fact has happened? Since the advent of flexible exchange rates, world trade has not only continued but expanded. Over a one-year period, the world economy adjusted to the shock of a fourfold increase in the price of its most important internationally traded commodity, oil. Although the OPEC oil cartel's price increase certainly had adverse economic effects, it did so without paralyzing the economy of any one nation.

The most important advantage of the flexible-rate system is that the recurrent crises that led to speculative rampages and major currency revaluations under the fixed Bretton Woods system have significantly diminished. Under the fixed-rate system, price changes in currencies came infrequently, but when they came, they were large: 20 percent or 30 percent changes overnight were fairly common. Today, price changes occur daily or even hourly, but each change is much smaller, with major changes in exchange rates typically occurring only over periods of months or years.

Fixed Exchange Rates Can Result in Currency Shortages

Perhaps the most significant problem with a fixed-rate system is that it can result in currency shortages, just as domestic price and wage controls lead to shortages. Suppose we had a fixed-rate system with the price of one euro set at $1, as shown in Exhibit 1. In this example, the original quantity of euros demanded and supplied is indicated by curves D_0 and S, so $1 is the equilibrium price. That is, at a price of $1, the quantity of euros demanded (by Canadian importers of European products and others wanting euros) equals the quantity supplied (by European importers of Canadian products and others).

Suppose that some event happens to increase Canadian demand for Dutch goods. For this example, let us assume that Royal Dutch Shell discovers new oil

section 15.4
Exhibit 1   **How Flexible Exchange Rates Work**

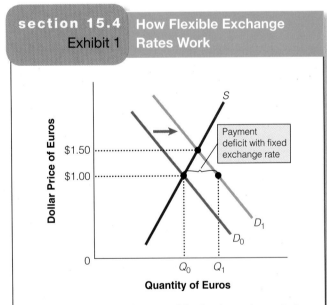

An increase in demand for euros shifts the demand curve to the right, from D_0 to D_1. Under a fixed-rate system, this increase in demand results in a shortage of euros at the equilibrium price of $1, because the quantity demanded at this price, Q_1, is greater than the quantity supplied, Q_0. If the exchange rate is flexible, however, no shortage develops. Instead, the increase in demand forces the exchange rate higher, to $1.50. At this higher exchange rate, the quantity of euros demanded doesn't increase as much, and the quantity of euros supplied increases as a result of the now relatively lower cost of imports from Canada.

reserves in the North Sea and thus has a new product to export. As Canadian consumers begin to demand Royal Dutch Shell oil, the demand for euros increases. That is, at any given dollar price of euros, Canadian consumers want more euros, shifting the demand curve to the right, to D_1. Under a fixed exchange rate system, the dollar price of euros must remain at $1, where the quantity of euros demanded, Q_1, now exceeds the quantity supplied, Q_0. The result is a shortage of euros—a shortage that must be corrected in some way. As a solution to the shortage, Canada may borrow euros from the Netherlands, or perhaps ship the Netherlands some of its reserves of gold. The ability to continually make up the shortage (deficit) in this manner, however, is limited, particularly if the deficit persists for a substantial period of time.

Flexible Rates Solve the Currency Shortage Problem

Under flexible exchange rates, a change in the supply or demand for euros does not pose a problem. Because rates are allowed to change, the rising Canadian demand for European goods (and thus for euros) would lead to a new equilibrium price for euros, say, at $1.50. At this higher price, European goods are more costly to Canadian buyers. Some of the increase in demand for European imports, then, is offset by a decrease in quantity demanded resulting from higher import prices. Similarly, the change in the exchange rate will make Canadian goods cheaper to Europeans, thus increasing Canadian exports and, with that, the quantity of euros supplied. For example, a $40 software program that cost Europeans 40 euros when the exchange rate was $1 per euro costs less than 27 euros when the exchange rate increases to $1.50 per euro ($40 divided by $1.50).

Flexible Rates Affect Macroeconomic Policies

With flexible exchange rates, the imbalance between debits and credits arising from shifts in currency demand and/or supply is accommodated by changes in currency prices, rather than through the special financial borrowings or reserve movements necessary with fixed rates. In a pure flexible exchange rate system, deficits and surpluses in the balance of payments tend to disappear automatically. The market mechanism itself is able to address world trade imbalances, dispensing with the need for bureaucrats attempting to achieve some administratively determined price. Moreover, the need to use restrictive monetary and/or fiscal policy to end such an imbalance while maintaining a fixed exchange rate is alleviated. Nations are thus able to feel less constraint in carrying out internal macroeconomic policies under flexible exchange rates. For these reasons, many economists welcomed the collapse of the Bretton Woods system and the failure to arrive at a new system of fixed or quasi-fixed exchange rates.

WHAT ARE THE DISADVANTAGES OF A FLEXIBLE EXCHANGE RATE SYSTEM?

Despite the fact that world trade has grown and dealing with balance-of-payments problems has become less difficult, flexible exchange rates have not been universally endorsed by everyone. Several disadvantages of this system have been cited.

Flexible Rates and World Trade

Traditionally, the major objection to flexible rates was that they introduce considerable uncertainty into international trade. For example, if you order some perfume from France with a commitment to pay 1000 euros in three months, you are not certain what the dollar price of euros, and therefore of the perfume, will be three months from now because the exchange rate is constantly fluctuating. Because people prefer certainty to uncertainty and are generally risk-averse, this uncertainty raises the costs of international transactions. As a result, flexible exchange rates can reduce the volume of trade, thus reducing the potential gains from international specialization.

Proponents of flexible rates have three answers to this argument. First, the empirical evidence shows that international trade has, in fact, grown in volume faster since the introduction of flexible rates. The exchange rate risk of trade has not had any major adverse effect. Second, it is possible to, in effect, buy insurance against the proposed adverse effect of currency fluctuations. Rather than buying currencies for immediate use in what is called the *spot market* for foreign currencies, one can contract today to buy foreign currencies in the future at a set exchange rate in the forward or future market. By using this market, a perfume importer can buy euros now for delivery to her in three months; in doing so, she can be certain of the dollar price she is paying for the perfume. Since floating exchange rates began, booming futures markets in foreign currencies have opened in Toronto, Chicago, New York, and other foreign financial centres. The third argument is that the alleged certainty of currency prices under the old Bretton Woods system was fictitious because the possibility existed that nations might, at their whim, drastically revalue their currencies to deal with their own fundamental balance-of-payments problems. Proponents of flexible rates, then, argue that they are therefore no less disruptive to trade than fixed rates.

Flexible Rates and Inflation

A second, more valid criticism of flexible exchange rates is that they can contribute to inflationary pressures. Under fixed rates, domestic monetary and fiscal authorities have an incentive to constrain their domestic prices because lower domestic prices increase the attractiveness of exported goods. This discipline is not present to the same extent with flexible rates. The consequence of a sharp monetary or fiscal expansion under flexible rates would be a decline in the value of one's currency relative to those of other countries.

Advocates of flexible rates would argue that inflation need not occur under flexible rates. Flexible rates do not cause inflation; rather, it is caused by the expansionary macroeconomic policies of governments and central banks. Actually, flexible rates give government decision makers greater freedom of action than do fixed rates; whether decision makers act responsibly is determined not by exchange rates but by domestic policies.

SECTION CHECK

- Today, rates are free to fluctuate based on market transactions, but governments occasionally intervene to increase or depress the price of their currencies.
- Changes in exchange rates occur more often under a flexible-rate system, but the changes are much smaller than the large overnight revaluations of currencies that occurred under the fixed-rate system. Under a fixed-rate system, the supply and demand for currencies shift, but currency prices are not allowed to shift to the new equilibrium leading to surpluses and shortages of currencies.
- The main arguments presented against flexible exchange rates are that international trade levels will be diminished due to uncertainty of future currency prices and that the flexible rates would lead to inflation. Proponents of flexible exchange rates have strong counterarguments to those views.

For Your Review

Section 15.1

1. Indicate whether each of the following represents a credit or debit on the Canadian current account.

   a. A Canadian imports a BMW from Germany.

   b. A Japanese company purchases software from a Canadian company.

   c. Canada gives $100 million in financial aid to Afghanistan.

   d. A Canadian company sells lumber to the United Kingdom.

2. Indicate whether each of the following represents a credit or debit on the Canadian capital account.

   a. A French bank purchases $100 000 worth of Canadian government bonds.

   b. Research in Motion (RIM) purchases U.S. telecommunications company.

   c. A Canadian resident buys company shares in the Japanese stock market.

   d. A Japanese company purchases a shopping mall in Vancouver.

3. How is each of the following events likely to affect the Canadian merchandise trade balance?

   a. The European price level increases relative to the Canadian price level.

   b. The Canadian dollar appreciates in value relative to the currencies of its trading partners.

   c. The Canadian government offers subsidies to firms that export goods.

   d. The Canadian government imposes tariffs on imported goods.

   e. The United States experiences a severe recession.

4. How is each of the following classified, as a debit or as a credit, in the Canadian balance-of-payments accounts?

	Credit	**Debit**
a. Canadians buy autos from Japan.	_____	_____
b. Canadian tourists travel to Japan.	_____	_____
c. Japanese consumers buy rice grown in Canada.	_____	_____
d. Canada gives foreign aid to Rwanda.	_____	_____
e. RIM, a Canadian company, earns profits in France.	_____	_____
f. Royal Dutch Shell earns profits from its Canadian operations.	_____	_____
g. RIM builds a new plant in Vietnam.	_____	_____
h. Japanese investors purchase Canadian government bonds.	_____	_____

Section 15.2

5. Assume that a product sells for $100 in Canada.

    a. If the exchange rate between British pounds and Canadian dollars is $2 per pound, what would be the price of the product in the United Kingdom?

    b. If the exchange rate between Mexican pesos and Canadian dollars is 8 pesos per dollar, what would be the price of the product in Mexico?

    c. In which direction would the price of the $100 Canadian product change in a foreign country if Canadians' tastes for foreign products increased?

    d. In which direction would the price of the $100 Canadian product change in a foreign country if incomes in the foreign country fell?

    e. In which direction would the price of the $100 Canadian product change in a foreign country if interest rates in Canada fell relative to interest rates in other countries?

6. Why is a strong Canadian dollar a mixed blessing?

Section 15.3

7. How is each of the following events likely to affect the value of the Canadian dollar relative to the euro?

    a. Interest rates in the European Union increase relative to those in Canada.

    b. The European Union price level rises relative to the Canadian price level.

    c. The Bank of Canada intervenes by buying Canadian dollars on the foreign exchange market.

    d. The price level in Canada rises relative to the price level in Europe.

8. What happens to the supply curve for Canadian dollars in the foreign exchange market under the following conditions?

    a. Canadians want to buy more Japanese consumer electronics.

    b. A Canadian mutual fund wants to buy shares of Microsoft.

9. How would each of the following affect the supply of euros, the demand for euros, and the dollar price of euros?

Change	Supply of Euros	Demand for Euros	Dollar Price of Euros
Reduced Canadian tastes for European goods			
Increased incomes in Canada			
Increased Canadian interest rates			
Decreased inflation in Europe			
Reduced Canadian tariffs on imports			
Increased European tastes for Canadian goods			

10. How would each of the following events impact the foreign exchange market?

    a. Canadian travel to Europe increases.

    b. Japanese investors purchase Canadian company shares.

    c. Canadian interest rates abruptly increase relative to world interest rates.

    d. Other countries become less politically and economically stable relative to Canada.

Section 15.4

11. What happens to the supply curve for dollars in the currency market under the following conditions?

    a. Canadians want to buy more Japanese consumer electronics.

    b. Canada wants to prop up the value of the yen.

12. If the demand for a domestic currency decreases in a country using a fixed exchange rate system, what must the central bank do to keep the currency value steady?

CourseMate

Access an interactive eBook and chapter-specific interactive learning tools, including flashcards, quizzes, a glossary, and more in CourseMate, accessed through **www.sextonmacro3ce.nelson.com**

Answers to Odd-Numbered Problems

CHAPTER 1

1. The definition of *economics* must recognize the central parts of the economist's point of view: Resources are scarce, scarcity forces us to make choices, and the cost of any choice is the cost of the lost opportunity with the highest value.

3. **a.** Both normative and positive statements. The first statement (a positive statement) expresses a fact or a testable theory that a higher income tax rate would generate increased tax revenues. The second statement (a normative statement) expresses opinion regarding how any additional tax revenues should be used.
   b. Normative statements. Both statements are expressions of opinion, the first regarding the relative value of studying physics as opposed to sociology, and the second regarding the value of studying either physics or sociology.
   c. Positive statements. Both statements are expressions of facts or testable theories regarding the relationship between the price of wheat and how much wheat will be purchased and produced.
   d. Both normative and positive statements. The first statement (positive) expresses a fact or testable theory regarding the relationship between the price of butter and how much will be purchased. The second statement (normative) is an expression of opinion about the social value of buying butter.
   e. Positive statements. Both statements are expressions of fact or testable theory regarding demographic change.

5. The statement illustrates the fallacy of composition—it assumes that what is true for one person must be true for all others.

7. Being poor means that you have access to few resources, which limits the goods and services you consume. Scarcity means you don't have enough resources to do everything you want to do, so you have to make choices. Everyone experiences scarcity, because we can always think of more things that we want than we can produce with our resources.

9. Scarce goods are those that people pay for in either time or money or, in other words, have an opportunity cost. Garbage and dirty air in the city are not scarce goods since we either pay to get rid of them or pay with the consequences of their presence. Similarly, salt water is not a scarce good—although it is in limited supply; there is no price you need to pay to obtain some (assuming you are on the shore). Clothes, clean air, and public libraries are scarce goods because their production requires the use of scarce resources that could be used for the production of other goods.

11. No. First of all, Pizza Pizza uses scarce resources to produce the pizza slices, so a slice of pizza is not "free" to Pizza Pizza. Secondly, if people value their time at all, ten minutes standing in line to get the slice carries an opportunity cost equal to the value to those people of whatever else they could have done with the ten minutes.

13. **a.** $50; $25.
   b. 3; 5. Mark would go as long as his marginal benefit was greater than the admission price.
   c. Yes; 6. Mark would buy the pass because his total benefits would exceed his total cost. Once he has the pass, the marginal cost of attending one more day becomes zero, so he will go as long as his marginal benefits exceed zero.

15. The marginal benefits of jaywalking are the time savings and convenience of crossing the street where you want. The marginal costs are the additional risk of being hit by a car and the risk of being fined for jaywalking.
   a. Increases cost by increasing the risk of being hit by a car.
   b. Lowers cost by lowering the risk of being hit by a car and the risk of being fined.
   c. Increases the benefit because of the higher value of time savings.
   d. Increases cost because of a higher risk of receiving a fine.
   e. The time and convenience benefits are smaller.

17. Singapore's tough drug-trafficking penalty would clearly impact the cost–benefit ratios of would-be smugglers. Lighter sentences would probably result in more drug smuggling because the overall cost of breaking the law would be reduced.

19. The opportunity cost of growing soybeans is the lost value because Fran can't grow corn worth $60. The opportunity cost of growing corn on her land is the lost opportunity to grow and sell soybeans, which equals $75. Fran should specialize in soybeans, which is the crop with the lowest opportunity cost. For each acre of corn Fran converts to soybeans, she will gain $15.

21. If the country or region with the lower opportunity cost produces the good, the opportunity cost of consuming that good is minimized. Trade allows people, countries, and regions to specialize in producing those goods in which they have the lowest opportunity cost, so reducing trade restrictions will encourage specialization, thereby increasing efficiency.

23. **a.** Price of Jack Russell Terriers rises;   **b.** price of housing in Tampa rises;   **c.** price of coffee rises;   **d.** price of wheat rises;   **e.** wages of Canadian doctors fall;   **f.** price of gasoline rises.

CHAPTER 2

1. The three basic economic questions are: What is to be produced? How are these goods to be produced? For whom are the goods produced? Scarcity requires that these questions be addressed in some way by every economy. Market economies answer these questions in a decentralized way through the interaction of millions of buyers and sellers. In command economies, decisions are made largely through planning boards. The manner in which an economic system answers these questions helps determine the allocation of limited resources.

3. No, Karl is wrong. Markets provide important signals, and the signal being sent in this situation is that Adam should look for some other means of support—something that society values. Remember the function of consumer sovereignty in the marketplace. Clearly, consumers were not voting for Adam's art.

5. **a.** Product market;   **b.** factor market;   **c.** product market;   **d.** factor market. Furniture is a good purchased in the product market from firms. Labour is a resource that households sell to firms in the factor market. Restaurant food is a good purchased by consumers in the product market. Finally, Billy's entrepreneurial resource is paid a profit, which is the amount left over after all his other costs have been paid. This takes place in the factor market.

7. **a.** A production possibilities curve, which applies to a specific period of time, is drawn assuming that resources and the level of technology are held constant.
   b. The opportunity cost of another gun, when moving from point B to point C, is 4 units of butter. The opportunity cost of another gun, when moving from point D to point E, is 8 units of butter.
   c. These combinations are exhibiting increasing opportunity cost—the more guns you have, the higher the opportunity cost of obtaining additional guns.

9. **a.** Double-digit unemployment would not affect the production possibilities curve itself. An economy experiencing double-digit unemployment would be operating at a point inside the production possibilities curve.
   b. The production possibilities curve shifts outward whenever the economy experiences economic growth.
   c. Assuming resources are being used efficiently, the economy moves from one point along the production possibilities curve to another in the direction of more food production (requiring a sacrifice of shelter).
   d. Assuming resources are being used efficiently, the economy moves from one point along the production possibilities curve to another in the direction of more shelter (requiring a sacrifice of food).

11. Investment in capital goods increases the future productive potential of an economy. Economy A will grow more rapidly, shifting the production possibilities curve outward to a greater extent over time, if it invests in a higher proportion of capital goods than does Economy B.

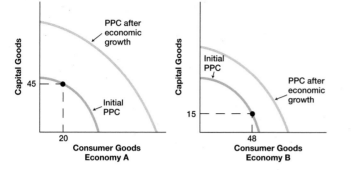
Economy A / Economy B

13. The politician would be able to keep her promise if the economy was operating inside the production possibilities curve. It would then be possible to have more of both schools and prisons by better utilizing available resources. Alternatively, an advance in technology or an increase in available resources (perhaps due to immigration) would also make it possible to have more of both goods by shifting the production possibilities curve in an outward direction.

CHAPTER 3

1. The definition of a market focuses on the process of exchange, not on the physical location where the exchange takes place. Therefore, even though online buyers and sellers are never actually in the same place, their behaviour still constitutes a market transaction due to the fact that goods and services are being exchanged.

3. a.

P	Q_D
5	4
4	8
3	12
2	16
1	20

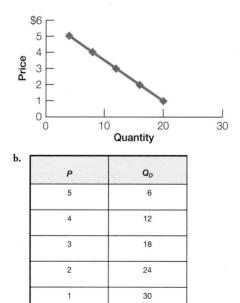

b.

P	Q_D
5	6
4	12
3	18
2	24
1	30

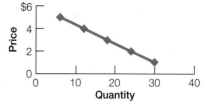

c.

P	Q_D
5	5
4	10
3	15
2	20
1	25

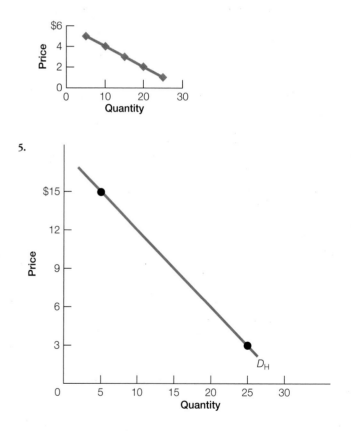

5.

7. a. Demand decreases (determinant: price of substitute falls); **b.** demand decreases (determinant: price of complement rises); **c.** demand increases (determinant variable: taste increase); **d.** demand increases (determinant: number of consumers increases).

9. a. Point B represents an increase in quantity demanded; **b.** point E represents an increase in demand; **c.** point F represents a decrease in demand; **d.** point C represents a decrease in quantity demanded.

11. a. Hamburger and ketchup are complements. An increase in the price of hamburger will decrease the demand for ketchup.

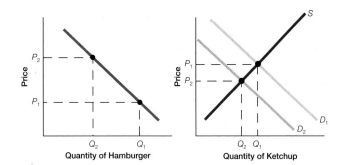

b. Coca-Cola and Pepsi are substitutes. An increase in the price of Coca-Cola will increase the demand for Pepsi.

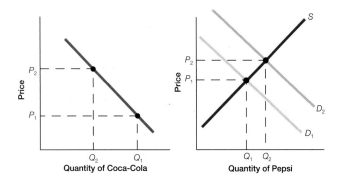

c. Cameras and film are complements. An increase in the price of a camera will decrease the demand for film.

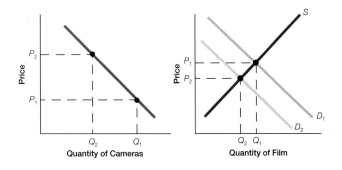

d. Golf clubs and golf balls are complements. An increase in the price of golf clubs will decrease the demand for golf balls, *ceteris paribus.*

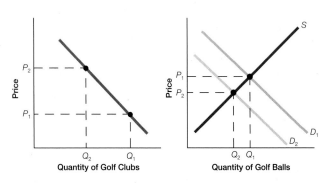

e. Assuming that skateboards and razor scooters are substitutes, an increase in the price of skateboards will increase the demand for razor scooters.

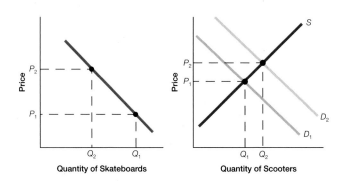

13. a. The shift from D_0 to D_1 is called an *increase in demand.*
b. The movement from (b) to (a) is called a *decrease in the quantity demanded.*
c. The movement from (a) to (b) is called an *increase in the quantity demanded.*
d. The shift from D_1 to D_0 is called a *decrease in demand.*
15. The market price of wheat would have to rise for Felix to have the incentive to produce from the second field. Because costs are higher in the second field, Felix must receive a higher price to compensate him for his higher costs.

17.

Quantity Supplied (barrels per month)				
Price ($ per barrel)	Rolling Rock	Armadillo	Pecos Petroleum	Market
$5	10 000	8 000	2 000	20 000
10	15 000	10 000	5 000	30 000
15	20 000	12 000	8 000	40 000
20	25 000	14 000	11 000	50 000
25	30 000	16 000	14 000	60 000

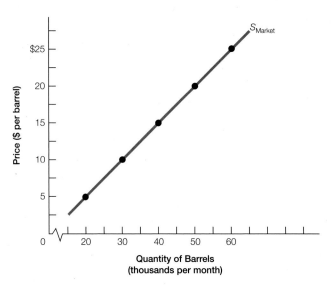

19. a. The shift from S_0 to S_1 is called an *increase in supply;*   **b.** the movement from (a) to (b) is called an *increase in the quantity supplied;*   **c.** the movement from (b) to (a) is called a *decrease in the quantity supplied;*   **d.** the shift from S_1 to S_0 is called a *decrease in supply.*

21. a. Supply decreases (determinant: input prices increase);   **b.** supply decreases (determinant: taxes increase);   **c.** supply increases (determinant: technology advances);   **d.** supply increases (determinant: an increase in the number of suppliers).

23. a. Point B represents an increase in quantity supplied;   **b.** point C represents an increase in supply;   **c.** point D represents a decrease in quantity supplied;   **d.** point E represents a decrease in supply.

CHAPTER 4

1. When a price is above the equilibrium price, the quantity of a good or service willingly supplied by sellers exceeds the quantity willingly demanded by buyers. If sellers want to sell a greater quantity of goods or services, it is necessary to reduce the price (or otherwise improve the terms of sale, such as with free delivery or lower interest rate financing) in order to induce buyers to make additional purchases. Market forces thus exert a downward pressure on price in the direction of equilibrium price. A surplus is eliminated once price falls to the equilibrium price.

If a price is below the equilibrium price, then the quantity of a good or service willingly demanded by buyers exceeds the quantity willingly supplied by sellers. In order to induce sellers to provide a greater quantity to the marketplace, it is necessary for buyers to offer a higher price for the good or service. Market forces exert upward pressure on price in the direction of the equilibrium. A shortage is eliminated once price increases to the equilibrium price.

3. a.

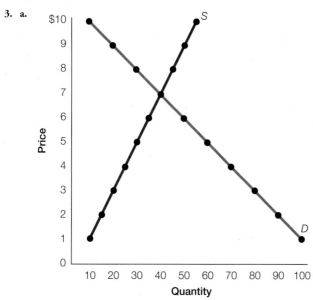

b. $7; 40 units traded.
c. Surplus. At $9, above the equilibrium price, there will be a surplus of 30 units of Z [the quantity supplied at $9 (50) minus the quantity demanded at $9 (20)].
d. Shortage. At $3, below the equilibrium price, there will be a shortage of 60 units of Z [the quantity demanded at $3 (80) minus the quantity supplied at $3 (20)].
e. $8, with 45 units traded (at the new supply and demand intersection).
f. $6, with 50 units traded (at the new supply and demand intersection).

5. The deputy parks commissioner may be correct. Fewer young people may want to be lifeguards now than in the past. An economist, however, knows that shortages are caused by prices that are below equilibrium. Since the number of lifeguards demanded in Vancouver exceeds the supply, it would seem that wages are too low. An economist would advise the City to raise lifeguards' wages in order to eliminate the shortage.

7. a.

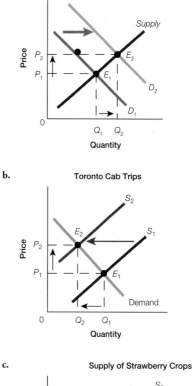

b.

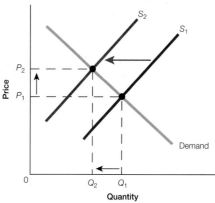

c.

Supply of Strawberry Crops

9. Even though the tuition "price" is the same in both cases, student demand for 10 A.M. classes is typically greater than for 8 A.M. classes. College students often prefer to sleep in later than punctual attendance at an 8 A.M. class would allow. A shortage of 10 A.M. class space relative to demand is the likely result. There may be a surplus of class spaces in 8 A.M. courses if the demand for early morning classes is sufficiently low.

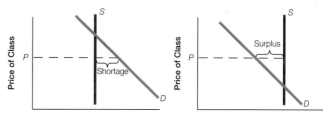

11. a. To get to point A would require a decrease in supply; to get to point B would require a decrease in supply and an increase in demand; to get to point C would require an increase in demand; to get to point D would require a decrease in supply and a decrease in demand; point E is the current equilibrium; to get to point F would require an increase in supply and an increase in demand; to get to point G would require a decrease in demand; to get to point H would require an increase in supply and a decrease in demand; to get to point I would require an increase in supply.

b. F, because it is an increase in supply and an increase in demand.

c. Indeterminate, because one of the changes decreases supply and the other increases supply, we don't know what the net effect is on supply. If the effects were of the exact same magnitude, the result would be E; if the increase in supply was greater than the decrease in supply, the answer would be I; if the decrease in supply was greater than the increase in supply, the answer would be A.

d. C; A; A.

e. G; I; G.

13.

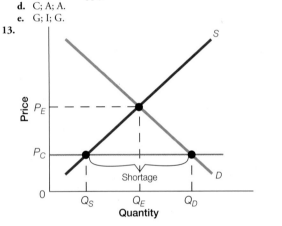

a. If the price ceiling is raised, the quantity supplied increases, the quantity demanded decreases, and the shortage is reduced; if the price ceiling is lowered, the quantity supplied decreases, the quantity demanded increases, and the shortage is increased.

b. The quantity supplied does not change, the quantity demanded increases, and the shortage is increased.

c. The quantity supplied increases, the quantity demanded does not change, and the shortage is decreased.

15. A price floor set above the equilibrium price for dairy products would result in a surplus. A price floor set below the equilibrium price would have no impact on the price or quantity of dairy products traded. (A price floor is a minimum allowed price, not a mandated market price.)

CHAPTER 5

1. Answers will vary based on information obtained at the time.

3. a. 80 percent (160 million/200 million)

b. 70 percent (140 million/200 million)

c. The labour force participation rate would become 55 percent (110 million/200 million).

d. Nothing; neither the adult population nor the size of the labour force would change.

5. a. Sam is a discouraged worker who is not actively seeking work and is therefore not considered to be unemployed.

b. The 12-year-old is under 15 years of age and therefore is not considered to be part of the labour force.

c. The factory worker is unemployed as long as she is looking for work.

d. The receptionist is considered to be employed, even though she would like to work more hours each week.

e. The high-school graduate is not actively seeking work and therefore is not considered to be unemployed.

7. Structural unemployment: b
Frictional unemployment: c, d
Cyclical unemployment: a

9. a. The natural rate of unemployment equals the sum of frictional and structural unemployment; cyclical unemployment is zero.

b. i. Unemployment increases; the natural rate of unemployment is unchanged.

ii. Both unemployment and the natural rate of unemployment would increase.

iii. Unemployment is unchanged, and the natural rate of unemployment decreases.

iv. Unemployment decreases, and the natural rate of unemployment increases.

v. Both unemployment and the natural rate of unemployment are unchanged.

11. If union bargaining raises the union wage above the equilibrium level, the quantity of unionized labour demanded will decrease and the quantity of unionized labour supplied will increase. Some union workers will be unemployed as a result and will either seek nonunion work or wait to be rehired in the union sector. Union workers who are still employed are better off due to their higher earnings.

13. a. Retirees on fixed incomes: Hurt
Workers: Hurt (unless wages kept up with inflation)
Debtors: Helped
Creditors: Hurt
Shoe-leather costs: Increased
Menu costs: Increased

b. Workers, debtors, and creditors would be unaffected. If retirees stayed on their fixed incomes, they would be hurt. Shoe-leather costs would be unaffected but menu costs would rise.

15. If the slowing of the rate of inflation is unexpected, then there is a redistribution of income from borrowers to lenders (assuming the borrowers do not default on their loans as a result). If the slowing of the rate of inflation is fully anticipated at the time the loan is taken out, then there is no redistribution of income associated with the student loan. The interest rate of a loan will be based on the anticipated inflation rate. If the parties had been aware that inflation would slow, there would have been a lower interest rate.

17. Price index 2008 = $16/$16 × 100 = 100
Price index 2009 = $17.28/$16 × 100 = 108
Price index 2010 = $20/$16 × 100 = 125

Inflation rate 2008–2009 = (108 − 100)/100 = 8 percent
Inflation rate 2008–2010 = (125 − 100)/100 = 25 percent
Inflation rate 2009–2010 = (125 − 108)/108 = 15.7 percent

19. Expansion phase

CHAPTER 6

1. The following are included in Canadian GDP calculations:

a. cleaning services performed by a cleaning company

d. prescription drugs manufactured in Canada and sold at a local pharmacy

g. toxic waste cleanup performed by a local company

h. car parts manufactured in Canada for assembly of a car in Mexico

3. Gross domestic product measures the total value of production, which can be determined by either the expenditure or income approach. Both approaches will deliver an equivalent result since every buyer must have a seller. The use of the expenditure approach to measure total production is based on the understanding that the total value of what is bought (the expenditure of the buyer) will be equal to the total value of what has been produced (considering only final goods and services). And since everything that is bought must be purchased (thereby creating income for the seller), the income approach is based on the understanding that the total value of factor payments generated from production will be equal to the total value of what has been produced.

5. a. Ministry of Transportation snow-clearing services: consumption

b. automobiles exported to Europe: exports

c. a refrigerator: consumption (consumer durables)

d. a newly constructed four-bedroom house: investment

e. a restaurant meal: consumption

f. additions to inventory at a furniture store: investment

g. purchases of new computers by Statistics Canada: government spending

h. a new steel mill: investment

7.

Consumption	$5400
Consumption of durable goods	1200
Consumption of nondurable goods	1800
Consumption of services	2400
Investment	1400
Fixed investment	800
Inventory investment	600

Government expenditures on goods and services	$1600
Government transfer payments	500
Exports	500
Imports	650
Net exports	−150
GDP	$8250

9. Output creates income of equal value.
11. One cannot say that production has increased in Nowhereland from 2010 to 2011 by just looking at nominal GDP. Production may have increased. However, nominal GDP could increase due to inflation while production remains unchanged (as would be the case with a 10 percent inflation rate) or even decreases (with a greater than 10 percent inflation rate).
13.

Year	GDP Deflator	Nominal GDP (in billions)	Real GDP (in billions)
2007	90.9	$ 700	$ 770
2008	100.0	800	800
2009	125.0	1000	800
2010	140.0	1400	1000
2011	150.0	1800	1200

15. a. Next year's real GDP can exceed next year's nominal GDP, but only if the price level falls. If the price level rises, next year's nominal GDP will exceed next year's real GDP.
 b. Yes. It will happen when the population growth rate exceeds the growth rate of real GDP.
 c. Since only what is produced can be consumed, if we measured all sources of output accurately, real per capita consumption possibilities could expand only when real per capita GDP grows. However, if, say, the underground (therefore, unmeasured) economy grew fast enough, real per capita consumption possibilities could increase despite measured decreases in real per capita GDP.
 d. Leisure is valuable, but its value is not counted in GDP. So changing amounts of leisure over time will not be incorporated into GDP measures. Further, while a decrease in leisure (an increase in market work) would increase measured GDP, people would be better off only if their real after-tax wages were higher than the value of the leisure they gave up, which need not always be the case (especially when workers are fooled by inflation).

CHAPTER 7

1. a.
0.5 percent	140	years
1.0 percent	70	years
1.4 percent	50	years
2.0 percent	35	years
2.8 percent	25	years
3.5 percent	20	years
7.0 percent	10	years

 b.
1.4 percent	$200 billion
2.8 percent	$400 billion
7.0 percent	$3200 billion

3. a. Using the rule of 70, Country A's real per capita GDP would double every 50 years (70/1.4) and Country B's real per capita GDP would double every 25 years (70/2.8). In the course of 100 years, Country B's real per capita GDP would double 4 times, while Country A's would double only 2 times. If they started at the same size, Country B's real per capita GDP would be 4 times that of A after that period of time, but since B started out one-fourth as large as A, their real per capita GDP would end up the same size in 100 years.
 b. At 2.8 percent annual growth, Country A's real per capita GDP would double every 25 years, or 4 times in a century. At 3.5 percent annual

growth, Country B's real per capita GDP would double every 20 years, or 5 times in a century. As a result, Country B's real per capita GDP would be twice that of Country A after a century.
5. d. The annual percentage change in real GDP per capita best measures economic growth.
7. It depends. Both capital investment and human capital investment increase productivity, so the answer depends on which is more productive in a given case. If education (human capital investment) is more productive, shifting from capital investment to human capital investment would increase the growth rate of real per capita GDP. If education (human capital investment) is less productive, shifting from capital investment to human capital investment would decrease the growth rate of real per capita GDP.
9. Each of the following will likely improve the productivity of labour:
 a. on-the-job experience
 b. college education
 d. improvements in management of resources
11. When patent and copyright laws are only weakly enforced, it reduces the incentive of individuals and firms to innovate by reducing the reward for innovation. Economic growth, which is enhanced by technological change and innovation, is likely to suffer as a result.
13. a. Real GDP will grow while real GDP per capita falls whenever the population growth rate exceeds the growth rate of real GDP.
 b. Country A has a higher real per capita GDP growth rate of 2 percent (4 percent real GDP growth minus 2 percent population growth). Country B's real per capita GDP growth rate is 1 percent (6 percent real GDP growth minus 5 percent population growth).

CHAPTER 8

1. a. 0.90
 b. 0.80
 c. 0.60
 d. $300 000; 0.75
 e. $120 000; 1.2
3. a. The quantity of investment demanded increases but the investment demand curve does not shift.
 b. The investment demand curve shifts to the left.
 c. The investment demand curve shifts to the right.
 d. The quantity of saving supplied increases but the saving supply curve does not shift.
 e. The saving supply curve shifts to the right.
5. An increase in current disposable income would increase the saving supply curve, shifting it to the right. A decrease in new technologies creating investment opportunities would shift the investment demand curve to the left, moving the equilibrium down along the saving supply curve but not shifting it.
7. a. decrease; decrease; decrease
 b. decrease; decrease; increase; increase
 c. decrease; decrease
9. a. increase
 b. indeterminate
 c. decrease
 d. increase
 e. indeterminate
 f. no change (change in quantity of RGDP demanded)
 g. no change (change in quantity of RGDP demanded)
11. Of the choices available, only option b, an increase in taxes, both decreases consumption and shifts the aggregate demand curve to the left.
13. a. Exports; aggregate demand will shift to the right.
 b. Investment and consumption; aggregate demand will shift to the right.
 c. Consumption and investment; aggregate demand will shift to the right.
 d. Investment; aggregate demand will shift to the right.
 e. Consumption; aggregate demand will shift to the left.

CHAPTER 9

1. This is an example of the misperception effect. The misperception effect implies an upward-sloping short-run aggregate supply curve.

3.

Change	Short-Run Aggregate Supply	Long-Run Aggregate Supply
An increase in aggregate demand	No change	No change
A decrease in aggregate demand	No change	No change
An increase in the stock of capital	Increase (right shift)	Increase (right shift)
A reduction in the size of the labour force	Decrease (left shift)	Decrease (left shift)
An increase in input prices (that does not reflect permanent changes in their supplies)	Decrease (left shift)	No change
A decrease in input prices (that does reflect permanent changes in their supplies)	Increase (right shift)	Increase (right shift)
An increase in usable natural resources	Increase (right shift)	Increase (right shift)
A temporary adverse supply shock	Decrease (left shift)	No change
Increases in the cost of government regulations	Decrease (left shift)	Decrease (left shift)

5. a. Shift *LRAS* to the right
  b. Shift *LRAS* to the right
  c. No effect on *LRAS* unless it reflects permanent changes in the supply of labour
  d. Shift *LRAS* to the left

7. a.

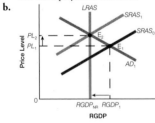

The price level increases, real output increases, employment increases, and unemployment decreases.

  b.

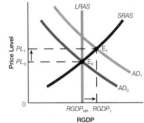

The price level ends up higher, real output ends up back where it began at potential output, employment ends up back where it began at full employment, and unemployment ends up back where it began at the natural rate of unemployment.

9. a.

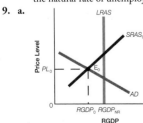

  b.

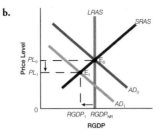

In the long run, the price level will end up lower than before, but real output and unemployment will return to their long-run equilibrium levels.

11. Cost-push inflation occurs when the short-run aggregate supply curve shifts to the left, pushing up prices. Demand-pull inflation occurs when the aggregate demand curve shifts to the right, pulling up prices. Examples will vary. Cost-push inflation may be caused by an increase in input prices, such as the price of crude oil or wages. Demand-pull inflation may be caused by an increase in consumer confidence or a decrease in taxes.

13. An increase in aggregate demand will have the following impact: output increases; unemployment decreases; the price level increases. A decrease in short-run aggregate supply will have the following impact: output decreases; unemployment increases; the price level increases.

CHAPTER 10

1. a. An increase in government spending would decrease a budget surplus.
  b. An increase in government spending would increase aggregate demand.
  c. When the threat of a recession is developing.

3. a. An increase in taxes would decrease a budget deficit.
  b. An increase in taxes would decrease aggregate demand.
  c. When the threat of an unsustainable, inflationary boom is likely.

5. Suppose the government places an additional $1 per package tax on cigarettes. For individuals who have an income of $50, this amounts to 2 percent of their income, however, for individuals who have an income of $100, the tax amounts to only 1 percent. Uniform taxes, such as excise taxes on cigarettes, have a greater impact on lower-income individuals.

7. a. $MPC = 0.25$, multiplier value is 1.33, the tax multiplier value is 0.33
  b. $MPC = 0.5$ multiplier value is 2, the tax multiplier value is 1
  c. $MPC = 0.75$ multiplier value is 4, the tax multiplier value is 3

9. The multiplier, which is one divided by one minus the *MPC*, could also be written as one divided by the *MPS*, because the *MPS* is equal to one minus the *MPC*.

11. a. GDP will increase.
  b. GDP will decrease.
  c. GDP will increase.
  d. GDP will decrease.

13.

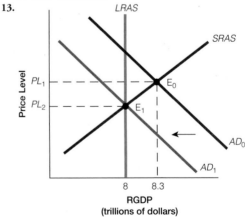

An economy can operate above the full employment level of output temporarily by using resources intensively. For example, factories may run three shifts per day, instead of two. Employees may be asked to work more hours each week. Firms may attempt to lure workers away from other firms by offering higher wages. As firms compete for scarce resources to maintain high levels of production, there will be upward pressure on input prices. When that occurs, the short-run aggregate supply curve will shift to the left, moving the economy back toward full employment and the economy will experience inflation. The government may be able to prevent inflation from occurring by decreasing government spending by $25 billion, eliminating the expansionary gap.

15. a. At point E_3.
  b. The economy would end up at a long-run equilibrium at point E_2.
  c. The economy would end up at a long-run equilibrium at point E_0.
  d. At point E_1.
  e. The economy would end up in long-run equilibrium at E_0.
  f. The economy would end up in long-run equilibrium at E_2.

17. Discretionary fiscal policy requires new policies to be made, so it is subject to time lags in deciding what the problem is and what to do about it, and in implementing a solution. Since automatic stabilizers do not require new policy to be adopted, those lags do not handicap it in the same way.

19. Government spending may crowd out private investment by increasing interest rates. Firms faced with higher interest payments on their borrowings may scale back plans to build new factories, introduce new products, etc. To the extent that the increase in government spending adds less to the value of the nation's capital stock than the private investment that is crowded out would have, long-term economic growth may be negatively impacted.

21. In the short run, deficit reduction is contradictory fiscal policy; either tax increases and/or a reduction in government purchases will shift the aggregate demand curve to the left, and a lower price level and lower RGDP will result.

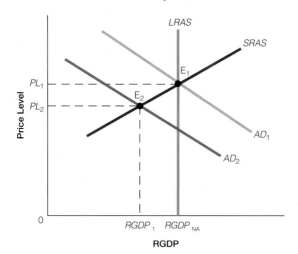

CHAPTER 11

1. An economics professor may find it difficult to locate a trading partner willing to listen to economics lectures or receive economic advice in exchange for a new car. There may be significant search costs involved in locating such a trading partner. The professor might have to provide lectures in exchange for goods that are not desired, hoping that ultimately, after perhaps a series of trades, to be able to obtain a new car.

3. a. savings deposit
  b. six-month Treasury bill
  c. demand deposit
  d. savings account

5.

Change	M2	M2+
An increase in currency in circulation	Increase	Increase
A decrease in demand deposits	Decrease	Decrease
An increase in savings deposits	Increase	Increases
A transfer of demand deposit balances from credit unions to chartered banks	Increase	No change

7. Money is both an asset and a liability. It is an asset to those who possess it, but it is a liability of the banking system.

9. a.

10 percent desired reserve ratio

Bank Balance Sheet			
Assets		**Liabilities**	
Desired reserves	$10 000	Demand deposits	$100 000
Excess reserves	$90 000		

20 percent desired reserve ratio

Bank Balance Sheet			
Assets		**Liabilities**	
Desired reserves	$20 000	Demand deposits	$100 000
Excess reserves	$80 000		

25 percent desired reserve ratio

Bank Balance Sheet			
Assets		**Liabilities**	
Desired reserves	$25 000	Demand deposits	$100 000
Excess reserves	$75 000		

50 percent desired reserve ratio

Bank Balance Sheet			
Assets		**Liabilities**	
Desired reserves	$50 000	Demand deposits	$100 000
Excess reserves	$50 000		

b.

10 percent desired reserve ratio

Bank Balance Sheet			
Assets		**Liabilities**	
Desired reserves	$10 000	Demand deposits	$100 000
Loans	$90 000		

20 percent desired reserve ratio

Bank Balance Sheet			
Assets		**Liabilities**	
Desired reserves	$20 000	Demand deposits	$100 000
Loans	$80 000		

25 percent desired reserve ratio

Bank Balance Sheet			
Assets		**Liabilities**	
Desired reserves	$25 000	Demand deposits	$100 000
Loans	$75 000		

50 percent desired reserve ratio

Bank Balance Sheet			
Assets		**Liabilities**	
Desired reserves	$50 000	Demand deposits	$100 000
Excess reserves	$50 000		

    c.   10 percent $1 000 000
           20 percent   500 000
           25 percent   400 000
           50 percent   200 000

11. a. 10
    b. 50
    c. 5
    d. 12.5

13. The value of the money multiplier would equal 1. Banks would not be able to create money in such a case because they would be unable to issue loans using customer deposits, and thereby generate new demand deposit accounts.

15. Excess reserves equal $75 000. The potential expansion in demand deposits from loaning out these excess reserves equals $500 000 ($75 000 × 1/0.15).

15 percent desired reserve ratio

Bank Balance Sheet (revised)			
Assets		**Liabilities**	
Reserves	$ 300 000	Demand deposits	$1 500 000
Loans	1 200 000	Demand deposits (new)	500 000
Loans (new)	500 000	**Total Liabilities**	**$2 000 000**
Buildings	500 000	**Capital**	**500 000**
Total Assets	**$2 500 000**	**Total Liabilities and Capital**	**$2 500 000**

CHAPTER 12

1. The following are functions of the Bank of Canada:
    b. supervise banks
    d. issue currency
    e. regulate the money supply
    f. loan reserves to banks
    g. act as the bank for the Canadian government

3.

Nonbank Public			
Assets		**Liabilities**	
Securities	–$10 million		
Demand deposits	+$10 million		

Banking System				Bank of Canada			
Assets		**Liabilities**		**Assets**		**Liabilities**	
Reserves	+$10 million	Demand deposits	+$10 million	Securities	+$10 million	Reserves of banking system	+$10 million

5 percent desired reserve ratio

Banking System			
Assets		**Liabilities**	
Reserves	$ 500 000	Demand deposits	$10 million
Excess reserves	$9 500 000		

Potential money creation
(bank system lending)   = $190 million ($9.5 million × 1/0.05)
Initial demand deposit   = $ 10 million

Total increase in money supply = $200 million

25 percent desired reserve ratio

Banking System			
Assets		**Liabilities**	
Reserves	$2 500 000	Demand deposits	$10 million
Excess reserves	$7 500 000		

Potential money creation
(bank system lending)   = $30 million ($7.5 million × 1/0.25)
Initial demand deposit   = $10 million

Total increase in money supply = $40 million

5. The potential change in the money supply is –$100 000 (–$10 000 × 1/0.10).

7. If the bank increases the desired reserve ratio to 12.5 percent, there would be insufficient reserves for the $1 000 000 in deposits by an amount of $25 000. The $100 000 in reserves would support only $800 000 in deposits, so this would decrease the money supply by $200 000.

9. When the Bank of Canada pays for an open market purchase and its cheque (electronic payment) clears, it will add that amount of new reserves to the bank where the payment is deposited by the seller. The excess reserves created by that process leads to an expansion of bank loans of those reserves, creating additional demand deposits and therefore additional money.

11. a. $M \times V = P \times Q$
    b. The Nominal GDP would double.
    c. The price level would double.
    d. Nominal GDP would double.
    e. Nominal GDP would remain unchanged.

CHAPTER 13

1. The higher the price level, the more money will be needed to conduct a given real value of transactions or for "just in case" precautionary purposes, so the demand for money for such purposes will be roughly proportionate to the price level. People will want to hold less money for either purpose when the opportunity cost of holding money—the interest rate—is higher.

3. When the demand for money increases, if there is no change in the money supply, interest rates will rise. Alternatively, to keep interest rates from rising will require an increase in the money supply.

5.

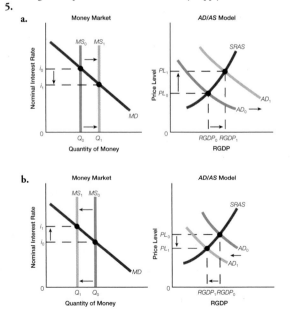

7.

a.

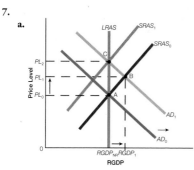

The short-run result is indicated by the movement from point A to point B in the diagram above.

b.

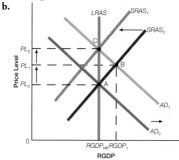

The long-run result is indicated by the movement from point B to point C in the diagram above.

9. The more excess capacity there is in the economy, the flatter the short-run aggregate supply curve over that range of output. Therefore, the more excess capacity there is in the economy, a given shift in aggregate demand will result in a larger effect on real output and a smaller effect on the price level.

11. In Canada, fiscal policy is implemented by the Government of Canada while monetary policy is delivered by the Bank of Canada. The separation between these two economic decision-making bodies introduces the possibility of conflicting policy initiatives being introduced simultaneously.

13. A movement up and to the left along a Phillips curve indicates an increase in inflation and a reduction in unemployment. A movement up and to the right along a short-run aggregate supply curve (achieved by a rightward shift in aggregate demand) indicates a price level increase (higher inflation) and an increase in RGDP (lower unemployment).

CHAPTER 14

1. The nature of Canadian exports has been, and continues to be, predominantly natural resource-based products (agricultural, energy, and forestry products). As for imports, the Canadian economy imports predominantly finished goods (automotive products, consumer goods).

3. a.

	Fish per Day	Buckets of Berries per Day
Bud	16	8
Larry	8	8
Total	24	8

b. Bud is better off because he can produce and consume more fish, while producing the same quantity of berries.

c.

	Opportunity Cost of a Bucket of Berries	Opportunity Cost of a Fish
Bud	2 fish	1/2 bucket of berries
Larry	1 fish	1 bucket of berries

d. Bud has a comparative advantage in fishing and Larry has a comparative advantage in picking berries.

e. A total of 32 fish and 16 buckets of berries will be produced. There will be 8 more fish and no fewer berries produced if they both completely specialize according to their comparative advantage.

5. Country B has a comparative advantage over the production of Good X because its opportunity cost of producing 1 unit of Good X is only 1.5 units of Good Y versus 2 units of Good Y in country A. Country A has a comparative advantage in the production of Good Y.

7. a. The opportunity cost of producing X in Freeland is 2Y. The opportunity cost of producing X in Braveburg is 1.5Y.

b. Since Braveburg has a comparative advantage in producing X, it will ship X to Freeland in exchange for Y produced in Freeland.

c. The terms of trade will have to be between 1.5Y per X and 2Y per X (the opportunity costs of producing X in the two countries).

d. Transaction costs, transportation costs, or tariffs greater than the net gains from trade (0.5 units of Y per X traded) would eliminate trade between Freeland and Braveburg.

9. a. The price will fall from P_{BT} to the world price, P_{AT}, because any higher price would attract additional exports, eliminating the price differential with the rest of the world.

b. The new Q_{DT} will be where the $S_{Domestic}$ curve intersects the world price curve. Imports will equal the difference between the Q_{AT} consumption level and the Q_{DT} domestic production level.

c. The lost producer surplus area b is the area below P_{BT} and above P_{AT}, out to the domestic supply curve $S_{Domestic}$.

d. The net gains from trade are measured by the area between $S_{Domestic}$ and $D_{Domestic}$ from the old P_{BT} and the world price P_{AT}.

e. Since consumers gain more than producers lose (as shown in part d above), they could compensate the producers and leave both consumers and producers better off than before.

11.

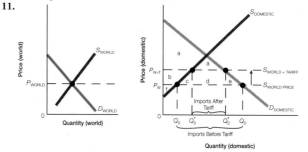

Gains and Losses from Tariffs			
Area	**Before Tariff**	**After Tariff**	**Change**
Consumer surplus (*CS*)	a + b + c + d + e	a	– (b + c + d + e)
Producer surplus (*PS*)	f	b + f	+ b
Government revenues (tariff)	0	d	+ d
Total welfare from tariff (*CS* + *PS* + Tariff revenues)	a + b + c + d + e + f	a + b + d + f	– (c + e)

13. Even though the total harm to all consumers from the imposition of a tariff or quota may be significant, the harm to an individual consumer may be relatively small. In addition, the average consumer may not be aware that she is paying a higher price for goods as a result of a tariff. As a result, consumers often do not oppose such protectionist policies.

15. a. In favour of freer trade, which will increase demand for your exports.

b. Against freer trade, which will decrease the price you can get for your output.

c. In favour of freer trade, which will decrease the cost you must pay for imported parts.

CHAPTER 15

1. a. debit
b. credit
c. debit
d. credit

3. a. Canadian exports will increase, imports decrease, and the trade deficit (surplus) will decrease (increase).

   b. Canadian exports will decrease, imports increase, and the trade deficit (surplus) will increase (decrease).

   c. Canadian exports will increase and the trade deficit (surplus) will decrease (increase).

   d. Canadian imports will decrease and the trade deficit (surplus) will decrease (increase).

   e. Canadian exports will decrease, imports increase, and the trade deficit (surplus) will increase (decrease).

5. a. 50 pounds

   b. 800 pesos

   c. The Canadian dollar would depreciate, making the Canadian product cheaper in the other country.

   d. The Canadian dollar would depreciate, making the Canadian product cheaper in the other country.

   e. The Canadian dollar would depreciate, making the Canadian product cheaper in the other country.

7. a. Likely to weaken the value of the Canadian dollar relative to the euro

   b. Likely to strengthen the value of the Canadian dollar relative to the euro

   c. Likely to weaken the value of the Canadian dollar relative to the euro

   d. Likely to strengthen the value of the Canadian dollar relative to the euro

9.

Change	Supply of Euros	Demand for Euros	Dollar Price of Euros
Reduced Canadian tastes for European goods	No change	Decreases	Decreases
Increased incomes in Canada	No change	Increases	Increases
Increased Canadian interest rates	Increases	Decreases	Decreases
Decreased inflation in Europe	Decrease	Increases	Increases
Reduced Canadian tariffs on imports	No change	Increases	Increases
Increased European tastes for Canadian goods	Increases	No change	Decreases

11. a. The supply curve for dollars shifts to the right.

   b. The supply curve for dollars shifts to the right.

Index

Chapter In Review

The Role and Method of Economics

Section 1.1 Economics: A Brief Introduction

- *What is economics?*

  Economics is the study of the allocation of our limited resources to satisfy our unlimited wants.

- *Why study economics?*

  Economics is a problem-solving science that teaches you to ask intelligent questions.

- *What distinguishes macroeconomics from microeconomics?*

  Macroeconomics deals with the aggregate, or total, economy, while microeconomics focuses on smaller units within the economy.

Section 1.2 Economic Theory

- *What are economic theories?*

  Economic theories are statements used to explain and predict patterns of human behaviour.

- *Why do we need to abstract?*

  Economic theories, through abstractions, provide a broad view of human economic behaviour.

- *What is a hypothesis?*

  A hypothesis makes a prediction about human behaviour and is then tested.

- *What is the* ceteris paribus *assumption?*

  In order to isolate the effects of one variable on another, we use the *ceteris paribus* assumption: holding everything else constant.

- *Why are observations and predictions harder in the social sciences?*

  With its focus on human behaviour, which is more variable and less predictable, observation and prediction are more difficult in the social sciences.

- *What distinguishes between correlation and causation?*

  The fact that two events are related does not mean that one caused the other to occur.

- *What is the fallacy of composition?*

  What is true for the individual is not necessarily true for the group.

- *What are positive analysis and normative analysis?*

  Positive analysis is objective and value-free, while normative analysis involves value judgments and opinions about the desirability of various actions.

- *Why do economists disagree?*

  Most disagreement among economists stems from normative issues.

Section 1.3 Scarcity

- *What is scarcity?*

  Scarcity exists when our wants exceed the available resources of land, labour, capital, and entrepreneurship.

- *What are goods and services?*

  Goods and services are things that we value.

Key Terms and Concepts

economics the study of the allocation of our limited resources to satisfy our unlimited wants p. 1

resources inputs used to produce goods and services p. 1

the economic problem scarcity forces us to choose, and choices are costly because we must give up other opportunities that we value p. 1

macroeconomics the study of the aggregate economy including the topics of inflation, unemployment, and economic growth p. 3

aggregate the total amount—such as the aggregate level of output p. 3

microeconomics the study of the smaller units within the economy including the topics of household and firm behaviour and how they interact in the marketplace p. 3

theory an established explanation that accounts for known facts or phenomena p. 4

hypothesis a testable proposition p. 4

empirical analysis the examination of data to see if the hypothesis fits well with the facts p. 4

ceteris paribus holding everything else constant p. 5

correlation two events that usually occur together p. 6

causation when one event causes another event to occur p. 6

fallacy of composition even if something is true for an individual, it is not necessarily true for a group p. 7

positive analysis an objective, value-free approach, utilizing the scientific method p. 7

normative analysis a subjective, biased approach p. 7

scarcity the situation that exists when human wants exceed available resources p. 9

labour the physical and mental effort used by people in the production of goods and services p. 10

Section 1.4 Opportunity Cost

- *Why do we have to make choices?*

  Scarcity means we all have to make choices.

- *What do we give up when we have to choose?*

  When we are forced to choose, we give up the next highest-valued alternative.

- *Why are "free" lunches not free?*

  Because the production of any good uses up some of society's resources, there is no such thing as a free lunch.

Section 1.5 Marginal Thinking

- *What do we mean by marginal thinking?*

  Economists are usually interested in the effects of additional, or incremental, changes in a given situation.

- *What is the rule of rational choice?*

  The rule of rational choice states that individuals will pursue an activity if they expect the marginal benefits to be greater than the marginal costs, or $E(MB) > E(MC)$.

Section 1.6 Incentives Matter

- *Can we predict how people will respond to changes in incentives?*

  Incentives change the expected marginal benefits and expected marginal costs of certain behaviour. Therefore, when people are acting rationally, they respond to incentives in predictable ways.

- *What are positive and negative incentives?*

  A negative incentive increases costs or reduces benefits, thus discouraging consumption or production, while a positive incentive decreases costs or increases benefits, thus encouraging consumption or production.

Section 1.7 Specialization and Trade

- *Why do people specialize?*

  Specialization is important for individuals, businesses, regions, and nations. It allows them to make the best use of their limited resources.

- *How does specialization and trade lead to greater wealth and prosperity?*

  Specialization and trade increase wealth by allowing a person, a region, or a nation to specialize in those products that it produces at a lower opportunity cost and to trade for those products that others produce at a lower opportunity cost.

Section 1.8 Market Prices Coordinate Economic Activity

- *How does a market system allocate scarce resources?*

  Through voluntary exchange and the price system, the market system provides a way for producers and consumers to allocate scarce resources.

- *What are the effects of price controls?*

  Price controls sometimes force prices above or below what they would be in a market economy.

- *What is a market failure?*

  A market failure occurs when an economy fails to allocate resources efficiently on its own.

Chapter In Review

Scarcity, Trade-Offs, and Production Possibilities

Section 2.1 The Three Economic Questions Every Society Faces

- *What is to be produced?*

   Every economy has to decide what to produce. In a decentralized market economy, millions of buyers and sellers determine what and how much to produce. In a mixed economy, the government and the private sector determine the allocation of resources.

- *How are the goods and services to be produced?*

   The best form of production is the one that conserves the relatively scarce (more costly) resources and uses more of the abundant (less costly) resources. When capital is relatively scarce and labour is plentiful, production tends to be labour-intensive. When capital is relatively abundant and labour is relatively scarce, production tends to be capital-intensive.

- *Who will get the goods and services?*

   In a market economy, the amount of goods and services one is able to obtain depends on one's income. The amount of an individual's income depends on the quantity and the quality of the scarce resources that the individual controls.

Section 2.2 The Circular Flow Model

- *What are product markets?*

   In the product market, households are buyers and firms are sellers.

- *What are factor markets?*

   In the factor markets, households are the sellers and firms are the buyers.

- *What is the goods and services flow?*

   The goods and services flow represents the continuous flow of inputs and outputs in an economy.

- *What is the income flow?*

   The income flow represents the continuous flow of income and expenditure in an economy.

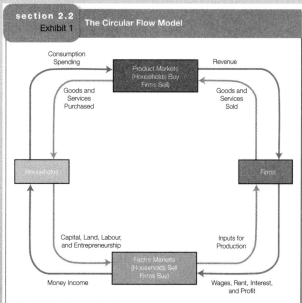

section 2.2 Exhibit 1 The Circular Flow Model

Households and firms continuously trade goods and services and payments between themselves. For example, households receive income from firms in exchange for working and providing other inputs. Households then recycle that income to the firms in exchange for goods and services. Dollars flow clockwise and goods and services flow counterclockwise.

- *What is the circular flow model?*

   The circular flow model illustrates the flow of goods, services, and payments among firms and households.

Section 2.3 The Production Possibilities Curve

- *What is a production possibilities curve?*

   A production possibilities curve represents the potential total output combinations of any two goods available to a society, given its resources and existing technology.

Key Terms and Concepts

consumer sovereignty consumers vote in economic affairs with their dollars in a market economy p. 37

command economies economies where the government uses central planning to coordinate most economic activities p. 37

market economy an economy that allocates goods and services through the private decisions of consumers, input suppliers, and firms p. 37

mixed economy an economy where government and the private sector together determine the allocation of resources p. 37

labour-intensive production that uses a large amount of labour p. 38

capital-intensive production that uses a large amount of capital p. 38

product markets the markets for consumer goods and services p. 40

factor (input) markets the market where households sell the use of their inputs (capital, land, labour, and entrepreneurship) to firms p. 40

goods and services flow the continuous flow of inputs and outputs in an economy p. 40

income flow the continuous flow of income and expenditure in an economy p. 40

circular flow model of income and output an illustration of the continuous flow of goods, services, inputs, and payments between firms and households p. 40

- *What is efficiency?*

  Efficiency requires society to use its resources to the fullest extent—no wasted resources. If the economy is operating within the production possibilities curve, the economy is operating inefficiently.

- *How is opportunity cost measured?*

  The cost of altering production within the production possibilities curve framework, at efficiency, is measured in forgone units of the sole alternative.

- *What is the law of increasing opportunity costs?*

  A bowed production possibilities curve means that the opportunity costs of producing additional units of a good rise as society produces more of that good (the law of increasing opportunity costs).

Section 2.4 Economic Growth and the Production Possibilities Curve

- *How do we show economic growth on the production possibilities curve?*

  Economic growth is represented by an outward shift of the production possibilities curve, indicating the possibility of producing more of all goods. Despite this, scarcity inevitably remains a fact of life.

- *How can we summarize the production possibilities curve?*

  The production possibilities model is an effective way of illustrating the economic concepts of scarcity, choice, opportunity costs, efficiency, and economic growth.

section 2.4
Exhibit 3   The Effects of Change on the Production Possibilities Curve

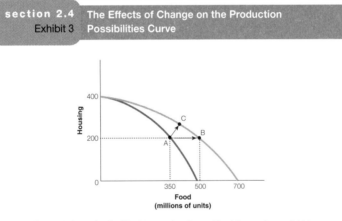

A move from point A to point C will lead to more housing and food. A move from point A to point B will lead to more food and the same level of housing.

section 2.4
Exhibit 4   Production Possibilities Curve

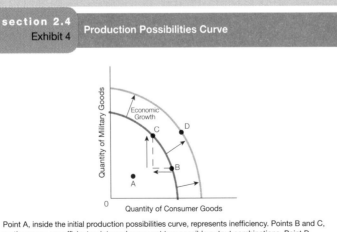

Point A, inside the initial production possibilities curve, represents inefficiency. Points B and C, on the curve, are efficient points and represent two possible output combinations. Point D can be attained only with economic growth, illustrated by the outward shift in the production possibilities curve.

Supply and Demand

Section 3.1 Markets

- *What is a market?*

  A market consists of buyers and sellers exchanging goods and services with one another.

- *What are the roles of buyers and sellers in a market?*

  Buyers determine the demand side of the market and sellers determine the supply side of the market.

Section 3.2 Demand

- *What is the law of demand?*

  The law of demand states that when the price of a good falls (rises), the quantity demanded rises (falls), *ceteris paribus.*

- *What is an individual demand schedule and curve?*

  An individual demand schedule is a table that shows the relationship between the price of a good and the quantity demanded. An individual demand curve is a graphical representation of the relationship between the price and the quantity demanded.

- *What is a market demand curve?*

  A market demand curve shows the amount of a good that all the buyers in the market would be willing and able to buy at various prices.

Section 3.3 Shifts in the Demand Curve

- *What is the difference between a change in demand and a change in quantity demanded?*

  A change in demand shifts the entire demand curve in response to a change in some determinant of demand. A change in the quantity demanded describes a movement along a given demand curve in response to a change in the price of the good.

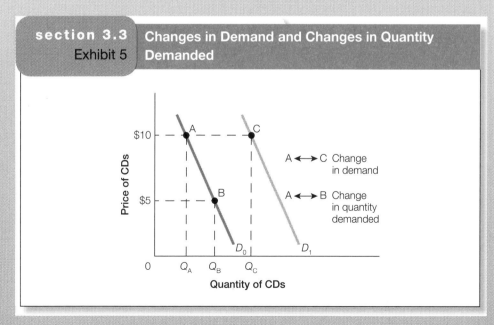

section 3.3
Exhibit 5
Changes in Demand and Changes in Quantity Demanded

Key Terms and Concepts

market the process of buyers and sellers exchanging goods and services   p. 55

competitive market a market in which there are a number of buyers and sellers offering similar products, and no single buyer or seller can influence the market price   p. 56

law of demand the quantity of a good or service demanded varies inversely (negatively) with its price, *ceteris paribus*   p. 56

substitution effect at higher prices, buyers increasingly substitute other goods for the good that now has a higher relative price   p. 57

income effect at higher prices, buyers feel poorer, causing a lowering of quantity demanded   p. 57

individual demand schedule a table that shows the relationship between price and quantity demanded   p. 57

individual demand curve a graphical representation that shows the inverse relationship between price and quantity demanded   p. 58

market demand curve the horizontal summation of individual demand curves   p. 58

change in quantity demanded a change in a good's price leads to a change in quantity demanded, a move along a given demand curve   p. 60

change in demand a change in a determinant of demand leads to a change in demand, a shift of the entire demand curve   p. 60

substitute an increase (a decrease) in the price of one good causes an increase (a decrease) in the demand for another good   p. 61

- *What are the determinants of demand?*

  Some possible determinants of demand (demand shifters) are the prices of related goods, income, number of buyers, tastes, and expectations.

- *Can we review the distinction between changes in demand and changes in quantity demanded?*

  The price of a substitute is positively related to the demand curve for the good in question; the price of a complement is inversely related to the demand curve for the good in question. For normal goods, income is positively related to the demand curve for the good in question; for inferior goods, income is inversely related to the demand curve for the good in question. The demand curve will vary according to the number of consumers in the market, taste changes will shift the demand curve, and changes in expected future prices and income can shift the current demand curve.

Section 3.4 Supply

- *What is the law of supply?*

  The law of supply states that the higher (lower) the price of the good, the greater (smaller) the quantity supplied.

- *What is an individual supply curve?*

  The individual supply curve shows the positive relationship between the price and quantity supplied of a given good or service.

- *What is a market supply curve?*

  The market supply curve is a graphical representation of the amount of goods and services that suppliers are willing and able to supply at various prices.

Section 3.5 Shifts in the Supply Curve

- *What is the difference between a change in supply and a change in quantity supplied?*

  A movement along a given supply curve is caused by a change in the price of the good in question. A shift of the entire supply curve is called a *change in supply*. As we move along the supply curve, we say there is a *change in the quantity supplied*.

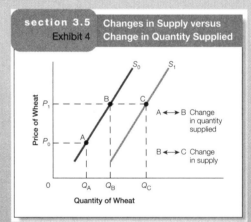

section 3.5
Exhibit 4
Changes in Supply versus Change in Quantity Supplied

- *What are the determinants of supply?*

  Input prices, the prices of related products, expectations, the number of suppliers, technology, regulation, taxes and subsidies, and weather can all lead to changes in supply (shifts in supply).

- *Can we review the distinction between a change in supply and a change in quantity supplied?*

  Input prices are inversely related to the supply curve for the good in question; the price for a substitute in production is inversely related to the supply curve for the good in question; the price for a complement in production is positively related to the supply curve for the good in question; changes in expected future prices can shift the current supply curve; the supply curve will vary according to the number of suppliers in the market; taxes (subsidies) are inversely (positively) related to the supply curve for the good in question; changes in technology can shift the supply curve for the good in question; and weather will shift the supply curve.

Chapter In Review

Bringing Supply and Demand Together

Section 4.1 Market Equilibrium Price and Quantity

- *What is the equilibrium price and the equilibrium quantity?*

  The intersection of the supply and demand curve shows the equilibrium price and equilibrium quantity in a market.

- *What is a shortage and what is a surplus?*

  A shortage is where quantity demanded exceeds quantity supplied at a price below equilibrium price. A surplus is where quantity supplied exceeds quantity demanded at a price above equilibrium price.

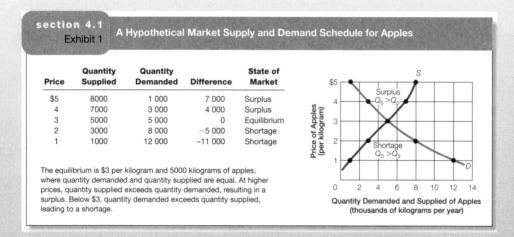

section 4.1 Exhibit 1 A Hypothetical Market Supply and Demand Schedule for Apples

Price	Quantity Supplied	Quantity Demanded	Difference	State of Market
$5	8000	1 000	7 000	Surplus
4	7000	3 000	4 000	Surplus
3	5000	5 000	0	Equilibrium
2	3000	8 000	−5 000	Shortage
1	1000	12 000	−11 000	Shortage

The equilibrium is $3 per kilogram and 5000 kilograms of apples, where quantity demanded and quantity supplied are equal. At higher prices, quantity supplied exceeds quantity demanded, resulting in a surplus. Below $3, quantity demanded exceeds quantity supplied, leading to a shortage.

Section 4.2 Changes in Equilibrium Price and Quantity

- *What happens to equilibrium price and equilibrium quantity when the demand curve shifts?*

  Changes in demand will cause a change in the equilibrium price and quantity, *ceteris paribus*. An increase (decrease) in demand will cause an increase (decrease) in both equilibrium price and equilibrium quantity.

- *What happens to equilibrium price and equilibrium quantity when the supply curve shifts?*

  Changes in supply will cause a change in the equilibrium price and quantity, *ceteris paribus*. An increase (decrease) in supply will cause a decrease (increase) in equilibrium price and an increase (decrease) in equilibrium quantity.

- *What happens when both supply and demand shift in the same time period?*

  When there are simultaneous shifts in both supply and demand curves, either the equilibrium price or the equilibrium quantity will be indeterminate without more information.

Key Terms and Concepts

market equilibrium the point at which the market supply and the market demand curves intersect p. 81

equilibrium price the price at the intersection of the market supply and demand curves; at this price the quantity demanded equals the quantity supplied p. 81

equilibrium quantity the quantity at the intersection of the market supply and demand curves; at this quantity, the quantity demanded equals the quantity supplied p. 81

surplus where quantity supplied exceeds quantity demanded p. 82

shortage where quantity demanded exceeds quantity supplied p. 82

price ceiling a legally established maximum price p. 89

price floor a legally established minimum price p. 89

unintended consequences the secondary effects of an action that may occur after the initial effects p. 92

Key Exhibits/ Graphs

Section 4.1, Exhibit 1

Section 4.2, Exhibit 7

Section 4.3, Exhibit 1

Section 4.3, Exhibit 2

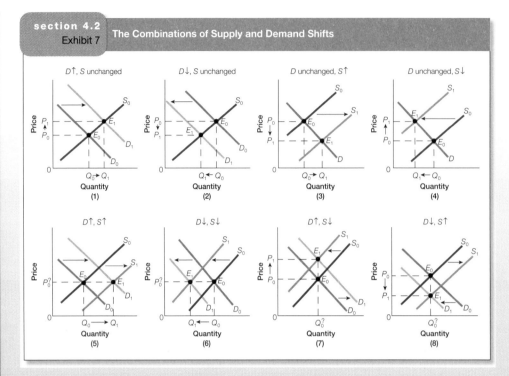

Section 4.3 Price Controls

- *What are price controls?*

  Price controls involve government man-dates to keep prices above or below the market-determined equilibrium price.

- *What are price ceilings?*

  Price ceilings are government-imposed maximum prices. When price ceilings are set below the equilibrium price, shortages will result.

- *What are price floors?*

  Price floors are government-imposed min-imum prices. When price floors are set above the equilibrium price, surpluses will result.

section 4.3
Exhibit 1
Rent Controls

The impact of a price ceiling (a rent-control law) set below the equilibrium price is a shortage.

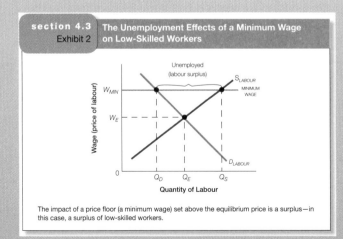

section 4.3
Exhibit 2
The Unemployment Effects of a Minimum Wage on Low-Skilled Workers

The impact of a price floor (a minimum wage) set above the equilibrium price is a surplus—in this case, a surplus of low-skilled workers.

Introduction to the Macroeconomy

Section 5.1 Macroeconomic Goals

- *What are the three major macroeconomic goals in Canada?*

  The three major macroeconomic goals in Canada are full employment, price stability, and economic growth.

- *Are these macroeconomic goals universal?*

  Individuals have their own reasons for valuing certain goals more than others. As a result, there is debate as to what is most important for an economy.

Section 5.2 Employment and Unemployment

- *What are the consequences of high unemployment?*

  The consequences of high unemployment to society include a reduction in potential output and consumption—a decrease in efficiency.

- *What is the unemployment rate?*

  The unemployment rate is found by taking the number of people officially unemployed and dividing by the number in the labour force. Unemployment rates are higher for teenagers, men, and those living in eastern Canada.

- *Are unemployment statistics accurate reflections of the labour market?*

  No. The overall accuracy of the unemployment rate is impacted by factors such as; discouraged workers, the treatment of part-time work, and the underground economy.

- *What are the categories of unemployment?*

  There are four main categories of unemployed workers: job losers, job leavers, re-entrants, and new entrants.

- *What is the labour force participation rate?*

  Labour force participation measures the percentage of the adult population that is participating in the labour force. In Canada, women's labour force participation has increased dramatically over the past 40 years.

Section 5.3 Different Types of Unemployment

- *What is frictional unemployment?*

  Frictional unemployment results when a person moves from one job to another as a result of normal turnovers in the economy.

- *What is structural unemployment?*

  Structural unemployment results when people who are looking for jobs lack the required skills for the jobs that are available, or a long-term change in demand occurs.

- *What is cyclical unemployment?*

  Cyclical unemployment is caused by a recession.

- *What is the natural rate of unemployment?*

  When cyclical unemployment is eliminated, our economy is said to be operating at full employment, or at a natural rate of unemployment.

Key Terms and Concepts

real gross domestic product (RGDP) the total value of all final goods and services produced in a given time period such as a year or a quarter, adjusted for inflation   p. 97

labour force persons 15 years of age and over who are employed or are unemployed and seeking work   p. 99

unemployment rate the percentage of the people in the labour force who are unemployed   p. 100

discouraged workers people who have left the labour force because they could not find work   p. 100

job loser an individual who has been laid off or fired   p. 102

job leaver a person who quits his or her job   p. 102

re-entrant an individual who worked before and is now re-entering the labour force   p. 102

new entrant an individual who has not held a job before but is now seeking employment   p. 102

underemployment a situation in which workers have skills higher than necessary for a job   p. 102

labour force participation rate the percentage of the population (aged 15 years and over) in the labour force   p. 103

frictional unemployment unemployment from normal turnovers in the economy, such as when individuals change from one job to another   p. 104

structural unemployment unemployment that occurs due to a lack of skills necessary for available jobs   p. 105

Section 5.4 Inflation

- *Why is the overall price level important?*

  Price level stability is a desirable goal because it limits inflationary costs.

- *How is inflation measured using the Consumer Price Index (CPI)?*

  A price index allows us to compare prices paid for goods and services over time. The Consumer Price Index (CPI) is the best known price index.

- *Who are the winners and losers during inflation?*

  Inflation generally hurts creditors and those on fixed incomes and pensions; debtors generally benefit from inflation.

- *What are the costs of inflation?*

  Unanticipated inflation causes unpredictable transfers of wealth and reduces the efficiency of the market system by distorting price signals.

- *What is the relationship between inflation and interest rates?*

  The nominal interest rate is the actual amount of interest you pay. The real interest rate is the nominal rate minus the inflation rate. Wage earners attempt to keep pace with inflation by demanding higher wages each year or by indexing their annual wage to inflation.

Section 5.5 Economic Fluctuations

- *What are short-term economic fluctuations?*

  Business cycles (or economic fluctuations) are short-term fluctuations in the amount of economic activity, relative to the long-term growth trend in output.

- *What are the four stages of a business cycle?*

  The four phases of a business cycle are expansion, peak, contraction, and trough.

- *How long does a business cycle last?*

  Recessions occur during the contraction phase of a business cycle. Severe, long-term recessions are called depressions, while prolonged expansions are referred to as *booms*. The economy often goes through short-term contractions even during a long-term growth trend. Overall, the duration of any one business is uncertain.

Chapter In Review

Measuring Economic Performance

Section 6.1 National Income Accounting: Measuring Economic Performance

- *Why do we measure our economy's performance?*

  We measure our economy's status in order to see how its performance has changed over time. These economic measurements are important to government officials, private businesses, and investors.

- *What is gross domestic product (GDP)?*

  Gross domestic product (GDP) is the value of all final goods and services produced within a country during a given time period. The two different ways to measure GDP are the expenditure approach and the income approach.

section 6.1
Exhibit 1
The Expanded Circular Flow Model

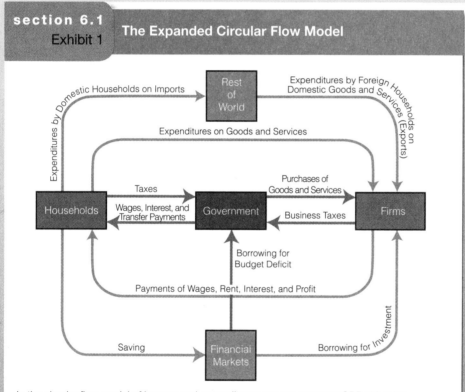

In the circular flow model of income and expenditures, we can measure GDP either by calculating the total value of expenditures or the total value of aggregate income because for the economy as a whole, expenditures must equal income. GDP equals the total amount spent by households in the market—to buy goods and services, to pay taxes, and to save. To produce goods and services, the firm uses the factors of production (labour, land, capital, and entrepreneurship), and it pays these factors wages, rent, interest, and profit. These payments are total income, which is also equal to GDP. Governments and firms borrow the funds that flow into the financial system from households.

Section 6.2 The Expenditure Approach to Measuring GDP

- *What is the expenditure approach to measuring GDP?*

  The expenditure approach to measuring GDP involves adding up the purchases of final goods and services by market participants. Four categories of spending are used in the GDP calculation: consumption (*C*), investment (*I*), government purchases (*G*), and net exports (*X − M*).

Key Terms and Concepts

national income accounting a uniform means of measuring economic performance   p. 124

gross domestic product (GDP) the measure of economic performance based on the value of all final goods and services produced in a country in a given period of time   p. 125

double counting adding the value of a good or service twice by mistakenly counting intermediate goods and services in GDP   p. 125

expenditure approach calculation of GDP by adding up how much market participants spend on final goods and services over a period of time   p. 127

consumption purchases of consumer goods and services by households   p. 127

nondurable goods tangible consumer items that are typically consumed in a relatively short period of time, such as food   p. 128

durable goods longer-lived consumer goods, such as automobiles   p. 128

services intangible items of value provided to consumers, such as haircuts   p. 128

investment the creation of capital goods to augment future production   p. 128

fixed investments all new spending on capital goods by producers   p. 128

producer goods capital goods that increase future production capabilities   p. 128

inventory investment all purchases by businesses that add to the stocks of goods kept by the firm to meet consumer demand   p. 128

Key Exhibits/ Graphs

- *What is consumption?*

  Consumption includes spending on nondurable consumer goods—tangible items that are usually consumed in a relatively short period of time; durable consumer goods—longer-lived consumer goods; and services—intangible items of value.

- *What is investment?*

  Fixed investment includes all spending on capital goods, such as machinery, tools, and buildings. Inventory investment includes the net expenditures by businesses to increase their inventories.

- *What are government purchases?*

  Purchases of goods and services are the only part of government spending included in GDP. Transfer payments are not included in these calculations because that spending is not a payment for a newly produced good or service.

- *What are net exports?*

  Net exports are calculated by subtracting total imports from total exports.

Section 6.3 The Income Approach to Measuring GDP

- *What is the income approach to measuring GDP?*

  The income approach to measuring GDP involves summing the incomes received by the producers of goods and services. These payments to the owners of productive resources are also known as *factor payments*. The income approach to GDP adds together wages and salaries, corporate profits, interest income, and net income of farm and unincorporated businesses to obtain net domestic income at factor cost. Adding indirect taxes less subsidies and depreciation to net domestic income gives GDP.

- *What do personal income and disposable income measure?*

  Personal income measures the amount of income received by households (including transfer payments) before taxes. Disposable income is the personal income available after taxes.

Section 6.4 Issues with Calculating an Accurate GDP

- *What are the problems with GDP in measuring output?*

  It is difficult to compare nominal GDP over time because of the changing value of money over time.

- *How is real GDP calculated?*

  The GDP deflator is a price index that measures the average level of prices of all final goods and services produced in the economy. It is used to convert nominal measures of GDP into equivalent real measures of GDP.

- *What is real GDP per capita?*

  Per capita real GDP is real output of goods and services per person. In some cases, real GDP may increase, but per capita real GDP may actually drop as a result of population growth.

Section 6.5 Problems with GDP as a Measure of Economic Welfare

- *What are some of the deficiencies of GDP as a measure of economic welfare?*

  Several factors make it difficult to use GDP as a welfare indicator, including nonmarket transactions, the underground economy, leisure, and externalities. Nonmarket transactions are the exchange of goods and services that do not occur in traditional markets, so no money is exchanged. The underground economy is the unreported production and income that come from certain legal and illegal activities. The presence of positive and negative externalities also make it difficult to measure GDP accurately.

Economic Growth in the Global Economy

Section 7.1 Economic Growth

- *How does economic growth differ from the business cycle?*

  Economic growth refers to the long-run trend rate of growth for an economy. *Business cycles* refer to the short-run fluctuations in economic activity around this trend rate of growth.

- *What is economic growth?*

  Economic growth is usually measured by the annual percentage change in real output of goods and services per capita. Improvements in and greater stocks of land, labour, capital, and entrepreneurial activity will lead to greater economic growth and shift the production possibilities curve outward.

- *What is the Rule of 70?*

  According to the Rule of 70, if you take a nation's growth rate and divide it into 70, you have the approximate time it will take to double the income level.

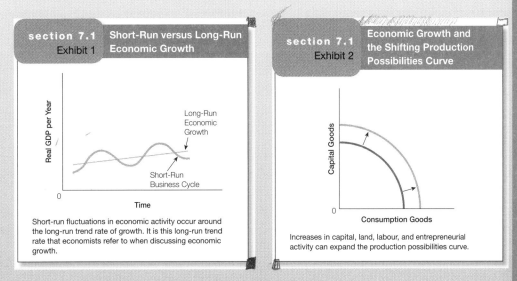

section 7.1 Exhibit 1 — Short-Run versus Long-Run Economic Growth

Short-run fluctuations in economic activity occur around the long-run trend rate of growth. It is this long-run trend rate that economists refer to when discussing economic growth.

section 7.1 Exhibit 2 — Economic Growth and the Shifting Production Possibilities Curve

Increases in capital, land, labour, and entrepreneurial activity can expand the production possibilities curve.

Section 7.2 Determinants of Economic Growth

- *What factors contribute to economic growth?*

  The factors that contribute to economic growth are the same factors that determine growth in productivity. They include increased quantity and quality of labour; natural resources; physical capital; and technological advances.

Section 7.3 Public Policy and Economic Growth

- *Why is the saving rate so important to economic growth?*

  Generally speaking, higher levels of saving will lead to higher rates of investment and capital formation and, therefore, to greater economic growth.

- *Why are research and development so important to economic growth?*

  Larger rewards for research and development would spur even more rapid economic growth.

Key Terms and Concepts

economic growth an upward trend in the real per capita output of goods and services p. 144

productivity the amount of goods and services a worker can produce per hour p. 146

human capital the productive knowledge and skill people receive from education and on-the-job training p. 147

innovation applications of new knowledge that create new products or improve existing products p. 148

research and development (R&D) activities undertaken to create new products and processes that will lead to technological progress p. 150

Key Exhibits/Graphs

Section 7.1, Exhibit 1

Section 7.1, Exhibit 2

- *Why are property rights so important to economic growth?*

  Economic growth rates tend to be higher in countries where the government enforces property rights more vigorously.

- *What impact will free trade have on economic growth?*

  Allowing free trade can also lead to greater output because of the principle of comparative advantage.

- *Why is education so important to economic growth?*

  Education, investment in human capital, is important to improving standards of living and economic growth.

Section 7.4 Population and Economic Growth

- *What is the effect of population growth on per capita economic growth?*

  Population growth may increase per capita output in resource-rich countries such as Canada, the United States, Australia, and Saudi Arabia, because they have more resources for each labourer to produce with. They are more likely to be able to exploit economies of large-scale production, and they are more likely to have rapidly expanding technology.

- *What is the Mathusian prediction?*

  The Malthusian prediction was that, due to limited productive resources and rapid population growth, eventually per capita economic growth would become negative.

Chapter In Review

Aggregate Demand

Section 8.1 The Determinants of Aggregate Demand

- *What is aggregate demand?*

  Aggregate demand is the sum of the demand for all final goods and services in the economy. It can also be seen as the quantity of real GDP demanded at different price levels.

- *What is consumption?*

  Consumption—the purchases of consumer goods and services by households—is the largest component of aggregate demand. Empirical evidence suggests that consumption increases directly with any increase in income.

- *What is investment?*

  Investment spending refers to the purchases of investment goods such as machinery and equipment. Changes in investment spending are often responsible for changes in the level of economic activity.

- *What are government purchases?*

  Government purchases are made up of federal, provincial and territorial, and local purchases of goods and services.

- *What are net exports?*

  Net exports are the difference between the value of exports and the value of imports.

Section 8.2 The Investment and Saving Market

- *What is the investment demand curve?*

  The investment demand curve is downward sloping, reflecting the fact that the quantity of investment demanded varies inversely with the real interest rate. At high real interest rates, firms will pursue only those few investment activities with still higher expected rates of return. At lower real interest rates, projects with lower expected rates of return become profitable for firms, and the quantity of investment demanded rises. Technology, inventories, expectations, and business taxes can shift the investment demand curve at a given real interest rate.

- *What is the saving supply curve?*

  The supply of national saving is composed of both private saving and public saving. The saving supply curve is upward sloping. At a higher real interest rate, there is an increase in the quantity of saving supplied. At a lower real interest

section 8.2
Exhibit 6

Equilibrium in the Saving and Investment Market

Desired investment equals desired national saving at the intersection of the investment demand curve and the saving supply curve, the equilibrium in the saving and investment market. The intersection of these two curves shows the real equilibrium interest rate. At higher than the real equilibrium interest rate, the quantity of savings supplied would be greater than the quantity of investment demanded; there would be a surplus of savings at this real interest rate. As savers (lenders) compete against each other to attract investment demanders (borrowers), the real interest rate falls. If the real interest rate, r_2, is below the equilibrium real interest rate, r_E, the quantity of investment demanded is greater than the quantity of saving supplied at that interest rate and a shortage of saving occurs. As investment demanders (borrowers) compete against each other for the available saving, the real interest rate is bid up to r_E.

Key Terms and Concepts

aggregate demand (*AD*) the total demand for all the final goods and services in the economy   p. 159

average propensity to consume (*APC*) the fraction of total disposable income that households spend on consumption   p. 160

marginal propensity to consume (*MPC*) the additional consumption resulting from an additional dollar of disposable income   p. 160

open economy a type of model that includes international trade effects   p. 161

net exports the difference between the value of exports and the value of imports   p. 161

private saving the amount of income that households have left over after consumption and taxes   p. 164

public saving the amount of income that the government has left over after paying for its spending   p. 164

national saving the sum of both private and public saving   p. 164

dissaving consuming more than total available income   p. 166

aggregate demand curve a graphical representation that shows the inverse relationship between the price level and RGDP demanded   p. 168

Key Exhibits/ Graphs

Section 8.2, Exhibit 6

Section 8.4, Exhibit 1

rate, there is a decrease in the quantity of saving supplied. Two noninterest determinants of the saving supply curve are disposable (after-tax) income and expected future earnings.

- *How is equilibrium determined in the investment and saving market?*

  In equilibrium, desired investment equals desired national saving at the intersection of the investment demand curve and the saving supply curve. If the real interest rate is above the equilibrium real interest rate, the quantity of saving supplied is greater than the quantity of investment demanded at that interest rate; lenders will compete against each other to attract borrowers and the real interest rate falls. If the real interest rate is below the equilibrium real interest rate, the quantity of investment demanded is greater than the quantity of saving supplied at that interest rate; borrowers compete with each other for the available saving and drive up the real interest rate.

- *What effect do budget surpluses and budget deficits have on the investment and saving market?*

  Budget surpluses lead to an increase in national saving, a lowering of the real interest rate and an increase in the quantity of saving and investment. Budget deficits reduce national saving, increase the real interest rate, and lower the quantity of saving and investment.

Section 8.3 The Aggregate Demand Curve

- *How is the quantity of real GDP demanded affected by the price level?*

  An increase in the price level causes RGDP demanded to fall. Conversely, if there is a reduction in the price level, quantity demanded of RGDP increases.

- *Why is the aggregate demand curve negatively sloped?*

  The aggregate demand curve is downward sloping because of the real wealth effect, the interest rate effect, and the open economy effect.

Section 8.4 Shifts in the Aggregate Demand Curve

- *What variables cause the aggregate demand curve to shift?*

  Aggregate demand is made up of total spending, or $C + I + G + (X - M)$. Any change in these factors will cause the aggregate demand curve to shift. A change in the price level causes a movement along the aggregate demand curve, but not a shift in the aggregate demand curve.

- *Can we review the determinants that change aggregate demand?*

  Any nonprice-level variable that causes C, I, G, or X to increase, or M to decrease, will cause the aggregate demand curve to shift to the right. Any nonprice-level variable that causes C, I, G, or X to decrease, or M to increase, will cause the aggregate demand curve to shift to the left.

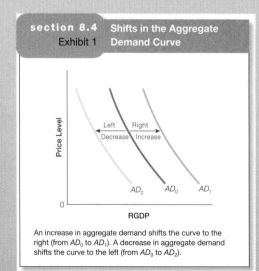

section 8.4 **Shifts in the Aggregate**
Exhibit 1 **Demand Curve**

An increase in aggregate demand shifts the curve to the right (from AD_0 to AD_1). A decrease in aggregate demand shifts the curve to the left (from AD_0 to AD_2).

Chapter In Review

Aggregate Supply and Macroeconomic Equilibrium

Section 9.1 The Aggregate Supply Curve

- *What is the aggregate supply curve?*

  The aggregate supply curve is the relationship between the overall price level and the total quantity of final goods and services that suppliers are *able* and *willing* to produce.

- *Why is the short-run aggregate supply curve positively sloped?*

  The short-run aggregate supply curve measures how much RGDP suppliers are willing to produce at different price levels. In the short run, producers supply more as the price level increases because wages and other input prices tend to change more slowly than output prices. For this reason, producers can make a profit by expanding production when the price level rises. Producers also may be fooled into thinking that the relative price of the item they are producing is rising, so they increase production.

- *Why is the long-run aggregate supply curve vertical at the natural rate of output?*

  In the long run, the aggregate supply curve is vertical. In the long run, input prices change proportionally with output prices. The position of the *LRAS* curve is determined by the level of capital, land, labour, entrepreneurship, and technology at the natural rate of output, $RGDP_{NR}$.

Section 9.2 Shifts in the Aggregate Supply Curve

- *What factors of production affect the short-run and the long-run aggregate supply curves?*

  Any increase in the quantity of any of the factors of production—capital, land, labour, entrepreneurship, or technology— available will cause both the long-run and short-run aggregate supply curves to shift to the right. A decrease in any of these factors will shift both of the aggregate supply curves to the left.

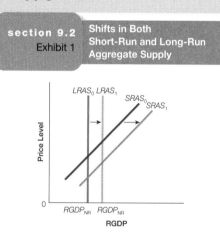

section 9.2 Exhibit 1	Shifts in Both Short-Run and Long-Run Aggregate Supply

Increases in any of the factors of production—capital, land, labour, or entrepreneurship—can shift both the *LRAS* and *SRAS* curves to the right.

- *What factors exclusively shift the short-run aggregate supply curve?*

  Changes in wages and other input price, productivity, and temporary supply shocks shift the short-run aggregate supply curve but do not affect the long-run aggregate supply curve.

- *Can we review the determinants that change aggregate supply?*

  A given factor can shift either the short-run aggregate supply curve, the long-run aggregate supply curve, or both, depending on whether the effects are temporary or permanent.

Section 9.3 Macroeconomic Equilibrium

- *How is macroeconomic equilibrium determined?*

  Short-run macroeconomic equilibrium is shown by the intersection of the aggregate demand curve and the short-run aggregate supply curve. A short-run equilibrium is also a long-run equilibrium only if it is at potential output on the long-run aggregate supply curve.

Key Terms and Concepts

aggregate supply curve (*AS*) a graphical representation that shows the positive relationship between the price level and real gross domestic product supplied p. 177

short-run aggregate supply curve (*SRAS*) the graphical relationship between RGDP and the price level when output prices can change but input prices are unable to adjust p. 177

long-run aggregate supply curve (*LRAS*) the graphical relationship between RGDP and the price level when output prices and input prices can fully adjust to economic changes p. 177

shocks unexpected aggregate supply or aggregate demand changes p. 184

recessionary gap an output gap that occurs when the actual output is less than the potential output p. 184

inflationary gap an output gap that occurs when the actual output is greater than the potential output p. 184

demand-pull inflation a price level increase due to an increase in aggregate demand p. 185

stagflation a situation in which lower growth and higher prices occur together p. 185

cost-push inflation a price level increase due to a negative supply shock or increases in input prices p. 185

wage and price inflexibility the tendency for prices and wages to only adjust slowly downward to changes in the economy p. 187

Key Exhibits/Graphs

- **What are recessionary and inflationary gaps?**

  If short-run equilibrium occurs at less than the potential output of the economy, $RGDP_{NR}$, there is a recessionary gap. If short-run equilibrium temporarily occurs beyond $RGDP_{NR}$, there is an inflationary gap.

- **How can the economy self-correct to a recessionary gap?**

  It is possible that the economy could self-correct through declining wages and prices. For example, during a recession, labourers and other input suppliers are willing to accept lower wages and prices for the use of their resources, and the resulting reduction in production costs increases the short-run supply curve. Eventually, the economy returns to the long-run equilibrium, at $RGDP_{NR}$, and a lower price level.

- **Why can the self-correction to a recessionary gap be slow?**

  Wages and other input prices may be very slow to adjust, especially downward. This downward wage and price inflexibility may lead to prolonged periods of recession. Firms might not be willing to lower nominal wages in the short run for several reasons, leading to downward wage and price inflexibility or sticky prices. Firms may not be able to legally cut wages because of long-term labour contracts (particularly with union workers) or due to a legal minimum wage. In addition, efficiency wage and menu costs may lead to sticky wages and prices.

- **How can the economy self-correct to an inflationary gap?**

  It is possible that the economy could self-correct to an inflationary gap by increasing wages and prices. For example, during inflation, labourers and other input suppliers will experience a loss of purchasing power as output prices rise and input prices remain constant. When production costs eventually do increase, this will decrease the short-run aggregate supply curve, ultimately returning the economy to the long-run level of output, $RGDP_{NR}$, at a higher price level.

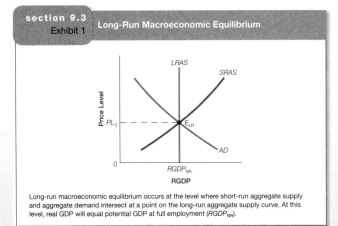

section 9.3 Exhibit 1 Long-Run Macroeconomic Equilibrium

Long-run macroeconomic equilibrium occurs at the level where short-run aggregate supply and aggregate demand intersect at a point on the long-run aggregate supply curve. At this level, real GDP will equal potential GDP at full employment ($RGDP_{NR}$).

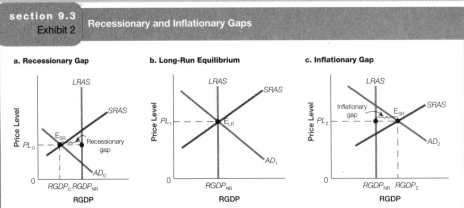

section 9.3 Exhibit 2 Recessionary and Inflationary Gaps

a. Recessionary Gap

b. Long-Run Equilibrium

c. Inflationary Gap

In Exhibit 2(a), the economy is currently in short-run equilibrium at E_{SR}. At this point, $RGDP_0$ is less than $RGDP_{NR}$; that is, the economy is producing less than its potential output and the economy is in a recessionary gap. In Exhibit 2(c), the economy is currently in short-run equilibrium at E_{SR}. At this point $RGDP_2$ is greater than $RGDP_{NR}$. The economy is temporarily producing more than its potential output and we have an inflationary gap. In Exhibit 2(b) the economy is producing its potential output at the $RGDP_{NR}$. At this point the economy is in long-run equilibrium and is not experiencing an inflationary or recessionary gap.

Chapter In Review

Fiscal Policy

Section 10.1 Fiscal Policy

- *What is fiscal policy?*

  Fiscal policy is the use of government spending on goods and services and/or taxes to affect aggregate demand and to alter RGDP and the price level.

- *How does fiscal policy affect the government's budget?*

  Expansionary fiscal policies will increase the budget deficit (or reduce a budget surplus) through greater government spending, lower taxes, or both. Contractionary fiscal policies will increase a budget surplus (or reduce a budget deficit) through reduced government spending, higher taxes, or both.

Section 10.2 Government: Spending and Taxation

- *What are the major categories of government spending?*

  Over 30 percent of federal government spending goes to social services, such as Employment Insurance and Old Age Security programs. Provincial, territorial, and local government spending is much more balanced, with the majority of the expenditure going to health care and education.

- *What are the major sources of government revenue?*

  The largest source of federal revenue is income tax on individuals and corporations. Provincially and territorially, income and consumption taxes are the largest sources of revenue, whereas locally, property taxes represent the major revenue source.

Section 10.3 The Multiplier Effect

- *What is the multiplier effect?*

  The multiplier effect is a chain reaction of additional income and purchases that results in a final increase in total purchases that is greater than the initial increase in purchases.

- *What impact does the multiplier effect have on the aggregate demand curve?*

  Initially, the *AD* curve shifts rightward by the amount of the original increase in expenditure. The multiplier effect has the effect of shifting the *AD* curve further rightward.

- *What impact does the multiplier effect have on tax cuts?*

  Because taxes have only an indirect impact on aggregate demand, the tax multiplier is smaller than the government spending multiplier.

- *What factors can potentially reduce the size of the multiplier?*

  Because of a time lag, the full impact of the multiplier effect on GDP may not be felt until a year or more after the initial purchase. Also, the ultimate size of the multiplier may be reduced by increases in savings rates, taxes, and money spent on imported goods.

Section 10.4 Fiscal Policy and the *AD/AS* Model

- *How can fiscal policy alleviate a recessionary gap?*

  A government decision to spend more and/or cut taxes would increase total purchases and shift out the aggregate demand curve. If the correct magnitude of

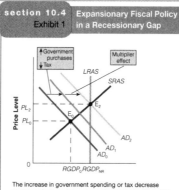

section 10.4 Exhibit 1 — Expansionary Fiscal Policy in a Recessionary Gap

The increase in government spending or tax decrease causes an increase in aggregate demand from AD_0 to AD_1. This triggers the multiplier effect (AD_1 to AD_2) and the result is a new equilibrium at E_2, reflecting a higher price level and a higher RGDP. Because this result is on the *LRAS* curve, it is a long-run, sustainable equilibrium.

expansionary fiscal policy is used in a recession, it could potentially bring the economy to full employment at a higher price level.

- *How can fiscal policy alleviate an inflationary gap?*

  Use of the correct magnitude of contractionary fiscal policy in an inflationary boom could potentially bring the economy back to full employment at a lower price level.

Section 10.5 Automatic Stabilizers

- *What are automatic stabilizers?*

  Automatic stabilizers are changes in government transfer payments or tax collections that happen automatically and have effects that vary inversely with business cycles.

- *How does the tax system stabilize the economy?*

  The tax system is the most important automatic stabilizer; it has the greatest ability to smooth out swings in GDP during business cycles. Other automatic stabilizers are Employment Insurance and social assistance payments.

Section 10.6 Possible Obstacles to Effective Fiscal Policy

- *How does the crowding-out effect limit the economic impact of expansionary fiscal policy?*

  The crowding-out effect states that as the government borrows to finance the budget deficit, it drives up the interest rates and crowds out private investment spending. If crowding-out causes a higher Canadian interest rate, it will attract foreign funds. In order to invest in the Canadian economy, foreigners will have to first convert their currencies into Canadian dollars. The increase in the demand for dollars relative to other currencies will cause the dollar to appreciate in value, making imports relatively cheaper in Canada and Canadian exports relatively more expensive in other countries. This will cause net exports $(X - M)$ to fall. This is the crowding-out effect in the open economy.

- *How do time lags in policy implementation affect policy effectiveness?*

  The time lag between when a fiscal policy may be needed and when it eventually affects the economy is considerable. Time lags are generally grouped in three classifications: recognition lags, implementation lags, and impact lags.

Section 10.7 The Federal Government Debt

- *How is the budget deficit financed?*

  The budget deficit is financed by issuing debt.

- *What has happened to the federal budget balance?*

  Improvement in the federal budget balance since the mid-1990s resulted from economic growth, increased tax revenues, and the efforts of the federal government to control the growth of government spending.

- *What is the impact of reducing a budget deficit?*

  In the short run, reducing a budget deficit can lead to a recession (if not offset by expansionary monetary policy). In the long run, however, deficit reduction increases economic growth and lowers the price level.

- *How much is the burden of government debt in Canada?*

  With greater fiscal responsibility and increased economic growth, Canada has managed to lower its debt–GDP ratio (the international measure of debt burden).

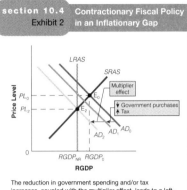

section 10.4
Exhibit 2   Contractionary Fiscal Policy in an Inflationary Gap

The reduction in government spending and/or tax increases, coupled with the multiplier effect, leads to a leftward shift in aggregate demand and a change in the short-run equilibrium from E_0 to E_2, reflecting a lower price level and a return to full-employment RGDP ($RGDP_{NR}$).

Chapter In Review

Money and the Banking System

Section 11.1 What Is Money?

- *What is money?*

  Money is anything that is generally accepted in exchange for goods or services.

- *What are the four functions of money?*

  The four important functions of money are money as a medium of exchange, money as a store of value, money as a unit of account, and money as a means of deferred payment.

Section 11.2 Measuring Money

- *What is currency?*

  Currency refers to the coins and paper notes that are issued by institutions and governments to facilitate the trading of goods and services and the payment of debts. Canadian currency consists of Government of Canada-issued note and coins, and demand and savings deposits held in various financial institutions.

- *What are demand and savings deposits?*

  While both demand and savings deposits are considered money, only demand deposits can be accessed on demand.

- *What is liquidity?*

  The ease with which one asset can be converted into another asset or into goods and services is called *liquidity*.

- *How is the money supply measured?*

  M2 is made up of currency outside chartered banks plus demand and savings deposits at chartered banks. M2+ includes M2 plus demand and savings deposits at trust companies, mortgage loan companies, credit unions, caisses populaires, and other financial institutions.

- *What backs the money supply?*

  Money is backed by our faith that others will accept it from us in exchange for goods and services.

Section 11.3 How Banks Create Money

- *What types of financial institutions exist in Canada?*

  While a variety of financial intermediaries exist in the Canadian financial system, the financial sector is dominated by deposit-accepting institutions—banks. The Canadian banking industry itself is dominated by six large chartered banks. The "Big Six" hold the majority of the financial assets in the banking industry.

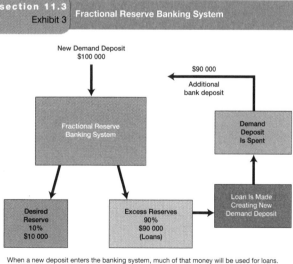

section 11.3
Exhibit 3   Fractional Reserve Banking System

New Demand Deposit
$100 000

$90 000
Additional
bank deposit

Fractional Reserve
Banking System

Demand
Deposit
Is Spent

Desired
Reserve
10%
$10 000

Excess Reserves
90%
$90 000
(Loans)

Loan Is Made
Creating New
Demand Deposit

When a new deposit enters the banking system, much of that money will be used for loans. Banks create money when they increase demand deposits through the process of creating loans.

Key Terms and Concepts

money anything generally accepted in exchange for goods or services   p. 225

medium of exchange the primary function of money, which is to facilitate transactions and lower transaction costs   p. 225

barter direct exchange of goods and services without the use of money   p. 225

measure of value money as a common "ruler" of worth allowing for the comparison of diverse goods and services   p. 226

store of value how money provides a means of saving or accumulating purchasing power from the present and transferring it to the future   p. 226

means of deferred payment the attribute of money that makes it easier to borrow and to repay loans   p. 226

currency consists of coins and paper notes that an institution or government has created to be used in the trading of goods and services and the payment of debts   p. 227

legal tender refers to coins and paper notes officially declared to be acceptable for the settlement of debts incurred in financial transactions   p. 227

fiat money a means of exchange established by government declaration   p. 227

demand deposits balances in bank accounts that depositors can access on demand   p. 228

savings deposits financial institution accounts containing funds that cannot be used for payment directly   p. 229

liquidity the ease with which one asset can be converted into another asset or into goods and services   p. 229

Key Exhibits/ Graphs

- *How do banks create money?*

  Money is created when banks make loans. Borrowers receive newly created demand deposits.

- *What does a bank balance sheet look like?*

  A bank balance sheet is a financial record that indicates the balance between a bank's assets and its liabilities plus capital. A bank's largest asset is loans and its largest liability is deposits.

- *What is a desired reserve ratio?*

  A desired reserve ratio is the percentage of deposits a bank chooses to keep on hand in the form of cash reserves.

Section 11.4 The Money Multiplier

- *How does the multiple expansion of the money supply process work?*

  New loans mean new money (demand deposits), which can increase spending as well as the money supply. New loans also create excess reserves in other banks, which leads to still further increases in both loans and the money supply.

- *What is the money multiplier?*

  The money multiplier is equal to one divided by the desired reserve ratio.

- *Why is it only "potential" money creation?*

  The banking system as a whole can potentially create new money equal to several times the amount of new reserves—as determined by the money multiplier. However, due to various leakages and time lags, the actual monetary impact of an initial deposit created out of excess reserves within a short period of time will be less than that calculated by the money multiplier.

section 11.4 Exhibit 1   The Multiple Expansion Process

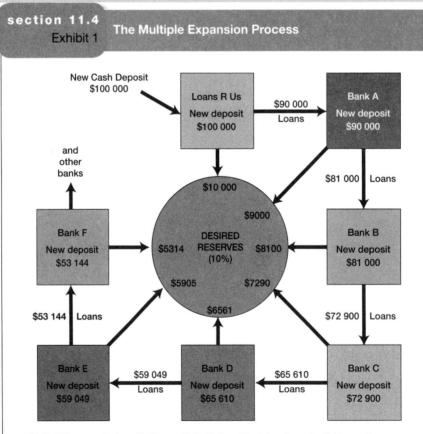

A $100 000 new cash deposit at Loans R Us National Bank has the potential to create $1 000 000 in new demand deposits in a chain reaction that involves many banks. The process repeats itself, as the money lent from one bank becomes a new deposit in another bank.

Chapter In Review

The Bank of Canada

Section 12.1 The Bank of Canada

- *What is the Bank of Canada?*

  The Bank of Canada is Canada's central bank. It is owned by the federal government, which has final responsibility for the Bank of Canada's policies. Despite this goal dependence, the governor of the Bank of Canada has considerable independence in formulating the Bank of Canada's monetary policy.

- *What are the functions of the Bank of Canada?*

  The Bank of Canada has five main functions: currency maintenance, banker of the federal government, bank to the chartered banks, lender of last resort, and money supply management. Of the five main functions of a central bank, the most important is its role in regulating the money supply.

Section 12.2 Tools of the Bank of Canada

- *What are the tools of the Bank of Canada?*

  The two major tools of the Bank of Canada are open market operations and changing the target for the overnight interest rate.

- *How does the Bank of Canada influence the money supply?*

  If the Bank of Canada wants to stimulate the economy (increase aggregate demand), it will increase the money supply by buying government bonds and/or lowering the target for the overnight interest rate. If the Bank of Canada wants to restrain the economy (decrease aggregate demand), it will lower the money supply by selling bonds and/or raising the target for the overnight interest rate.

Section 12.3 Money and Inflation

- *What is the equation of exchange?*

  The equation of exchange is expressed as $M \times V = P \times Q$, where M is the money supply, V is the velocity of money, P is the average level of prices of final goods and services, and Q is real GDP in a given year.

- *What is the quantity theory of money and prices?*

  The theory that draws a connection between the money supply and the price level when the velocity of money is constant is referred to as the *quantity theory of money and prices*.

Key Terms and Concepts

open market operations purchase and sale of government securities by the Bank of Canada   p. 248

bank rate interest rate that the Bank of Canada charges chartered banks for the loans it extends to them   p. 249

overnight interest rate interest rate that chartered banks charge each other for one-day loans   p. 249

bankers' deposit rate the interest rate the Bank of Canada pays chartered banks on their reserve deposits at the Bank of Canada   p. 250

velocity of money (V) the average number of times that a dollar is used in purchasing final goods or services in a one-year period   p. 253

quantity theory of money and prices a theory of the connection between the money supply and the price level when the velocity of money is constant   p. 253

Key Exhibits/ Graphs

Section 12.2, Exhibit 1

Open Market Operations: Bank of Canada Buys Securities from Investment Dealer

a. Investment Dealer (nonbank public)

Assets		Liabilities	
Securities	−$10 000		
Demand deposits	+$10 000		

b. Loans R Us Bank

Assets		Liabilities	
Reserves	+$10 000	Demand deposits	+$10 000

10 percent desired reserve ratio

c. Bank of Canada

Assets		Liabilities	
Securities	+$10 000	Reserves of Loans R Us Bank	+$10 000

d. Loans R Us Bank

Assets		Liabilities	
Reserves	$1000	Demand deposits	$10 000
Loans	$9000		

When the Bank of Canada buys securities from the nonbank public in the open market, it creates reserves. The nonbank public exchanges its securities for deposits, as seen in Exhibit 1(a). These additional deposits increase bank reserves, as seen in Exhibit 1(b). The additional bank reserves, along with the original purchase of securities, increase both assets and liabilities at the Bank of Canada, as seen in Exhibit 1(c). The increase in bank reserves will likely trigger additional lending and therefore money creation, as seen in Exhibit 1(d).

Chapter In Review

Monetary Policy

Section 13.1 Money, Interest Rates, and Aggregate Demand

- *What determines the money market?*

  The money market is the market where money demand and money supply determine the equilibrium interest rate. Money demand has three possible motives: transaction purposes, precautionary reasons, and asset purposes. The quantity of money demanded varies inversely with interest rates and directly with income. The supply of money is effectively almost perfectly inelastic with respect to interest rates over their plausible range, as controlled by Bank of Canada policies.

- *How does the Bank of Canada affect RGDP in the short run?*

  When the Bank of Canada sells bonds to the private sector or raises its target for the overnight interest rate, there is a reduction in the money supply, which in turn leads to a higher interest rate and a reduction in aggregate demand, at least in the short run. When the Bank of Canada buys bonds or lowers its target for the overnight interest rate, the money supply increases. The increase in the money supply will lead to lower interest rates and an increase in aggregate demand.

- *Does the Bank of Canada target the money supply or the interest rate?*

  Since the Bank of Canada cannot completely control both the growth of the money supply and the interest rate, it must choose which target to manage.

- *Which interest rate does the Bank of Canada target?*

  The Bank of Canada signals its intended monetary policy through the overnight interest rate target that it sets.

- *Does the Bank of Canada influence the real interest rate in the short run?*

  Since a change in the nominal interest rate tends to change the real interest rate by the same amount in the short run, most economists believe the Bank of Canada can control both the nominal and real interest rates (in the short run).

Section 13.2 Expansionary and Contractionary Monetary Policy

- *How does expansionary monetary policy work in a recessionary gap?*

  An expansionary monetary policy can combat a recessionary gap. By increasing the money supply, the Bank of Canada can lower interest rates, thereby causing an increase in real GDP and the price level.

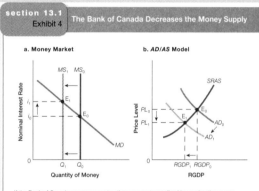

section 13.1 Exhibit 3 — The Bank of Canada Increases the Money Supply

a. Money Market
b. AD/AS Model

If the Bank of Canada is pursuing an expansionary monetary policy (increasing the money supply), this will lower the interest rates, as seen in Exhibit 3(a). At lower interest rates, households and businesses will invest more and buy more goods and services, shifting the aggregate demand curve to the right, as seen in Exhibit 3(b).

section 13.1 Exhibit 4 — The Bank of Canada Decreases the Money Supply

a. Money Market
b. AD/AS Model

If the Bank of Canada pursues a contractionary monetary policy (decreasing the money supply), this will lead to a reduction in the money supply or a leftward shift, as seen in the money market in Exhibit 4(a). The reduction of the money supply leads to an increase in the interest rate in the money market. The higher interest rate, or the rise in the cost of borrowing money, then leads to a reduction in aggregate demand for goods and services, as seen in Exhibit 4(b).

Key Terms and Concepts

money market market in which money demand and money supply determine the equilibrium interest rate   p. 258

Key Exhibits/ Graphs

Section 13.1, Exhibit 2

Section 13.1, Exhibit 3

Section 13.1, Exhibit 4

Section 13.2, Exhibit 1

Section 13.2, Exhibit 3

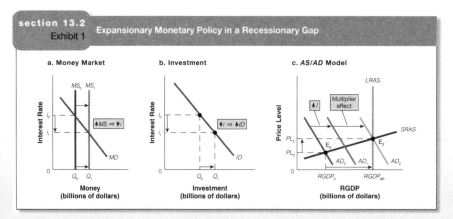

- *How does contractionary monetary policy work in an inflationary gap?*

  A contractionary monetary policy can close an inflationary gap. By reducing the money supply, the Bank of Canada can raise interest rates, thereby causing a decline in real GDP and the price level.

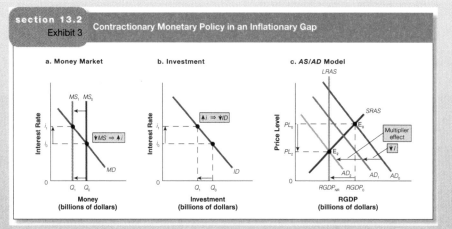

- *How does monetary policy work in the open economy?*

  In the open economy, interest rate changes can impact exchange rates. Higher interest rates produced by contractionary monetary policy lead to an appreciation of the Canadian dollar. This appreciation can cause net exports to decline and RGDP to be reduced in the short run. Expansionary monetary policy, having the opposite effect, can increase net exports and expand RGDP in the short run.

Section 13.3 Problems in Implementing Monetary and Fiscal Policy

- *What problems exist in implementing monetary and fiscal policy?*

  Monetary policy faces somewhat different implementation problems than fiscal policy. Both face difficult forecasting and lag problems, but the Bank of Canada can take action much more quickly. However, its effectiveness depends largely on the reaction of the private banking system to its policy changes. In Canada, monetary and fiscal policy are carried out by different decision makers, thus requiring cooperation and coordination for effective policy implementation.

Section 13.4 The Phillips Curve

- *What is the Phillips curve?*

  The inverse relationship between the rate of unemployment and the rate of inflation is called the *Phillips curve.*

- *How does the Phillips curve relate to the aggregate supply and demand model?*

  When the aggregate supply curve is positively sloped, an increase in aggregate demand will cause higher prices and higher output (lower unemployment). A decrease in aggregate demand will cause lower prices and lower output (higher unemployment).

Chapter In Review

International Trade

Section 14.1 Canada's Merchandise Trade

* *Who are Canada's trading partners?*

   Our most important trading partner, the United States, accounts for 73 percent of our exports and 64 percent of our imports. Trade with Japan and the countries of the European Union is also particularly important to Canada.

* *What does Canada import and export?*

   Exports of natural resource-based products make up over one-half of our exports of goods. Our imports are concentrated in finished goods, like machinery and equipment, automotive products, and consumer goods.

Section 14.2 International Trade Agreements

* *What has been the impact of international trade on Canada?*

   The volume of international trade has increased substantially in Canada over the past 50 years. During that time, exports and imports have grown from about 20 percent of GDP to over 30 percent.

* *What international trade agreements is Canada involved in?*

   The numerous trade agreements in which Canada is an active participant range from multilateral global trade agreements (such as GATT/WTO) to regional agreements (such as the Canada–Costa Rica Free Trade Agreement). This substantial involvement is a major reason why Canada has experienced a rise in international trade.

Section 14.3 Comparative Advantage and Gains from Trade

* *Why do economies trade?*

   Voluntary trade occurs because the participants feel that they are better off because of the trade.

* *What is the principle of comparative advantage?*

   A nation, a geographic area, or even a person can gain from trade if the good or service is produced relatively cheaper than anyone else can produce it. So, an area should specialize in producing and selling those items that it can produce at a lower opportunity cost than others can. Through trade and specialization in products in which it has a comparative advantage, a country can enjoy a greater array of goods and services at a lower cost.

Section 14.4 Supply and Demand in International Trade

* *What is consumer surplus and producer surplus?*

   The difference between what a consumer is willing and able to pay and what a consumer actually has to pay is called *consumer surplus*. The difference between what a supplier is willing and able to receive and the price a supplier actually receives for selling a good or service is called *producer surplus*.

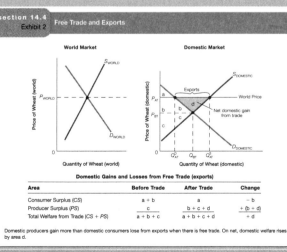

section 14.4
Exhibit 2 Free Trade and Exports

Domestic Gains and Losses from Free Trade (exports)

Area	Before Trade	After Trade	Change
Consumer Surplus (CS)	a + b	a	− b
Producer Surplus (PS)	c	b + c + d	+ (b + d)
Total Welfare from Trade (CS + PS)	a + b + c	a + b + c + d	+ d

Domestic producers gain more than domestic consumers lose from exports when there is free trade. On net, domestic welfare rises by area d.

- *Who benefits and who loses when a country becomes an exporter?*

  With free trade and exports, domestic producers gain more than domestic consumers lose.

- *Who benefits and who loses when a country becomes an importer?*

  With free trade and imports, domestic consumers gain more than domestic producers lose.

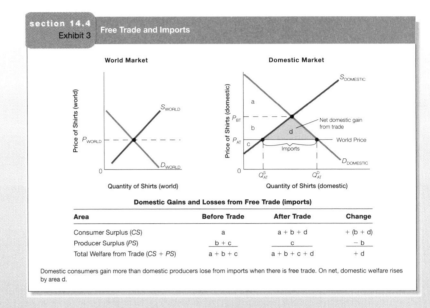

section 14.4
Exhibit 3 — **Free Trade and Imports**

Domestic Gains and Losses from Free Trade (imports)

Area	Before Trade	After Trade	Change
Consumer Surplus (CS)	a	a + b + d	+ (b + d)
Producer Surplus (PS)	b + c	c	− b
Total Welfare from Trade (CS + PS)	a + b + c	a + b + c + d	+ d

Domestic consumers gain more than domestic producers lose from imports when there is free trade. On net, domestic welfare rises by area d.

Section 14.5 Tariffs, Import Quotas, and Subsidies

- *What is a tariff?*

  A tariff is a tax on imported goods.

- *What is the impact of tariffs on the domestic economy?*

  Tariffs bring about higher prices and revenues to domestic producers, and lower sales and revenues to foreign producers. Tariffs lead to higher prices and reduce consumer surplus for domestic consumers. Tariffs result in a net loss in welfare because the loss in consumer surplus is greater than the gain to producers and the government.

- *What are some arguments in favour of tariffs?*

  Arguments for the use of tariffs include: Tariffs help infant industries grow, they can reduce domestic unemployment, they are necessary for national security reasons, and they protect against dumping.

- *What are import quotas?*

  Import quotas are legal limits on the quantity of an imported good that can be produced abroad and sold in domestic markets.

- *What is the impact of import quotas on the domestic economy?*

  Like tariffs, import quotas restrict imports, lowering consumer surplus and preventing countries from fully realizing their comparative advantage. There is a net loss in welfare from quotas, but it is proportionately larger than for tariffs because there are no government revenues.

- *What is the economic impact of subsidies?*

  Sometimes a government tries to encourage production of a certain good by subsidizing its production with taxpayer dollars. Because subsidies stimulate exports, they are not a barrier to trade like tariffs and import quotas are. However, they do distort trade patterns and cause overall inefficiencies.

Chapter In Review

International Finance

Section 15.1 The Balance of Payments

- *What is the balance of payments?*

  The balance of payments is the record of all of the international financial transactions of a nation for any given year.

- *What is the current account?*

  The current account is a record of a country's imports and exports of goods and services, net investment, and net transfers. If the sum of credits exceeds the sum of debits for all transactions of goods, services, investment income, and transfer payments, the current account is in surplus. If the opposite is true, the account is in deficit.

- *What is the capital account?*

  The capital account records the foreign purchases or assets in Canada and Canadian purchases of assets abroad. Capital account surpluses finance current deficits.

- *What is the statistical discrepancy?*

  To ensure that the balance of payments account does in fact balance, an "error" category—the statistical discrepancy—is included.

Section 15.2 Exchange Rates

- *What are exchange rates?*

  The price of a unit of one foreign currency in terms of another currency is called the *exchange rate*.

- *How are exchange rates determined?*

  The exchange rate for a currency is determined by the supply of and demand for that currency in the foreign exchange market.

section 15.2
Exhibit 2 **Equilibrium in the Foreign Exchange Market**

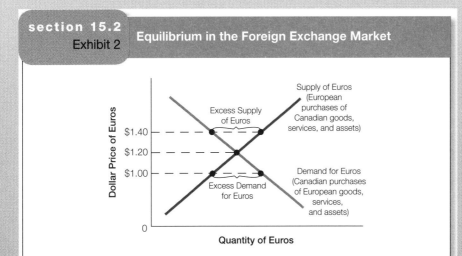

Suppose the foreign exchange market is in equilibrium at 1 euro = $1.20. At any price higher than $1.20, there will be a surplus of euros. At any price lower than $1.20, there will be a shortage of euros.

Key Terms and Concepts

balance of payments the record of international transactions of a nation over a year p. 301

current account a record of a country's imports and exports of goods and services, net investment income, and net transfers p. 301

capital account a record of the foreign purchases or assets in the domestic economy (a monetary inflow) and domestic purchases of assets abroad (a monetary outflow) p. 303

exchange rate the price of one unit of a country's currency in terms of another country's currency p. 305

appreciation an increase in the value of a currency p. 305

depreciation a decrease in the value of a currency p. 305

derived demand the demand for an input derived from consumers' demand for the good or service produced with that input p. 307

dirty float system a description of the exchange rate system that means that fluctuations in currency values are partly determined by market forces and partly influenced by government intervention p. 313

Key Exhibits/Graphs

Section 15.3 Equilibrium Changes in the Foreign Exchange Market

- **What are the major determinants in the foreign exchange market?**

  Any force that shifts either the demand or supply curves for a foreign currency will shift the equilibrium in the foreign exchange market and lead to a new exchange rate. Changes in tastes, tariffs, income levels, relative interest rates, relative inflation rates, or speculation will cause the demand for and supply of a currency to shift.

Section 15.4 Flexible Exchange Rates

- **How are exchange rates determined today?**

  Today, rates are free to fluctuate based on market transactions, but governments occasionally intervene to increase or depress the price of their currencies.

- **What are the advantages of a flexible exchange rate system?**

  Changes in exchange rates occur more often under a flexible-rate system but the changes are much smaller than the large overnight revaluations of currencies that occurred under the fixed-rate system. Under a fixed-rate system, the supply and demand for currencies shift, but currency prices are not allowed to shift to the new equilibrium, leading to surpluses and shortages of currencies.

- **What are the disadvantages of a flexible exchange rate system?**

  The main arguments presented against flexible exchange rates are that international trade levels could be diminished due to uncertainty of future currency prices and that the flexible rates would lead to inflation. Proponents of flexible exchange rates have strong counterarguments to those views.

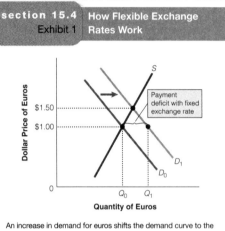

section 15.4 Exhibit 1 How Flexible Exchange Rates Work

An increase in demand for euros shifts the demand curve to the right, from D_0 to D_1. Under a fixed-rate system, this increase in demand results in a shortage of euros at the equilibrium price of $1, because the quantity demanded at this price, Q_1, is greater than the quantity supplied, Q_0. If the exchange rate is flexible, however, no shortage develops. Instead, the increase in demand forces the exchange rate higher, to $1.50. At this higher exchange rate, the quantity of euros demanded doesn't increase as much, and the quantity of euros supplied increases as a result of the now relatively lower cost of imports from Canada.

Notes